ROUTLEDGE LIBRARY EDITIONS: THE ENGLISHWOMAN'S REVIEW OF SOCIAL AND INDUSTRIAL QUESTIONS

Volume 3

THE ENGLISHWOMAN'S REVIEW OF SOCIAL AND INDUSTRIAL QUESTIONS

THE ENGLISHWOMAN'S REVIEW OF SOCIAL AND INDUSTRIAL QUESTIONS

1870

Advisory Editors
JANET HOROWITZ MURRAY AND
MYRA STARK

LONDON AND NEW YORK

First published in 1985 by Garland Publishing, Inc.

This edition first published in 2017
by Routledge
2 Park Square, Milton Park, Abingdon, Oxon OX14 4RN

and by Routledge
711 Third Avenue, New York, NY 10017

Routledge is an imprint of the Taylor & Francis Group, an informa business

All rights reserved. No part of this book may be reprinted or reproduced or utilised in any form or by any electronic, mechanical, or other means, now known or hereafter invented, including photocopying and recording, or in any information storage or retrieval system, without permission in writing from the publishers.

Trademark notice: Product or corporate names may be trademarks or registered trademarks, and are used only for identification and explanation without intent to infringe.

British Library Cataloguing in Publication Data
A catalogue record for this book is available from the British Library

ISBN: 978-1-138-20875-9 (Set)
ISBN: 978-1-315-39366-7 (Set) (ebk)
ISBN: 978-1-138-22088-1 (Volume 3) (hbk)
ISBN: 978-1-138-22091-1 (Volume 3) (pbk)
ISBN: 978-1-315-41169-9 (Volume 3) (ebk)

Publisher's Note
The publisher has gone to great lengths to ensure the quality of this reprint but points out that some imperfections in the original copies may be apparent.

Disclaimer
The publisher has made every effort to trace copyright holders and would welcome correspondence from those they have been unable to trace.

THE
ENGLISHWOMAN'S
REVIEW
of
Social and Industrial Questions

1870

GARLAND PUBLISHING, INC.
New York & London
1985

Bibliographical Note

This facsimile has been made from
a copy in the collection of
the Bodleian Library.

The volumes in this series are printed on
acid-free, 250-year-life paper.

ISBN 0-8240-3727-8

Printed in the United States of America

THE ENGLISHWOMAN'S REVIEW.

No. I.—January, 1870.

I.—FUTURE PLANS.

Much regret having been expressed at the discontinuance of the ENGLISHWOMAN'S REVIEW, especially of the Record of Events, and "Now-a-Days," which it was hoped would supply its place, having been suspended, I have determined to start the REVIEW again.

In all directions busy workers are engaged in enlarging the sphere of women's usefulness, and in extending their influence. A correct record of these efforts ought to be kept, otherwise only an indistinct and confused recollection will remain some years hence of the important events now happening around us.

It has often been remarked that, after a long pause, rapid progress will be made for several years in some particular direction, to be followed by another long pause, during which no advance is made. For example, during some hundreds, or, to speak more correctly, thousands of years, wool was spun by the distaff and spindle. Suddenly the distaff was superseded by the spinning wheel, and then the wheel by Arkwright's spinning-jenny, driven by steam. This occurred about sixty years ago, and since then no equally great improvements have been made in this direction. So in the case of railroads. In 1825, the belief in the possibility of driving an engine at so rapid a rate as twelve miles an hour was regarded an extravagant opinion; but by 1845, the speed attained was not much inferior to that of the present day, and from that time to this, no considerable improvements have been made in the convenience or safety of railway travelling.

As in mechanics, so in morals, our progress has been by fits and starts. The grammar and other endowed schools, with which England is so thickly dotted, were almost all founded within the century that commences with the conclusion of the reign of Henry VII., and terminates with the first years of James I.

The Reformation itself spread to its widest limits in Europe during the space of fifty years.

From the days of chivalry until lately, little or no advance has been made in improving the position of women. Indeed it is a matter of doubt whether women did not stand higher in the estimation of men 500 years ago than they do now.

That women, in common with the lower animals, have benefitted by the spread of humane sentiments and the softening of manners, and have in consequence been better protected from brutal treatment, cannot be disputed; but there are strong reasons for believing that they had less influence and were less respected fifty years ago than in the days of the Plantagenets. If it is true, as antiquaries say, that women burgesses had votes in the election of borough officers and members of Parliament for boroughs, that women freeholders voted at the election of knights of the shire, that peeresses in their own right voted by proxy in the House of Lords, and abbesses attended the sittings of the House, and voted in person, there can be no doubt that women have lost much ground in public estimation since "the good old times."

During the last twenty years the influence of women has been increasing perceptibly, probably owing to their admission to the lighter walks of literature, and this influence has continued to grow stronger and stronger, until the present time.

Now, almost every year shows some barrier thrown down, which had been put up to fence them out from education, or employment, or some other means of happiness. In the last year three very important events have taken place:—

(1.) Women householders have been placed by

Parliament on an equality with men householders, as far as regards the election of municipal officers.

(2.) Parliament has decided that women are to enjoy a share in the educational endowments of the country.

(3.) The University of Edinburgh has admitted women as medical students.

Indeed, a month seldom passes without the occurrence of some minor event favourable to women. In the last quarter the University of Oxford has extended its local examinations to girls, and a college for women has been opened at Hitchin, in which professors from Cambridge are not too proud to give lectures to the pupils.

These events are called "minor," because they are not of such great magnitude as the three events spoken of previously, but in themselves they are not small events at all. And little incidents are continually occurring which are not only pleasing in themselves, but are significant as showing the course of public opinion. In fact, the workers in the women's cause are making history, and making it very fast. For 500 years no advance has been made in raising the position of women; but now the progress is rapid, and we may hope that the good cause will continue to advance with ever increasing velocity for some years to come.

As circumstances prevent me from being a worker at present, it shall be my humble task to chronicle the doings of others, and if it is true that lookers-on see most of the game, perhaps the fact of my not being a worker may make me better qualified to act as chronicler. I shall at any rate endeavour to keep an accurate record, in which, as in the log-book of a ship, the events that mark our progress will be noted down from day to day. This log-book will, I hope, be found of present interest to the workers, for the workers in one department know but little of what is being done in other departments, and they may perhaps be glad of a publication, by the perusal of which for half-an-hour once a quarter, they can become acquainted with what is being done for women in all directions. That this record will be valuable in future years I have no doubt at all.

The present number is in all respects incomplete, except as regards the record, but if the number of subscribers will allow of it, the next will be arranged on the plan of the former ones, with the addition of a foreign letter, containing information of the progress of the women's movement abroad; and under any circumstances the record will be continued.

JESSIE BOUCHERETT.

II.—PRACTICAL SUGGESTIONS ON BOARDING-OUT.

IN ANSWER TO MANY INQUIRIES.

By LOUISA BOUCHERETT.

IT is now about seven years since my attention was first directed by Mrs. David Archer, of Kingsdown House, Swindon, Wilts, to the unhappy and forlorn condition of children in most of our workhouse schools.

In July, 1863, I asked and obtained leave to take two girls, twelve and fourteen years of age, out of the workhouse school of the district in which I then resided. Their physical condition I found to be very miserable. One had had a cough for six months and was very thin. Both were unhealthy. I have no reason to suppose they were worse than others in the same workhouse. Some were better in health than they were, but others were worse. Morally, these children were neither honest, truthful, cleanly, nor active; nor did I find others more so. I have had altogether twenty-five under my care during the past six years; nine of these are still in the receipt of relief, the rest have gone to service. The result of my observations is that a child cannot be placed out too young, if a suitable home can be found, and if the supervision be careful and efficient.

Personal correction is sometimes absolutely unavoidable with children who have been ill brought up till seven or eight years of age, but the earlier they are removed from the workhouse, the less likely is this ever to be necessary. I need hardly observe, that though in a few exceptional cases it may be absolutely necessary, and should therefore never be quite forbidden, yet it is a practice which should be as much as possible discouraged; and I am persuaded that where the children are placed in good hands from their early infancy, the cases in which it may occur will be very rare indeed.

Greediness I found to be a constant fault with these children. Having been entirely deprived of sugar and all sweet things for years in the workhouse, their craving for all kinds of sweets seemed rather the result of a necessity than of ordinary greediness. It was quite impossible in many instances to keep it within bounds, and long before Christmas-day the mince meat had often mysteriously disappeared where a child old enough to scheme such depredations had been received. It is hardly to be wondered at in such cases if a whipping ensued, but in no case was a child cruelly or injuriously punished. If left long in the workhouse their tempers often become very unmanageable indeed. The tempers of girls are not worse, naturally, than those of boys, but so much more is expected from them that they often appear so. When a boy has done his work or returned from school he may go out to play, but a girl is expected to sit down to her needle, or to perform some household drudgery. Needlework is often very wearisome to young girls, yet it is absolutely necessary they should be good needle-women, and it is best to accustom them to take a pride in their skill as early as possible. I think prizes for needle-work very useful in schools, and especially for these friend-less little ones, who will often if skilful make friends of their mistresses, and sometimes may be able to take lighter places in consequence. But care should be taken to prevent them from ever depending entirely on needlework for a maintenance, and, therefore, as they grew older, I have been at much pains to have them taught to milk and to be handy with cattle, as a girl who can milk a cow and rear a calf is always sure of good employment at fair wages. No doubt there are many other trades in manufacturing towns in which they might advantageously be instructed.

I see that good-tempered, calm-looking women and men make the best foster-parents. Those who are lively and excitable, or over-anxious in character, don't do well, however high principled and well intentioned, as all children require much patience, and workhouse bred ones more than others.

But no system of education will succeed without constant superintendence. The supervision of the village schoolmistress may be very useful, as she must constantly see the children. Any irregularity in their attendance at school should be noticed at once and inquired into.

I do not insist that children should attend school both in the morning and afternoon. Once a day will be found enough if the school is a good one, or they may attend twice a day on alternate days. I believe this, if regular, would be found the best of all for boys. Had I remained at home I should have endeavoured to place two boys in the same home, and make them go after the age of nine to school and work on alternate days. Such a plan would require the earnest co-operation of an intelligent farmer. I hear it has been tried near Leicester with much success, with the children of labourers.

With respect to allowances, I do not think it wise in any case to take a child for less than it would cost in the workhouse exclusive of staff expenses, or such allowance would be too small. If a small allowance was accepted and supplemented by charity, a bad example of taking too little would be set, which might be followed in cases where no charity could be obtained to assist. I, therefore, do not think it wise to give the foster-parent anything beyond what is allowed by the Board of Guardians, though I have done it. The allowance for board and lodging may vary in different places from 2s. 9d. to 3s. 6d. per week. School expenses should always be paid by the board; an outfit given, and 7s. a quarter at least allowed for repairing and renewing their clothing. Medical attendance and drugs should also be supplied by the board. If accident or illness befell the family where a child is boarded, then some aid might wisely be given by those who placed the child there; and where there was illness, the child, if old enough to be of use, should be allowed to remain at home to help for a time.

I have never placed more than one pauper child in a house at one time; but I have often placed them where there are other children belonging to the family, and found advantage in it. I see no objection where the bedroom accommodation is sufficient. In the case of boys no inconvenience can arise; nor can it even with girls when they are older than the boys of the family. They act as little nursemaids, and often become tenderly attached to their young charges. When I sent a child to a cottage I always looked at the accommodation; and, sometimes, by merely putting up a wooden partition, at the expense of a few shillings, I added greatly to the comfort of the whole family, by giving the girls a separate room. Should any report arise of a child being ill-treated, it should be immediately inquired into, and the person who reported it to the proper authorities should be thanked, whether it proved true or not. If untrue the report should be traced to its originator, who should be the *only* person reproved —otherwise, ill-treatment might be concealed.

I have, however, known false reports spread by low persons, who wished to have the child themselves, that they might work it or starve it, and so make a profit of it. This fact has been noticed by others interested in the subject besides myself, and may occur in any place where the labour of children can be made remunerative.

In reply to the inquiry—Do I exclude illegitimate children when I board out paupers? I reply that I do not. But the state of the law has occasioned me great difficulty, nor could I understand it at all for a long time. There is no legal difference between orphans and illegitimate children with respect to out-relief.

All children, whether legitimate or not, are divided by the Poor Law into two classes—those whose parents are able-bodied, technically called able-bodied children, and deserted children, or orphans; deserted children being classed with the orphans because their parents, not being discoverable, the child cannot be classed as able-bodied.

All whose parents are to be found are classed as able-bodied. Thus an infant in arms may be reckoned able-bodied, because its mother is so.

Now, by the law, relief to a child is construed as

relief to the parent, and is so truly, as the parent is always the guardian of the child, and may sell its clothes and enjoy the fruits of its labour, if it is capable of working at all. Parents have very extensive authority over their children, and cannot be deprived of it by any misconduct short of such violence as would send them to jail—and even then, on their release, the child is as much their helpless slave as ever. My own experience affords an example of this. I had once two illegitimate girls under my care, aged ten and eleven. Their mother had not been heard of for years. She was a very wicked woman. Suddenly, she came to me, and asked where her children were, saying, she was now married to a steady man, and would take them home and bring them up in honest industry. I would not give the address till I had seen the relieving officer. He said the mother was not married, but was still leading a disreputable life, and the children would be lost at once if I gave them up. So I sent them back to the workhouse, where the dreadful mother did not dare try to follow them. I think it would be an immense blessing if children were protected from their own parents. I think that no woman leading a disreputable life ought to have property in her children's clothing, when it has been supplied by others, or to have any authority over them after they have once become chargeable to the public. And I think that compelling or inducing a child to leave its foster-parents, without the consent of the authorities, should be made a punishable offence. I know not if there is any provision of this nature in Mr. Goschen's Poor Law Amendment Act for 1870, but I am quite satisfied there ought to be.

I have had, besides these two girls, several other illegitimate children under my care, but then the parents were dead, or had totally disappeared and could not be found. If they could be found they would probably be obliged either to maintain the children, or to bring them into the workhouse and to remain there themselves, as it is not lawful to give out-relief to the able-bodied, whether adults or able-bodied children.

An exception is made with respect to widows, and also, I believe, to deserted wives and their children; but the allowance is usually miserably small, and unless the mother has very good employment besides, their sufferings are often cruel.

The Rev. W. W. Cooper, of West Rasen, a magistrate and *ex officio* guardian, writes thus—"In a very few words, all children may be boarded out to whom out-door relief may legally be given, and out-door relief is very constantly given to widows, who, though able-bodied, cannot maintain their children, and it *must* be given for all children under seven years of age, unless the workhouse contains accommodation for them with their mothers. The guardians cannot separate a child from its mother till it is above seven."

III.—A PLEA FOR WOMEN FARMERS.

IN different parts of England various customs prevail in the letting of farms.

One of these customs is very advantageous to women, and as a great number of proposals are constantly being made for settling the difficulties of tenant right in Ireland, we will add one more to the number by suggesting that this custom which [is so advantageous to women should be adopted in Ireland.

The plan is rarely followed with regard to large farms, but is found to work well for small ones. In a northern district of Lincolnshire, as soon as a small farm is vacant, several candidates are sure to appear, each of whom is ready to show excellent reasons why he should be the new tenant. The best candidate is of course selected; the best candidate meaning the most sober and industrious man who possesses the requisite capital. The farm is then let to him nominally for a year, the landlord having the legal right to turn him out at a year's notice, but in reality the farm is let to him for life, and for the life of his wife if she survives him.

The rate of rent asked is somewhat higher than that demanded of the larger tenants, but as long as the man or his widow live it will never be raised. A farm may thus be held at the same rent for forty or even fifty years, and as the value of money keeps continually falling, the loss to the landlord in the event of a tenant proving extraordinarily long-lived may be considerable; but on the whole, taking all the small farms together, and comparing them with the larger farms, it is thought by those competent to judge that the loss to the landlord is but slight, if, indeed, there is any. On the death of the tenant and his widow the farm is let again at an increased rent.

Some landlords out of kindness diminish the rent to the widow, but this is not necessary, and is, in our opinion a mistake; for where this is done the system becomes distinctly disadvantageous to the landlord, and consequently falls into disfavour.

We say that it is not necessary to lower the rent to a widow because infirm old men, who are past work, contrive while paying the same rent they did when they were young to live comfortably, and even to leave a little money behind them, and there is no reason why infirm old women should not do the same; we know that in one instance where the rent was lowered to a widow she was reported by her neighbours to have saved a great deal of money.

Now, if the Irish are unable to make reasonable contracts about their farms, so that it is necessary for Parliament to make a universal legal rule to guide them, would not this custom form a good rule?

Some changes would be required, to suit the peculiarities of the Irish. For instance, no English farmer would dream of marrying to spite his landlord, but an Irish farmer might do so, and marriages between men of seventy and girls of fifteen would probably become common in Ireland if widows had a legal right to keep the farm for their lives, at the same rent. Some restriction would therefore have to be made, and the widow of a tenant ought not to be legally entitled to keep the farm, unless she was married to him when he took it, or had married him within ten years from his taking it.

In England, too, improvements are made by the landlord, and as the contrary is the case in Ireland, it would have to be provided that if a tenant died, leaving no widow, before he had enjoyed the full benefit of his improvements, his heirs should receive compensation for them from the landlord. It appears not to be unusual in Ireland at present for widows to keep their husbands' farm, and every one must feel that the widow of a working farmer, who has helped her husband to manage it, and has with her own hands milked the cows and made the butter, which is perhaps the chief profit of the farm, has morally a better claim to succeed her husband in its occupation than any one else, but in all the discussions which have taken place on this subject, we do not remember to have seen this stated.

It has been urged more than once that a son has a moral right to succeed to the farm which his father has held. This may, or may not be the case, if there is no widow, but we maintain that the widow's claim is far stronger than the son's. A young man, or a middle-aged man, can maintain himself by his own labour, but if a feeble old woman was put out of her husband's farm she must, in all probability, go to the workhouse, for though the tenant of a large farm can often save a great deal of money, the tenant of a small one can rarely save much, and Irish farms are, generally speaking, small.

If, therefore, an Act was passed, giving to sons the legal right of succession to their fathers' farms, it would be a very bad thing for widows.

It may be said that under such circumstances a son would be sure to keep his mother, out of charity. Probably most sons would do so, but some might not, and others, though they might keep their mother, would consider her a burden, and let her see that they thought so. In other cases the daughter-in-law might be unkind to the old woman. The bread of charity is proverbially bitter, and it is hard that industrious women should be compelled to eat it in their old age, when, under a more just arrangement, they might have lived in independence.

If a law is to be made for the purpose of compelling landlords to dispose of their farms in such a manner as shall be consistent with justice, let us take care that the law itself is not unjust.

When a widow succeds to her husband's farm she often takes her son to live with her. Her position in this case is very different from having to live as a dependent on her son's charity. The farm is hers, and she is doing her son a favour in allowing him to live with her. Both the young man and his wife are kept on their good behaviour, for if they behaved ill the old woman could turn them out of doors. In one case she is certain of kind and respectful treatment, in the other case she may be oppressed and ill-used in the house of which she was once the mistress.

We have purposely avoided expressing any opinion on tenant right, for it is not our business to defend either landlords or tenants, both parties being perfectly well able, to tell their own story and make themselves heard by the public. Our object has been to put in a plea for helpless old women, who, having no money, no political power, and no education, must be quite unable to make their voice heard, and who therefore may be terribly oppressed by accident without any one being conscious of it, just as a dumb man might be run over on a dark night, by the most careful and considerate of coachmen.

RECORD OF EVENTS.

For the two quarters from July 1st, to the end of December, 1869.

QUARTER FROM JULY TO OCTOBER.

MARRIED WOMEN'S PROPERTY BILL.

THIS Bill made shipwreck in the House of Lords. Their lordships read it the second time, and then dropped it, on account of the lateness of the season, for they would not pass it without alteration, and there was not time to consider what the alterations should be.

Lord Penzance, in proposing the second reading of the Bill, said he was anxious that their lordships should read it the second time in order to show their sympathy with a suffering class, but he was quite aware that it could not become law this year.

It was very evident from his speech that Lord Penzance himself did not approve of the Bill, but thought it went too far. He appears to be in favour of securing their own earnings to wives, and is willing to allow wives who have obtained separations from their husbands, the use of their own property, but he seems to be of opinion, that as long as husband and wife live together, the due subordination of the wife can only be secured by giving the husband the entire control of her money.

After hearing Lord Penzance's speech, the Duke of Northumberland withdrew his notice to oppose the second reading of the Bill. The Lord Chancellor said he approved of its principle, but thought some of the details required investigation. Lord Cairns spoke to the same effect. Lord Dufferin said a strong feeling prevailed in Ireland in favour of the Bill. Lord Romilly also expressed his approbation of the principle of the Bill. The Earl of Harrowby disapproved of it. The Earl of Shaftesbury spoke warmly in favour of securing a married woman's earnings to herself.

The Bill was then read a second time.

The Executive Committee, formed to promote the passing of the Bill, have laboured assiduously to carry out their object. They have also had most valuable assistance from the Local Secretaries, whose names are given below, and from Miss Robertson, the Hon. Sec. of the Dublin Committee, who sent up five petitions with an aggregate of 4837 signatures; and from Miss Tod, the Hon. Sec. of the Belfast Committee.

The Committee did not, however, possess the power necessary for success. Mr. Russell Gurney has given notice that, unless the Government should take up the subject, he will bring forward another Bill on the subject early next session. If he should be supported by an influential London committee, a large measure of success is highly probable. The names of the Committee and others, who have so nobly fought the battle this session, are as follows:—

Executive Committee:—Jacob Bright, Esq., M.P., Mrs. Jacob Bright, Thomas Chorlton, Esq., Rev. Alfred Dewes, B.D., LL.D., Mrs. Moore, Dr. Pankhurst, Mrs. Pochin, Miss Alice Wilson. *Treasurer*—Miss Becker, 28, Jackson's Row, Albert Square, Manchester. *Hon.*

Secs.—Mrs. Butler, 280, South Hill, Park Road, Liverpool; Miss Wolstenholme, Moody Hall, Congleton, Cheshire.

Local Secretaries:—Bath, Miss Le Geyt, Miss L. Ashworth; Bristol, Miss Florence Hill; Edinburgh, Mrs. Daniell; Leeds, Miss T. L. Marshall; Lichfield, Mrs. Kingsford; Oxford, Mrs. Mark Pattison; St. Andrew's, Mrs. Robertson; Leamington, Mrs. Feast; and at Nottingham, Mrs. Ransom—has practically been *Local Secretary.*

Birmingham Committee:—Mrs. C. D. Sturge, Miss Sturge, Mrs. W. Kenrick, Mrs. W. Taylor, W. Goodrick, Esq. *Hon. Sec.*—Miss J. M. Hill, 3, Hagley Grove, Edgbaston.

The Committees for Dublin and Belfast contain a large number of influential names. The *Hon. Sec.* for Dublin is Miss A. Robertson, of 2, St. James's Place, Blackrock, Dublin; the *Hon. Secs.* for Belfast are Mrs. Thomson, 17, University Square, and Miss Tod, University Square East.

The following petitions in favour of the Married Women's Property Bill were presented during the session of 1869:—

Date.	From	Presented by	No. of Sigs.
Feb. 26	Inhabitants of Waterford...	....	18
Mar. 10	,, Barnstaple .	Mr. T. Cave	1531
,, 13	Caleb Wright and others...	Mr. Jacob Bright	85
,, ,,	Inhabitants of Kingston ...	Mr. J. T. Hamilton	531
,, ,,	,, Blackrock...	Colonel Taylor ...	134
,, ,,	,, Donabate ...	,, ...	108
,, 16	S. Charlesworth and others	Mr. Cowen.........	272
,, ,,	Inhabitants of Middleton (Lanc.) ...	....	202
,, 17	,, Newton-le-Willows ...	Mr. Rylands	156
,, 18	,, Bridgwater .	Mr. Gilpin	58
April 1	,, Waterford..	Mr. Blake	25
,, 6	,, Southport...	Mr. Turner	354
,, 9	,, Edgbaston...	Mr. Dixon	983
,, ,,	,, Burnley ...	....	208

Date.		From	Presented by	No. of Sigs.
April 12		Inhabitants of Sunderland.	Mr. Candlish......	1098
,,	,,	,, Luddenden Foot	Sir F. Crossley...	43
,,	,,	Eleanor Boon and others...	Mr. W. M. Torrens	27
,,	13	Inhabitants of Macclesfield	Mr. Chadwick ...	60
,,	,,	,, Tiverton ...	Mr. Denman......	47
,,	,,	,, Charlesworth	Mr. Lefevre	220
,,	,,	,, Nottingham	Mr. Mundella ...	1951
,,	,,	,, Rochdale ...	Mr. Potter.........	1529
,,	,,	,, Liverpool ...	....	173
,,	,,	,, Lakefield ...	....	20
,,	14	A. Challis Lakefield ...	Mr. Barnes	1
,,	,,	Inhabitants of Whalley Range ...	Mr. Jacob Bright	97
,,	,,	,, Manchester.	,, ...	3181
,,	,,	,, Altrincham & Bowdon	,, ...	147
		,, Alderley & Chorley ...	,, ...	468
,,	,,	,, Wakefield...	,, ...	360
,,	,,	,, Dyffryn......	,, ...	17
,,	,,	,, Haslingden .	,, ...	163
,,	,,	,, Leek	Sir E. Buller......	107
,,	,,	,, Bath	Mr. Dalrymple ...	2104
,,	,,	A. Biggar and others	Mr. Dowse.........	2
,,	,,	Inhabitants of Liverpool ...	Mr. Graves	152
,,	,,	,, Oxford	Mr. R. Gurney ...	76
,,	,,	,, Bolton	,, ...	174
,,	,,	Women of Boston Spa......	,, ...	132
,,	,,	J. B. Roberts and others...	,, ...	67
,,	,,	Law Amendment Assoctn .	,, ...	1
,,	,,	R. G. Johnston and others	Mr. Kirk	41
,,	,,	John Stuart Mill and others	Mr. Lefevre	1386
,,	,,	Inhabitants of Newby	....	151
,,	,,	Ellen Evans and others ...	Mr. M'Laren......	1558
,,	,,	Inhabitants of Belfast	Mr. M'Clure	2302
,,	,,	,, Ballymena and Larne	,, ...	367
,,	,,	,, Bristol	Mr. Morley	2355
,,	,,	,, Dublin	Mr. Pim	2347
,,	,,	,, Williamstn., co. Dublin	,, ...	123
,,	,,	,, Bray, co. Dublin ...	,, ...	63
,	,,	,, Cork	,, ...	85

Record of Events.

Date.	From	Presented by	No. of Sigs.
April 14	Inhabitants of Ballyroan & Rathsaran	Mr. Pim	54
,, ,,	,, Booterstown	,,	65
,, ,,	,, Dalkey	,,	102
,, ,,	,, Longford	Mr. O. Reilly	60
,, ,,	,, Stroud	Mr. Winterbotham	235
,, ,,	,, Leamington	Mr. Wise	1338
,, ,,	,, Darlington		43
,, ,,	,, Newtownards		389
,, ,,	Susannah Palmer		1
,, 15	Inhabitants of Leeds	Mr. Baines	116
,, ,,	,, ,,	,,	224
,, ,,	,, Lichfield	Colonel Dyott	164
,, 16	Working Women of Street, Somerset	Mr. Jacob Bright	193
,, ,,	James Moreton and others	,,	56
,, ,,	Baldwin Lloyd and others	,,	20
,, ,,	Inhabitants of London	Mr. R. Gurney	1154
,, ,,	Adelaide Taylor and others	Mr. Sartoris	386
,, ,,	Inhabitants of Street		31
,, 19	,, Saxmundham, Aldeburgh, Woodbridge, & Framlingham	Mr. Gurney	56
,, 21	Members of Burnley Reform Club	Mr. Shaw	112
,, ,,	Ellen Ince	Rt. Hon. J. Bright	1
,, 26	Emilia Gurney and others	Mr. R. Gurney	34
,, 29	Inhabitants of Carlisle	Sir W. Lawson	38
May 3	,, Salford	Mr. Charley	152
,, 27	,, Royston	Mr. Taylor	78
,, 31	,, Melton Mowbray	Lord J. Manners	61
,, ,,	,, Rock Ferry	Mr. Rathbone	324
,, ,,	,, St. Asaph	Mr. Fawcett	45
June 11	,, Rhyl	Mr. Taylor	78
,, 15	,, Haslingden	Mr. Holt	15
,, 16	,, Manchester	Mr. Jacob Bright	2820
,, ,,	,, Huddersfield	,,	346
,, ,,	,, Ockley	,,	13
,, ,,	,, Cheltenham	,,	79
,, ,,	,, London	Mr. R. Gurney	753
,, ,,	,, Dover	,,	98
,, ,,	,, Edgware	,,	41
,, ,,	,, Preston	,,	45
,, ,,	,, Lancaster	,,	59
,, ,,	,, Gt. Stanmore	Mr. Lefevre	17

Date.	From		Presented by	No. of Sigs.
June 16	Inhabitants of	Harrow	Mr. Lefevre	81
,, ,,	,,	Hendon	,,	49
,, ,,	,,	Monk Coniston	,,	105
,, ,,	,,	,, ,,	,,	67
,, ,,	,,	Grantham	,,	19
,, ,,	,,	Carmarthen	,,	295
,, ,,	,,	Dublin	Mr. Pim	1211
,, ,,	,,	Liverpool	Mr. Rathbone	226
,, ,,	,,	Kidderminster		116
,, ,,	George Grundy and others			669
,, 17	Inhabitants of Manchester		Mr. Charley	1010
,, ,,	,,	Teignmouth	Visct. Courtenay.	440
,, 21	,,	Bruree	Mr. Pim	23
,, ,,	,,	Denbigh	Mr. W. Williams	20
,, 22	,,	Carlisle	Sir W. Lawson	27
,, 29	,,	Hayward's Heath	Mr. Fawcett	47
,, ,,	Arundel and Snape		,,	53
July 21	Isaac Gault and others		Mr. Jacob Bright	287
,, ,,	Inhabitants of Liverpool		Mr. Rathbone	95
,, 26	,,	Coventry	Mr. Taylor	26

Total number of petitions............ 113
,, ,, signatures 42,654

[*Extracted from the Report of Committee of Parliamentary Petitions.*]

DECEASED WIFE'S SISTER.

THE Bill for legalising the marriage of a widower with his former wife's sister did not pass through the House of Commons, although the motion for reading it the second time was carried by a large majority. Without entering into the question of whether it is in itself desirable that the law should be altered, we must express our satisfaction that the Bill has not passed Parliament, for as at present constituted it is not competent to legislate on the subject.

It is especially a woman's question, and until some means have been found for ascertaining the opinion of women, no legislation ought to take place.

The Bill brought in was moreover one-sided, for it proposed to permit a man to marry his deceased wife's sister, while continuing to forbid a woman to marry her deceased husband's brother.

MUNICIPAL FRANCHISE BILL.

ON June 9 Mr. Jacob Bright moved an amendment to this Bill, the effect of which was to give women the right to be enrolled as burgesses, and to vote at the election of councillors, auditors, and assessors. The Bill thus amended received the royal assent on August 2, and women ratepayers became entitled to vote in the municipal elections in November.

The work of obtaining and spreading information, and promoting petitions in favour of restoring to women ratepayers their ancient rights was undertaken by the Committee of the Manchester National Society for Women's Suffrage, and the efforts of this Committee have been declared, by the members who were promoting the measure in Parliament, to have been indispensable to their success. This should encourage all friends of the cause of justice to women, to persevere in strenuous endeavours to forward measures tending to this object, and not to think that any earnest effort can be made without doing some good. About forty petitions were presented in favour of this municipal franchise for women, with between 2000 and 3000 signatures, and about 1500 copies of articles conveying information on the subject, and reports of Mr. Jacob Bright's speech were distributed to members of both Houses of Parliament, and the friends of the cause.

WOMEN'S SUFFRAGE.

A MEETING of the London Women's Suffrage Society took place at 9, Conduit Street, Regent Street, on the 17th of July.

Mrs. P. A. Taylor took the chair. The speakers were Mr. Mill, Rev. Charles Kingsley, Sir C. W. Dilke, Mr. Morley, of the *Fortnightly Review*, Professor Fawcett,

Mrs. Fawcett, Miss Biggs, Lord Houghton, **Professor** Masson, and Mr. Stansfield, M.P.

The room was crowded, and the meeting applauded the speeches with enthusiasm. Ladies slightly preponderated over gentlemen in numbers. The company included Mr. McLaren, M.P. for Edinburgh, Mr. P. A Taylor, M.P., Mr. Boyd Kinnear, Mr. Thomas Hare, Sir W. Lawson, M.P., Mr. Price, M.P., Sir David Wedderburn, M.P., Mr. Winterbotham, M.P., Hon. Auberon Herbert, Mrs. Charles Kingsley, M. Louis Blanc, &c., &c.

Miss C. Biggs read the report, and it was resolved to bring in a Bill next session. During the session 257 petitions in favour of Women's Suffrage were presented in the House of Commons, with an aggregate of 61,705 signatures. These petitions were all, or almost all, presented through the Societies for Women's Suffrage, established in London, Manchester, Edinburgh, Dublin, Bristol, Birmingham, and Belfast. The report of the London Society states that 111 petitions were presented through its means, including one from London with 12,000 signatures, and that it had put in circulation 18,500 pamphlets, written by Mr. Mill, Miss Cobbe, Madame Bodichon, and Professor Newman.

Miss Becker, the Secretary of the Manchester Society, informs us that eighty-seven petitions were sent through the society to which she belongs, with 21,132 names attached to them. Miss A. Robertson, of Dublin, says that nine petitions, with 4160 signatures, were sent up for presentation from Ireland.

The Executive Committee of the London Society is composed of the following ladies:—Mrs. Brewer, Mrs. Donkin, Mrs. H. Fawcett, Miss Hare, Mrs. F. Hill, Miss E. Keary, Mrs. Boyd Kinnear, Mrs. Lucas, Mrs. F. Malleson, Mrs. R. Martineau, Mrs. Stansfeld, Mrs. Westlake. *Secretaries and Treasurers*:—Mrs. P. A. Taylor, Aubrey House, Notting Hill, W., and Miss C. A. Biggs.

The members of the Manchester Committee are:—Mr. Jacob Bright, M.P., Mrs. Jacob Bright, Miss Barton, Mrs. Butler, Mr. T. Chorlton, Mr. T. K. Greenbank, Dr. Pankhurst, Mr. R. D. Rusden, Mrs. R. Sutcliffe, Mr. T. P. Thomason, Miss A. Wilson, Miss Wolstenholme. *Secretary*:—Miss Becker, 28, Jackson's Row, Albert Square, Manchester. *Treasurer*:—Rev. S. A. Steinthal, 107, Upper Brook Street, Manchester.

Miss Agnes M'Laren, of Newington House, is the Secretary of the Edinburgh Society. We do not know the names of the Committee.

We doubt if there is a Committee in Dublin, but the two Misses Robertson, of 2, St. James' Place, Blackrock, do the work of getting up petitions. Miss Tod is Secretary to the Belfast Society; Miss Johnson, Linda Villa, to the Birmingham Society; and Professor Newman to the Bristol Society.

The following list of petitions in favour of Women's Suffrage presented to Parliament during the Session of 1869 is taken from the Parliamentary Report of Petitions.

THE FOLLOWING PETITIONS

FOR THE

PARLIAMENTARY SUFFRAGE FOR WOMEN,

Were presented to the House of Commons during the Session of 1869.

DATE.	DESCRIPTION OF PETITION.	BY WHOM PRESENTED.	NO. OF NAMES.
Feb. 18	Inhabitants of Ramsgate	Mr. P. A. Taylor	15
,, 22	,, Scarborough	,,	412
,, 22	,, Deal	,,	72
,, 25	,, Bolton	Colonel Gray	713
,, 26	,, Reigate	Mr. P. A. Taylor	16
,, 26	,, Shrewsbury	,,	63
Mar. 1	,, Barmouth	Mr. J. Bright	36
,, 2	,, Dyffryn	,,	40
,, 4	,, Pinner	Mr. P. A. Taylor	127
,, 5	,, Matlock Bank	,,	29
,, 8	,, Swansea	Mr. Dillwyn	61
,, 8	Jane Wigham	Mr. Mc Laren	1
,, 8	Margaret Armour	,,	1
,, 8	Lilias Craig, &c.	,,	2
,, 8	Jane Meik	,,	1
,, 8	Margaret & Elizabeth Hunter	,,	2
,, 8	E. Annie Macqueen	,,	1
,, 10	Inhabitants of Sabden	Mr. Starkie	42
,, 11	Mary Park	Mr. Miller	1
,, 11	Elizabeth Wilson	,,	1
,, 11	Mary Cockburn	,,	1
,, 11	Mary Veitch	,,	1
,, 11	Inhabitants of Petersfield	Mr. P. A. Taylor	115
,, 11	,, Tunbridge	,,	31
,, 15	,, Sunderland	Mr. Candlish	20
,, 15	,, Blackrock	Mr. J. T. Hamilton	121
,, 15	,, Kingston	Colonel Taylor	528
,, 15	,, Leominster	P. A. Taylor	36
,, 16	,, Hendon, Middlesex	Viscount Enfield	57
,, 16	,, Grt. Stanmore	,,	16
,, 17	,, Canterbury	Sir W. Lawson	78
,, 17	,, South Shields	Mr. Stevenson	58
,, 18	Elizabeth King	Mr. Mc Laren	1
,, 18	Mobena Moffat	,,	1
,, 18	Helen Steel	,,	1

Date.	Description of Petition.	By whom Presented.	No. of Names.
Mar. 18	Christiana and Jesse Bartholomew	Mr. Mc Laren	2
,, 22	Anne Chalmers	,, ...	1
,, 23	Women of Edinburgh	,, ...	153
,, 23	Inhabitants of Margate	Mr. Lusk	59
,, 23	,, Stranraer	Mr. George Young ...	40
April 1	,, Rivington	Mr. Jacob Bright.......	8
,, 5	Public Meeting, Carlisle	Sir W. Lawson.........	(Seal) 1
,, 5	Inhabitants of Monmouth ...	Mr. P. A. Taylor	11
,, 5	,, Bridgewater ...	,, ...	27
,, 7	,, Ambleside ...	Colonel Patten..........	78
,, 8	,, Woodbridge ...	Dr. Brewer	31
,, 8	,, Tavistock	Mr. A. Russell	68
,, 8	,, Thetford	Mr. P. A. Taylor	48
,, 9	Public Meeting, Newcastle ...	Mr. Headlam	(Seal) 1
,, 12	,, Choppington .	Sir George Grey	(Seal) 1
,, 13	Inhabitants of Merthyr Tydvil	Mr. C. Talbot .:......	102
,, 13	,, Tiverton	Hon. G. Denman......	46
,, 13	Margaret Scott	Mr. Mc Laren	1
,, 13	Emelia Wright	,, ...	1
,, 13	Isabella Hogg	,, ...	1
,, 14	Public Meeting, Dukinfield...	Mr. Jacob Bright.......	(Seal) 1
,, 14	Inhabitants of Bradford	Mr. W. E. Forster ...	52
,, 14	,, Hertford		58
,, 14	,, Frome	Mr. T. Hughes.........	87
,, 14	,, Lichfield	Mr. P. A. Taylor	218
,, 14	,, Peterborough .	Mr. Whalley.............	52
,, 16	,, Darlington ...	Mr. Backhouse..........	297
,, 16	,, Nottingham ...	Sir R. Clifton	170
,, 16	Mary Neal and others	Colonel Patten..........	8
,, 19	Public Meeting, Cheetham Hill	Mr. Jacob Bright.......	(Seal) 1
,, 19	Inhabitants of Cheetham Hill	,, ...	27
,, 19	G. J. Holyoake and others ...	Mr. Sartoris.............	108
,, 20	Inhabitants of Douglas..........	Mr. P. A. Taylor......	7
,, 20	,, Tunbridge Wells	,, ...	91
,, 22	,, Harrow	Viscount Enfield......	59
,, 22	,, Reading.........	Mr. P. A. Taylor......	9
,, 23	,, Framlingham .	,, ...	54
,, 23	,, Cockermouth .	Hon. P. Wyndham...	29
,, 23	,, Bootle	,, ...	54
,, 23	,, Whitehaven ...		81
,, 26	,, Stroud	Mr. Dickinson	27
,, 26	,, Wigan	Mr. Lancaster	262
,, 26	,, Teignmouth and Shaldon	Mr. P. A. Taylor......	38
,, 27	,, Mossley..........	Mr. Jacob Bright......	51
,, 27	,, Leicester	Mr. P. A. Taylor	200
,, 28	,, Rusholme	Hon. A. Egerton	64
,, 28	Public Meeting, Longsight ...	,, ...	(Seal) 1
,, 29	J. Wilson and others	Sir W. Lawson.........	39
,, 29	H. Hill and others	,, ...	31
,, 29	J. Thornton and others	Mr. Leatham	33

Date.		Description of Petition.	By whom Presented.	No. of Names.
April	30	Inhabitants of Morpeth	Sir George Grey	30
,,	30	Inhabitants of Edinburgh	Mr. M'Laren	1,813
,,	30	Women Ratepayers of Stranraer	,,	43
,,	30	Inhabitants of Trudoxhill	Mr. P. A. Taylor	9
May	3	,, Ipswich	Mr. Adair	116
,,	3	,, Oxfordshire	Mr. Henley	180
,,	3	,, Lancaster	Mr. Stanley	31
,,	3	,, ,,	,,	28
,,	4	,, Gloucester	Mr. W. Price	128
,,	4	,, Ottenfell	Mr. Stanley	48
,,	4	Harriet Rigbye	,,	1
,,	4	Inhabitants of Chesterfield	Mr. Strutt	17
,,	4	,, Hertfordshire	Mr. Taylor	17
,,	4	,, St. Columb	Mr. Trelawney	15
,,	5	,, Derby	Mr. A. Bass	26
,,	5	,, Bath	Mr. Tite	771
,,	6	,, Croydon	Mr. Locke King	422
,,	7	,, Choppington	Sir G. Grey	113
,,	7	,, Matlock Bath	Mr. Taylor	14
,,	10	,, Windsor	Mr. Eykyn	66
,,	10	,, Middleton and Tonge	Mr. Hibbert	98
,,	10	,, Stow-on-the-Wold	Mr. Taylor	13
,,	10	,, London	Mr. Torrens	11,834
,,	11	,, Manchester	Mr. Jacob Bright	1,494
,,	11	Women Householders of Manchester	,,	442
,,	11	George and Josephine Butler	Mr. Graves	2
,,	11	Robert Trimble, &c.	Lord Sandon	2
,,	11	Robert Beales, &c., Congleton	Mr. Whiteside	3
,,	11	Inhabitants of King's Lynn	Lord Stanley	375
,,	11	,, Kendal	Mr. Whiteside	16
,,	12	M. Martindale	Mr. Jacob Bright	1
,,	12	Alice Wood and others	Mr. J. S. Henry	5
,,	12	Inhabitants of Cheltenham	Mr. Samuelson	17
,,	12	,, Lincoln	Mr. Seeley	113
,,	12	Jane Townson	Mr. Stanley	1
,,	12	Inhabitants of Ipswich	Mr. Taylor	130
,,	13	,, Southampton	Mr. R. Gurney	30
,,	13	,, Street	Mr. Gore Langton	16
,,	13	,, Plymouth	,,	65
,,	27	,, Aberdeen	Colonel Sykes	229
,,	31	Public Meeting, Holbeck	Mr. Baines	(Seal) 1
,,	31	,, Hunslet	,,	(Seal) 1
June	1	Inhabitants of Manchester	Mr. Bazley	1,247
,,	1	Women of Manchester	Mr. Birley	1,005
,,	1	Inhabitants of Salford	Mr. Charley	148
,,	1	,, Longsight	Hon. A. Egerton	111
,,	1	,, Hayward's Heath	Mr. Fawcett	65
,,	1	,, Moffatt	Mr. M'Lean	18

Date.		Description of Petition.	By whom Presented.	No. of Names.
June	1	Ellen Ferguson	Mr. M'Lean	1
,,	1	Inhabitants of Liverpool	Mr. Rathbone	285
,,	1	,, Tynemouth ...	Mr. J. Smith	234
,,	1	Mary Hudson and others	Mr. Turner	119
,,	1	John Robinson and others ...	Mr. Whitwell	34
,,	3	Inhabitants of Ely	Dr. Brewer	13
,,	3	,, Norwich	,, ...	50
,,	3	,, Newcastle	Mr. Cowen	258
,,	3	,, LittleStanmore	Viscount Enfield......	33
,,	3	,, St. Asaph	Mr. Fawcett............	31
,,	3	,, Walsall.........	Mr. C. Forster	32
,,	3	,, Dewsbury......	Mr. J. Simon	58
,,	3	,, Carmarthen ...	Colonel Stepney	103
,,	7	,, Carlisle.........	Sir W. Lawson	99
,,	7	,, Cambridge ...	Mr. Jacob Bright......	34
,,	7	Fellows of Colleges, ,, ...	,, ...	8
,,	7	Women Ratepayers, M'chestr.	,, ...	292
,,	7	Inhabitants of Richmond ...	Mr. Dixon...............	100
,,	7	,, Rhyl	Mr. Taylor	19
,,	7	,, Broadway, Worcester	,, ...	21
,,	10	,, Retford	Mr. Barron	138
,,	11	,, Garstang	Colonel Patten.........	24
,,	11	,, Clayton-le-Moors	Mr. Starkie	23
,,	11	,, Penzance	Mr. Taylor	19
,,	11	,, Clitheroe	,, ...	18
,,	11	,, Grantham......	,, ...	19
,,	14	,, Sandwich	Mr. Brassey	51
,,	14	Eliza Jones and others	Sir Stafford Northcote	45
,,	14	Inhabitants of Cinque Ports.	Baron M. Rothschild.	94
,,	15	Women Ratepayers of Oxford	Mr. V. Harcourt	12
,,	15	Inhabitants of Oxford	,, ...	38
,,	15	,, Beverley	,, ...	30
,,	15	Fellows of Colleges, Oxford ...	,, ...	21
,,	16	Inhabitants of Malton, Yorkshire.........	Mr. Cowen	144
,,	16	,, Gravesend......	Sir C. Wingfield	39
,,	16	,, Manchester ...		1,235
,,	17	,, Cirencester ...	Mr. Bathurst	22
,,	17	,, Salford	Mr. Charley............	500
,,	17	,, Northampton..	Mr. Gilpin	319
,,	17	,, Newcastle	Mr. Headlam	244
,,	17	,, Huntingdon ...	Mr. Hughes	14
,,	17	,, Dover	Mr. Jessel...............	14
,,	18	,, Chatham	Mr. Otway	151
,,	18	,, Yarmouth	Mr. Taylor	38
,,	21	,, Pontefract......	Mr. Childers............	78
,,	21	,, Dalkey	Mr. Ion T. Hamilton..	106
,,	21	,, Bootherstown..	,, ...	56
,,	21	,, Williamstown..	,, ...	124
,,	21	,, Ballyroan	Mr. Pim	20
,,	21	,, Cork	,, ...	24

DATE.	DESCRIPTION OF PETITION.		BY WHOM PRESENTED.	NO. OF NAMES.
June 21	,,	Bruree, county Limerick...	Mr. Pim	21
,, 21	,,	Dublin	,, ...	3,164
,, 21	,,	Denbigh	Mr. W. Williams......	13
,, 22	,,	Haslingden ...	Mr. Holt	41
,, 23	,,	Manchester ...	Mr. Birley.............	985
,, 23	R. Whitelegge and others ...		Hon. A. Egerton	3
,, 24	Inhabitants of Thirsk		Sir C. W. Dilke	90
,, 23	,,	Argyleshire ...	Mr. M'Laren............	54
,, 24	J. Brine and others		Mr. Solicitor-General	327
,, 24	Inhabitants of Tenterden ...		Mr. Taylor	33
,, 24	,,	Watford	,, ...	5
,, 28	English residents in Lisbon...		Sir C. W. Dilke	5
,, 28	Inhabitants of Burnley		Mr. Stansfeld	56
,, 29	,,	Salford	Mr. Cawley	601
,, 29	,,	Brighton	Mr. Fawcett.............	112
,, 30	,,	Middlesborough	Mr. Bolckow	132
,, 30	Women Ratepayers of Salford		Mr. Charley............	50
,, 30	Inhabitants of Stockton-on-Tees		Mr. Dodds...............	149
July 1	,,	Manchester ...	Mr. Birley...............	1,000
,, 1	,,	Cowbridge, Glamorgan ...	Mr. C. Talbot	44
,, 1	,,	Birkenhead ...	Mr. Taylor	80
,, 2	,,	Waterloo	Mr. Cross	76
,, 2	,,	Co. Durham ...	Mr. Henderson	53
,, 2	,,	Brecon	Major Morgan	16
,, 6	,,	Truro............	Sir W. Lawson.........	23
,, 6	,,	Portsmouth ...	Mr. Stone	83
,, 7	,,	Wednesbury...		16
,, 9	Louisa Carbutt		Mr. W. Egerton	1
,, 9	Inhabitants of Battle		Mr. Taylor	17
,, 9	,,	Evesham	Mr. Taylor	14
,, 13	,,	Salford	Mr. Charley............	613
,, 14	,,	Hartlepool ...	Mr. Stevenson	285
,, 15	Women Householders of Manchester		Mr. Jacob Bright......	400
,, 15	Inhabitants of Greenwich ...		Rt. Hon. W. E. Gladstone	103
,, 15	,,	Bournemouth .	Mr. Haviland Burke .	31
,, 16	,,	Bury St. Edmunds	Mr. Hardcastle	37
,, 16	,,	Dumfries	Mr. Jardine	120
,, 16	,,	Kingston-on-Thames ...	Mr. Locke King	31
,, 16	,,	Helstone	Mr. A. Young	16
,, 19	,,	Newport	Mr. Taylor	9
,, 20	,,	London	Sir C. W. Dilke	10,835
,, 20	,,	Ripon	Lord J. Hay	33
,, 20	,,	Fifeshire	Mr. M'Laren.............	33
,, 21	,,	Manchester ...	Mr. Jacob Bright......	628
,, 22	,,	Ashton-under-Lyne.........	Mr. Mellor	230
,, 22	,,	Stockport......	Mr. Smith...............	750

Date.	Description of Petition.	By whom Presented.	No. of Names.
July 22	Inhabitants of Preston	Sir C. W. Dilke	87
,, 23	,, Knaresborough	Mr. Illingworth	100
,, 26	,, Salisbury	Dr. Lush	158
,, 26	,, Worcester	Mr. Sherriff	271
,, 27	,, Moulsey	Mr. Briscoe	34
,, 27	,, Ashton-under-Lyne	Mr. Mellor	540
,, 27	,, Stoke-on-Trent	Mr. O'Reilly	105
,, 29	,, Southport	Mr. Jacob Bright	242
,, 29	,, Manchester	,,	506
,, 9	Alderley and Chorley	,,	297
,, 9	Salford	Mr. Charley	700
,, 9	Swindon	Mr. Taylor	17
,, 9	Darwen	,,	102
,, 9	York	Mr. Brown Westhead.	26
,, 30	J. S. Mill and others	Sir C. W. Dilke	1,170
Aug. 2	Birmingham	Rt. Hon. John Bright	1,512
,, 2	Manchester	Mr. Jacob Bright	424
,, 9	,,	,,	3
,, 9	Women Householders of Manchester	Mr. Bazley	12
,, 9	,, ,,	,,	68
,, 9	,, ,,	Mr. Jacob Bright	100
,, 9	Inhabitants of Salford	,,	508
,, 9	,,	,,	473
,, 9	Scotland	Mr. M'Laren	26
Aug. 10	Salford	Mr. Charley	205

HIGHER EDUCATION OF WOMEN.

Lectures to ladies on English literature are to be given by Professor Morley, at Winchester, in the autumn. The professor is also to give two lectures on the same subject in Newcastle. Classes for young ladies are to be opened at Windsor in October on two afternoons in the week; Mr. William Johnson, of Eton, teaching Latin, and Mr. Oscar Browning, English history; while the Rev. Stephen Hawtrey takes elementary geometry, and Mr. W. H. Harris physical geography and geology. If these succeed, other classes will follow. For the scholarships at the Women's College, at Hitchin, there were ten candidates.

The University of Dublin has established examinations for women.

The following letter appeared in the *Spectator*, and several daily newspapers:—

"22, Manor Place, Edinburgh, July 26, 1869.

"Will you allow me to state that it is probable that classes will be opened this winter for the medical instruction of ladies in the University of Edinburgh, as the Medical Faculty, Senators and University Court have approved of the admission of women to the preliminary examination in Arts, and their subsequent matriculation as medical students.

"As arrangements are already in progress, it would be well for any ladies intending to join these classes to communicate at once with me on the subject.

"Sophia Jex-Blake."

RECORD OF EVENTS

QUARTER ENDING DECEMBER 31, 1869.

OPENING OF THE UNIVERSITY OF EDINBURGH TO WOMEN.

Last March Miss Jex-Blake applied to the Medical Faculty of the University of Edinburgh for permission to attend the summer courses of lectures in botany and natural history; and this permission was, after some discussion, accorded and subsequently confirmed by the majority of the Senatus (or whole body of professors). Strong opposition to the measure was made, however, by a few of the professors, and a petition against it was signed by a large number of the medical students, though there is good reason for believing that it did not originate with them. The pressure thus brought to bear induced the University Court to make use of the supreme authority vested in them to forbid the admission of a lady to the general classes, "considering the difficulties at present standing in the way," and thus the measure was for the time lost.

A month or two later, however, Miss Jex-Blake, having been joined by some other ladies desirous of medical education, renewed her application in a modified form, requesting that the sanction of the University might be given to the formation of *separate classes* for ladies. This proposal was approved by the Medical Faculty, Senatus, and University Court, and was in October submitted to the General Council consisting of all the graduates of the University. Great efforts were made to prevent its meeting with approval here; but, though a certain Edinburgh doctor distinguished himself by regretting that "women were increasing at a tremendous rate and could not be diminished like Norway rats," a favourable vote was given by a very large majority of the Council after some magnificent speeches by Professor Masson and other chivalrous supporters of the movement.

Five ladies have taken advantage of the permission thus accorded, and having passed with marked credit the preliminary examination in arts, are now studying medicine in the University. It is difficult to know whether most to congratulate the women who have gained so important a step, or the University which has thus won for itself the palm of liberality, and the certainty of fame in a future age, which will find it hard to believe how fierce a battle has now to be fought to procure for women leave either to toil or learn.—*From a Correspondent.*

The *Scotsman*, of November 12, in commenting on this

decision of the General Council of the University, says—

"The resolution to admit females as candidates for medical degrees was no more than was reasonable and to be expected It is manifestly too late in the day to resist this innovation. The movement has vindicated its propriety elsewhere by the irresistible logic of success; and when such a body as the University of Paris had recognised it, Edinburgh could gain nothing by refusal except the distinction of being old-fashioned, and the loss of an important class of students. . . . In short, the principle is unequivocally proclaimed that there should be no legal barriers in women's way towards any calling. If women are not to be judges or legislators, let it be for the same reason that they are not boiler-makers or drivers of stage-coaches—simply because, on trial, they are found not to have the power or taste for doing the work well. Nature can settle the matter without the help, or rather the encumbrance, of Statute."

HIGHER EDUCATION OF WOMEN.

The University of Oxford will admit girls to the local examinations next June. For the Cambridge local examinations 515 girls were entered as candidates at the examinations held just before Christmas.

The number of candidates at the Christmas examination last year was 401, and the year before 231.

The College at Hitchin was opened on October 16, under the direction of Mrs. Manning. The College is designed to be in relation to girls' schools and home teaching, what the Universities are towards the public schools for boys. The charge for students for board, lodging, and instruction, is 35*l*. per term. Ladies who may be unable to take the whole course, which would occupy three years, may be received for shorter periods.

The *Executive Committee*, by whom the college has been started, consists of the following ladies and gentlemen:—Lady Augusta Stanley, Lady Goldsmid, Mrs. Bodichon, Mrs. Russell Gurney, G. W. Hastings, Esq., James Heywood, Esq., Mrs. Manning, Miss F. Metcalfe, Hon. Mrs. Ponsonby, H. J. Roby, Esq., Professor Seeley, Sedley Taylor, Esq. *Treasurer*—H. R. Tomkinson, Esq., 24, Lower Seymour Street, London, W. *Honorary Secretary*—Miss Davies, 17, Cunningham Place, London, N.W., from whom further particulars can be obtained.

The School of Art at Edinburgh has been opened to female students, owing, we are informed, to the exertions of Miss Burton, of Tiverton Bank.

The University of Stockholm has decided to admit women to study medicine.

Lectures for ladies, in connection with the Universities, are now held in many of the large towns of England and Scotland.

We have much pleasure in calling attention to three new societies just established for the purpose of promoting the higher education of women. We give the London Society precedence.

ASSOCIATION FOR PROMOTING THE APPLICATION OF ENDOWMENTS TO THE EDUCATION OF WOMEN.

An Act " to Amend the Law relating to Endowed Schools and other Educational Endowments in England, and otherwise to provide for the Advancement of Education," was passed in Parliament last Session, and is known as the "Endowed Schools' Act, 1869."

H.M. Commissioners to carry out this Act are:—Lord Lyttelton, Rev. Canon Robinson, and Arthur Hobhouse, Q.C.,* and they are now beginning their work.

The Act contains the following clause:—" In framing schemes under the Act, provision shall be made, as far as conveniently may be, for extending to Girls the benefits of Endowments."

An Association is being formed, with a view to rendering such aid as may be found desirable in carrying out the directions of this clause, and the persons whose names appear below have consented to act as its first Committee.

This Committee will be glad to assist Trustees of Schools and other persons interested in Education, by supplying information, and by suggesting plans, whereby available funds may be most advantageously applied to the Education of Women. It is hoped that Local Committees will also be formed for mutual assistance, and as a means of awakening public interest in the matter. As regards London, the Committee desire to act, so far as lies in their power, as a local organisation, and to facilitate the action of the Commissioners, by collecting the most recent information respecting the Educational needs of each part of the

---

* We remarked in a former number of the *Review* that as Mr. Hobhouse had been a Charity Commissioner, we were afraid he would not be favourable to the education of women. We are now informed that Mr. Hobhouse is a strong friend to female education.

Metropolitan district, the wishes of the inhabitants, and the funds applicable to the Education of Girls.

The Committee desire to urge the importance of seizing the opportunity which this Act affords, of securing, by means of new schemes for the application of Endowments, a better provision than now exists for the Education of Women.

Committee.—Miss Bostock, Mrs. H. A. Bruce, James Bryce, Esq., Miss A. J. Clough, Miss Davies, J. E. Gorst, Esq., J. G. Fitch, Esq., T. H. Green, Esq., E. G. Herbert, Esq., Miss M. B. Smedley, with power to add to their number. *Honorary Secretary.*—Miss E. Bonham-Carter, Ravensborne, Beckenham.

An educational association has been formed at Manchester for the advancement of the education of women. The object of the Association is to unite in one society all friends of female education. It aims at the improvement of schools as well as of private education. It would watch the course of parliamentary legislation with a view to the application of public educational funds to girls as well as boys in fair proportion. It would provide lectures, similar to those which the universities offer to their undergraduates, at the cheapest rate compatible with real excellence. It would open classes to embrace all the subjects proposed in the Cambridge Local Examinations for women and girls; and establish libraries for female students similar to the free libraries of our large towns, or the reading room of the British Museum. It would also initiate and support such other measures or educational objects as may best tend to afford women, of whatever rank or previous education, advantages similar to those so profusely enjoyed by the other sex. Without promoting any extravagant changes, it is believed there is but too much room for improvement in every branch of female education, not only to supply the demand for duly qualified teachers, but even to ensure the solid mental culture necessary to every Englishwoman.

With a view to interesting and uniting as many as possible in so desirable an object, the committee has been constructed on a broad basis. The subscription required is small; and it is confidently hoped that a sufficient number of members will be at once enrolled to enable the executive committee to take immediate steps towards the attainment of some of the above objects during the present winter.

The minimum subscription is 2s. 6d. per annum.

Executive Committee.—Mrs. Anson, Birch Rectory; Rev. Canon Beechy, Worsley; T. Blacklock, Esq., Pendleton; Mrs. R. D. Darbishire, Victoria Park; Mrs. Durnford, Rectory, Middleton; Miss Gaskell, 84, Plymouth Grove; Mr. Principal Greenwood, Owen's College; Rev. W. Herford, 48, Dover Street, Oxford Road; Miss Higgins, Stocks, Cheetham; Mrs. W. J. Kennedy, 19, Ardwick Green; Mrs. Micholls, Grove House, Oxford Road; Rev. Canon Richson, 31, Shakspeare Street, Ardwick; Miss Wolstenholme, Moody Hall, Congleton. *Treasurer*—Mrs. Anson, Birch Rectory, Fallowfield. *Honorary Secretaries*—Miss Gaskell, 84, Plymouth Grove; Miss Higgins, Stocks, Cheetham.

The Ladies' Institute has been established at Belfast for the purpose of promoting the higher education of women throughout Ulster. It consists of ladies connected with all parts of the province, who are interested in the subject. Information respecting conditions of membership may be obtained from any of the lady-superintendents, or from the secretary. The number of members at present is about fifty.

The senate of the Queen's University having consented to establish senior and junior examinations for women, the Ladies' Institute intend, in future sessions, to provide classes in all the subjects required for the senior examinations. It is hoped that many schools will avail themselves of the opportunities of the junior Examinations.

President—The Lady Dufferin and Clandeboye; *Lady-Superintendents* — Mrs. Duffin, Queen's Elms; Mrs. Bushell, Strandtown; Mrs. M'Ilwaine, Hampton; Mrs. J. Scott Porter, College Square East; Mrs. J. Thompson, 17 University Square; Miss Tod, College Park. *Treasurer*—Mrs. Duffin. *Hon. Secretary*—Miss Tod. *Secretary*—Miss Connery, 35, Victoria Place.

A fourth plan for promoting the higher education of women has been set on foot at Cambridge.

For some time past it has seemed to many influential persons living in Cambridge, that it offers exceptional facilities for an attempt to extend the education of women, since it contains a large number of trained and practised teachers. The present time seems favourable for the experiment, as the University has recently instituted an examination for women on various subjects. Accordingly, a general committee has been formed of resident members of the University engaged in tuition, who have adopted a scheme of arrangement for lectures during the ensuing Lent Term. This committee comprises Professor Adams, C. C. Babington, Cayley, Liveing, and Maurice, and about twenty other Fellows, and tutors, or lecturers of their respective colleges. The lectures will, for the most part, commence in the first week in February, and will comprise English history, English language and literature, Latin, Greek, German, French, algebra, and the principles of arithmetic, practical arithmetic, geometry, logic, political economy, botany, geology, and physical geography, chymistry, harmony, and thorough bass, and the theory of sound in its application to music. The lectures will be delivered, generally speaking, twice a week within the period of University residence, and in the afternoon between the hours of two and five. The fee for a single course of lectures will be one guinea, and any women, having attained the age of seventeen, are eligible for attendance. It is intended that the scheme shall be self-supporting; but the committee will be glad to accept any funds offered for the formation of exhibitions. The executive committee are Mr. Bonney, St. John's; Mr. Ferrers, Caius; Professor Maurice and Mr. Peile, Christ's; Mrs. Adams, the Observatory; Mrs. Bateson, St. John's Lodge (treasurer); Mrs. Fawcett, Paston House; and Mrs. Venn, 11 Trumpington Street, the Rev. T. Markby, 10, Regent Street, and Mr. Sidgwick, of Trinity College, are the secretaries.—*Times*, December 18.

MUNICIPAL ELECTIONS.

The admission of women to vote at municipal elections for the first time (at least in modern days) is an event of no small importance. It is satisfactory to find that female householders have generally availed themselves of their new rights whenever a contested election has taken place. In the majority of towns, however, there has been no contest. In Bodmin two ladies voted, one aged ninety-two, the other ninety-four years.*

The following table sent by Miss Becker, will show the proportion in which women voted. The list of towns is, however, incomplete, as in many instances

---

* Report, Manchester Suffrage Society.

the town clerks did not furnish her with the necessary information.

It will be observed that as a general rule the proportion of men householders who voted compared to those who did not vote is larger than the proportion of women householders who voted compared to those who did not vote. This was to be expected, for it is so new an idea for women to vote that many would doubtless be prevented by timidity, as the votes had to be given in person.

In some towns, however, the proportion was equal—and in a few the proportion of women votes was the largest. This was the case at Ruthin where the proportion of women to men on the register was 1·0 to 3·9, while the proportion of women to men who voted was 1·0 to 2·6. At Bristol the proportion is still larger, the proportion of women to men on the register being 1·0 to 7, and the proportion who voted 1·0 to 4·6. At Bolton nearly the same thing occurred. At Leicester and Newark a slightly larger proportion of women voted. At Manchester, Preston, Wells, Maidstone, Guildford, and Exeter, the proportion of men was only a little larger than the proportion of women.

The proportion in which women voted shews pretty clearly in which towns what is called "strong-mindedness" has spread most widely. Brighton is not given in the list, but a local paper states that 400 women voted. On the whole list the proportion of women on the register is about one woman to eight men, the proportion of women who voted to men who voted, about 1·0 to 13.

A rough estimate shows that about one man voted out of every three men on the register; and one woman voted out of every five women on the register.

At Leeds a complimentary tea was given to the women voters in Holbeck Ward, when a time-piece was presented to the first woman who recorded her vote. The time-piece was purchased by the subscriptions of working men. It was stated in one of the speeches which followed the tea that the election in Holbeck Ward was conducted in so orderly a manner as to set a good example to other wards, and this was attributed to the influence of the large number of women who voted.

MUNICIPAL ELECTIONS, 1869.

Name of Borough.	Total No. of Voters on Register.	Number of Women on Register.	Proportion of Women to Men on Register.	No. of Wards in Borough.	No. of Wards Contested, Nov. 1, 1869.	Total No. of Persons who Voted.	Number of Women who Voted.	Proportion of Women to Men who Voted.
Abingdon	793	83	1 to 8·5	1	1	622	49	1 to 11·7
Banbury	683	83	1 to 7·2	1	0	0	0	
Basingstoke	727	93	1 to 6·7			422	26	1 to 15·2
Bath	5,980	1,250	1 to 3·8	7	2	832	111	1 to 6·5
Bedford	2,305	243	1 to 8·4	2	2	643	5	1 to 127·6
Berwick-on-Tweed	1,652	173	1 to 7·5	3	0	0	0	
Bewdley	397	32	1 to 11·4	1	0	0	0	
Bideford	1,037	140	1 to 6·4	1	1	731	73	1 to 9
Bodmin	600	93	1 to 6·1	1	1	473	53	1 to 7·9
Bolton	19,656	1,533	1 to 11·9			9,707	1,112	1 to 7·8
Bridport	1,134	128	1 to 7·8	2	2	838	78	1 to 9·7
Bristol	19,880	2,465	1 to 7	10	1	1,355	242	1 to 4·6
Bury St. Edmunds	1,613	250	1 to 5·4	3	0	0	0	
Canterbury	2,948	360	1 to 7·2	3	1	27	0	
Cardiff	3,819	317	1 to 11	2	1	304	3	1 to 100·3
Carmarthen	1,260	234	1 to 4·4	2	2	818	107	1 to 6·6
Chard	162	33	1 to 4	1	1	107	7	1 to 14·2
Chester	5,525	698	1 to 6·9	5	4	1,865	150	1 to 11·4
Clitheroe	1,335	224	1 to 5	1	0	0	0	
Colchester	3,419	324	1 to 9·5	3	0	0	0	
Coventry	6,572	799	1 to 7·2	5	3	36	1	1 to 85
Dartmouth	631	72	1 to 7·7	1	1	337	13	1 to 24·9
Deal	1,065	147	1 to 6·2	2	1	288	21	1 to 12·2
Denbigh	917	84	1 to 9·9	1	0	0	0	
Derby	8,904	970	1 to 8	6	0	0	0	
Devizes	757	60	1 to 11·4	2	0	0	0	
Dorchester	769	74	1 to 9·4	1	0	0	0	
Dover	3,202	352	1 to 8·1	3	2	1,328	98	1 to 12·5
Droitwich	591	35	1 to 15·9	1	0	0	0	
Durham	2,053	314	1 to 5·5	3	1	561	53	1 to 9·5
Evesham	711	100	1 to 6·1	1	0	0	0	
Exeter	4,780	699	1 to 5·8	6	6	3,345	396	1 to 7·4
Falmouth	427	61	1 to 6	1	1	176	9	1 to 18·5
Faversham	873	110	1 to 6·9	1	0	0	0	
Flint	688	53	1 to 11·9	1	1	144	0	
Gateshead	3,754	327	1 to 10·4	3	0	106	0	
Godalming	284	0		1	1	428	73	1 to 4·8
Great Torrington	495	86	1 to 4·7	1	1	1,765	60	1 to 28·4
Grimsby	3,298	198	1 to 15·6	1	1	826	104	1 to 6·9
Guildford	1,082	171	1 to 5·3	1	1	242	13	1 to 17·5
Harwich	663	62	1 to 9·7	1	1	647	62	1 to 9·4
Haverfordwest	934	128	1 to 6·3	1	1	370	0	
Helston	418	0		1	1			
Hereford	2,648			3	1	715	91	1 to 6·8
Hereford (1 ward)	1,035	160	1 to 5·4			540	59	1 to 8·1
Hertford	667	89	1 to 6·4	1	1	260	7	1 to 37·1
Ipswich	5,045	503	1 to 9	5	1	0	0	
King's Lynn	2,869	462	1 to 5·2	3	0	0	0	
Lancaster	1,424	0		3	0	3,570	265	1 to 12·4
Leicester	12,160	870	1 to 12·9	7	3	477	18	1 to 25·5
Leominster	910	119	1 to 6·6	1	1	0	0	
Lichfield	1,195	169	1 to 6	2	0	0	0	
Lincoln	4,153	397	1 to 9·4	3	0	416	22	1 to 17·9
Liskeard	729	96	1 to 6·6	1	1	79	6	1 to 13·1
Lyme Regis	359	67	1 to 4·3	1	1	246	14	1 to 16·5
Maidenhead	418	51	1 to 7·2			379	33	1 to 10·5
Maidstone	3,337	344	1 to 8·7	4	1	0	0	
Maldon	809	80	1 to 9·8	1	0			
Manchester	53,903	7,618	1 to 6	15	9	16,262	1,869	1 to 7·7
Manchester (9 Wards)	28,365	3,599	1 to 6·8					

Name of Borough.	Total No. of Voters on Register.	Number of Women on Register.	Proportion of Women to Men on Register.	No. of Wards in Borough.	No. of Wards Contested, Nov. 1, 1869.	Total No. of Persons who Voted.	Number of Women who Voted.	Proportion of Women to Men who Voted
Marlborough	514	35	1 to 14·2	1	1	393	17	1 to 22
Morpeth	694	129	1 to 4·3	1	1	81	4	1 to 19
Neath	1,082	0		1	1	804	0	
Newark	2,060	233	1 to 7·8	3	1	473	49	1 to 8
Newcastle-on-Tyne	12,693	1,370	1 to 8·2	9	3	1,170	64	1 to 17·2
Northampton	5,609	394	1 to 13·2	3	2	2,209	78	1 to 27·5
Oswestry	1,230	196	1 to 5·2	2	0	0	0	
Penryn	624	49	1 to 11·8	1	1	363	16	1 to 21·7
Penzance	1,462	306	1 to 3·7	2	2	527	46	1 to 10·4
Pontefract	714	69	1 to 9·3	1	1	331	7	1 to 46·2
Preston	12,317	1,735	1 to 6	6	3	4,771	521	1 to 8·1
Reading	3,461	482	1 to 6·1	3	0	0	0	
Richmond (Y.)	572	69	1 to 7·2	1	0	0	0	
Ripon	820	0		1	1	523	0	
Rochester	2,393	178	1 to 12·4	3	0	0	0	
Ruthin	666	135	1 to 3·9	1	1	110	30	1 to 2·6
Ryde, Isle of Wight	1,631	298	1 to 4·4	2	2	788	93	1 to 7·4
Rye	583	43	1 to 12·5	1	1	492	26	1 to 17·9
Salford	19,552	2,769	1 to 5·6	8	5	7,544	1,123	1 to 5·7
Scarborough	3,487	528	1 to 5·6	2	2	1,674	97	1 to 16·3
Southport*	2,624	656	1 to 3	4	4			
Southwold	630	80	1 to 6·8	1	0	0	0	
Stafford	2,058	171	1 to 11	2	2	49	0	
Stamford	1,289	158	1 to 7·1	2	0	0	0	
St. Ives, Cornwall	1,019	0		1	0	0	0	
Stockton	3,550	350	1 to 8·5	4	4	2,524	193	1 to 12
Stratford-on-Avon	558	86	1 to 5·8	1	0	0	0	
Truro	1,636	268	1 to 5·1	2	2	922	64	1 to 13·4
Wallingford	304	35	1 to 9·4	1	1	270	19	1 to 13·2
Walsall	5,892	246	1 to 22·9	3	1	1,662	47	1 to 34·4
Wells	611	68	1 to 8·2	1	1	450	40	1 to 10·2
Welshpool	1,278	89	1 to 13·3	1	0	0	0	
Winchester (1 Ward)	1,863	231	1 to 7	3	1	263	7	1 to 36·3
Wisbech	1,605	290	1 to 4·5	2	2	902	103	1 to 7·9
York	7,316	1,044	1 to 7	6	0	0	0	

* The Town Clerk made no definite report as to the women voting, but writes "A goodly number. The number who polled surprised us all."

THE SUFFRAGE.

The following Bill is to be introduced into Parliament next session—

1. That in all Acts now in force regulating or appertaining to the qualification and registration of voters or persons entitled or claiming to be registered and to vote in the election of Members of Parliament, wherever words occur which import the masculine gender, the same shall be held to include females for all purposes connected with and having reference to the right to be registered as voters, and to vote in such election.

Great exertions will be made by the various Suffrage Committees to elicit expressions of public opinion on the subject by petitions and public meetings. Hopes are confidently entertained in some quarters that the Bill will pass the House of Commons this session. In other quarters opinions are less favourable. There seems, however, to be no doubt that a very much larger number of members will vote for the measure this session (should a division take place) than voted for it two years ago.

The fact that so many women have shown themselves glad to make use of the municipal franchise, has removed the strongest argument against giving them the Parliamentary franchise, viz., that they did not wish for it, and would not use it.

A great meeting of the Manchester Suffrage Society was held in the Town Hall at Manchester, on December 15. The mayor, Mr. John Grave, presided, and the meeting was addressed by the Rev. S. A. Steinthal, Mr. Rylands, M.P., Mr. Charley, M.P. for Salford, Dr. Pankhurst, Miss Lilias Ashworth, Mr. Jacob Bright, M.P., Mr. B. Whitworth, Mr. Hopwood, Miss A. Wilson, Mr. Rusden, and Mrs. Josephine Butler.

Miss Becler read the report. The room was crowded, chiefly by ladies. It was resolved to request Mr. Jacob Bright, Sir C. Dilke, and Mr. Rylands to introduce a Bill into Parliament, next Session, to remove the electoral disabilities of women.

The following ladies and gentlemen were appointed to form the Executive Committee for the year 1870:—

Miss Barton, Miss Becker, Jacob Bright, Esq., M.P., Mrs. Jacob Bright, Mrs. Butler, Thomas Chorlton, Esq.; T. R. Greenbank, Esq.; Mrs. R. R. Moore, Dr. Pankhurst, R. D. Rusden, Esq.; Rev. S. A. Steinthal, Mrs. Sutcliffe, Mrs. J. P. Thommasson, Miss A. Wilson, Miss Wolstenholme.

It is stated in the report of the Manchester Society that a new branch of the National Women's Suffrage Society was formed at Carlisle last summer, of which Miss Smith is the secretary.

In the territory of Wyoming, United States, the elective franchise has been bestowed on women. They will vote henceforth at the election of members of Congress.

MARRIED WOMEN'S PROPERTY BILL.

The following petition is being extensively circulated.

To the Right Honourable the Lords Spiritual and Temporal in Parliament assembled,

The Humble Petition of the undersigned
SHEWETH,

1. That the common law of England, which gives the personal property and earnings of a wife to her husband, is unjust and inexpedient, and that the consequent injury presses with especial hardship on the poor.

2. That there is nothing in the nature of the marriage contract from which it can naturally result that wives should be deprived of the rights, privileges, and responsibilities of property, or of the enjoyment of their earnings.

3. That marriage settlements, by which the rich protect themselves from some of the consequences of the injustice, and which under the proposed alteration of the law they will be able to retain if they prefer them, are wholly unsuited to the case of earnings, as well as to the circumstances of the less wealthy possessors of property, who need and desire the utmost freedom in its disposition.

4. That no extension of the system of protection orders can adequately protect the earnings of wives, which in every case belong of right, and ought to be declared by law to belong to the earner, and not only in the case of the husband being unscrupulous and untrustworthy, of which besides the wife would be properly reluctant to adduce public proof.

Your Petitioners, therefore, humbly pray that your Lordships will pass the Bill entitled "A Bill to Amend the Law with respect to the Property of Married Women.

And your Petitioners will ever pray.

[This Petition to be signed by Men and Women, with the full Christian and Surname. It must be forwarded, when signed, to Miss Wolstenholme, Moody Hall, Congleton.]

Ladies of high standing can greatly assist the passage of this Bill by privately calling the attention of Peers to the cases of hardships that so often occur under the present law.

Several excellent pamphlets can be obtained from Miss Wolstenholme.

The case of Kelly *v.* Kelly, reported in the newspapers of December 8, curiously illustrates the tendency of the present law to create dissension in families. A legacy of 5000*l.* is left to Mrs. Kelly by her sister. Mr. Kelly loses the greater part of it in a speculation. Mrs. Kelly becoming anxious to save the remainder, asks a relative to examine the will to ascertain if she has power to prevent her husband from disposing of it. The correspondence falls into Mr. Kelly's hands, who is rendered furious by what he considers undutiful and deceitful conduct on his wife's part, and treats her with systematic cruelty for two years. At last Mrs. Kelly sues for a judicial separation and obtains it.

Is it not perfectly clear that if Mr. Kelly had had no power over the money, and if Mrs. Kelly had been able to dispose of it openly in whatever manner she thought best, the chances of a quarrel ensuing would have been much diminished? Mrs. Kelly felt that she had a moral right to preserve the legacy her sister had left her for herself and her son if she could. Mr. Kelly knew that he had the legal right of disposing of it as he pleased, and when moral right and legal right are opposed to each other, collisions are pretty sure to occur.

EMPLOYMENT OF WOMEN.

The following letter, written by the Hon. Mrs. Locke King, has appeared in the *Times*:—

To the Editor of the Times,

SIR,—Assured of your sympathy in all that commends itself to thoughtful intelligence, I am anxious to enlist your powerful aid on behalf of educated women in indigent circumstances, daughters of professional men and others, on whom indigence too often suddenly comes entirely unprovided for, and whose cause has been advocated during the last ten years, by a society called "The Society for Promoting the Employment of Women."

Statistics have laid bare the fact that in England, in modern times, there is a large surplus of women over men, and it has been calculated that about two millions of these women are dependent for their bread on their own exertions.

To become either a governess or a dressmaker was formerly the only prospect that lay before these two millions of more or less educated women.

This society, started at the suggestion of an energetic lady, has been successfully, to a certain extent, endeavouring to pave the way for women either themselves willing, or whose parents are willing for them, to undertake other occupations than these, with a view of obtaining their livelihood.

At the present time much could be done in the way of training girls, and helping them with premiums, if the income of the society permitted.

It may be well to state that, among the occupations now open for women, some of which can be carried on under the domestic roof, are law copying, bookkeeping, glass engraving, jewel-case making, carving, artistic work in wood, hair-dressing, telegraphing, dispensing, and various other resources may be originally traced to this society.

May we not hope that the English public will take this society into consideration more than it has yet done, and, following the example of Her Majesty, the Crown Princess of Prussia, and the Princess Louise, come liberally forward either with donations or with annual subscriptions?

In conclusion, I will only add that the tenth annual report of the society and full particulars of the work in all its branches may be had at 23, Great Marlborough Street, between the hours of ten and five.

I have the honour to be, Sir, your faithful servant,

Dec. 6. LOUISA ELIZABETH KING.

There are now two large and fashionable hairdressers' establishment in London where women are employed. These are Douglas's at 21 and 23 Bond Street, and Truefit's at 20 and 21 in the Burlington Arcade.

The *Times* reprints a favourable notice of the Edinburgh Employment Society from the *Scotsman*, giving an abstract of its eighth annual report.

A School for Telegraphy has been established in London, where young men and young women are taught.

A technical school, where girls are taught handicrafts, has been established at Warsaw, and is said to be highly successful.

A Horticultural School for girls is about to be established in Ithaca, New York. They are to be taught agricultural chemistry, gardening, how to preserve fruits and manage bees, besides housekeeping and needlework. The object is to make good farmers and farmers' wives. Nothing is said about milking, cheesemaking, or poultry keeping, but perhaps these may be included in the grand phrase, " Technical Knowledge." It seems to be an excellent scheme. We are well convinced that Industrial and Technical Education is much needed by women. It is intended that the work of the farm should be as much as possible performed by the pupils.

THE PEASANTRY OF CUMBERLAND AND WESTMORELAND.

THERE is one chapter in the report of the Agricultural Commission—*i.e.* that which relates to Cumberland and Westmoreland—the life, habits, and education of the labourers in these northern counties—which deserves a separate notice. It contains much that will sound to southern ears novel and almost incredible, and presents an array of facts which are of a kind that, on a superficial view, might drive an educationalist or a moralist to despair. Before entering on the question of the propriety of forbidding female and children's out-door labour, it may be as well to see how matters are with the Cumbrian peasantry on this and cognate subjects. The people referred to have been for the last century, and are at this moment, able to compare favourably in education with those of any county in England. The children are sent to school with more or less regularity up to the age of thirteen or fourteen. The labourers, both men and women, are well fed, well paid, simple and contented in their habits and disposition, of an independent turn of mind, prudent and thrifty, and—very immoral. It should be borne in mind that in old times the word Northumbria was used to signify the whole country from the Humber up to the Firth of Forth. The Scottish lowlands, Northumberland, Yorkshire, North Lancashire, and the dales of Cumberland and Westmoreland were inhabited by the same hardy, independent race. It is not, therefore, surprising that the yeomen and dalesmen of these counties have in many respects the same characteristics, or that they present a marked contrast to the agriculturists in the southwest of England, for which the difference in race fully accounts. When the report on agricultural Scotland is published we feel tolerably sure that our remarks will be borne out. Cumberland and Westmoreland are thinly populated counties, consisting mostly of small estates and small farms. The cattle, which last century were the principal support of the people, fed on the moors or hill sides, were more remarkable for their hardiness and activity than their fitness for food. Oat cake, porridge, bacon, dried legs of mutton, rye bread, and skim-milk cheese, were the ordinary articles of diet, and the Commissioners seem to think it poor fare, but it made bone and muscle, and produced a strong and healthy peasantry. It is mentioned that in 1795 Mr. Curwen, then member for Carlisle, to show the inability of the labouring population to bear any more taxation, entered the House of Commons dressed as a Cumbrian labourer, in a grey homespun coat, wearing the wooden clogs of the country rimmed with iron, carrying under one arm a brown " groudie," or loaf made of mixed barley and rye, and under the other a "whellimer," or skim-milk cheese, and bearing in his hand a " gully," or large knife, with which, when he cut the black loaf and the cheese he had placed on the table, he produced a sound in the one resembling the crushing of cinders, and in the other that of planing a deal board.

In 1805 farms under fifty acres were by far the most numerous, but though the land is still much divided, the old statesmen, or those who are owners of about thirty acres, and with the assistance of their families, work this bit of land so as to support themselves, are, as a class, dying out. So much of the country is barren mountain or moorland that in such districts many hands are not required, and a few shepherds with their dogs do all that is necessary. But everywhere labour is scarce, and in great demand both for men and women, and high wages and excellent food are given. A Westmoreland farmer stated, in reply to the question whether he employed any women but his own farm servants in field labour, that he would willingly do so if he could get them, but that if he wanted a single extra female hand he should have to go to Carlisle, a distance of thirty miles, to hire her. In all the farms the women servants help in the out-door work. This Mr. Tremenhere seems to lament, but we see little to deplore in it. A case was indeed mentioned by him of one young woman who contracted a complaint from the hardships to which she had been exposed by working in a farmyard, and from which she died. But against a solitary instance of this kind it may be reasonably urged that many hundreds of girls occupied in sedentary and unwholesome employments, pursued in close and ill-ventilated rooms, contract consumption and other fatal complaints, or linger out a shortened life in a state of permanently debilitated health. Moreover it ought to be remembered that these women are to be wives and helpmates of the men, and the Commissioners quite admit that with respect to this class of servants, both male and female, "sickness is very rare, their excellent diet and regular hours keeping them in excellent health." The great majority of these labourers are boarded in the farm houses, and four ample and nourishing meals per diem leave nothing to be desired on that score. Beer and tea are but little used, but porridge is as common as it is among the Scotch. The wages of an in-door male farm servant are from 18*l.* to 30*l.*, everything found; strong young girls from 5*l.* to 12*l.*; out-door men from 12*s.* to 21*s.* per week, with free cottage, potatoes, or keep of a cow. Harvest wages are extra. Even children can at some work earn from 1*s.* 6*d.* to 2*s.* a day. The population increases slowly, and early marriages are the exception and not the rule. "These servants are not like the agricultural labourers of some other parts of England, a well-defined portion of the community, who marry without regard to consequences, and multiply beyond the requirements of the labour market." This is no doubt greatly owing to the natural thrift and forecast of the people. They see plainly that though an out-door labourer receives high wages, single men resident in the house are more advantageously situated. Reckoning the cost of a man's board at about 15*l.* 12*s.*, and his wages at 20*l.*, it gives, it is true, only an average of 14*s.* 6*d.* per week, or 35*l.*; but he is much better fed, warmed, and lodged than he would probably be in a cottage of his own, and he is employed in preference by the farmers because, as the latter state, "such men are always at hand, and less particular about hours; they not only do more and better work in a given time, but work longer and harder. On many farms the farmer's sons and the farmer himself work with the men, who can't object to labour which the master's family share with themselves." It is said also that many of the farmers take considerable pains to provide amusement and recreation for the men after hours. Farm servants here are both able and willing to save money. In the Morland branch of the Carlisle Savings Bank alone fifteen of these men had placed to their credit various sums of from 100*l.* to 182*l.* each, and six women had saved from 106*l.* to 189*l.* each. In the Penrith Branch Bank 260 male farm servants had upwards of 9259*l.* and 240 women had laid by nearly 8000*l.* Many of them have purchased small farms, chiefly grass or pasture land, but this is not so commonly done as formerly, and in such cases these small farmers and their families work harder and are more pinched than the labourers. The cottages are of stone, solidly built and warm, but to southern eyes they wear a bare, grey, and desolate appearance. Often the farmhouses have been made out of the remains of small domestic fortresses, which were built in troublesome times, when the border raids were something more than common, and the outbuildings for cattle are sometimes of a very superior description. The people do not care much for gardens or allotments; these require more labour to yield profit than the men are inclined to give after a hard day's work. The women make their own terms, and receive high wages as we have seen. They do not work much in wet weather, and are quite independent about what they will do; they are exceedingly strong and robust, and hoe turnips or reap corn— shear it, as it is there termed—nearly as well as men. Some of the Commissioners regret that they should be thus employed, and seem to think the prevalence of unchastity, which undeniably exists, has something to do with it. But there are other reasons which are to our minds more cogent. Many of these persons are exceedingly respectable and orderly, and the Cumbrian women have the reputation of being quite strong enough and able to defend themselves from any undue precipitancy on the part of the men if they choose.

We intimated before that in some respects these people present characteristics which it is difficult to make square with all the theories usually entertained on such subjects. A high value is placed on education, and it is quite certain that these counties are in this particular more advanced than most parts of England, but excessive laxity of morals is the rule, the per centage of illegitimate births is very large, and what is the worst part is that this state of things is not considered either extraordinary or disgraceful. A girl who has had what is usually termed there "a misfortune"—*i.e.* a chance child, or even several—is hardly thought of as being at all the worse for it, and in some districts the workhouses bear a great resemblance to lying-in hospitals. On the other hand, there is a remarkable absence of crime. Burglaries and highway robberies are unknown, and the chief constable reports that in the returns furnished to him a year ago by his superintendents there was not recorded a single person or a house under the respective designations of "known thieves," "receivers of stolen goods," "prostitutes," "suspected characters," "houses for receivers of stolen goods," "beer-houses of bad character," "coffee-shops, ditto," "houses of ill-fame," and other "suspected houses." But after attentively reading the report we find at p. 146 some observations which go a long way to explains this apparent anomaly.

"The sleeping accommodation in the farmhouses has long been a disgrace to these counties, and although some improvement has taken place in this respect within the last twenty years, the same stairs often lead to the rooms of both male and female servants. Only a few years ago, in one of the largest farmhouses in the district, belonging to one of its principal landed proprietors, the men and women servants slept in the same room, the men at one end, the women at the other, with not even a curtain to separate them; and in another case, a farmer, apologising for the domestic arrangements of his house, said he had done the best he could for the protection of his female servants by putting curtains to their beds."

It therefore appears to us that it is not because the women

work in the fields that unchastity prevails, for physical fatigue is in itself a corrective to riotous conduct, but because a great number of young and well-fed single farm servants of both sexes are lodged together in the farmhouses without proper separation, supervision, or discipline. Congregated together in this fashion, distant from large towns or even villages, and having no companions but each other, what follows is hardly unnatural and certainly not surprising. As long as these causes remain the results will be the same, until men and women too can keep their bodies in more temperance, soberness, and chastity than town folks do. It would almost seem that we are driven to choose one of three evil things: a state of general immorality among the men and women alike, which is esteemed neither scandalous nor even very objectionable; or the majority of the women are chaste, but there is abundance of prostitution; or we get to virtuous poverty, that particular form of virtue which is quite apart from prudence and self-denial, and culminates in early marriages, eight children, and about as many shillings a week to maintain them. Still, among the people we have been describing there seems such a solidity and independence of character, and the elements of so much that is excellent and entirely worthy of respect, that we believe that if their intelligence and attention were directed to the matter, the larger farmers would make alterations and arrange for a better system, which would be both possible and easy, and that the best of their servants, men and women alike, would understand and approve of the change.—*Pall Mall Gazette*, December 18.

We have been requested to publish the following circular—

EMPLOYMENT FOR WOMEN.

Some months since a few gentlemen, interested in improving the art of printing and in introducing women into the trade, quietly employed a young woman from one of our Lancashire mills, who had never before seen printer's types. She spent ten days in study upon a plan devised to give with rapidity and thoroughness, the knowledge needed by the type setter. At the end of this time she commenced to set type, and in two weeks could earn double her ordinary wages at the usual rates paid to men. The quality of the work challenges comparison with that of the best newspaper offices. This young woman was considered a fair average of the intelligent young women to be found all over the United Kingdom to whom this work would be a priceless boon.

The success attending this single experiment led to a trial with a small class of young women under the tuition of the first, and for this purpose a school-room was rented for a number of weeks. The class gave sufficient evidence of aptitude to warrant the taking of premises for the prosecution of the printing business, and now some twenty-five young women have been trained and are ready to take in hand newspaper or other plain work. An evening class has also been organised among those who attend daily work, but are willing to sacrifice their too few hours of leisure to learn a new business that promises to give them a higher position in life. It is now proposed to give this enterprise a permanent organization by forming a limited liability company, the shares of which shall be 1*l*. each, so that every person employed may have an opportunity to participate in the profits by investing her surplus wages.

The Company if well managed, cannot fail to become a good investment, for it can be demonstrated that by organising a printing-office thoroughly, and introducing all the latest appliances, the work can be done at one third present prices, while paying good wages to those employed.

Further particulars may be learned of

CHARLES WILSON FELT,

5, CROSS-STREET, MANCHESTER.
DECEMBER 10, 1869.

P. S. This office will be organised for the purpose of showing the advantage of employing women; and as soon as the advantages are acknowledged, efficient plans will be promulgated for teaching and placing women in any and every office in the Kingdom.

A meeting was held was held at Manchester to consider the plan. The propriety of employing women was warmly disputed, but it seems to have been generally admitted that the new system of combined printing was an improvement on the old one, and a vote of thanks was given to Mr. Felt the inventor.

BOARDING OUT OF PAUPER ORPHANS.

Mr. Goschen has sent Mr. Henley, the Poor Law Inspector, to Scotland to inquire into the working of the boarding out system in that country where it has long been in practice.

It has been adopted in England in twenty-one Unions. The following account of the scene that occurred early this winter at Weymouth on the adoption of the plan will nterest our readers.

"At the Board meeting a large number of applicants to take charge of the children presented themselves, and it was most satisfactory to observe that they were of the best class of the working people in the rural districts, several of whom were themselves related to the children.

For instance, a grandmother applied for the care of her three orphan grandchildren, an aunt for three children of her deceased sister, deserted by their father. Again, the wife of a seaman in Her Majesty's Service, who had just lost an only child, wished for one to fill that void, and fixed her choice upon one about three years old. I was informed by the matron that it was the sweetest tempered child in the house, without either father or mother or known relative. Each applicant's name and means were inquired into, and it was resolved that the application should be referred to the guardians of each parish for their report of the fitness of the applicants to receive the children, such report to be supplemented by the clergyman of the parish. After these preliminaries had been duly settled, a rather amusing scene took place. The applicants asked leave to see the children, and to the surprise of the board, very soon returned, each leading a child or two by the hand and exclaiming that these were their children, and that they would have taken them at once if it had been so permitted. At the end two came in with a girl between them, one saying, 'This is the one I should like.'

'I don't like to say anything to make things unpleasant,' says the other, 'but I knew her mother and father, and for their sakes I should like to have this one.' And if report be true they came to rather high words on the subject. I know not if a Solomon will be required to settle the dispute. It is hoped that at the commencement of the new year the arrangements will be completed, and the system of boarding out the orphan and deserted children in full operation."—*From a Weymouth Newspaper.*

LIST OF UNIONS IN WHICH THE BOARDING-OUT SYSTEM HAS BEEN ADOPTED, IN ENGLAND AND WALES, DECEMBER, 1869.

Leominster
Highworth and Swindon
Eton
Caistor

Warwick
Ludham
Yardley Gobion and Stony Stratford

Horncastle
King's Norton
Chorlton
Evesham
Bath
Clifton
Dartford

Newport Pagnell
Colchester*
Berwick-on-Tweed*
Merthyr Tydvil*
Buckingham
Weymouth
Southampton

The plan is under consideration in several other Unions.

MEDICAL.

Miss Garrett, F.S.A., has just passed the third examination for the M.D. of Paris. The subjects of the examination were chemistry, zoology, natural philosophy, and botany. The examiners were M.M. Wurtz, Baillon, and Lutz. Miss Garrett's note was "bien satisfait," the highest, it is stated, that has been gained for these subjects since the commencement of the session. *Pall Mall Gazette*, December 20.

At Zurich, when medical education was first opened to women three years ago, four ladies entered as pupils, next year there were eight, last year the number had risen to sixteen. The year 1870 will probably see a further increase.

Our readers will be interested in hearing that the first woman who ever received a medical diploma in modern times is now practising in London. Elizabeth Blackwell is an Englishwoman, a native of Bristol, where her father was extensively engaged as a sugar refiner. In 1832, Mr. Blackwell was so heavy a loser by the failure of several commercial houses that he determined on removing to the United States; but such was the esteem in which he was held by his fellow townsmen that a nunber of merchants met in the Exchange and offered to lend him as much capital as he might require to carry on his business. Mr. Blackwell, however, declined the offer and went to New York, where he established a sugar refinery, and was for some years exceedingly successful, and took an active part in the organisation of the American Anti-slavery Society.

---

* Not absolutely certain.

The commercial crisis of 1837-8 caused him such heavy losses, that at his death, which occurred in the year following, he left his family in poverty. The widow and her elder children were thus thrown upon their own exertions for the support of themselves and the younger children. The elder daughters became teachers, the only career open to them. This profession was, however, extremely distasteful to Elizabeth, then in her eighteenth year. And as soon as the younger children could provide for themselves, she commenced saving money for the purpose of entering the medical profession. In 1847 she endeavoured without success to obtain admittance to the medical schools at Philadelphia.

She had better success at the College of Geneva in the State of New York, and in 1849 she there obtained her diploma.

She afterwards studied medicine in Paris and London, and in 1851 returned to New York, where she established a dispensary for women and children, and some years afterwards a hospital for women.* Since she opened the way, many women in the United States have become physicians. It is stated that there are no less than 300, all earning good incomes.† Dr. Elizabeth Blackwell is at present practising at 37 York Place, Portman Square.

MISS CARPENTER,

AT the Social Science Congress, it was resolved by the Council to elect Miss Carpenter an Honorary Member of the Association. In the farewell address of that lady, previous to her return to India, she stated that much interest in female education had been aroused among educated Hindoos.

MISCELLANEOUS.

MRS. POVALL, a lady at the Cape of Good Hope, has

---

* This account of Dr. E. Blackwell is abridged from the *Englishwoman's Journal* of April, 1858.
† See "The College, the Market, and the Court," by Mrs. Dall. Page 429.

for several years been engaged in rearing silk worm. She returned to England some months ago with specimens of silk. These were pronounced to be of very good quality, but of little value on account of having been badly reeled. On this Mrs. Povall went to Berlin, and worked in a silk factory till she learned the art of reeling perfectly well. She is now returning to the Cape to teach the women there how to reel, and hopes to establish a good trade.

THERE is an excellent article in *Macmillan's Magazine* for October, by Canon Kingsley, on "Women and Politics." Everybody should read it.

MR. MILL'S book on "The Subjection of Women," has reached several editions. It has been favourably reviewed in Russia, and is said to be much read there. This work has given a great impulse to the woman's movement all over the world.

MISS RYE'S Home for Children at Niagara was formally opened on the 1st instant. In the course of some remarks explaining the objects of the Home, Miss Rye said it was not the lack of money that prevented a larger flow of young emigrants to Canada. The British public only wanted to see that a suitable outlet could be had for its homeless little ones, and the means for sending and maintaining them for a time would not be wanting. More than 100,000 could be had at once if the colony could find homes for them. Miss Rye said she did not ask the people of Canada for money, but for their sympathy and moral support in finding places for the orphan children. The arrangements of the Home and the appearance of the children seem to have created a very favourable impression upon the visitors.—*Echo*, December 22.

THE Canadian papers, in speaking of the arrival at Niagara of Miss Rye with the seventy orphan children she has taken out from England, refer in favourable terms to the appearance of the youthful emigrants. There are seven boys in the party, and a few grown up girls; but the majority are girls between five and seven years of age. "What struck the spectator on their arrival at Niagara," says the *Toronto Globe*, "was the unlimited confidence of these children in Miss Rye, and the affection they endeavoured to show in many artless ways." The *Niagara Mail* is of opinion that Miss Rye has done more to promote the cause of emigration than all the societies of the colony put together. The Government of Ontario cannot, it thinks, but recognize this "great benevolent work" as one claiming its sympathy and support.— *Campden Herald*, December 11, 1869.

MISS STARR'S picture "Wandering Thoughts" at the Dudley gallery is much admired.

WOMEN'S CLUB AND INSTITUTE.—An interesting social meeting was held last night at the rooms of this institution, 77, Newman Street, Oxford Street. This club —the subscription to which is only five shillings a year— offers the advantage of reading room, supplied with newspapers and periodicals, and a gradually increasing selection of books; a drawing room, a visitor's room, and a dining room, where refreshments are supplied at a moderate price. The club already numbers 230 members, chiefly young ladies engaged in art, literature, or tuition, and it may be expected to make rapid progress as it becomes more widely known. — *Echo*, December 22.

A LADIES' ASSOCIATION has been formed for the purpose of procuring the repeal of the Contagious Diseases Acts. A protest has been published against the principles of the Acts in question, and the promoters of the movement say that the necessity for such an association as they have started becomes more urgent from the fact that a society is already in existence for procuring the extension of the obnoxious measures to the women of the whole kingdom. "We earnestly entreat our countrywomen," they say, "of every class and party, to help us in the difficult and painful task which only a deep sense of duty could have forced us to undertake. We have not entered lightly upon it, nor shall we lightly abandon it, because we believe that in its attainment are involved, not only the personal rights of our sex, but the morality of the nation." The first name on the list of signatures is that of Harriet Martineau. Among those who have signed are Miss Nightingale and Miss Lydia Becker. Ladies who wish to join are to send their names to the Honorary Secretary, Mrs. George Butler, 280, South Hill, Park Road, Liverpool.—*Pall Mall*, December 31.

MISS MULOCK is bringing out a charming story in *Macmillan's Magazine*, entitled "A Brave Lady," in which the injustice of the laws of marriage is illustrated.

"THE MINISTER'S WIFE," by Mrs. Oliphant, a most delightful tale, also contains some good remarks on the subject.

VI.—CORRESPONDENCE.

MENDING.

"How do you get your clothes mended?" asked a lady artist of another whose genius draws admiring crowds to see and hear her whenever she appears in public.

"I wear them till they drop off, and then I get others; I have tried long and vainly to find a mender, and now I do without." Such was the resigned reply.

Asking the same question of a foreign authoress, we found that she sacrificed one day in the week to this dull business.

"In France," said she, "I used to have a woman in once a fortnight, to put all the linen in order, my own wardrobe and my mother's, and the house linen; but here in England there is no such thing as a professional mender."

We speak in the interests of both classes—those who want their mending done for them, and those who might make a livelihood by doing it—when we say that this useful art is not sufficiently studied by those who maintain themselves by needlework, neither does it meet with the attention it deserves as a necessary branch of industrial education. Why should not girls who learn to sew at school learn especially to mend? It is surely a most desirable accomplishment for a girl who is to be a domestic servant or a poor man's wife, or who, under whatsoever circumstances, has to earn her own clothes and make them last as long as possible.

In France and Germany, mending is a trade, a separate branch of industry which some women carry to considerable perfection, and by which they make their living. We have seen stockings and pieces of muslin, linen, and other fabrics, so well mended by a German, that it was difficult to find the place where the hole had been, and that in a shorter time than a less skilled needlewoman would have taken to cobble up the torn or worn place in the clumsiest manner.

Why should we not have regular menders in England? There are hundreds, perhaps we should be nearer the mark if we said thousands, of persons in London alone, who would be thankful to pay *anything* in reason to a competent woman, who would come on stated days, with clean hands and a clean apron, and look over all the buttons and tapes, and put in the many single stitches, each of which "saves nine." We have plenty of dressmakers of every degree of fashion and every scale of expense; plenty of sempstresses to make new clothes; but where is the mender?

A sempstress who goes out for the day earns two shillings, but generally she can't or won't mend. A charwoman also earns two shillings a day besides her food. We venture to assert that a mender might earn at least double. A lace-mender earns whatever she chooses to ask; we grumble, but we value our lace, we must have it well mended, we don't like the labour of doing it for ourselves, possibly our eyes are not equal to such fine work, so we patronise the mender. But a mender for all our clothes! where is she?* A. B. C. D.

---

* Menders can be obtained from the office of the Society for the Employment of Women, 23, Great Marlborough Street, London, W. We are sorry to say they are not paid the magnificent wages which our correspondent thinks they could earn.

THE ENGLISHWOMAN'S REVIEW.

(NEW SERIES.)

No. II.—APRIL, 1870.

ART. I.—NEW OBJECTIONS TO WOMEN'S SUFFRAGE.

THAT determined enemy to women's suffrage, the *Pall Mall Gazette*, has brought forward two new objections to it. The first objection is that the manner in which women voted at the municipal elections shows them to be entirely unfit for political power.

The *Pall Mall Gazette* is pleased to say it has discovered that at the municipal elections the women voters always voted for the candidate who was supported by the clergy of the town, except where they voted in favour of the candidate who was supported by the dissenting ministers, and that they are thereby clearly convicted of being under clerical influence.

We are inclined to think that exactly the same thing may be said of almost all male voters. Every candidate of tolerably good character was sure to be supported, either by the clergy, or by the nonconformist ministers, and it would have been difficult to avoid voting for one or the other, if one voted at all. There may have been some unlucky candidates, who, owing to the badness of their characters, or to some other cause, were opposed by the clergy of all denominations; it is not likely that women would support these men, for the same reasons which caused the clergy to oppose them would also cause women to oppose them.

In one instance we saw the address of a candidate, in which he appealed to women voters to support him, on the ground that he was opposed to a multiplicity of public-houses, and that he would use his power, if elected, to diminish their number.

No doubt a good many women voted for him, and it is almost certain that these principles of his would also secure for him the support either of the clergy, or of the dissenting ministers. Women suffer so much from the intemperance of men, that those among them who had votes were almost certain to vote for the temperance candidate, whenever there was one, and as the clergy are well aware of the great evils which arise from drinking, it is likely enough that the same candidate would obtain their support also.

It does not follow, therefore, that women are specially under clerical influence, because they voted for the same candidate as the clergyman. It would be just as reasonable to say that a man was under *medical* influence because he voted for the same candidate as the doctor. If the list of male voters was looked into, it would probably be found that men had always voted for the candidate who received the support of some doctor or other, if not an allopath, then an homœopath. Just in the same way women have always voted for the candidate supported by some minister of religion, if not a clergyman of the Church of England, then a nonconformist minister.

The other objection which the *Pall Mall* has discovered against giving women the suffrage, is that the excitement of engaging in politics would drive them mad! This objection is admirably disposed of by the *Spectator*,* as follows:—

"Even if the assertion were true, the argument would not be final; but where is the evidence of its truth? The very few women in modern history who can be shown to have taken an intense personal interest in politics have been women of unusually sane minds and healthy physique. Catherine de Medicis surely took an interest in politics, and who except the first Bourbon ever defied her wit successfully? Her pupil, Mary of Guise, the woman whom Scotchmen will persist in talking of as if she were a Scotchwoman, whereas she was from toque to boots, in virtues and in vices, in her strong passions and her cold heart, in her brain for business and her incapacity of sympathy, Parisienne, lived and died for politics, and to her death was Burleigh's equal

---

* February 19, 1870.

in statecraft. Her rival, Elizabeth, a woman of the typical sort, vain, mean, vacillating, and given to intrigue, lived fifty years of active life, during which she subordinated every interest to politics, and died to leave behind, throughout a race like ours, the tradition of large-hearted competence. Did Anne of Austria go mad, or Adelaide of Orleans? or Louisa of Prussia, who really ruled the kingdom through that awful tempest of French invasion? or Catherine II. of Russia, or any one of the dozen or so women whom modern history classes as rulers and politicians? Why the Pompadour, with the Parc aux Cerfs upon her conscience, and that horrible 'unamusable,' keen-sighted, heartless voluptuary perpetually upon her hands, did not go mad, because mainly of the interest with which politics invested her life; as they did that of the good bourgeoise Maria Theresa, who patronized her, and governed Austria, and fought Frederick, and dismembered Poland, and suppressed the Jesuits, and after a life of fierce political warfare died a comfortable, serene old lady at sixty-three. These were Empresses, or Queens, or Kings' mistresses. How old was Madame de Recamier? How old are the half-dozen women in Paris who still keep up the tradition of the political salon? We have them in England too, surely. Not to mention living names, though it is a certainty that among the best balanced intellects in England are half-a-dozen political dames, there was Lady Palmerston, steeped in politics throughout life, and at eighty, sanest of English mankind. We might multiply instances for ever, but we do not understand even the *à priori* argument? Why should one of the noblest, most varied, and least selfish of all interests, the one which if thoroughly felt of all others most widens the intellects of average men, tend to destroy the intellects of average women? Because it is an excitement? So is dress, so is intrigue, so is the social struggle, so above and before all is ambition outside the political circle, yet women who feel all these do not go mad. Those who go mad are governesses, whose minds are concentrated on their monotonous toil; old maids, whose affections cannot find the centre which would give their minds full play; women in whose brains from want of political or other intellectual interest religion has come to be a one idea, a monomania? and the women of vacant minds, minds which, like bandboxes, might, if filled by politics or anything else—the more solid the thing the better—keep their perfect form, but unfilled are crushed by the first blow, the most trifling accident. Excitement, intimates the *Pall Mall Gazette*, is very injurious to women. Is it? Why is it not beneficial, as Michelet, a very bad authority, but a well-known one, and every doctor in every country perpetually asserts? Of all excitement nothing is, we believe, quite equal to immense success at the opera; for the applause comes quick, and the applause gives all that is dear to all—money, position, personal worship; yet the great female singers of the world, Jenny Lind, Tietjens, Alboni, Patti, Lucca, Sessi, are certainly not among the women who create the impression of approximate insanity. Even if excitement were bad for women—a notion we believe to be born exclusively of the results of the one excitement our civilization promotes, the struggle against hot air, late hours, and injurious food, the struggle to buy the success of the salon at the price of physical health—that would not show that political excitement was specially bad. On the contrary, it would seem to be specially good, if only because its first condition is self-restraint, instead of *abandon*. The pursuit of politics hardly admits of the monomaniacal concentration of thought on a single object which tends to produce, or rather, as we should say, to develop, insanity; it is too varied, admits of too many interests, of too rapid an alternation of success and defeat. No doubt women who get interested in politics betray more interest in them than in anything else, get more excited, talk more at random, flush more deeply, are more carried out of their ordinary restraints than men are; but is not that true of all pursuits, or where it is specially true, is not the cause the law which prohibits them from action? Dumb men always seem, and usually are, very fierce men, but speech would not make them insane."

Art. II.—A LADY FARMER.

An admirable instance of what women can do in the farming way, is afforded by a young lady whom I had the pleasure of seeing last year in Ireland. Miss C—— is a farmer's daughter, and having inherited a little money four or five years ago she took a lease of one of my brother's farms, containing, I suppose, about 200 acres of wheat and pasture land. The previous tenants had sadly neglected both the house, offices, and land, but Miss C—— set at once about putting everything to rights. Fences and drains were looked after, and first-rate farm offices built, and when I went over the premises nothing was to be seen but order and prosperity. Splendid stacks of corn were in the hay yard, and a herd of really choice cattle, including some fancy stock, Spanish and Alderney, were being driven to pasture. A little pleasure garden in front of the house was resplendent with jacqueminots and celestine forrestier, and a dozen other show roses; and within doors the pretty little drawing-room had its piano, and its table covered with new books and newspapers. Among the sights of the farm, however, I must not omit a knowing little mare, on which Miss C—— is apt, I am told, to take a leading place in the hunting field, and last, not least, a merry tribe of dogs following at her heels. "How do you find living alone, Miss C——?" inquired I. "Do you ever feel solitary?" "I only feel the days are not nearly long enough," she replied, "for all I have to do, and all my enjoyment of them." Need I add two facts in conclusion—First, that Miss C—— pays her rent to the day and is the most valued of my brother's tenants, albeit she has no vote to throw into the scale of his political interest? Secondly, that this able and high-spirited woman entertains no manner of doubt about the capability of the female sex to discharge the duties entailed by the possession of the franchise, and eagerly signs every petition which I forward to her, intended to help its attainment. She observes very justly that, however good a tenant she may have proved, it was a mere chance that she met with a landlord who would grant her a lease, while legally incapacitated from recording a vote in the election of a representative for the country.

F. P. C.

Art. III.—PUBLIC OPINION ON QUESTIONS CONCERNING WOMEN.

IN *Fraser's Magazine* for February, there is a review by Sir Henry Taylor, of Mr. Mill's "Subjection of Women." Sir H. Taylor agrees with most of Mr. Mill's conclusions, though he forms his opinions on different grounds.

He thinks women ought to have the suffrage because they have generally clearer insight into character than men, and that they will therefore choose better members of Parliament, although he is somewhat afraid that women will be even more easily bribed than men.

He thinks that married women ought to have the use of their own property, because if there be a natural predominance of man over woman there is no need of laws to maintain the natural and inevitable superiority of husbands over wives; and if there be no natural predominance of man over woman an artificial one ought not to be created.

He also is of opinion that all legal disabilities should be removed which prevent women from engaging in any employment whatever; on the ground that, if women are found by experience to be incompetent to fill any situation, custom will exclude them from it as effectually as law.

He believes that women will be found incapable of filling many positions which they fancy would suit them well.

In the *Fortnightly Review* there is an article by Mr. A. Hobhouse, Q.C., on the "Forfeiture of Property by Married Women."

Mr. Hobhouse advocates the passing of Mr. Russell Gurney's Bill, commonly called the Married Women's Property Bill No. 1. He contends that the plan which is sometimes proposed of an extension of the protection order system would not be effectual, and would reach only one case out of scores which would be reached by a simple change in the principle of the law.

"The particular cases that appear are only the symptoms. But it is childish to treat the symptoms separately while the cause remains untouched. It is about as wise as to let your child go on with an unwholesome diet, but to make it very easy for him to see the doctor as each fit of sickness occurs."

To the other proposed plan of extending the system of settlement to the poor, he has a much stronger dislike, for, while the extension of protection orders would do a little good, the system of settlements would do a great deal of harm.

"The sum falling under such an Act as this would in few cases exceed 300*l.* or 400*l.* And sums of that or of much larger amount are far more beneficially applied when left free to be used for the exigencies of the family, than when tied up, and made available only by way of income. Rich people may afford to put by a sum of money, and say that there it shall lie for a term of years. The poor cannot; the possession of a little capital often makes to them the whole difference between getting a start in life and losing it, between moderate success and total failure; they have no margin, and no friends to fall back on for the critical occasions when money is necessary.

"Besides and beyond the crippling effect of tying up money comes the demoralising effect of expectations. They are peculiarly noxious to the poor and ignorant, who always exaggerate them, often relax their exertions on account of them, and not seldom discount them. When Eutrapelus wished to ruin a man he gave him fine clothes. If I wished to throw sore temptation in the way of a humble family, I would put a couple of hundred pounds in strict settlement for them.

"But if settlements are such good things why not extend them to men?

"When women ask that marriage may not operate as a forfeiture of their property, they are to be told that it must be kept for their children. It is difficult to see why the same principles should not be applied to men when they marry. If the arrangement is based on the good of the children, it must be the same to them from whichever parent the money comes. If based on the good of the wife, is it not rather wiser to let her be the judge, whether it is for her good or not? The argument must come ultimately to this—that women when they marry are such poor weak creatures that they cannot be trusted to deal with their own money; they cannot judge whether to keep it or spend it; whether to bestow it on their husbands or themselves, or their children, or elsewhere; therefore the law shall step in, assume in every case that a woman ought to settle money on herself and her children, and make that arrangement for her.

"To this I answer—First, the weakness is assumed without proof, or without better proof than some coarse dictum of Lord Thurlow's. Women know how to hold their own where they are accustomed to act. Give them legal rights, and wait to see whether or no they will use them. Secondly, that the circumstances and needs of people vary infinitely, and to apply one Procrustean rule of law to all will produce, first misery, and then revolt against the law. Thirdly, that the proposed legal assumption of what it is right for a woman to do with a small sum of money is so unwise that the weakest woman commanded by the most tyrannical husband could not do worse with it. Fourthly, that it is a somewhat hard measure for those who come complaining of their unprotected state to be told that they are quite right, but that they want a great deal more protection than they ask for, and shall for the future be protected not only against their husbands, but against themselves.

"I will only now add that for myself I would sooner see no measure at all carried than one establishing a system of settlements; and I believe the gentlemen who have given years of labour to the ripening of opinion for the reception of Mr. Russell Gurney's Bill are of the same opinion."

The *Pall Mall Gazette*, of February 17, contains an article against Women's Suffrage:—

"A provision was inserted in an Act of the last session of Parliament enabling women whose names are on the rate-books to vote in municipal elections. They did, in fact, vote at the municipal elections of last year in considerable numbers. What, then, was the character of their voting?—One small piece of experience has been gained which ought to be of the utmost value in a controversy which has hitherto been conducted nearly exclusively on *à priori* grounds. We believe it can be shown—though we admit that a larger comparison of facts should be made than it is in our power to institute—that the enfranchised ladies voted almost exclusively with and for the clergy. We do not mean to say that their votes were always given, strictly speaking, to the Conservatives. There are many cities and towns in England in which there are clerical questions which are independent of politics. In cathedral cities, for example, there are often quarrels about local taxation, in which the clergy take a side not on the score of their professional opinion, but on the ground of their professional interests. We are informed that in all such places the cathedral or clerical party won last year easy success through the votes of the ladies. It is getting to be clearly understood that the clergyman of the parish is becoming quite a new power for municipal purposes, through his having the votes of the female ratepayers at his command. No doubt the Dissenting minister has to a certain extent the same advantage, but it would appear that the number of Dissenting ladies on the rate-books is always much smaller than the number of those attached to the Established Church.

"If there were the smallest chance of Mr. Jacob Bright's bill becoming law, we should express a hope that the facts of the last municipal elections would be carefully collected and well pondered, especially by Liberal members of Parliament. They constitute, as we have said, the one small fragment of experience which has a bearing upon the measure. There is, however, another kind of evidence which it would be necessary to adduce before women were really admitted to the contests of the political arena. It is possible that, though social phenomena may teach us little as to the consequences of the enfranchisement of women, physiology may be in a position to teach us a good deal. What to themselves are likely to be the physical consequences of opening a new source of excitement to women? It is idle to say that the excitements of politics are more wholesome or healthy than the excitements of social or fashionable life. That is to beg the question under cover of ambiguous phrases. There cannot be a doubt that politics, when actively and personally engaged in, furnish a far stronger and keener excitement than almost any other known pursuit. We should like to know, then, what Sir James Simpson, or Dr. Gull, or Dr. Farre, or Dr. Priestley, or Mr. Paget thinks himself bound by past observation to predict as the probable consequence of kindling intense excitement on political subjects in that vast majority of women who now eschew them or give them but moderate attention. It is not altogether impossible that Mr. Mill, in aiming at the intellectual elevation of the human race, advocates that which would lead to its steady physical degeneration."

The *Journal of the Manchester Women's Suffrage Society* for March contains the following information—

"The following Newspapers have published articles advocating the principles of women's suffrage, or extracts from the Second Annual Report of the Society. The politics are indicated by the initial letters of the words Liberal, Conservative, Neutral, Independent:—The Manchester Examiner and Times (L), the Bath Express (C), the Surrey Comet (N), the Exeter Gazette and Daily Telegram (C), Brett's St. Leonards and Hastings Gazette (L), the Hereford Journal (C), the Bristol Daily Review (L I), the Penny Illustrated Paper (L), the Wellington Times (L), the Derbyshire Courier (L), the Newbury Weekly News (N), the Ulverston Advertiser (N), the Tunbridge Wells Gazette (N), the Tyrone Constitution (C), Newcastle-under-Lyme Weekly Times (I), the Londonderry Standard (L C), the Scarborough Gazette (N), the Barrow Herald (I), the North Wilts Herald (I), the Monaghan Northern Standard (C), the Sunderland Times (L), the Buchan Observer (I), the Western Daily Mercury (L), the Nenagh Guardian (C), the Armagh Guardian (C), Leeds Mercury (L), Western Daily Press (L), Daily Telegraph (L), Staffordshire Weekly Times (L)."

The *Echo* has a capital article on "Money in Women's Hands" *à propos* of a lawsuit caused by the extravagance of a certain Mrs. Hayter, who being allowed no money at all by her husband, though possessing 90*l.* a year of her own, which he appropriated, ran up awfully long bills at various shops.

"Now it is a fact to be borne clearly in mind by those who would throw all the blame of such disasters on the folly, vanity, and selfishness of women, that while extravagant wives are very common phenomena, extravagant old maids are almost unheard of. Persons who have paid attention to the subject have remarked, over and over again, that such a thing as a single lady of good character running into debt, or a small tradeswoman incurring bankruptcy by any fault of her own, are things they have rarely observed. When such women are bankrupt or insolvent, it nearly always is seen either that the catastrophe arises from some inevitable misfortune, or from the betrayal of their interests by some male relation in whom they have placed ill-judged confidence. In fact, the faults of old maids are notoriously in another direction. They are inclined to be stingy, penurious, and mean. Having few or no ways open to them of earning money, they are driven to invent instead a thousand petty devices to save it; and the result is that the tendency of their minds, nine times out of ten, is to err on the side of parsimony rather than of extravagance. Even young single women of independent fortune, who might be accused of too great earnestness in the pursuit of pleasure-seeking, rarely lavish their means on dress and other allurements, after the fashion of wives who have only vanity to be flattered, and no serious object to win by their display?

"How is this parodox then to be explained? Had Mrs. Hayter at seventeen remained unmarried and received her 90*l.* a year to provide for herself under the roof of some relative or friend, does any one suppose that at twenty-three she would have been running up bills of 99*l.* in six weeks at a linen-draper's, or buying eighteen-guinea sealskin jackets? She was almost as poor a woman, as the mother of a family, on 490*l.*, as a single woman on 90*l.* alone. But in one case the education of responsibility would have taught her how to manage her slender resources; and in the other, her condition of mere childish dependence left her exposed to every temptation to extravagance. . . . If a measure could have been devised by human ingenuity to make women extravagant, it would surely have been that of relieving wives from their personal responsibility, and the marvel is not that under the present law we have so many, but so few cases before the courts, like the one on which we have now briefly commented. We trust this great mistake in our legislation may be corrected by the revised Married Women's Property Bill of next session. Meanwhile, and always, to every husband and father, we say—If you desire your wife or your daughter to know the value of money, to resist the temptations to waste it, then give her from the first an independent allowance suitable to your means. Be persuaded that the study of the alphabet is not more necessary to teach her to read, nor the practice of scales to make her play the piano, than the uncontrolled expenditure of a little "pin-money" to train her to be the careful mistress of her household, and the mainstay, not the ruin and disgrace, of her family."

A SAD SUBJECT.

From the *Daily Telegraph*, March 14th.

'IN the House of Commons last week a question was asked which, for the first time, gave public intimation of a dispute enormously important and passionately debated, although its character has kept it hitherto out of general hearing. It can be suppressed no longer. The consideration and interests involved in the discussion whether the 'Contagious Diseases Acts' should be repealed, continued, or extended from military and naval towns to the civil population, concern the very life and future history of the nation, and must be carried, as is our wont, before the tribunal of national opinion. In arriving at this conclusion, we believe that the momentous problem may be discussed without failing in that reverence for purity and innocence which has thus far dictated silence to the leading organs of the press. We hope to wound no ear and to break the charm of no happy ignorance, while we place this question in its true light before the community. A woman, of whom Mr. Jacob Bright spoke on Thursday last, has been thrown into prison for refusing to submit to the regulation of the Acts which we have mentioned. These Acts, passed in 1864 and 1866, are the foundation, at our military and naval stations, for a system of inspection and sanitary superintendence which has been now for some time administered, on a small scale, by the Admiralty and the War Office, and which a certain number of persons would extend, not only more generally in garrison and seaport towns, but to the entire civil population. Now, how are the very serious powers of these enactments justified, and with what arguments do the advocates of the system demand its extension? It is clear that, even limited to their present range, the Acts confer upon the police and the medical officers an authority which even a fallen woman does find intolerable. The system sets aside that 'liberty of the individual' which has been held sacred even in the lowest. It introduces among us an approximation to the French practice of Government licences and supervision. It heals the disabled victim of sin only to replace her in most cases in her former pursuits. It says—in legislative language—that the physical injury concerns the State more than the moral and social offence. It changes the tone of English law from stern condemnation of infamous trades to tolerant acknowledgment of the fact that they exist and interfere with the general comfort. It treats only as a patient her whom it has received as a misdemeanant; for, whatever its apologies, it certainly recognises vice and aids it towards custom by abridging periods of incapacity. These considerations are grave, even when they are confined to experimental essays in a few notoriously immoral stations; but they appear more than grave, they become most pressing and disquieting, when the proposal is to make such purely foreign regulations co-extensive with the population of the kingdom, and to throw the tremendous power of denunciation and personal examination into the hands of the police and the medical officers.

"Justice must be done to the motives and arguments of those who have introduced these innovations, and who now desire to extend their area. They urge with much force that it is always, everywhere, and at all times, good to relieve human creatures from suffering. They expatiate upon the heavy loss which the State sustains by the disablement of its soldiers and its sailors; and, to justify their wish to extend the operation of the Acts, they paint in terrible colours the evils which they seek to mitigate. But, thus far, they would be answered, of course, by the glad consent of the community to establish more hospitals, since nobody doubts the duty of healing the sick, nobody denies the harm done by the existence of the specific complaints. The battle really gathers round the point of supervision, examination, and registration. This is the actual matter in dispute between an ardent band advocating the extension of the Acts and an equally ardent phalanx, composed of eminent men and women, protesting, with earnest voice and act, against that which they say is the abolition of individual rights, the practical licensing of professional infamy, and the "thin end" of a national policy fatal to purity, morality, domestic peace, and English characteristics—a policy not of pity but of cynicism, destined to degrade and corrupt the country submitting to it. The promoters of the innovation plead State necessities, precedent, and reason against these "sentimental" objections. They point out that we interfere already with sources of fever and cholera, local or individual; that we have Vaccination and other Laws which postpone the liberty and self-respect of the person to the welfare of the community; that, as to recognising the vice, they do no more than the hospital which cures a notorious thief and discharges him to his old pursuits, or than the existing asylums; while they cite figures to show that, under the edicts in question, they have diminished the extent of the evil, and therefore claim that those Acts, with their extraordinary powers, shall be gradually extended to the entire kingdom.

"Allowing that this is but a partial representation of the case presented by the promoters of such exotic ideas, we must, nevertheless, pronounce at once and plainly against them. It will prove impossible, and, were it possible, it would, we believe, be most mischievous, to make these secretly-commenced measures generally the law of the land. One such rebellion as that of the person now in prison at Maidstone throws us back upon principles higher than any invoked by the hygienists, and is much more calculated to suggest the repeal of the partial experiment than to lead to its extension. Carefully perusing, as we have done, the evidence for and against the Acts, we have been struck by the weakness of its advocates; even on their own ground, the diminution of evil which they have effected has been but little, despite their powers; and amid a civil population, where only one sex could be supervised, it would necessarily be less. Their representations are much controverted by the very ablest authorities. Mr. Simon, the chief medical officer of the Privy Council, has reported most distinctly against the proposal to enlarge the action of the Bill; and a most erudite and minute protest upon medical grounds, extremely difficult to answer, has appeared to the same effect, signed by some sixty scientific gentlemen of Nottingham and the midland counties. Meantime, a formidable movement, hostile even to the continuance of the Acts upon their present basis, has sprung up; and those who silently obtained the consent of Parliament to the experiment must rather seek, we think, to strengthen their pleas for its further duration than hope to expand it into an accepted policy. Emphatically we oppose that idea; for, apart from other reasons, what prisons are there wide enough to hold those who would resent legislative interference; and what Acts would survive the public indignation at the first case in which a respectable woman should be denounced to the authorities, either from corrupt or revengeful motives, on the part of the police? Foreign to all the tradition and all the tendency of our national feeling, the Extended Act would be torn to pieces within a year, amid failure and execration. The well-meaning people who support the contrary view must prepare rather to defend the ground already in their possession. They must be ready with a reply, when it is urged that the State has no business to guarantee a vicious citizen from the contingencies which surround his own indulgence. They must account for the failure of the supervisionary system in France, where, without greatly diminishing evil results, it has produced the shocking spectacle of medical statesmen asking the Government for 20,000 more recruits to the army of misery, and for an enactment preventing parents from reclaiming their children from vice. Such monstrous propositions—the fruit of the French system—have been publicly heard in Paris lately: and, were it all otherwise, the methods advocated stand condemned as permanent resources, because they are at best but partial remedies for a social evil which must be shortly dealt with from root to fruit. We are no advisers of silence and inaction in view of this "Great Sin," which cankers civilisation and blasphemes humanity and Christianity together. On the contrary, we should hail all rightful attempts to alleviate the sufferings of the vilest; and we not only allow but demand that the hideous facts of the day shall be confronted and boldly brought into the province of the Legislature. The hospitals which heal the sinner must not, however, have gates opening back into her miserable haunts; they must not destroy her last shred of feminine self-respect under the name of public safety; and they must not exist as the open and ratified confession that prostitution is a necessary provision and department of the State. When we have revised the laws which now connive at rather than punish seduction—when we have made the parents of the youthful ministress of debauchery answerable for the abandonment of their child—when emigration has hopelessly failed to restore the proportion of the sexes, and education is proved powerless, with the aid of righteous laws, to save the daughters of the poor from this 'death in life'—then, if there be still need, we may consent to put every woman into the power of ignorant policemen, and to establish institutions which cure the inconveniences, but heed nothing of the crime and pathos of this sale of soul and body. While nobler and larger laws, and efforts as practical and still more radical, are yet to be tried, however, we must regard any proposal to extend these Acts as rash and foolish; and even as concerns the military and naval services, the question will arise whether anything like a commensurate success has yet justified the outrageous invasion of individual liberty, against which even the lingering pride of a creature like Elizabeth Holt at last protests in the name of what is still womanly and human in her nature."

ACTIONS FOR BREACH OF PROMISE OF MARRIAGE.

From the *Daily Telegraph*.*

" IF any action for breach of promise be justifiable, it is in a case like that now before us, the defendant in which had exhausted almost every form of unmanly caprice. It has been sometimes suggested, from the Bench, and also in the press, that all actions of this kind are absurd, because a man should be allowed to change his mind; and that to be forced into marriage, if courtship provokes alienation, would be a fearful fate even for the injured party. But it must be borne in mind, that the law does not hinder a man from changing his mind; it merely awards compensation to the person who has suffered from the change, and imposes what is practically a penalty on the rash promises rather than on the prudent retractations. It should also be borne in mind, that a girl who is jilted suffers more or less in social esteem, and in her chance of obtaining an honourable alliance; money is a poor *solatium* for such loss, but it is some counterpoise to the injury sustained in material interests. If the matrimonial chances of a portionless girl are spoiled, the difference to her may be the difference between a comfortable home and lonely penury as an old maid; there is simple justice in saving her from at least the pecuniary troubles of undowered virginity. But arguments against the breach of promise action sometimes take the form of protests against the horrible profanity of unveiling lovers' secrets to the coarse ridicule of a public court, and of what has been called 'a ribald press.' No doubt this is an evil; but the evil is small compared with some that we avoid by force of the publicity. When a man now breaks a promise, and the young lady seeks redress, the public learns, as in this case of 'Mitchell *v.* Hazeldine,' that there is no imputation on the young lady's character, and that the fickleness of the man is the sole cause of the breaking off. But let us suppose these matters to be settled in some private court—what is to prevent malignant whispers from affecting the young lady's character? We know that as regards irresponsible society the Mrs. Candours can make a great deal of smoke without any fire; and perfect secrecy in the proceedings would leave room for any amount of scandal. It would then be known that young So-and-so had paid 2000*l.* sooner than consent to marry Miss Blank; and it would be easy for the man and his friends to hint unutterable things, 'to lie in silence,' to shake their heads, or sneer away a girl's reputation. Compelled

---

* Referring to a case in which the jury gave 2000*l.* damages.

to come into a public court, they must be careful—if they make imputations, they must either prove them, or withdraw them altogether. The damages in these cases vary according to the discretion of the jury, who take everything into consideration—the conduct of the young lady and of the man, his income and expectations. Above all, the girl has the opportunity of publicly proving beyond slander that she is not in fault. Of course, this necessity of obtaining public redress is painful. But it is also painful for a woman to give evidence that may convict a ruffian of an assault; yet does anybody affirm that a woman should shrink from bringing such an offender to justice? In more serious cases—such as those which come before Lord Penzance—full publicity is sometimes essential to justice. Persons are often collaterally implicated in a cause, to whom the verdict of the jury or the judgment of the Court may not apply; and if there were no impartial and ample report, private slanders might afterwards whisper away the good name of the party left at the mercy of their weapons."

THE EMPLOYMENT OF WOMEN AND GIRLS IN FARM WORK.

From the *Pall Mall Gazette*.

"WE must confess that, next to the pronounced indecency that flourishes so luxuriantly in some of the novels written by, and presumably for, women, we regard that prurient modesty which finds nature itself indelicate, and hastens to fasten on anything objectionable and to disquiet itself therewith. We find evidence of a good deal of this fidgety sensitiveness in the pages of the Agricultural Report whenever the witnesses or Commissioners enter on the subject of out-door employment for the wives, widows, and daughters of agricultural labourers; and the frank speech which characterizes Mr. Henley's remarks on this point is like a wholesome dose of common sense. When it is clearly proved that among the juvenile gangs, boys and girls were in the habit of bathing together indiscriminately stark naked, or that in a certain 'cockling' village in Lancashire the 'badger,' or master, was accustomed to collect his workers of both sexes, and shut them in a barn all night, to be ready for the tide in the early morning, it is impossible to expose the evil too plainly, or to denounce too strongly a system which permits anything so disgraceful and detestable. But we hardly see the wisdom of making it an indictable offence for a woman to ascend a ladder, unless we are also prepared to forbid her getting over a gate, and to cause all rural stiles—which are, indeed, often worse than either ladder or gate—to be done away with by Act of Parliament. The various restrictions as to female labour suggested by some witnesses are peculiar and diverting: that no young woman should be allowed to work in the fields at all; no unmarried woman no married woman with a family; no girl unless her mother were in the same field; no girl under thirteen; no girl over thirteen; no girl under eighteen; that female labour should be confined to harvest and hop-picking; that it should be prohibited on Saturday, and during the winter; lastly, and oddest of all, one gentleman wishes that no married woman should be allowed to work 'unless she had a daughter of thirteen who had obtained a certificate of education.' Our own opinion is that with so many women unable to obtain work on our hands it would be extremely injudicious to close to them any harmless employment which has up to this time been open to them. In the first place, from a sanitary point of view, out-door labour is excellent in its effects. On this head the medical evidence is decisive and all but unanimous. Dr. Paley, for twenty-six years physician to the Peterborough Hospital, says that the women who work in the fields are 'particularly healthy.' Dr. Francis, physician to the Northampton Infirmary, cannot recall 'a single instance of physical injury being caused by it.' The medical officer of Woburn Union says, 'It expands the chest, inures to hardness, confers good digestion and sound sleep.' Another states, 'A healthier set of women and girls is seldom to be met with.' Dr. Mackintosh, after twenty years' experience, declares that 'girls employed in the fields enjoy more robust health and a greater immunity from the complaints incident to the age of puberty than girls employed in indoor service.' We might multiply this kind of evidence, but what we have given is sufficient for the purpose. Again, the assistance of women is necessary. At certain seasons every hand is wanted that can be made available; and it would really be too ridiculous for Parliament to prevent women earning money by working in the same field as their husbands or even their sweethearts. Moreover, sometimes a young woman, by reason of being hampered with a baby not born in wedlock, can neither obtain a place as a domestic servant, nor could she attend to her child if she did so. It appears, however, that in Cheshire this sort of fault is passed over: 'the only question ever asked is, Can she make good cheese?' This reminds us of Dean Ramsay's old Scottish lady, who, seeking the character of a cook, exclaimed, 'D—n her morals, can she make collops?' It is surely better for a woman to work honestly in the fields than to be driven to the workhouse; and better, too, that a girl, even of imperfect morals, should be a dairy-maid if she can find any one to take her than that she should become a prostitute. Then there are widows with young families dependent on them, and widows living alone supporting themselves as they best can. It would be simply cruel to prevent them following any employment which they think suits them. Some witnesses fear the rain and the wet, and others the east wind; but it should be remembered that to work or not is optional: the east wind has small terrors for a healthy peasant woman; steady rain always sends men and women alike to shelter; and the latter can, and almost always do, refuse to go to work which will draggle and wet their dresses, simply because they find it does not pay them to do so. . . . . . Of the employments or performances denounced in the report as unsuitable and improper for women—are standing on ladders, helping with threshing machines, driving carts, spreading manure, and getting on stacks either of hay or straw. Respecting the ladder question we have already given our opinion. In some old-fashioned cottages a ladder is the only mode of access to the bedroom; and to forbid a woman to ascend it would be to emulate the noble member of the peerage who, as the guardian angel of servant-girls, has immortalized himself by his exertions to prevent them cleaning windows. To assist with threshing machines, or, indeed, any kind of machines, is unfit for women on account of their dress. Even in mills, where proper precautions are supposed to be taken, very sad accidents have occurred; and country women not being born fools are aware of the danger, and generally refuse this work. The reasons why a woman should not be permitted to drive a cart we profess ourselves unable to understand. Is it because she is believed to be unable to manage a horse? But in that case she might surely be suffered to conduct a donkey-cart. Is it because she would dangle her legs over the side or sit upon the shafts? But then male life is not less valuable than woman's, and men do this without restraint, and often fall off and get run over in consequence. Would she be guilty of driving carelessly and without reins? Not likely, for we have often observed that women always tug at the horses' heads when they are driving, as if that were one method of getting on; or, lastly, is it supposed that she cannot manage to get in and out without outraging propriety by a casual display of ankles? But if she must not mount to drive, neither must she mount to ride either in cart or gig; and really it is sometimes a greater feat than any of these things to clamber up into a railway carriage at a siding or at the end of a long train. Standing in the centre of a half-made stack to catch the sheaves as they are tossed up, and arrange them neatly, may not be precisely the amusement which a town-bred lady would prefer, still less that of 'tiffling muck;' but we do not see much harm in either, though the objectionable ladder would certainly be required for the descent, unless we could substitute for it some ingeniously arranged machine in the fashion of a fire-escape to be used instead. Surely all this is sad nonsense. It arises, as we believe, from a sentiment of spurious delicacy, which resembles prudery much more than it does modesty, and it would be in our mind much better that a woman's ankles should be seen than that women should be always thinking about whether they are seen or not. Of other demoralizing influences attributed to farm occupations we shall speak on another occasion."

MARRIED WOMEN'S PROPERTY BILL.

From the *Manchester Examiner* of March 7, 1870.

"EVERY ONE now admits that some alteration in the law relating to the property and earnings of married women is desirable and even necessary. It is conceded on all hands that cruel injustice is worked by leaving careful and industrious wives at the mercy of dissolute and depraved husbands; by treating one section of the population as the living chattels of another; and by depriving of all legal rights the very persons who not unfrequently stand in most need of the protection of the law. There is, however, still a great difference of opinion as to the remedy which should be applied to the evil, and the rival schemes of those who propose to legislate on the subject are embodied in two Bills which have recently been introduced into the House of Commons. The first is that for which Mr. Russell Gurney stands sponsor. The measure was before Parliament last session, and as we then fully described and discussed its main provisions, it will not be necessary for us to do more than remind our readers of its nature, so far as may be requisite for the purpose of comparing it with the competing plan. It proceeds upon a clear and simple principle. The mischief to be dealt with being clearly traceable to the hard and rigid rule of the Common Law, by which the personality of the wife is completely absorbed in that of the husband, it goes directly to the root of the evil, restores to the wife the independent legal personality which she enjoyed as a single woman, and gives back to her the same right and control over her own property and her own earnings which she would possess apart from the confiscating effect now worked by the marriage service. If this Bill becomes law every wife would, without more ado, become the legal owner of what, morally speaking, belongs to her. It would be hers to do what she liked with; to save it, to spend it, to give it to or to withhold it from her husband—in a word, to employ it as she deemed most advisable for her family. In ninety-nine cases out of a hundred, the measure would leave things practically very much as it finds them, but that is not the least of its merits. Nature and affection are, as a rule, stronger than law. In the vast majority of instances there is a thorough community of goods between man and wife; they neither of them trouble their heads about the respective right of proprietorship; the one thought of both is how to do the best they can for each other and their children. To such couples Parliament can give nothing, since from them it has taken nothing away. Mr. Gurney's Bill would, however, come into immediate operation when the husband and wife are no longer one; when the natural protector and head of the family has become its worst enemy, and when the woman has thrown upon her shoulders the burthen of maintaining herself and her children. By recognising the wife's ownership of that which has been left to her or given to her, has been bought by her or earned by her, it would afford her exactly the same protection by which every other British subject is at present secured in the enjoyment of his property or the fruit of his industry. "Very different is the method adopted by Mr. Raikes. Shrinking, as he does, from altering the legal status of the wife; leaving her as he finds her, the mere creature of her husband; denying her legal personality on any other than the statutory rights which he proposes to confer upon her; withholding from her any power to protect herself,—he is, of course, compelled to surround her with a complicated system of artificial safeguards. In lieu of freedom he offers her a change of servitude. As a relief from the oppression of her husband he proffers her the fetters of the law. Instead of altering the Common Law, he proposes to leave it untouched, and to adopt for general use intricate machinery by which Equity lawyers have circumvented it in the interest of the more wealthy classes. This he does without the slightest reference to the fact that this machinery, and the settlement of property which it creates, are by their very nature adapted to the exclusive position and the wants of those who have hitherto resorted to them. When a family is rich enough to have a considerable portion of their property tied up, nothing can be more prudent than to make a settlement. The money thus set apart is invested in the names of trustees, who pay the interest to the wife during her life, and to the husband, if he survives her, for his life, dividing the principal, after the death of both parents, amongst the children of the marriage. In this way, if the sum settled be sufficient, the family is effectually secured against the necessities and misfortunes of life. But, suppose the sum does not yield any appreciable income; suppose that the family cannot afford the luxury of investing in the funds or on mortgage the money which was wanted for some trade or business, and which can be employed therein with far greater profit and advantage, is it not evident that a settlement is then a mere encumbrance? Its principal effect is to prevent a husband and wife from making the best use of their limited means. No doubt, if the husband is a spendthrift and the wife is a weak fool, a settlement may be the best thing for them. But it would be rather absurd to put all the world in leading strings because a few people cannot take care of themselves. That, however, is exactly what Mr. Raikes does. Instead of giving the wife her own property, he prefers to tie it up in strict settlement. Of course, to do this, trustees must be provided. Unless the wife objects, the husband will be the trustee, and will hold the property upon 'the trusts, and with the powers, provisions, agreements, and declarations usually inserted by the High Court of Chancery in settlements made under its direction.' If, however, the wife objects to her husband being the trustee, she may, on application to the County Court, have him divested of the trust, and have the judge of such court and one of the Vice-Chancellors substituted in his place; or the same step may be taken by any one interested in the property. So long as the husband is the trustee he will be unable to sell, transfer, or vary the investment of any property so held by him, without the consent of the County Court judge; and although it is true that with the consent of such judge the property, if personal property, may be advanced to the husband to be employed in his trade or business, it will be quite optional with his Honour to grant or to withhold this permission, and even he has no power to allow a wife to apply any money that may come to her directly for the advantage of her family. If, for instance, a wife living on affectionate terms with her husband were to have 20*l.* bequeathed to her, into settlement it must go; at most it might be lent to the husband, but by no possibility could it be applied to the purchase of additional furniture or comforts for the house, to the discharge of debts, to the education of a child, or to any of the hundred domestic purposes which such a woman might have at heart. On the other hand, if a wife and husband were on unfriendly terms, if he half-starved her, or even deserted her, she could not—unless she had obtained a protection order—get hold of a single sixpence of her money in order to supply her wants or set herself up in business. For the sake, therefore, of protecting against her husband the one woman in a hundred who needs protection, Mr. Raikes would deprive the other ninety-nine of the power of doing what they like with their own, and he would not even then give the hundredth woman the only power which would as a rule be of the slightest use to her. This is truly an admirable result at which to aim; nor is the process by which it is attained less worthy of note. It is certainly one that must make lawyers' mouths water. Only let any one picture to himself the incessant applications to the County Court, the hearings about this, and the litigation about that, which this system would involve, and then say how much of any small property which might come to a wife would ever reach the family, and how much would go to the 'profession.'

We have hitherto dealt with the wife's property on the supposition that it consists of money, securities for money, or land. It will hardly be believed, but it is strictly true, that although the measure is mainly intended for the benefit of the humbler classes, it confers absolutely no protection whatever upon any other kind of property which a wife may possess. As it expressly excepts from the operation of the trustee clause 'all chattels transferable by mere delivery,' it would leave a bad husband exactly the same power which he now possesses to seize and sell furniture, household goods, or stock in trade, which his wife, whether being with him or apart from him, might acquire or possess—that is to say, unless she had the protection order of which we shall now speak. If a wife can prove that for six months before she makes the application she has earned more than half the expense of her family, she may then obtain from the County Court judge an order of protection which will, so long as it is in force, enable her to sue and be sued, to hold property, and to keep her earnings to herself as if she were *femme sole*. That is to say, in order to get any protection for her earnings she must undergo the pain of making a full application in open court; and she will even then fail if she cannot show—in opposition, it may be, to the endeavours of her husband—that she has made more than half the income of the family. Here is of course another reason for more litigation. Experience, however, has proved that, in a large proportion of cases, a woman will endure almost anything rather than undergo such an ordeal; while it is evident that nothing can be more unjust than to make her property in her own earnings dependent upon the proportion they may bear to the income of the family. Let us take a case in which this injustice would be apparent, we should think, even to Mr. Raikes. Suppose the mother and her children were living together, and all contributing to their joint support, while the father was a good-for-nothing vagabond, and did nothing for them. It might well be that the mother's earnings did not amount to half their income, and in that case she would have no claim to a protection order, but would be entirely at the mercy of her husband! It would be easy enough to give other illustrations of the futility, or even worse than futility, of this crude and ill-digested measure. We have, indeed, dealt with it only in the most general way, while almost every detail invites hostile criticism. But considerations of space impose limits upon us, and we have probably said enough to show that it is open to almost every kind of objection which can be urged against a proposed piece of legislation. It is neither based on justice nor is it adapted to the exigencies which it is intended to meet. It ignores rights which it ought to recognise, and it offers people that which they do not want, instead of that which they do want. It is not bread but a stone. It would either prove utterly unworkable or would work infinite mischief and inconvenience; and we cannot therefore for a moment suppose that Parliament will prefer it to the simple, righteous, and effective measure to which the name of the Recorder of London is attached."

The great Suffrage Meeting on the 26th has called forth several expressions of public opinion.

The *Times*, *Pall Mall*, *Standard* and *Telegraph* have articles against removing the disabilities of Women. The *Echo* and several country newspapers have articles in favour of removing them.

ART. IV.—REVIEWS OF BOOKS.

Historical Sketches of the Reign of George II. By Mrs. Oliphant. William Blackwood & Sons. Edinburgh and London.

SINCE the brilliant Essays of Macaulay were given to the world, few books have appeared so worthy to take a place by their side as these admirable biographical sketches by Mrs. Oliphant. With her keen perception of character, and her power of vivid description, she makes a whole group of eighteenth century personages live again before us, showing each in turn " as he lived "

and with all his surroundings, while they unfold to us
the secrets of their hearts more fully than they did even
to their contemporaries. It may safely be affirmed that
a more correct idea of how our ancestors of that period
felt and thought, and of the kind of world in which they
lived, may be gathered from a perusal of these amusing
sketches than might often be gained from the hard study
of many ponderous historical volumes. The persons
treated of are admirably selected so as to afford a range
over every subject of interest, while the authoress displays such thorough acquaintance with each as enables
her to set it lucidly as well as eloquently before the
reader. Thus in "The Sceptic"—Hume, and "The
Reformer"—Wesley, we have a view of the times in
relation to religion, of the spiritual deadness into which
the nation had fallen, and the violent efforts made to
awaken it to new life. In "The Philosopher"—Berkely,
the conflict of the materialist and the idealist systems
is discussed. "The Painter"—Hogarth, gives scope
for a glance at Art; "The Novelist"—Richardson, and
"The Poet"—Pope, for a survey of literature. The
gay world is shown in chapters on Lord Chesterfield
and Lady Mary Wortley Montague, the "Man" and the
"Woman of Fashion." "The Sailor" brings us to Vernon's failure and Anson's sufferings and triumphs at sea;
"The Young Chevalier" touches on military affairs;
while "The Minister"—Walpole, and "The Queen,"
introduce us to politics and government. The last
named (though in the book it holds the first place) is
a peculiarly interesting chapter, since it sets in a truer
light one who has not always had justice done to her
great merits. In any question of female fitness for
sovereignty a Maria Theresa, an Elizabeth, a Catherine
and some others rise at once before us, but the figure
of Queen Caroline does not always follow in the august
procession. Yet not only was she the real ruler of
England during that period of her life when her husband
filled its throne, but she ruled it well and wisely, though
it was to her a foreign country, and all her native
instincts must have been opposed to the principles of
its government. If it be said of her as it sometimes is
of Queen Elizabeth, that her success was due, not to

herself, but to the instruments she employed, yet more forcible in her case is the rejoinder that it was in this selection her great sagacity was shown. The Virgin Queen was surrounded by a galaxy of worthies too brilliant to be possibly overlooked, and who, great as they were, yet strove for her personal favour, and fed her with unceasing flattery. Moreover, she had but to please herself, to judge if her servants' plans were good and then order their fulfilment. At the court of Caroline, on the other hand, there was but one man of ability among a host of incapables; his talents were not so shining that no discernment was needed to appreciate him, for Walpole's power lay rather in avoiding great mistakes than achieving great exploits; while so far from having a claim on her feelings as a favourite, he had long been personally opposed to her, and even when they were allies was accustomed to speak his mind to her with a bluntness which sometimes amounted even to insult. Yet when the Prince and Princess of Wales became King and Queen, and all the world looked for the dismissal of the late sovereign's minister as a matter of course, it was Caroline who forgot all animosity, forgave all previous affronts, and persuaded her reluctant husband to keep at his post him whom she saw to be the one man competent to fill it. When she knew the measures he proposed and had approved of them, the most difficult part of her task had yet to come, for she then had so cunningly to enfilter them into George's mind as to lead him to believe they were his own original conceptions, for thus only could he be induced to consent to them, "losing no opportunity to declare that the queen never meddled with his business." For ten long years this was her daily work, the worst feature of it being, that she was thus compelled to pass so many hours in her husband's society; a burden so wearisome, that when one of his mistresses retired from the court, she is recorded to have been "sorry to have so much more of her husband's time thrown on her hands," a sentiment endorsed by the Princess Royal's exclamation " I wish with all my heart that he would take somebody else, that mamma might be a little relieved from the *ennui* of seeing him always in her room!" It was not a very moral suggestion, but Caroline, though virtuous herself, did not exact virtue from others, and least of all from her consort. Under so little restraint, indeed, did he feel himself from any jealousy on her part, that he made her the confidante of his amours, and decorated her sitting-room with portraits of her rivals. Whether strict observance of so much of the marriage vow as refers to "love" and "honour" could be possible with such a spouse may be open to question, but that third article— to "obey"—sometimes more important in marital eyes than either of the other two—was fulfilled with unswerving fidelity by Queen Caroline. According to Horace Walpole she had so firmly resolved "never to refuse a desire of the king's," that "more than once when she had the gout in her foot, she dipped her whole leg in cold water to be able to attend him" when he wished for her company in a walk. Ready to sacrifice morals, health, life itself, rather than thwart her husband's merest caprice, here, truly, we have the ideal wife of many men, and alas! even of some women too. But the effect upon the master thus submitted to is hardly encouraging. Vain and ill-tempered, selfish and sensual, George might not have been a much better man had his wife shown a little more self-assertion, but he could hardly have been a worse one. And the reward she won was worthy of her obsequient servility, and of him to whom it was rendered, for when on her death-bed she advised him to marry again—conscious, too late, that he was losing one whom he could never replace he sobbed out, "*Non,— j'aurais des maîtresses.*" With a bitter humour she rejoined—"*Ah, mon Dieu! cela n'empêche pas.*"

But if Caroline as a wife was "perfect," according to a popular, though not unquestioned, idea of perfection, as a mother she has incurred much censure from those advocates of the crushing process, who would fain have the maternal relation, as far at least as boys are concerned, a mere variation of the conjugal, so that, "The sons may finish what the sire began." Caroline is admitted to have "despised and disliked her son." When however, we know what Prince Frederic was, and how he treated her; that "the weak and treacherous young profligate had forfeited every claim upon her affection" by avowed enmity and studied insult, no blame can reasonably attach to his mother for at length becoming alienated from him. It should be sufficiently satisfactory to learn, that, despite all provocation, there cannot be found throughout her history "one trace of wilful unkindness to Prince Frederick;" and her maternal character is fully vindicated by the fact that to all her other children, seven in number, she proved "a tender and judicious mother."

As regards her religious feelings, the first act recorded of Caroline, when a maiden Princess of Anspach, is, that on being chosen to be the wife of the King of Spain, on condition of changing her faith from Protestant to Catholic, according to the custom of royal German brides, she refused to purchase the honour at this price, and preferred her creed to a crown. Again, the last word she uttered when a prelate was brought to her dying bed was "Pray." Between the youthful act and the expiring word, however, we fear there was very little in her life in keeping with either. Indifference was the spirit of the age, and the queen, though on the best level of that age, was not beyond it. Let one instance suffice. "It was the pious custom of the period to read prayers in the ante-room while the queen dressed, thus saving at once time and appearances."

As a wife, a mother, or a woman, Caroline may be variously estimated according to the predilections of her judges, but in her professional capacity, as we may say, that is, as a sovereign—and were she of the other sex, it is thus that she would be chiefly viewed—her great ability is unquestionable. "The queen's power was unrivalled and unbounded," says Lord Hervey, whose memoirs afford the fullest information on the period; and he describes at length by what unceasing efforts she maintained her rule. While admitting that she sometimes felt indignant at the restraints imposed upon royalty in our free England, he bears testimony, too, to the strong good sense with which she reconciled herself to them, albeit brought up in the midst of German despotism; and even records her expressing an opinion most remarkable from a foreigner owning no prejudice in our favour, and a sovereign who was personally hampered and inconvenienced by the system she could yet thus sagaciously criticize.

"I had as lief," he reports her as saying, "be Elector of Hanover as King of England, if the government was the same. *Quel Diable*, that had anything else would take you at all, or think you worth having, if you had not your liberties? Your island might be a very pretty thing in that case for Bridgman and Kent to cut out into gardens; but for the figure it would make in Europe it would be of no more consequence here in the West than Madagascar in the East; and for this reason, as impudent and as insolent as you all are with your troublesome liberty, your princes, if they are sensible, will rather bear with your impertinences than cure them —a way that would lessen their influence in Europe full as much as it would increase their power at home."

A painful disorder aggravated by neglect cut short Caroline's reign at the age of fifty-two. Her husband worried and scolded her to the last, his vile temper and brutal manners turning even what he meant for attentions into irritating annoyances; while her unnatural son kept away, consoling himself with the hope, "we shall soon have good news, she cannot hold out much longer." But other, better children were by her side—a boy not yet outgrown his mother's love, and an elder daughter to receive a tender charge of younger sisters. The Minister, too, to whom she had been so faithful that she had transmitted his views to the king, and secured their adoption even when she had found herself unable to share them; he, too, knelt beside her, while with dying lips she recommended "the king, my children, and the kingdom to your care." He did his best to care for them, but with his able colleague much of his power departed, and it was not very long before it ceased altogether. Since that time many other influences have swayed England and her destinies, purer and more high-minded, perhaps, in accordance with our moral progress; but that elevation could hardly have been attained in the early Georgian days, and if it had, might have proved ineffectual to cope with surrounding circumstances. Caroline was fitted for the period in which she appeared; she succeeded where a more refined and lofty-spirited woman might have failed; but let it not be forgotten that if her defects did not prevent her success, it was her many excellences that ensured it, and that she may well be deemed a credit to her sex, of whom it may be affirmed—She was far from a bad woman and she was a thoroughly good queen.

E. G. BERNARD.

The Food Journal; a Review of Social and Sanitary Economy. March Number. Price 6d. J. M. Johnson, publisher, 3, Castle Street, Holborn.

THIS number contains several interesting articles. That "On Fasting and Fasting People" gives authentic stories of various persons who went without food, or almost without it, for extraordinary lengths of time.

A wretched being, known as "The living Skeleton," existed on a biscuit a day for years. A man residing near Stamford made a bet that he would live for seven weeks without solid food, and though hard pressed won his bet; he seems to have had an unlimited allowance of liquids of all sorts. A madman at Haarlem is said to have fasted for forty days in imitation of the Saviour. During this period he took nothing but water and tobacco smoke. Ann Moore, of Tutbury, about 1813, pretended to live without food. She was watched and actually held out for nine days, when she gave in and confessed the imposture.

In another article a curious account is given of adulterations of coffee. It is a very comforting account, however, as generally nothing worse is used than roasted grain and chicory. One grain sometimes used is called "coffina," and this name, no doubt, accounts for a revolting theory held by some people.

Information is given in other articles on brandies and wines, on potatoes, on chestnuts, and on various other descriptions of food.

Finally, two or three pages of useful recipes are given. The mistress of many a household would find this journal of use, especially if her husband happened to be an epicure.

On the Laws Relating to the Property of Married Women. By Arthur Hobhouse, Q.C. Manchester: Alexander Ireland & Co.

THIS small pamphlet is a remarkably clear exposition of the evils arising from the present law, and although written by a learned Q.C., it contains no technical expressions or legal phrases hard to be understood; but while the language is simple, the reasoning is close and convincing. It is admirably well calculated for distribution among M.Ps, men of business, and other persons who may be supposed to possess rather more than an average amount of intelligence.

As, however, it contains no stories of oppression, and is not at all sensational, it is less likely to impress that very numerous class of readers who reason with their hearts, than some other pamphlets of far less real power. One of its great merits is, that it enters fully into the feelings and reasons of those who object to any change in the law, as the following passage will show—

"To my mind it is abundantly clear that there should be an alteration of the law under discussion. But it must not be forgotten that we are speaking of a law probably cöeval with the very beginnings of English society; part of the Common Law, whose origin is lost in the darkness of antiquity, and which has been handed down to us as part and parcel of the institutions that have helped to preserve our liberties and to form our national character; a law, moreover, that relates to the most necessary and sacred of all connexions, the union of man and wife, the root of the family, the origin and rudiment of all social stability and progress. No wonder if by all who are timid, by all who are superstitious, by the majority of those who obey sentiment rather than reason, and by many who possess a large share of reason and judgment, any alteration of such a law is regarded, according to the character of the mind, with fear, with horror, with disgust, or with calm disapproval. It is of no use to disguise or to extenuate the difficulties which meet a reformer on the very threshold of such a subject as this."

Mr. Mill's Subjection of Women from a Woman's point of view. Clayland's Debating Society, London. Published by request of the Club. Manchester: John Heywood, 141 Deansgate.

THE object of the writer of this clever, amusing pamphlet is to explain why it is that women, whom she believes to be by Nature intellectually *superior* to men, have achieved so little in the world of Art and Science. Her profession of faith is thus made:—

"For my part I strongly conjecture that woman is the highest known order of intelligence, but in an undeveloped, immature condition; and that the poet Burns divined a very deep truth (a deeper truth than he would perhaps have endorsed in his less inspired moods,) when he sang of Nature—

"Her 'prentice han' she tried on a man,
An' then she made the lasses O!"

I do not expect that any of you will agree with me in this opinion, nor do I affirm it dogmatically or as capable of demonstration. I fully admit that the evidence is incomplete, and must be so by the conditions of the problem; since women have never been allowed to put forth their power in their own way, and by virtue of their own inherent laws, but have always been subject to powerful deflection through masculine control. Yet there are some reasons to justify my view of the case, which, if this were the subject before the meeting, I should be happy to adduce. Meantime I may point out that men appear to have a presentiment of a similar kind, either latent or carefully suppressed, else why are they always so reluctant to undertake competition on equal terms with women? The latter, except where great physical strength is required, are always ready to stand the test of open competition. No one has even dared to ask for privileges, protection, or favour in their behalf. The most that is ever asked for them is a fair field and no favour, and that arbitrary restrictions against the use by them of their own faculties should be withdrawn. Now it is notorious that men as against women, have had to call in the power of special legislation. They have had to be helped, and protected, and endowed, and privileged, and promoted, and combined in large numbers. Even now with all these advantages, many would not be content unless women were driven out of the field altogether, so afraid are they of standing the test of competition."

A few extracts will show the line of argument—

"It is quite a mistake, however, to suppose that either Mr. Mill or any one else wishes, by any means whatsoever, to convert women into men; on the contrary, we think the world is considerably over-weighted with masculinity. Our theology, politics, and prevalent opinions on all topics, are almost painfully and exclusively masculine. It is to give freer play to the purely *feminine* elements that we advocate the present changes; and though we propose tentatively to adopt what have been hitherto masculine forms and methods, it is not because men have adopted them, but because men have found them to *answer*, that we give the preference to known and tried, rather than to unknown and untried paths. It is quite possible that they may not fully answer for women; but all experiments hitherto made in the same direction have been attended with reasonable success;

and in a boundless wilderness of possibilities, we take the path which leads within the experience of humanity, to a well-ascertained goal."

"Some one has propounded the idea that woman is '*a great idea—spoiled.*' It strikes one as rather odd that no one should ever have seriously proposed to *realise* the *idea.*"

"Among all the true things that Mr. Mill has said of us—and one is almost lost in wonder that a man should be found capable of so accurately divining the situation—one of the most true is, that women have little or no *consecutive* time, and have to do their thinking at odd moments. The demands upon their attention are incessant, and make up in number for what they want in importance. So various are they, so conflicting, and so unexpected the quarters from whence they come, that life from this cause alone is apt to lose all its coherence, and become a mere rope of sand; added to which, there is the bewildering duty laid upon us of being agreeable to every one, at all times, even to people of diametrically opposite tastes; of being always well-dressed and presentable, and able to do a multiplicity of incongruous things with a lady-like air—(for no one ever excuses a woman for doing *badly* whatever she has to do). I think when these things are fairly taken into consideration that even the most confirmed misogamist would admit that our life is by no means an easy one, although to him so barren of valuable results."

"With regard to art, no less an authority than Göethe has declared that no great work can be produced merely at odd times, which, owing to the disruption of their lives already pointed out, is all that women have to give."

The tone throughout is good-tempered, and there is no touch of bitterness in the twenty-three pages of which the pamphlet consists.

The author is not one of "the women who shriek," but is rather a laughing philosopher, and though a most thorough-going champion of womankind, is a very good-natured one.

We recommend this little work to those who complain, not without reason, that the literature on the women's question is "so awfully dull."

Art. V.—RECORD OF EVENTS.

PROPERTY OF MARRIED WOMEN.

As soon as the Parliamentary session opened, Mr. Russell Gurney gave notice that he would bring forward his Bill again.

Mr. Raikes also gave notice that he would bring forward another Bill on the same subject.

The Manchester Executive Committee thus describes the two Bills in a circular:—

There are two Bills now before Parliament dealing with the question of the property of married women. The Bill to amend the law with respect to the property of married women, prepared and brought in by Mr. Russell Gurney, Mr. Headlam, and Mr. Jacob Bright, proposes to abrogate the rule of the Common Law, which gives the personal property and earnings of a married woman absolutely to her husband. If this measure should become law, the effect will be that marriage will no longer operate as a gift to the husband of the property and earnings of the wife, and that a wife will be solely liable for her own debts. Men and women, before they marry, or afterwards, will still be able to make binding settlements or agreements as to the way in which the property of either or both of them is to be administered. Without such express agreement, a woman's property will not by marriage be taken from her. *She* may make the property her husband's by gift; but the law will not give it to him. This measure passed the House of Commons last session by a very large majority. It passed the second reading in the House of Lords without a division ; but was postponed for want of time to consider the details. It has, therefore, to go through all its stages over again, during the present session.

A second Bill, known as the Married Women's Property Bill No. 2, the full name of which is "The Bill to *protect* the Property of Married Women," has been prepared and brought in this session by Mr. Raikes, Mr. Staveley Hill, and Mr. West. It is the very object of this Bill to preserve the rule of the Common Law, which has worked so much injustice—and it only proposes to mitigate some of its worst abuses—even this it proposes to do by such an amount of interference with individual right, as to disposition of property, as would of itself introduce most serious evils.

Mr. Raikes's Bill proposes to make every husband a trustee of all the real and personal property of his wife; but no payment to him under the trust is to be valid unless made in pursuance of an order signed by his wife, and he is not to be free (even with the full consent of his wife apparently) to sell, transfer, or vary the investment of any property held by him under the trust *without the consent of a county court judge.* Such a measure might suit lawyers, since it would compel the waste upon legal expenses of the better half of any small property belonging to a wife; but it will not suit anybody else, least of all the class (nine-tenths of the people of this country) to whom freedom in the disposition of property is necessary to make the possession of property any real advantage to them.

The Bill further provides that a married woman may obtain protection for her earnings from the county court judge of the district in which she lives, when she can show that for the last six months before her application she has been earning more than half the expenses of her family. It is quite certain that such a remedy will meet only a very few cases, and a rule so wholly arbitrary is a mere mockery of justice.

Whether the 1,100,000 married women earning wages in England and Ireland have a legal right to their earnings or not, their moral right is unquestionable. This right is fully recognised by the habitual practice of the better order of the working classes. It should be the part of legislation to conform to the higher social morality, and not to demoralise a people by legalising injustice, and then providing partial and ineffectual remedies for consequent injury.

All persons who approve the principle of Mr. Russell Gurney's Bill must equally disapprove the purpose and the provisions of Mr. Raikes's. Such persons should immediately petition Parliament in favour of the former measure, and against the latter. Better far no legislation at all, than legislation based upon injustice.

    Elizabeth C. Wolstenholme,
     Moody Hall, Congleton.
    Josephine E. Butler,   Hon. Secs.
     280, South Hill, Park Road, Liverpool.
    Lydia E. Becker, Treasurer,
     28, Jackson's Row, Albert Square, Manchester.

Wednesday, the 23rd of March, was the day appointed for reading both the Bills a second time; but, unfortunately, such a long discussion took place on the Bill, which had to be considered previously,* that no time was left, and the House adjourned without a word having been said on the subject. This is what is very liable to happen when non-party questions have to be considered, particularly when the question concerns the interests of unrepresented portions of the community. The following

---

* The Burials Bill. The *Pall Mall* describes the division which took place as a "purely party division."

is part of a letter on the subject which appeared in the *Echo*:—

Sir,—"A live dog," the saying runs, "is better than a dead lion." But in the eyes of members of the House of Commons a dead Dissenter is better than a live woman. Yesterday was the day appointed for the second reading of Mr. Russell Gurney's bill to amend the law with respect to the property of married women, but the grievance of the Dissenters in being forbidden to have their own form of service said by their own minister in the parish churchyard over a departed brother, so entirely occupied the time and attention of the House that the Recorder had to postpone his Bill. Wednesday is the only day on which the House can entertain matters of such trifling importance, and the first vacant one is May 18th. If it be permitted to gain a hearing then, we shall probably be told that it is too late in the session for the Bill to go into committee, and the question will be shelved again for another year; and yet we are perpetually being told that there is not the smallest need for women having the privilege of the suffrage!

A great number of petitions in favour of Mr. Gurney's Bill and against Mr. Raikes' Bill have been presented.

On the day when it was expected that the discussion would take place, the *Times* records that forty-two petitions were presented in favour of Mr. Gurney's Bill and fourteen *against* Mr. Raikes'. Not one petition was presented in favour of Mr. Raikes' or against Mr. Gurney's Bill.

The total number of petitions presented in this session up to March 22 were sixty-two signatures, 9673.*

Including the petitions presented on the 23rd, the number of petitions was 118. The number of signatures attached to these last is not known yet.

---

* It had been intended to give the lists, but they have not been sent, and we will delay our publication no longer.

DUBLIN SOCIETY FOR MARRIED WOMEN'S PROPERTY BILL.

It was stated in error, in our last number, that only five petitions were sent last year by this Society in favour of the Married Women's Property Bill. There were thirteen petitions sent by the Dublin Society to the House of Commons in 1869; and five petitions (including one signed by upwards of four thousand persons from Dublin) sent to the House of Lords.

During the first week of the present session the Dublin Society sent to the House of Commons five petitions—presented on 11th February by Mr. Pim—and three petitions to the House of Lords, presented on 8th February by the Earl of Kimberley—in favour of amending the law relating to Married Women's Property.—*Hon. Sec.*, Miss Anne J. Robertson.

THE KELLY CASE.

Mr. KELLY having appealed against the decision of Lord Penzance, the case was tried again before Lord Penzance and two other judges—Mr. Baron Channell and Mr. Justice Hannen. Mr. Baron Channell thus delivered judgment:—

This is an appeal to the full Court from a decision of the Judge Ordinary. Lord Penzance is desirous that my brother Hannen and myself should first state our views. I proceed, therefore, to deliver our joint opinion. The appeal is by the Rev. James Kelly against a decree whereby the Judge Ordinary, on the petition of the appellant's wife, Francis Kelly, decreed in favour of the petitioner for a judicial separation from her husband on the ground of cruelty. Mr. and Mrs. Kelly were married in Ireland in the year 1841. There was issue of the marriage a child, deceased, and a son, now living, who was born in 1845. With the exception of a visit made by Mrs. Kelly to Wales and Ireland, Mrs. Kelly lived under the same roof with Mr. Kelly from the time of the marriage until January, 1869. Since that time Mr. and Mrs. Kelly have ceased to cohabit, Mrs. Kelly having left her husband's home, and claimed from this Court the decree for judicial separation now appealed against. There is some evidence that on one or two occasions Mr. Kelly laid hands on Mrs. Kelly against her consent. But the evidence is so slight on this head that we think it safer to treat the case (as it was considered by the Judge Ordinary) as one on which there is an absence of any proof of such physical violence towards the wife on the part of the husband as would justify a decree. The question then arises whether the decree is erroneous in holding that, although there was not such actual physical violence on the part of the husband towards the wife, there is shown to be that cruelty which will entitle her to ask this Court for a decree for a judicial separation. The appellant seeks the reversal of the decree on two grounds—first, that the Judge Ordinary has erred in point of law in the definition which he has given of cruelty; and, secondly, that the evidence does not establish that the appellant has been guilty of legal cruelty. The passages in the judgment of the Judge Ordinary in which he has laid down the principles upon which his decision is based are the following:—"The peculiar and distinguishing feature of this case is the adoption by the respondent of a deliberate system of conduct towards his wife with the view of bending her to his authority. If force, whether physical or moral, is systematically exerted for this purpose in such a manner, to such a degree, and during such a length of time, as to break down her health and render serious malady imminent, the interference of the law cannot be justly withheld by any Court which affects to have charge of the wife's personal safety." "Moreover," says his Lordship, "the decisions have imparted this further proposition as a condition of the Court's interference, that the troubles of the wife are not owing to her own misconduct." We are of opinion that the above cited passages contain an accurate and, so far as was necessary for the determination of the case, a complete statement of the law on the subject. It would be difficult to frame a definition of legal cruelty which should be applicable to all the cases which may arise. The object of the Matrimonial Court in exercising its jurisdiction in decreeing for judicial separation for cruelty is to free the injured consort from a cohabitation which has been rendered, or which there is imminent reason to believe will be rendered, unsafe by the illusage of the party complained of. It is obvious that the modes by which one of two married persons may make the life or the health of the other insecure are infinitely various, but as often as perverse ingenuity may invent a new manner of producing the result the Court must supply the remedy by separating the parties. The most frequent form of ill-usage which amounts to cruelty is that of personal violence; but the Courts have never limited their jurisdiction to such cases alone, as will be clearly seen by reference to some of the authorities. His Lordship then cited several decisions on the question of cruelty, and afterwards referred in detail to the evidence in the case, which he said had satisfied the Court that the acts imputed to Mr. Kelly as amounting to legal cruelty were established. The Court adopted the view of the evidence taken by the Judge Ordinary, and dismissed the appeal.

Lord Penzance then made some further remarks, concluding with these words:—

The appellant affirms that a new law has been made to meet

his case, and that it will form a dangerous precedent. I hope
not. To the best of my judgment it is the case which is new, and
not the law. I have searched the recorded decisions of the Matrimonial Courts in vain for a case the features of which in any
considerable degree resemble the present. It has no parallel in
the past, and as to becoming a precedent it is hardly likely to find
one in the future. So much injustice, so much perversion of
mind, such abiding rancour for so trifling a cause, so much
deliberate oppression under provocation so slight, moral chastise-
ment so severe administered with so much system, maintained
with such tenacity up to the brink of so perilous a danger to
health, with so utter a disregard of consequences, and all to
extort confession of acts never committed and force repentance
without consciousness of wrong, will probably never be exhibited
again. That such a case should recur it would be necessary that
to an inflexible will should be added the power of self-deception
in an inordinate degree, so that the promptings of angry resent-
ment should be mistaken for the voice of duty, and that while
religion should be put forward to sanction and even enjoin a
harsh and cruel retaliation, the leading precepts of religion,
humility, and forgiveness, should be altogether forgotten or but
little heeded.—*Times*, February 22nd.

Mrs. Kelly having asked for alimony, Lord Penzance
issued the following decree after some days of consideration :—

The Judge-Ordinary announced that in this case he should
decree alimony to the petitioner at the rate of 164*l*. a year. In
the first instance, the alimony *pendente lite* had been computed
upon an income of 468*l*. derived by the respondent. Of this
228*l*. accrued from his wife's property, and the yearly value
of his benefice, after payment of a curate, did not exceed 100*l*.
Upon these data the Court fixed the respondent's income at 328*l*.,
and awarded the wife half, as the greater portion of it arose from
her property, which had been in great part wasted by the ill-
judged litigation of the respondent.—*Pall Mall Gazette*.

It seems to us very hard that Mrs. Kelly should not
obtain the whole of her property. It is difficult to see
what meritorious action of Mr. Kelly's deserves to be
rewarded by a gift of £64 a year out of his wife's
fortune; nor what offence Mrs. Kelly has committed
that she should be fined.

It appears, too, that Mr. Kelly retains control over the
principal of his wife's fortune, so that it is but too probable
that it will share the fate of the portion which he has
already squandered.

At a meeting of the Juridical Society on the 26th of

January, a paper was read by Mr. Droop, advocating a change in the law to give married women greater control over their property. Sir Roundell Palmer spoke against Mr. Droop's plan. He must, therefore, be regarded as an opponent to Mr. Gurney's Bill.

It has been distinctly established that a husband is not under the obligation of paying his wife's debts. He takes her income, but she has no power to pledge his credit in order to make purchases, as the following case shows:—

A silk mercer of Kingston recently brought an action in the Court of Common Pleas against a Mr. Hayter to recover the sum of 128*l.*, for goods supplied to the defendant's wife. The question was whether the wife, who was now living apart from her husband, had any authority to pledge his credit to the extent represented by the amount of this bill. Mr. Justice Keating explained to the jury that a wife, even when living with her husband, had no absolute right to pledge his credit. The jury found for the defendant."—*Campden Herald*, February 12th.

The *Droit des Femmes* of March 5, states that some opposition members in the Chamber of Deputies have undertaken to bring in a Bill for improving the condition of women in France. One of the clauses provides that a woman, who obtains a separation from her husband, shall have control over the whole of her own property, and be able to dispose of it as she thinks fit.

It does not seem at all probable that the proposed amendment in the French law will be adopted.

SUFFRAGE.

SEVERAL public meetings have been held during the past quarter in support of women's suffrage.

The first was held in Edinburgh, on the 17th of January. The meeting was much crowded, and hundreds were obliged to leave who could not obtain admittance. It was computed that about 1200 persons were present. Among those on the platform were:—Principal, Sir Alexander Grant, Bart.; Sir David Wedderburn, Bart., M.P.; Mr. Duncan M'Laren, M.P.; Mr. Jacob Bright, M.P.; Dr. Lyon Playfair, C.B., M.P.; Mr. Miller, M.P.; Rev. Dr. Robert Wallace; Professors Masson,

Kelland, and Calderwood; Mr. Adam Gifford, advocate;
Mr. W. F. Bedford, D.C.L.; Councillors Mossman,
Greig, Millar, Bladworth, Wormald, and Murray; Messrs.
Hugh Rose, W. M'Crie, Edward Blyth, Robert Cox,
W.S.; Wm. Smith, Duncan M'Laren, jun., John
Carmichael, &c.

On the motion of the Principal of the University, Mr.
D. M'Laren, M.P., was called to the chair.

The chairman read letters from Sir Robert Anstruther,
M.P., Sir John Murray, and several other gentlemen,
regretting their inability to be present, and approving
the object of the meeting. He also explained that it was
not proposed to give votes to *all* women, but only to
householders, landholders, and others who fulfil the
conditions which bestow the suffrage on men.

Professor Calderwood read the report of the Edinburgh branch of the National Society for Women's
Suffrage. The report stated that nearly one hundred
petitions in favour of women's suffrage had been sent
from Scotland, signed by upwards of 19,000 names.
Two hundred and thirty-nine qualified women had sent
in claims to be registered under the new Reform Act in
Wigton and other places, and in Aberdeen the whole of
the women householders had been placed on the electoral
roll by the assessor, but all the claims were rejected.

Professor Calderwood moved the adoption of the report. Councillor Mossman seconded the motion, and
the Chairman declared it carried. This being disputed,
a show of hands was taken, when only a few hands were
held up against it, and the resolution was carried almost
unanimously.

Mr. Jacob Bright, M.P., moved the following resolution:—

That the ownership or occupation of lands or houses, being
the basis of representation in this country, it is unjust in principle
to make sex a ground of disqualification, therefore. excluding a
large number of intelligent persons well qualified to exercise the
electoral franchise.

After a few remarks, Mr. Bright said:—

Nobody will deny that women are injured by bad and benefited by good laws, precisely as men are. They have as deep an
interest as men in the wise progress of our legislation—nay, I

would undertake to show, if it were necessary, that they have a deeper interest than men, because they are the weaker portion of society, and the weak are more interested than the strong in impartial and just laws. Some three years ago, a great Act of Parliament was passed—the last Reform Act. It was called the Household Suffrage Act. I do not know how it got that name, for the name does not characterise the measure. It was not a Household Suffrage Act—it was a Male Household Suffrage Act. A very considerable proportion of the houses of the whole kingdom were passed over by that Act—something like one in six, I suppose, speaking generally. On an election day, the doors of these houses are closed—they are passed over because a woman happens to be at the head of the household instead of a man. Nobody comes forth to the polling booth to register a vote in the interest and for the protection of the family. In regard to the inmates of these houses, any law may be passed, however injurious, however dangerous it may be to personal security; and it must not be supposed that we are past the time when laws pernicious to certain classes of society may be enacted. We have had recent legislation which, in my opinion, throws down the safeguards of the personal liberty of women in such a manner, that if any Government, however powerful, had dared to interfere in the same way with the personal liberty of men, that Government would have been instantaneously destroyed. Now, as has already been shown, women, although denied the privileges, are not shielded from the burdens, of citizenship. The whole weight of taxation falls equally on both sexes. We have a tax called the inhabited house duty. I have no fault to find with the name, for it does actually characterise the tax; it is not an inhabited male house duty. It does not pass over any house; it comes equally on all, and the tax-gatherer, directly or indirectly, enters the house of every widow and every spinster in Edinburgh; and I think our Chairman, with his great political information, would agree when I say there are hundreds of poor women in Edinburgh paying, in proportion to their incomes, a greater amount of taxation than is paid by the greatest houses in the land. (Cheers.)

Mr. Bright pointed out that women were not fairly dealt with in the matter of education, and in some other matters, especially in respect to the property of married women.

Mr. Bright concluded by saying :—

Speaking as an English politician, I will tell you with all sincerity that we in England are grateful to Scotland for the powerful aid she always gives in the settlement of national questions; and looking at this meeting, knowing the influence of this platform, seeing how many of your members of Parliament are present to-night, I may confidently predict that when this question comes up for discussion in the House of

Commons, Scotland will give no doubtful vote in your favour. (Loud cheering.)

Professor Masson seconded the motion in a magnificent speech, of which our space will only allow us to quote a fragment. In speaking of occupations for women he said:—

The theory is—and it is the theory of our opponents, or at least they are bound to make it their theory—that every woman in the world is supported by men—(cheers and laughter)—that all women are supported by the labour of the other sex; the one sex living entirely without working, living on the labour of the other. That is the theory; and, observe, all people who take the opposite side argue on that theory. But what is the fact? The fact is that the theory is a sheer delusion, one of the greatest hallucinations ever propounded. (Laughter and cheers.) The saying in the well-known song is—

"Men must work and women must weep
While the harbour bar is moaning."

But the fact is, that, though the men work, they do not devolve the mere duty of weeping upon the women. Women have to do much of the work and nearly all the weeping too. (Cheers and laughter.) I have looked at the census of 1861 for England and Scotland; and, as there is a committee appointed in this city for regulating the census which is to take place next year, I will give my experience of the last census to this effect, that it might be vastly improved upon,—that a great deal of new information might be obtained along with the census in various subjects of social importance, and especially in regard to women's employments. I find, slumping together England and Wales and Scotland, that there are 11,900,000 females of all sexes. (Laughter.) Sometimes one hits on a truth by a blunder, and if you do not know, I know that there are a great many "old women" in the other sex. (Laughter and cheers.) The number of females of all ages, according to the census of England and Wales and Scotland in 1861, was 11,900,000; and, doing my best to make a calculation, I find that 3,800,000 of these were working for their bread—not only working domestically as members of families, as wives and daughters, but working in the ordinary sense in which we understand work. Now, if you take that proportion of the 11,900,000 of all ages, you will see what a vast proportion of the grown-up women are working—sometimes not working for themselves, but for people that are depending on them—nay, sometimes working for wretches of men who ought to be hurled beyond the frontier where good bread is given to hungry mouths. (Cheers.) But I find also the fact that there is a general tendency to keep women out of the higher occupations. So long as it is menial work, or anything approaching that, they are allowed to do it, notwithstanding the beautiful theory that every woman reposes in a cushioned chair, and is ministered to. (Cheers and laughter.) But the moment they want to get themselves educated, to get to higher duties, then there is a dead-set made against them, as there has been here till recently. I saw in one paper, when there was a desire expressed by some women to become medical practitioners—(cheers and hisses)—I saw in one medical newspaper a letter with this argument:—There are a great many medical men that are not in practice—(laughter)—and what will be the consequence if we bring in women? (Loud laughter.) Observe what that means. It means that before you begin to help a woman, or allow her to help herself, all the men must be exhausted. (Laughter and cheers.) How different is that from our so-called gallantry! Let there be a dinner party in any part of the kingdom, and is it not the rule that the women shall be helped first? (Laughter and cheers.) I daresay the women would be prepared to part with that privilege, and to let all be helped simultaneously on such occasions, if justice were allowed to them in other respects, and if they were allowed to suit their own tastes and cultivate and exercise their own faculties equally with men. (Cheers.) In regard to education, it seems to me so strange that the world should have come to this time and all but forgotten one half of the human species. When we have endowments and State helps of all sorts for the superior education of men—not only primary schools, but middle schools, grammar schools, and universities; with systems of scholarships, rewards, fellowships, everything that can encourage young men and push them forward—why, on earth, I wonder, should there not be something of all this for women too? (Hear, hear.) Have not women minds? Is there anything in astronomy, in mathematics, or in any other branch of knowledge that would not make the soul or mind of a woman as much nobler than that of an uneducated woman as it would make that of a man nobler than that of an uneducated man? (Cheers.) The time will come—I prophesy it—(cheers and laughter)—when universities and great schools, or at all events the precise equivalents to these, will be provided for our sisters and daughters. (Cheers.) But what is necessary towards all this is a little power on the part of women. A little of that power which consists of the right of giving or refusing a vote will be of great use; and I hold that those who have strong opinions on this question ought to begin to consider whether on the occasion of elections they will not make this a testing question—whether, when two men come before us as a constituency, if the one is not thoroughly right on this question, we should not rather give our vote to the other, though he may not be so favourable to our views in other respects. Then as to the objections. I have heard an argument which has come from one or two of the extreme Liberal party, and perhaps I ought not to state this objection, because it has not been publicly stated before. It is like lending a sword to the enemy, and it may be used against us. (Laughter.) But there is nothing like frankness. It is said that the result of this vote will probably be a great increase of Conservative power. Well, now, as this is not a political meeting, and has nothing to do with party, I will just say that, so far as that argument may be deterrent to the one political party, it ought to be good news to the other. I have no opinion myself on the subject of the probability hinted at; but considering the many advantages of other kinds, I am quite willing—without saying which side I take myself—I am quite willing to risk all that. (Hear, hear.)

Professor Lyon Playfair, M.P., in the course of an excellent speech related the following history:—

Permit me to state one instance, as it happens to be that which first aroused my slumbering conviction as to the injustice of our laws in regard to women. Some years since, I was in a steamer, going from Hull to St. Petersburg, when one of the lady passengers presented to me a letter of introduction. This unfortunate lady was flying from her husband, in order to seek that protection in a despotic country which the law refused to give her in England. She had a fortune when she married, but that had been squandered by her husband, who was then resorting to infamous practices for support. He lived in Germany, and used their children as a means of enticing governesses from England. When they crossed the Channel, provided with money for their journey, this rascal met and robbed them of their slender funds, leaving them destitute in a foreign country. The wife refused to share his guilt, and herself went out as a governess, but lost each situation by his demands on her earnings and threats of conjugal rights. For years she was protected in Russia, as the swindler was known to the police, who prevented his entrance into that country. A short time since the poor lady again visited me in London, in order to ask my aid in procuring the liberation of her boy, who was then in prison at Munich along with the father. I represented the case to some eminent Bavarian friends, who did their best to separate father and son; but bad law was more powerful than equity, and the young boy went out of prison with the father to pursue a career of iniquity, when the good mother, whose rights the law ignored, was standing by eager to rescue her lost child. Can you be surprised, with instances like these, that there are now many men and women who demand that they shall both be made equal in all legal and social relations of life? Women have long waited for such a recognition of their equality at the hands of men, and I for one am not surprised that it is now being sought in another and more effective way. There are few doctrines upon which liberal politicians are more agreed than that representation should be co-extensive with taxation; though, in application, the doctrine is limited to men. Women have not, and never can have, their just equality, unless they share with men the right to elect those who impose taxation.

Dr. Wallace, Sir D. Wedderburn, Bart., M.P., Mr.

Edward Blyth, and Mr. Miller, M.P., also spoke. A more successful meeting could not be held.

The names of the Edinburgh Committee for Women's Suffrage are—Mrs. M'Laren, Newington House, *President;* Miss Burton, Miss Craig, Miss A. Craig, Mrs. Crudelius, Miss Dick Lauder, Mrs. Furguson Home, Miss Hunter, Mrs. Lemmi, Mrs. Low, Mrs. M'Queen, Miss E. Stevenson, Miss Walker, Mrs. Wigham, Mrs. Nichol, Huntley Lodge, Merchiston, *Treasurer;* Miss Wigham, 5, South Gray Street, and Miss Agnes M'Laren, Newington House, *Secretaries.*

A large audience assembled in the Guildhall, Bath, on January 28th, to hear Professor F. W. Newman give an address on the Parliamentary Suffrage for Women. The Mayor took the chair.

The lecture was very eloquent. The following passage is striking—

If you, ladies, are happy, remember that others are unhappy. If you have kind and just husbands, remember that thousands of women have selfish or wicked husbands. If you have enough of this world's good, remember that scores of thousands of women and girls can scarcely get bread and shelter even by an excess of toil. If you have been tenderly watched over from childhood, learn that thousands of your sisters are untaught and untrained, and many hundreds wickedly sold by parents or kinsfolk to the shambles of the voluptuous rich. It is a grievous fact that men possessed of political power, and fully aware of things concerning which we fear to speak very plainly, have enacted in a course of many centuries just enough law against these horrors to salve their own consciences, but never have so enforced any enactment as to make the law a reality; much less have they enacted all that the case demands. I boldly say that history, and the voice of God sounding through its miserable pages, call upon purehearted and happier women to succour their unhappy sisters, whom the ruder and less virtuous sex tramples down. You cannot succour them without some power to mould the law and incite its enforcement.

A public meeting was held in the Athenæum, Bristol, on the 4th of February, in support of the Bill to remove the electoral disabilities of women.

The following resolutions were moved by Mr. F. W. H. Myers, Fellow of Trinity College, Cambridge, and Professor Sheldon Amos, and carried:—

That by the deprivation of the parliamentary franchise not

only do women suffer much grievous social injustice, but the State loses an influence which would tend to soften and purify laws and morals.

That the basis of the English constitution, and the actual municipal suffrage, attest the constitutional right of women to vote on a par with men.

On the 8th of February, a large meeting was held in the Corn Exchange, Crewe. Mr. John Eaton took the chair. A resolution approving of the principle of the Bill, about to be introduced into Parliament by Mr. Jacob Bright, was proposed by the Rev. S. A. Steinthal, in an able speech, and seconded by Miss Becker.

Amongst other remarks Miss Becker said—

At a time when the Government of the nation was in few hands, there was not such a great difference between men and women as to their political status as to make women feel that they were in a degraded position. But every advance which was made in the direction of giving more extended influence to men depressed the condition of women politically. Under the reign of Louis Philippe, in France, women were accustomed to hold many civil offices, such as being post-office and other clerks, but of these privileges they had since gradually been deprived, the reason being that, as they did not hold votes, they were destitute of that political influence which had become necessary to obtain government appointments. The same thing was felt in England; and, as illustrating this remark, she might quote the case which frequently arose in the agricultural counties, where the widow of a farmer, being able and anxious to carry on a farm after the death of her husband, was thrown out of this means of earning her livelihood because her landlord wanted a vote, which he could not command when his tenant was a woman. Such instances had occurred over and over again, where women had been compelled to part with their farm stock at great sacrifices, and had been reduced to comparative poverty for these political reasons. (Hear.) Again, in the case of the Married Women's Property Bill, which would be introduced into Parliament, that question must be referred to an assembly which was composed entirely of men, and from the election of which the voice of every woman was carefully excluded. Were women likely to feel much confidence in such an assembly doing justice in a question between men and women? Would working men like a question between capital and labour to be settled in an assembly from the election of which the voice of every working man was carefully excluded. (Hear, hear, and cheers.) It was certainly possible that such an assemblage would do justice to working men, but if something less than justice was done, would working men be satisfied with it? With regard to the education question, Mr. Steinthal had pointed out that women had been excluded from the benefits of endowed schools. It appeared to her that the education of the women of the nation was not thought of at all. Certainly it was proposed to give girls the benefit of primary education. As regarded the secondary education to be obtained in the higher schools and the universities, it did not seem to be thought of that a poor girl should be given the opportunity of rising through these schools to be qualified for any high office of trust or emolument. She saw no reason why a sharp clever girl should not have the opportunity of going through the higher schools, and obtaining such offices under Government as she was qualified to fill in the same way as her brothers were enabled to do. (Cheers.) The general effect of the exclusion of women from political power had been to make women thought of less consequence than men even in matters of education. The education of women was of less consequence to politicians than the education of men so long as women did not have electoral privileges. (Hear.) An instance of this came under her own eye nearly every day in Manchester. There was the Manchester Free School, which, as far as it went, was an admirable institution, and in which a great number of poor boys, who would otherwise be what was called street Arabs, having been taken off the streets, were educated, and, perhaps, provided for in other respects. But the girls, who were sisters to these boys, were left in a friendless and neglected state, and the first direct lesson of that fact was to make the boys think they were of more consequence than the girls. Every day the thought occurred to her what became of the sisters of the boys taken care of in that Free School. Was it not likely they would grow up a greater curse to the community than their brothers who had been taken care of would have done? (Hear, hear and cheers.) It was proposed by the National Education League, of which she had the honour of being a member, to establish schools all over the country, and to make the attendance at them compulsory upon all children of school age. She supposed it would be necessary, if this proposal obtained legislative sanction, to appoint officials to see that the children did attend the schools to be provided for them, and to look after absentees. She wondered if it had ever occurred to any one that anybody but men should be appointed to be these school-inspectors. It seemed to her that the establishment of this new branch of the civil service might be made a means of providing for great numbers of educated women who were now struggling to obtain starvation wages as governesses. Such employment was entirely suited to the capacities of these ladies, who would make better school visitors and school-inspectors than men could. Their employment was further commended by this reason. It seemed to be overlooked that the father of a family had practically little to do with the matter of education, because during school hours he was engaged at work, and the duty of looking after the children devolved entirely upon the mother of the family. Let them suppose the case of a poor working woman with her husband's and half-a-dozen children's breakfasts to get ready, and the whole burden of housekeeping on her shoulders, and what the effect would be if a man who could not know or sympathise with her difficulties came round as a school-inspector to complain that her children were not regular in their school attendance. Would not a lady inspector be far more effectual for good in such cases than any other kind of policeman or Government inspector? (Cheers.) A good deal was said about unmarried women, as if they were the only women who earned their own living. It was supposed that when a woman was married she entered into a kind of haven, where she had nothing to do but to live upon her husband. (Laughter.) That was a thing which she disputed. She thought there were a great many married women who maintained their husbands. (Renewed laughter and cheers.) Moreover, she was perfectly certain that in a majority of cases where men had to go to work, but for the labour of his wife he would earn less wages. If a man had to get his own breakfast ready, and after his forenoon's work had to buy and cook his own dinner, to sweep up his house, wash his clothes, and do everything for himself, it would take up half his time, and a good deal of his strength, so that he would not be able to work so punctually or to earn the same wages. When a man entered into partnership, and gave his labour outside the house, and the woman her labour at home, they jointly earned the income of the family. (Cheers.) She regarded the position of the wives of the working men as extremely unjust, and regretted that the Married Women's Property Bill, even if it had passed into law, would not touch this particular injustice.

The resolution was carried with but one dissentient, and a petition in favour of Mr. Jacob Bright's Bill adopted.

Miss Becker's address appeared in several London papers.

Several lectures have been given on the same subject, which are thus noticed in the *Manchester Suffrage Journal*.

On February 8th, Miss Taylour delivered a lecture to a numerously-attended meeting at Newcastle-on-Tyne, and on the following day to a similar meeting at South Shields. Petitions in favour are being signed at these places.

On February 17th, the Rev. A. F. Macdonald delivered a lecture at Lincoln, which was well attended.

At Ipswich, on February 21st, a lecture was given by Miss Couperthwaite; and the same lady lectured the following day at Bury St. Edmund's.

Miss Craiger has lectured at Pleasley Vale, Bolton, Bacup, and Stackstead, in Lancashire.

On the 28th February, the Rev. A. F. Macdonald lectured at Leicester.

On Tuesday night, March 8, Mr. J. W. Fletcher

delivered a lecture at the Albert Rooms, Coronation Street, the meeting place of the Sunderland Conservative Association, on "Women's Suffrage." There was a good attendance, and a considerable number of ladies formed part of the audience. Ald. Tyzack occupied the chair.

Among other remarks Mr. Fletcher said :—

He advocated the enfranchisement of women because he believed the mind of the Legislature would be more frequently and fully fixed upon the social general condition of women; there were real grievances under which women laboured, which ought to be rectified, and would be much better ventilated had women direct political power. There were dozens of social questions concerning the poor outcast, the prodigal, alms-houses, asylums, &c., which, had women votes, would be more likely to be taken up by Parliament, for it was such departments of political economy which would be principally taken up by women.

On March 12, Professor Newman lectured on Women Suffrage, in the Masonic Hall, Birmingham. The Mayor, Mr. T. Prime, presided, and there was a good attendance.

On the 23rd of March, Mrs. Fawcett, wife of the member for that town, gave a lecture on the "Electoral Disabilities of Women," in the Town Hall. The occasion drew together the largest audience that has ever probably assembled in that room. Mrs. Fawcett combatted the various objections raised to women's voting, and thus spoke of one of the newly invented ones.

Let us now turn to the ninth objection, viz., that most women are Conservatives, and that their enfranchisement would consequently have a reactionary influence on politics. I have often heard this argument from the lips of men for whom I have the greatest respect, but I never hear it without astonishment and regret. What is representative government if not government by a national assembly chosen by the whole people to *represent* their views and to produce a corresponding influence on the state of the law ? Do those who object to the enfranchisement of women, on the ground that they are usually Conservatives, think that all Conservatives ought to be disfranchised ? Surely representative institutions require that all differences of opinion should have their due and proportionate weight in the Legislature. (Hear.) No class of persons should be excluded on account of their political opinions. What would be thought of a Conservative who gravely asserted that he thought all Dissenters should be disfranchised because they are generally Liberals ? I am almost afraid even to suggest the hard names which such a misguided person would be called by the very people who oppose women's suffrage, because most women are Conservatives. And yet the two cases are exactly parallel, and equally antagonistic to the fundamental principle of representative government. A representative system which excludes half the community from representation surely is a farce. In my opinion the question ought not even to be asked—"How would women vote if they had the franchise?" The only question ought to be, "Is representative government the best form of government that can be devised?"

The *Lincolnshire Chronicle* says that the Rev. A. F. Macdonald, M.A., of Lincoln, delivered a lecture in the room of the Liberal Association on Tuesday evening, the 29th of March, entitled "Education for all women: the franchise for some women."

A meeting of the National Society for Women's Suffrage was held on the 26th of March, at the Hanover Square Rooms, and was numerously attended.

Amongst those present were Lord Houghton, Lady Amberley, Lady Anstruther, Mrs. Jacob Bright, Mons. Louis Blanc, Sir D. Wedderburn, M.P., Professor Fawcett, M.P., Mr. John Morley, Mr. Eastwick, M.P., Mr. M'Laren, M.P., Mr. Charley, M.P., Mrs. M'Laren, Captain Maxse, Mr. P. A. Taylor, M.P., Miss Cobbe, Lady Eleanor Brodie, Mr. W. H. Ashurst, Mr. Bernard Cracroft, Mrs. Stansfeld, Miss C. A. Biggs, Lady Crompton, Countess Beauchamp, Lady Belper, Major and Mrs. Bell, Mrs. Crawshay, Professor Sheldon Amos, Miss Jewsbury, Herr Carl Blind, Syed Ameer Ali, Mr. James Heywood, Mr. F. T. Palgrave, Miss Motley, Mr. and Mrs. Russell Martineau, Mr. Lucas, Mr. M. D. Conway, Miss Elizabeth Garrett, Lady Lyell, Dr. Elizabeth Blackwell, &c., &c.

Mrs. P. A. Taylor, on taking the chair, was very warmly received. She expressed her gratification at the presence of so large an audience, which indicated the growing interest that was taken in this movement, but while the ranks of their opponents were being gradually thinned the fertility and variety of their arguments did not appear to lessen. There were social questions which touched women as nearly as men, and upon which women had a right to be heard. Some friends had expressed apprehension that the working classes would be opposed to this question, but out of a large number of petitions presented to Parliament on this subject from the metropolitan boroughs the half came from the working classes. (Hear, hear.) It had been asserted that women were unfit for the franchise, though they were not held to be unfitted for the payment of taxes and the other responsibilities of householders; and, further, that it would unfit them for domestic duties. The same argument was used when it was proposed to abolish slavery; it was said the negro was unfit for freedom. Slavery was, however, abolished, and the negro had proved himself fit for freedom. Let the electoral disabilities of women be removed, and they would at once prove themselves fit for the franchise (Loud applause).

Mr. John Stuart Mill, on rising to move the first resolution, was greeted with repeated cheers. He said that since their meeting in July last the society had ample reason to be satisfied with the progress they had made; that progress manifested itself not only in the increased number of its friends, but still more in the altered tone of its opponents. There was one particular in which the admission of women to the franchise might be expected to affect the character of Parliament, and that would be by infusing into the Legislature an increased disposition to grapple with the great physical and moral evils of society. (Hear, hear.) There were many men who regarded increased activity in this direction with alarm; but he was convinced that if the State used all the means it possessed of raising the standard of morality, and even in some respects the physical well-being of the community, they would find it had much more in its power than it was the fashion to believe. In this respect governments were blameable for neglecting the right means of compassing those objects. The time had passed away when governments were actively tyrannical; their favourite sins in these times were indolence and indifference. Whatever scruples they might have about doing evil, they had none about letting evil alone. (Hear). The consciences and feelings of men, which on these points were more indolent than those of women, needed rousing, and the stronger active impulses of women were needed to do this. They did not seek to disfranchise the men, there should be a mutual taking of council. The ship of the State needed both sail and ballast; at present it was too often the case that the vessel was all ballast and no sail (Laughter). In matters of government they did not fail for want of the curb, but for want of the spur, and women were quite equal to the performance of that office (Laughter). If they were admitted to their proper share of the functions of the State the many wrongs and grievances which especially affected their sex would no longer be considered too unimportant to require any serious effort to put an end to them. There would, for example, be a far sterner repression of those outrages upon women which at present disgraced the country, and less of that inexcusable leniency of our courts of justice towards the offenders (Hear). There were some men liberal and enlightened upon general topics, and whose feelings would incline them to be just to women, who dreaded that the immediate effect of admitting them to the suffrage would be greatly to increase the clerical power. He (Mr. Mill) was not likely to undervalue this objection; but how did it come to pass that the clergy possessed this power? Because they had addressed women through the only feelings and principles they had been encouraged to cultivate—because they had been the only persons who had taken pains with women's minds, and who had addressed them as if they had a moral responsibility—as if their souls and their consciences were their own; because they were the only men

G

who seemed to think it was of any consequence what women thought and felt. Those who showed this respect to women deserved to have influence with them, and would continue to do so until other men used the same measures of acquiring influence which they had done. If the fathers, brothers, and husbands of these women took the same pains with their minds, and invited them to interest themselves in the subjects in which they were interested, they would soon find themselves better judges upon those subjects than the clergy, whose influence over them would be weakened just in proportion as they took part in the general affairs of life. He concluded by moving the following resolution:—" That this meeting is of opinion that the extension of the franchise to women will tend to promote among them a more cogent sense of their special duties as citizens, and of their general responsibilities as concerned with the advancement of the highest moral interest of the whole community."

Professor Cairnes, in seconding the resolution, said—What would determine thoughtful people in deciding whether or not to support this movement would be, not so much the political results which would follow from it, but the effect of it upon the character of woman herself, and through that character on to the various departments of life which she so largely influences (Cheers).

Mrs. Grote, in supporting the resolution, said she had never been engaged in any cause in which her feelings were more completely seconded by her reason than this. She had always felt that the arguments against women's franchise were so feeble and limited and ineffective that it was a wonder they were ever put forth. (Hear, hear.) They had on their side an able counsel, an advocate, not a Q.C. (laughter), although she wore a silk gown—one who had pleaded the cause not before a court of Nisi Prius, but a court of common sense, in the pages of the *Westminster Review*, with arguments derived from the constitutional theory, developed with a clearness and a force which appeared to leave nothing unsaid (Cheers).

Sir Robert Anstruther, M.P., also supported the resolution, and said that women would be well qualified to take part in the administration of the Poor Law. Would all the evils that we had lately seen in our workhouses have taken place if women had had more concern in their management? Clearly not. There were many other evils with which men were almost powerless to grapple, but which might be materially diminished if women had a greater voice in the management of affairs.

The resolution was put and carried.

Mrs. Fawcett moved the following resolution:—" That this meeting regards with much satisfaction the introduction into the House of Commons of a Bill for removing the electoral disabilities of women." The objection constantly met with was that there was something repugnant to the feelings in the idea of women's suffrage. People did not think it necessary to state what the feeling was, or whether it was based on reason or justice, or the reverse. All they said was that it was repugnant to their feelings. Now the best way to meet such opposition as that was by full and frequent discussion of the claims of women to the suffrage, and by a constant reiteration of the basis of reason and equity upon which the claim rested. Some sanguine persons thought the Bill might be carried this year. Whether that prediction was to be fulfilled, or not, nothing but good could come from the introduction of this Bill, but if the Bill was lost this session it would be followed by an immediate notice of its reintroduction the first day of the next.

Lord Amberley, in seconding the resolution, said they ought to welcome as a thing good and desirable in itself the wish of any class for political equality. This was a time when social questions were becoming every day more important, and were more than ever engaging the attention of the Legislature. Upon such questions women were eminently competent to give advice and assistance. Another reason why women should be admitted to the franchise was that he did not think the law would ever do justice between man and woman unless they were placed on a footing of political equality. (Hear, hear.) The most grave objection urged was that a deteriorating influence might be exercised on the character of women. This was an imaginary undefined feeling which would not bear investigation. It was no doubt a very terrible prospect to think of women going about the country delivering speeches and lectures, and instead of amusing themselves by reading the latest novel, to be occupied in studying such pernicious and corrupting books as 'Mill on Logic' (Laughter). For his part, he had no fear of that dreadful result. There would, probably, always be a sufficient supply of frivolous women, as, notwithstanding all their advantages, there was a sufficient number of frivolous men. (Laughter and cheers.)

Miss Helen Taylor supported the resolution. After alluding to the different objects which the society had in view, she said that something was needed that should remind men that women were by their side in the affairs of life, with the same needs and desires as they had, and desired freedom and equality. How could it be said that women were men's companions in the affairs of life when they were only companions in one path and were shut out from the largest part—political affairs? There were some men who would say that women were too gentle and too sweet to be mixed up with all the vulgar realities of politics, and they would respect them a great deal more while they held aloof from the hard throes of life and lived in an atmosphere of sweetness and poetry; but this was a very fanciful idea of women's existence: they could not escape from the throes of human life whichever way they turned —they were to be met with in the ordinary common details of domestic life, in all the petty rivalries and jealousies which beset them, and which required from an upright and pure-minded woman quite as much exercise of conscience and self-control as in any sphere of life (Applause). They were told to confine their interests to their own homes, that they had but a small balance of judgment, that they seldom knew more than one side of a question, and so a long list might be gone through of their defects and the causes of those defects; but was it possible that the disabilities under which women suffered could do other than cause them to be regarded with less respect? For with whom did they share that disqualification? With criminals, with idiots, with lunatics, and minors. (Laughter and cheers.) There were some men of a reflective turn of mind, who, in the most kind and considerate language, said that it was the great superiority of women which shut them out from the franchise—that their gentleness and tenderness unfitted them for public affairs. Were kindness and gentleness, then, such drugs in the political life that they must be shut out for fear of being overdone with them? (Laughter and cheers.) Was not the great mass of poverty, corruption, and ignorance, that went on festering century after century in the depths of society, owing to the hardness, coldness, and selfishness of men; and might not woman's gentleness do much to remedy this? And what might be expected from the exclusion of one-half of human nature from all direct action on public affairs? Women's suffrage was not only wanted for the sake of its influence on society as a whole, but also to enable women to insist upon the carrying out of those reforms which all the world acknowledged to be desirable, but which were continually set aside while more pressing things which constituents demanded were being done. (Cheers.) When it was first proposed in the House of Commons to admit women to the franchise many members who discountenanced the idea yet expressed the greatest indignation against particular injustices to which women were subject; but what had those chivalrous gentlemen done since to protect women? Had they brought in a Bill for flogging men who ill-treated women. (Laughter.) It was worth notice that no Bill for the advantage of women had been brought in except by those who voted for giving them the suffrage. (Cheers.)

The Hon. Auberon Herbert, M.P., supported the resolution. It seemed to him perfectly impossible to refuse this claim of women's suffrage when once it had been seriously asked for by so large a number of women in this country.

The resolution was put and carried.

Mr. Jacob Bright, M.P., moved the next resolution, which was, "That the great extension of the suffrage, so long as women are excluded from it, is a positive injury to them, since it is rapidly making them the only excluded class.' He had, in conjunction with Sir Charles Dilke, undertaken to pilot the proposed Bill through Parliament. It was three years since Mr. Mill introduced this question into the House of Commons with great ability and success. Since then associations had been formed in many of the larger towns throughout the country, and many of the most scholarly and distinguished men in the universities were now on their side.

Sir Charles Dilke, M.P., in seconding the resolution, pointed out that the effect of the Bill which Mr. Jacob Bright and himself were to introduce was hardly wide enough to justify some of the arguments used either for or against it. It was not a Bill for giving a vote to every woman, but only to those women who fulfilled those conditions which were at present required of men, and it seemed to him so simple and easy a matter to justify such a proposal that he was sanguine enough to believe it would be carried during the present session and without a division. (Loud cheers.)

Miss Hare made a few remarks in support of the resolution, and was followed by Professor Hunter in a very effective and humorous speech, and it was put and carried unanimously.

A vote of thanks to Mrs. Taylor for her able conduct in the chair, moved by Sir Wilfrid Lawson, M.P., was carried by acclamation, and the meeting, which was throughout of a very enthusiastic character, was brought to a close.

The above report is taken from the *Standard* of March 28th, the report in that paper being very superior to the report in the *Times*.

The Dublin Branch of the Women's Suffrage Society, consists this year of Miss Sharman Crawford, Miss Craig, James Haughton, Esq., J.P., E. Richards, Esq., Mrs. Robertson, Miss Robertson, and Miss Anne Isabella Robertson, who acts still as hon. secretary.

Numerous petitions have already this session been sent through the Dublin Society, to the Houses of Lords and Commons.

The following is the Bill which has been prepared and brought forward by Mr. Jacob Bright, Sir Charles Dilke, and Mr. Eastwick.

A BILL TO REMOVE THE ELECTORAL DISABILITIES OF WOMEN.

Be it enacted by the Queen's most excellent Majesty, by and with the advice and consent of the Lords Spiritual and Temporal, and Commons in this present Parliament assembled, and by the authority of the same as follows:—

1. That in all Acts relating to the qualification and registration of voters or persons entitled or claiming to be registered and to vote in the election of members of Parliament, wherever words occur which import the masculine gender, the same shall be held to include females for all purposes connected with and having reference to the right to be registered as voters, and to vote in such election, any law or usage to the contrary notwithstanding.

We hear that the Edinburgh Town Council have resolved to petition Parliament in its favour. The 4th of May is the day fixed for the second reading of the Bill in Parliament.

THE SUMMARY OF PETITIONS FOR WOMEN'S SUFFRAGE PRESENTED TO THE HOUSE OF COMMONS SINCE FEBRUARY 10, UP TO MARCH 22, 1870.

	No. of Petitions signed officially or under seal.	Total No. of Petitions.	No of Signatures.
For Extension of the Elective Franchise to Women	5	19	1,496
Women's Disabilities Bill—In favour ...	13	112	44,269
	18	131	45,765

We had intended to give the list of petitions, but it has not been sent, and we will not delay our publication longer. The complete list will be given in our next number.

EDUCATION.

HITCHIN COLLEGE FOR WOMEN.—The next Entrance Examination will be held in London, and will occupy four days, beginning June 14. Forms of entry are now ready, and may be obtained on application to the Hon. Sec., Miss Davies, 17, Cunningham Place, London, N.W. These forms must be returned on or before April 30.

Scholarships tenable from October, 1870, will be awarded to the candidates who shall pass best in the entrance examination as follows:—

1. A Scholarship covering the whole fees for the College Course, *i.e.* of the annual value of 100 guineas for three years.

2. A Scholarship covering half the fees for the course, *i.e.* of the annual value of 50 guineas for three years.

It is reported that the establishment of classes for girls at Cambridge has proved remarkably successful. Upwards of fifty daughters of local tradesmen have availed themselves of the opportunity of receiving instruction from the most distinguished professors at the University. The lectures are a repetition of those which are delivered as part of the University course. It is probable that several scholarships for girls will be established at Cambridge.—*Campden Herald*, March 5.

For the convenience of persons not residing in Cambridge who may wish to avail themselves of the advantages of these lectures, Mrs. Masson is prepared to receive a certain number of young ladies to live with her during the next and subsequent terms. Information about this establishment may be obtained by applying to Mr. Sidgwick, or to Mrs. Masson, 5, The Avenue, Belsize Park, London, N.W. Mrs. Masson is allowed to refer to Mrs. Fawcett, Mrs. Venn, H. Sidgwick, Esq., M.A., of the Executive Committee, Cambridge; the Right Hon. Sir George Grey, Bart., 37, Eaton Place, London; the Rev. A. B. Barry, D.D., principal of King's College, London; the Rev. George Butler, M.A., principal of Liverpool College; Mrs. Myers, Brandon House, Cheltenham; Mrs. Luard, 4, St. Peter's Terrace, Cambridge.

Particulars regarding terms may be obtained by applying to Mrs. Masson, at her present address, 5, The Avenue, Belsize Park, London, N.W.

UNIVERSITY EXAMINATION FOR WOMEN.

To the Editor of the "Pall Mall Gazette."

SIR,—May I be allowed to draw the attention of your readers to the fact that the Cambridge University now offers a local examination to women over eighteen years of age, as I find it is by no means generally known to the public? To those who are familiar with the Cambridge local examinations for boys and girls it will be needless to explain the system on which these higher examinations are carried on, because they are but an extension of the same plan, and the decided success of the junior examinations was the strongest argument in favour of establishing a higher standard. The first examination was held last year in London and Leeds with satisfactory results; thirty-six candidates entered, of whom twenty-five passed. The second examination will be held this year, beginning July 4, in London and Leeds, and in any other locality where the required number of fees (25) are guaranteed. The examination is divided into groups of subjects; the first group, containing English subjects and arithmetic, is compulsory; other subjects, of which there is a large choice, are optional. The advantages offered by these examinations may be stated as follows: a standard by which to test the soundness of knowledge acquired, and a guide to future studies, and to professional teachers an opportunity for testing their proficiency, and of obtaining a certificate to which the authority of the University is attached. The regulations issued by the University require that a ladies' committee should superintend the local arrangements; one of the committee to act as local secretary. Information is given to committees by the secretary to the Syndicate at Cambridge; and candidates can obtain all particulars from several ladies and gentlemen who act as local secretaries in several towns, of which I name two only, in order not to trespass too much on your space — Miss E. Bonham-Carter, Ravensbourne, Beckenham; and Miss Wilson, Hilary Place, Leeds.

I am, Sir,
A LOCAL SECRETARY
For the Cambridge Examination for Women.

We regret to have to record the death of the Rev. Thomas Markby, Secretary to the Syndicate at Cambridge. In him the cause of the education of women has lost a true friend.

LOCAL EXAMINATION FOR GIRLS.—The resolution of the Oxford Delegacy to extend their local examinations to include girls has already stimulated local action. The London Committee of Ladies, who have for some years superintended the arrangements of the Cambridge examinations of girls in the metropolis, have undertaken the management of an Oxford examination also. Mrs. Roby, 48, St. George's Road, S.W., has consented to act as hon. secretary in respect of these new examinations, and will supply candidates or their friends with forms, and such information as may be required.

At a meeting of the Manchester Ladies' Educational Association, a paper was read by Mr. James Bryce, Fellow of Oriel College, Oxford, "On the Application of Endowments to the Education of Girls," in the course of which it was stated that in the last session of Parliament an Act was passed for the re-organisation of endowed schools, and the application to educational purposes of various charitable funds. Under that Act three commissioners had been appointed—Lord Lyttelton, the Rev. W. G. Robinson, and Mr. Hobhouse. A clause in the Act provided for girls in these words: "In forming schemes under this Act, provision shall be made, as far as may be found convenient, for extending to girls the benefit of endowments." Public opinion should be expressed in favour of this, so as to facilitate the labours of the commissioners. Though the value of the endowments was enormous, the girls would not be likely to receive anything like an equal share. In cases, however, where there had been so great a misapplication of charitable revenues that a wholly new scheme was needed, or where they were more than sufficient to maintain a boys' school, there we might expect to see the claims of girls considered; and as respected endowments not hitherto applied to any educational purpose, justice suggested that girls should be placed on a footing of perfect equality. But, after all, endowments were not essential to the success of schools, which were most satisfactory when self-supporting, and they should be placed under public management. Day schools for the poorer rather than the richer section of the middle class were the most needed, but boarding schools for the daughters of farmers were very desirable. The fees should be moderate in amount, varying according to the size of the town and numbers in the school. In Manchester we might have five or six schools of the third or lowest grade placed where the city passed into the suburbs, two or three schools of an intermediate grade, and one school of the highest grade. Incidentally Mr. Bryce expressed his belief that boys and girls might, with advantage to both, be taught in the same classes, up to the ages of fourteen or fifteen at least. The paper then dwelt on the desirableness of providing efficient mistresses by means of local colleges, and of some higher institution which might aim at doing for women what Oxford and Cambridge did for men. Schools could be more readily founded by the commissioners than by private individuals. Every effort should be made at once to hunt up cases of useless or mischievous non-educational endowments, to bring them before the notice of the commissioners.

Persons who wish to obtain funds from old endowments to establish middle class girls' schools in their neighbourhood should apply to Miss E. Bonham-Carter, Ravensbourne, Beckenham, Kent, who will tell them what steps should be taken.

It is proposed to establish a girl's day-school in London in connection with Christ's Hospital, the fee to be 1*l*. a quarter. We think the fee too high. Fathers will not pay as much for the education of their daughters as of their sons—so if 1*l*. is the right fee for a boy, 15*s*. only should be charged for a girl. Women teachers, moreover, do not require such high pay as men.

The *Droit des Femmes* states that an association of German ladies has petitioned the Saxon Chamber of Deputies to establish a normal school for women, also lectures for women on medical subjects, to prepare them for entering the medical profession. The Chamber unanimously voted that the petition should be forwarded to the Government.

The International Association of Women, whose headquarters are at Geneva, has petitioned the Italian Government to turn its attention to the neglected condition of female education in Italy. It is believed that the petition will not be without effect.

Miss MARY CARPENTER intends to open a female training school in Surat, after the model of the one already established at Ahmedabad.—*Campden Press*, March 12.

PETITION TO PARLIAMENT RESPECTING THE MEDICAL EDUCATION OF WOMEN.

As the subject of general medical education is to come before Parliament during the present session, it is desired to take advantage of this opportunity to obtain expression from women of their wish that facilities should be afforded for the study of medicine by women, it being often asserted that they in general have no sympathy with this movement.

It should be widely known that women have never been excluded from the Universities of Italy and Germany, and that lately those of Paris, Vienna, and Zurich, as well as medical schools in Sweden and in Russia, have been thrown open to them. In Great Britain women are unable to obtain medical education except as a matter of favour, no school being willing to admit them on the ordinary conditions, and it being impossible for them to obtain a degree except through some medical school.

It is proposed to send in some petitions, signed by *women* only, others signed by *medical men* only, and others signed by *all* who take an interest in the question. Forms for any of these purposes will be forwarded, on application to the *Hon. Sec.*, Mrs. Henry Kingsley, Morningside, Edinburgh.

It is announced that Earl de Grey will, on behalf of the Government, bring into the House of Lords a measure dealing with this question. It is therefore most important that petitions should be sent to the House of Lords as soon as possible after the Easter recess.

The report of the Edinburgh Ladies' Educational Association, for the second year of its existence, says that the work is well begun, but must not be considered to be completed.

Lady Dumfermline, having for private reasons resigned the Presidentship, has been succeeded by the Duchess of Argyll.

The total number of students in the classes of the three professors was 335.*

A small library has been established, and preparatory classes are wanted.

Professor Masson reports of the class in English literature—

I had a large and excellent class. It was conducted as nearly as possible as a University class of the same kind is conducted; and I applied much the same standard in judging of results. The average came fully up to the averages elsewhere within my memory, and the best here were closely comparable to the best there.

Professor Tait reports of the class in experimental physics that in spite of the want of preliminary training the answering of the working part of the class was very satisfactory.

Mr. Smith, his assistant, says that "the average marks gained, were decidedly higher than those gained on similar papers at the University."

Professor Fraser reports of the class of logic and mental philosophy—

* Some of these ladies merely listen to the lectures and do not attend the examinations or write papers.

Sixty-five students enrolled. Forty-eight of these shared more or less in the examinations and essays of the class. I found, as the session advanced, that I had at the outset underrated the mental power and persistency of as able and zealous a set of students as I have ever had the good fortune to conduct. It became evident, as far as the results of a session could make it so, that women were not inferior to the other sex in capacity for psychological and logical education, and that they might be animated with the enthusiasm for these studies which Scotchmen so often show.

Mr. Lindsay, his assistant, reports—

The papers of the Ladies' class were in no way inferior to the University papers. In spite of various disadvantages, want of previous experience in written examinations, want of the testing discipline of oral examination, and want of any definite aim, such as a Degree or Scholarship examination, to methodize reading, the average percentage was somewhat higher in the Ladies' class than in the University class, while one or two of the best papers were on the whole better than any in the University class.

The *Scotsman* of March the 29th contains the following singular statement:—

Yesterday, at the Chymistry Class in the University the results of the examinations held in the course of the Session were announced by Professor Crum Brown, who stated that 13 of the students had attained first-class honours. Their numbers stood as follows:—87, 86, 85, 84, 82, 81, 80, 80, 78, 76, 75, 75, 75. The third name on this list is that of Miss Mary Edith Pechey (85), the tenth that of Miss Sophia Jex Blake (76)—two of the six lady students who, in accordance with the decision of the University authorities at the beginning of the Session, had been admitted to study in the medical classes. To the four students whose names stand highest in the Chymistry Class for the Session the Hope Scholarships fall to be awarded, two of which entitle the holder to attend at the laboratory for the Winter and Summer Sessions, and two for six months only. Dr. Crum Brown, however, announced yesterday that the scholarships would be given, not to the four students highest on the list, but to Messrs. (1) Wilson, (2) Alston, (4) Young, and (5) M'Queen—Miss Pechey's name, which stood third, being thus dropped out; though it was at the same time announced that Miss Pechey was entitled to, and would receive, one of five medals awarded to the five highest students of the Session. This decision, which is not, we understand, likely to pass unchallenged, seems the more ungracious when the origin of the scholarships—of what seems her clear right to one of which Miss Pechey has thus been arbitrarily deprived—is considered. They arose out of the success of a course of lectures given a number of years ago by Dr. Hope, then professor of chymistry, to a ladies' class held in the University. Dr. Hope was so much gratified by the popularity of these lectures that, with their proceeds, amounting to about a thousand pounds, he founded the scholarships in question. It is rather remarkable that, on the first occasion on which ladies have had the chance of competing for these scholarships, one of them should have triumphantly entitled herself by her position in the class to this honour and reward—still more remarkable, surely, that she should not receive it? The facts as to Miss Pechey's eminence are even stronger than they appear, as stated above; for we understand that both the gentlemen whose names precede hers had attended a previous course of chymistry, so that Miss Pechey's position is absolutely the highest of all the students who may be classed as students of the year—the whole number of the class being about 236, inclusive of the six ladies.

EMPLOYMENT OF WOMEN.

THE Society for Promoting Technical Education among Women at Paris, has just opened a fifth Technical School at 25, Rue de Reuilly.

A banking house managed by ladies has been opened at New York. On the first day 4000 persons called at the offices. The ladies assert that in three months they shall have the largest business as bankers and brokers in New York.

The annual meeting for the distribution of prizes to pupils at the Female School of Art in Queen Square, was held at the South Kensington Museum, under the presidency of Sir Stafford Northcote. The Queen's gold medal was won by Miss Julia Pocock. Alice Ellis and Mary Webb also won prizes. The Committee announced that the school was free from debt.

The Eleventh Report of the London Society for Promoting the Employment of Women, office, 23, Great Marlborough Street, states that three young women who studied dispensing through the agency of the Society, are employed in three dispensaries, and are well spoken of by the doctors. There is a vacancy for an apprentice in this department.

The girls who were apprenticed to glass engraving can now execute orders, and have engraved glasses of various kinds to the satisfaction of those who furnished them with work. The following orders have been executed:—53 flower glasses, 42 wine glasses, 6 preserve dishes, 5 sugar basins, 2 olive jars, 1 cream jug, 1 water jug and 2 glasses to match, 1 water jug, 1 water bottle and tumbler, 1 goblet. Specimens of work are kept at the office for inspection.

In hairdressing, Mr. Truefitt has followed the example of Mr. Douglas,* and now employs women in his establishments, both in London and Brighton. The plan has also been adopted by another hairdresser at Brighton. The girls formerly apprenticed by the Society naturally find employment in these shops.

The report adds:—

Much satisfaction has been expressed by ladies at the manner in which the young women perform their work. The Committee earnestly hope that all ladies will support this movement. It rests with them to make the attendance of women in the ladies' rooms the general custom throughout the country.

When the telegraphs were taken by Government, fears were entertained lest the women clerks should be dismissed. The report shows that this has not occurred, and the pay and treatment of the clerks have been improved.

The report does not say that a larger number of women clerks are employed, but from what we hear we are inclined to think this may be the case.

The law copying office, 12, Portugal Street, at which women only are employed, continues its work steadily, and the number of women who obtain employment as law writers appears to increase.

The Commercial School for Girls continues to prosper. The average daily attendance throughout the year has been seventy. The adult class for bookkeeping is now held at the Society's office.

By means of the register sixty-three women have obtained permanent employment, and sixty-nine temporary employment, as follows:—

---

* Mr. Douglas's establishment is at 21 and 23 Bond Street, Mr. Truefitt's in the Burlington Arcade.

PERMANENT SITUATIONS.

Matrons	8
Housekeepers	10
Saleswomen	7
Nursery Superintendents	3
Companions	3
Needlewomen and Wardrobe Keepers	4
Photographers	2
Hospital Nurses	6
Bookkeepers	2
Governesses	3
Hairdressers	2
Telegraph Clerks	13
	63

TEMPORARY EMPLOYMENT.

Literary Work	1
Artistic Work	15
Photograph Tinting	4
" Mounting	2
Copying	17
Needlework	26
Sick Nursing	4
	69

The report adds:—

In the case of "temporary employments"—such as copying, reading aloud, photograph tinting, and needlework—one recommendation often leads to several subsequent engagements, for if the applicant has proved herself efficient in what she has undertaken, the employer naturally sends to her again without reference to the Society, whenever her services are required. In conclusion, the Committee beg to call attention to the Workmen's International Exhibition to be held during the summer, at the Agricultural Hall. The Council of the Exhibition have invited the co-operation of the Society, to obtain good specimens of women's work, and notices have been sent to all Institutions established for promoting the special training of women.

DESTITUTE GIRLS.

THE Committee of the Refuges for Homeless and Destitute Girls, states, in their report for 1869, that they have 400 boys under their care, and only 112 girls. They say they would be glad to extend their exertions in favour of poor girls, but that "the attention of the benevolent public has not been drawn to support plans for the rescue of destitute girls to anything like the extent that has been effected in the case of boys."

Miss Rye's young emigrants in Canada seem likely to do well. They are received at first into a general home, until they get situations or homes in farm-houses.

At a meeting at Niagara, in the winter, Miss Rye thus described her plan for providing for them:—

> She would bind them out to persons furnishing proper certificates of respectability, until they were eighteen years of age. The bond would be made in the name of the parties taking the children and of herself and the Mayor of this town. The children were to receive for their services until their fifteenth year, food, clothing, and education; from their fifteenth to their seventeenth year they were to receive $3 per month in lieu of clothing; and from their seventeenth to their eighteenth year, $4 per month; after that they were to be free to make what arrangements they pleased. Miss Rye's remarks were received with much sympathy and approval.—*Niagara Mail.*

Miss Rye writes from Canada on the 17th of March, to say that every child she took out has a home, and a hundred more good homes have been offered for as many children as soon as she can return to England to fetch them. Miss Rye intends to be back in England in the course of the present month, and to sail again for Canada with another ship-load of orphan girls at the end of May. We are sure that all our readers will wish her and her noble work, "God speed." Benevolent persons who may know of a destitute orphan girl of the working classes, who is in danger of being left to run wild, or of being shut up in a workhouse, should communicate with Miss Rye, or, if she is not in England, with Miss Jane Lewin, 12, Portugal Street, Lincoln's Inn, London, W.C. An excellent article has appeared in the *Telegraph*, showing how much more is done for destitute boys than for destitute girls.

LADIES' NATIONAL ASSOCIATION.

Mr. J. S. Mill, Professor Maurice, and Victor Hugo have written to the Secretary of this Association to say how cordially they agree in its objects. M. Victor Hugo bases his disapprobation of the Contagious Diseases Acts on his experience of their effects in France.

The following appeared in the *Pall Mall Gazette*:—

We are requested to publish the following list of ladies and gentlemen who, among many others, have expressed their earnest approval of the agitation for the repeal of the Contagious Diseases Acts:—Florence Nightingale, Harriet Martineau, Mary Howitt, Josephine Butler, Mr. John Stuart Mill, Mr. Herbert Spencer, the Bishop of Salisbury, Rev. F. D. Maurice, Professor Sheldon Amos, Dr. John Chapman, Dr. Elizabeth Blackwell, Miss Helen Taylor, Mrs. Jacob Bright, Sir George Grey, K.C.B., Lieutenant-Colonel Davidson, Dr. W. B. Hodgson, Dr. Bernays, Canon Babington, Rev. J. B. Lightfoot, D.D., Mrs. McLaren, Mrs. Pease Nichol, the Dean of Carlisle, Rev. Daniel Wilson, Mr. Jacob Bright, M.P., Mr. A. Mundella, M.P., Mrs. Charles Kingsley, Mrs. Bright Clark, the Lord Provost of Edinburgh, Rev. Dr. Guthrie, Mr. Alexander Moncrieff, Sheriff of Ross and Cromarty, Miss Louisa Twining, Rev. James Martineau, Victor Hugo, Hon. Auberon Herbert, M.P.

The names of the Bishops of Gloucester, Lichfield, and Norwich, and that of Professor Newman, are omitted from the above list, but they are nevertheless supporters of the Association.

Mrs. Butler, of 280, South Hill, Park Road, Liverpool, is Hon. Sec. to the Central Association. A Committee in connection with it has been formed in London consisting of the following ladies:—*Ladies' London Committee*—Mrs. McLaren, Mrs. Lucas, Mrs. William Hargreaves, Mrs. W. T. Malleson, Mrs. W. B. Hodgson, Mrs. William Howitt, Miss Helen Taylor, Mrs. F. Pennington, Mrs. P. A. Taylor, senr., Madame Venturi, Mrs. Jacob Bright, Mrs. Frank R. Malleson. *Hon. Secretary*—Mrs. Frank R. Malleson, 50, Great Marlborough Street, W. *Secretary*—Mrs. (Eliza) Hale. *Treasurer*—Mrs. Lucas, 32, Carlton Hill, St. John's Wood.

Ladies desirous of becoming members of the Association should send their names, addresses, and subscription to the Hon. Secretary, Mrs. Frank R. Malleson, 50, Great Marlborough Street, W., or to Mrs. (Eliza) Hale.

A pitiful letter appears in *The Shield* from a servant girl at Canterbury, which shows the consternation felt by women of the working classes at the operation of the Act which has just been put in force there. She says that two respectable shop girls have been put in prison. Another letter from a lady confirms the account. She says that young *ladies* of perfect respectability are followed and watched by the police to their great annoyance. She adds :—

> The effect of all this interference and espionage is that very many young females in situations, confined and working hard all day, are obliged to remain indoors at night, sacrificing their enjoyment and their health for fear of interference and insult from the Government spies.

Money to a considerable amount has been sent to the Association *anonymously* by persons who are unwilling to have their names appear in the matter.

Local Associations and Committees are springing up in several towns.

If our readers desire further information on this painful topic we refer them to *The Shield,* a weekly paper, price one penny, which can be obtained through any bookseller, or direct from the editor, care of Dr. Hooppell, South Shields.

MISCELLANEOUS.

THE *Philadelphia Post,* early in January, drew attention to the fidelity and ability of the women employed as government clerks, as follows :—

> In General Spinner's recent report to the Secretary of the Treasury, he makes some strong statements in relation to the female clerks employed by the government, and incidentally supplies proof of some of the assertions made by the advocates of suffrage for women. After stating that all the coupons and all the mutilated United States notes and fractional currency are assorted, counted, and prepared for destruction by female clerks, he adds that they not only do their work better, but also do more in a given time than the male clerks, who receive double the salary, possibly can. To prove this, the female clerks were required to recount the work of the male clerks, and it was found that they not only corrected errors in the count, but that they detected counterfeits that had not before been discovered, or known to any one connected with the Treasury department, in this city or elsewhere, and which had been overlooked by the male clerks in the offices where they were generally received, and by those in this office, who had counted them. But for the discovery of these counterfeit coupons, the Government would have

suffered great loss. Washington and Philadelphia, he states, are the only offices where female clerks are employed, and the best work is done in these offices by these clerks. "It has been remarked here, all along, that the remittances of mutilated currency to this office from the office in Philadelphia are better prepared, more neatly done up, with less mistakes in count, and containing less counterfeits than those from any other office. *The reason is that that office employs female clerks.*

At a meeting of the Church Convention in Dublin, the Rev. Mr. Hickley proposed that women, who were heads of families, should have votes. The motion was opposed by Sir William Osborne, on the ground that it might be inconvenient to husbands and fathers if their wives and daughters were to vote. The motion was lost by 158 Noes to 108 Ayes. When ladies are asked to subscribe towards the maintenance of the Irish Church, we hope they will remember this, and decline to give anything until women have votes.

The ground of the opposition was absurd, as wives and daughters are not "heads of families."

The Women's Club and Institute at 77, Newman Street, Oxford Street, is prospering; 260 members have joined, of whom 197 are known to maintain themselves. Of the remainder, some are ladies of private means. There is a conversation-room, a refreshment-room, and a library. A plate of meat costs 4d., vegetables 1d., bread ½d., ale or porter 1½d. a glass, so a good dinner may be obtained for 7d. A large cup of tea, with milk and sugar at discretion, and bread and butter costs 4d. The club appears to be likely to become self-supporting.

An interesting libel case was tried at Leeds yesterday. The plaintiff—Mrs. Eliza Banks—was a municipal voter at Nottingham. Last November she voted for the Liberal candidate—from which it appears that all women are not Tories. A few days later a local paper insinuated that she had received 10s. for her vote, and upon this she brought an action, which has resulted in a verdict in her favour with 40l. damages. We are glad that the first insinuation of corrupt practices against women voters has met with so emphatic a rebuff, and we hope that the present case may be an omen of the future.—*Echo,* end of March.

The following is from *The Revolution*, an American newspaper:—

The country has had its vulgar laugh at Wyoming for enfranchising woman and placing her in office as an intelligent, responsible being. And now there is time to call attention to the manner in which she was first inducted to the important office and position of the Grand Jury. It was in Laramie City, Wyoming. All the ladies drawn as grand jurors were present in the court-room punctually at eleven o'clock. A motion was made to quash the panel, but it was not sustained. At five minutes to twelve o'clock the first panel of lady grand jurors in the world were sworn. None of them asked to be excused. An able address was delivered by Chief-Justice Dowe, of which the following is an abstract:—

"Ladies and Gentlemen of the Grand Jury: It is an innovation and a great novelty to see, as we do to-day, ladies summoned to serve as jurors. The extension of political rights and franchise to women is a subject that is agitating the whole country. I have never taken an active part in these discussions, but I have long seen that woman was a victim to the vices, crimes, and immoralities of man, with no power to protect and defend herself from these evils. I have long felt that such powers of protection should be conferred upon woman, and it has fallen to our lot here to act as pioneer in the movement and to test the question. The eyes of the whole world are to-day fixed upon this jury of Albany county. There is not the slightest impropriety in any lady occupying this position, and I wish to assure you that the fullest protection of the Court shall be accorded to you. It would be a most shameful scandal that in our temple of justice and in our courts of law anything should be permitted which the most sensitive lady might not hear with propriety and witness. And here let me add that it will be a sorry day for any man who shall so far forget the courtesy due and paid by every American gentleman to every American lady as to ever by a word or act endeavour to deter you from the exercise of those rights of which the law has invested you. I conclude with the remark that this is a question for you to decide for yourselves. No man has any right to interfere. It seems to me to be eminently proper for women to sit upon grand juries, which will give them the best possible opportunities to aid in suppressing the dens of infamy which curse the country. I shall be glad of your assistance in the accomplishment of this object. I do not make these remarks from distrust of any of the gentlemen. On the contrary, I am exceedingly pleased and gratified with the indication of intelligence, love of law and good order, and the gentlemanly deportment which I see manifested here."

The *British Medical Journal* says that Miss Garrett has been admitted as a member of the medical staff of the East London Hospital for Children, and was appointed one of the physicians on Wednesday last. This is the first hospital in Great Britain which has recognized in this manner the female medical movement.—*Times*, March 22nd.

To show what may be done in getting up petitions, we will mention that one lady sent up this session thirteen petitions in favour of Married Women's Property Bill No. 1, and seven against Bill No. 2, and thirteen in favour of Women's Suffrage. The total number of signatures amount to 2494. The Misses Robertson of Dublin sent even more numerous petitions from Ireland last year, with a larger number of signatures.

Such noble workers ought to be gratefully remembered.

A petition from Chester, of which Mr. Raikes is the member, was sent to Parliament *through him*, against his own Bill, containing 500 signatures.

Madame Ollivier, the wife of the French Prime Minister, has intimated that at her receptions it is her intention to wear a high dress, and she hopes her friends will do the same.

The Manchester National Society for *Women's Suffrage Journal*, is edited by Miss Lydia Becker, and is published once a month, price one penny. It can be obtained through any bookseller.

POSTSCRIPT.

We particularly request attention to the following extract from the *Manchester Women's Suffrage Journal*, published April 1st:—

THE PROPERTY OF MARRIED WOMEN.

THIS Bill stood on the orders of the day for second reading in the House of Commons on Wednesday, March 23rd. About 100 petitions were presented in its favour, and a full House of the friends of the measure was ready to carry it through this its most critical stage. Never was a more favourable opportunity presented for carrying a great measure of justice, and never was a measure of relief so urgently needed by an oppressed class as this one. But between the suffering class and the decision which should have been an earnest of deliverance the Fates interposed the Burials' Bill. This had precedence of the Property Bill, and the rights of a few thousand dead Dissenters to dispense with the

Church of England service over their graves, took up all the time of the House, to the exclusion of the consideration of the rights of millions of living women to own the proceeds of their labour. So the second reading of the Property Bill is postponed till the 18th of May, and as it does not stand first on the list there is considerable danger lest the same fate may befall it.

Under these circumstances the friends of the Property Bill are earnestly exhorted to concentrate their present efforts on the Franchise Bill. If the second reading of the Women's Disabilities Bill pass the House of Commons, the strong probability that the next registry of Parliamentary voters will include women, will speak volumes to honourable members as to the necessity of looking to the interests of women. The impetus thus given would probably suffice to push the Property Bill through the House of Commons in time to secure full consideration in the other House. But if the Franchise Bill be lost it may be the deathblow of the Property Bill. There is no danger of a similar mischance in the case of the Disabilities Bill to that which rendered nugatory the exertions made on behalf of the Property Bill. The able and sagacious leader of the suffrage cause has taken care to secure a day for the second reading of his Bill, when it could stand first on the list, and in the ordinary course of events nothing can interpose to prevent its obtaining a hearing. If all persons who have signed petitions for the Property Bill will send similar petitions before the 4th of May in favour of the Women's Disabilities Bill, they will do the former the best service that now remains practicable.

Miss Wolstenholme, the indefatigable secretary of the Married Women's Property Bill Committee, desires to say that she entirely agrees with the above advice. The following is the form of petition to the House of Commons:—

To the Honourable the Commons of Great Britain and Ireland in Parliament assembled.

The humble Petition of the undersigned

SHEWETH,

That the exclusion of women, otherwise legally qualified, from voting in the election of Members of Parliament, is injurious to those excluded, contrary to the principle of just representation, and to that of the laws now in force regulating the election of municipal, parochial, and all other representative governments.

Wherefore your petitioners humbly pray that your Honourable House will pass the Bill entitled "A Bill to Remove the Electoral Disabilities of Women."

And your petitioners will ever pray, &c.

Directions for preparing a petition to the House of Commons.

Write out the form given above without mistakes, as no word may be scratched out or interlined, and sign it on the same piece of paper, obtaining as many signatures as you can to follow. After the written heading is signed extra sheets of paper may be attached to hold more names. The petition may be signed by men and women of full age, whether householders or otherwise.

Make up the petition as a book-post packet; write on the cover the words "Parliamentary Petition," and post it, addressed to the member who is to present it, at the House of Commons. No stamp is required, as petitions so forwarded go post free.

Write, and send along with the petition, a note (post-paid) asking the member to present it, and to support its prayer. Any member may be asked to present a petition, but it is desirable to select one in whose constituency the petitioners reside. Members of Parliament deem it their duty to present any petition from their constituency, whether they agree with its object or not; and as a rule they are very willing to take charge of any that may be entrusted to their care.

MDLLE. ROSA BONHEUR.—One of the later pictures of this gifted painter, "Shetland Ponies," has been engraved by Mr. C. J. Lewis, and is now in course of publication by Mr. F. Herbault, of the Strand. As the original work, now in possession of the Marquis of Lansdowne, to whom the print is dedicated, bears a date as recent as 1867, the interest and value of the transcript are enhanced by the freshness of the subject. Evidently studied from nature, as are all the compositions proceeding from the same hand, the wild group here depicted gives, with its wilder background of mist-shrouded landscape, a strikingly truthful idea of Shetland scenery. A kilted native of the island is dragging along by their halters two shaggy little shelties, whose unmanageable action, starting eyes, and unshod hoofs betoken very sufficiently their savage state. A gleam of light on the distant tarn somewhat relieves the gloomy aspect of the wet and barren waste; and the top of Mount Rona, or one of the highest of the not very high mountains of Shetland, rises imposingly above a drifting wreath of grey scud. Altogether the design is highly characteristic and picturesque, and the engraver has done his work excellently.

DIFFICULTIES having been thrown in the way of the

ladies obtaining anatomical instruction in Edinburgh, the professors of anatomy at two of the Scotch Universities have come forward to offer to the ladies the instruction which is denied them in their own college. Professor Struthers, of Aberdeen, and Dr. Bell, of St. Andrew's, are now willing to give them a course of lectures.—*Campden Herald*, February 5.

THE Princess of Wales has purchased an illuminated volume from Miss Elizabeth Wing. The work is beautifully executed in the style of the 15th century.—*Campden Herald*, February 12.

A MISS PITTS, of Ford Bend County, Texas, last year cultivated with her own hands seven acres of cotton, making five bales, worth 500 dollars. She supports several young children.—*Campden Herald*, February 26.

THE ENGLISHWOMAN'S REVIEW
(NEW SERIES.)

No. III.—JULY, 1870.

THE TESTIMONY OF HOLY SCRIPTURE CONCERNING THE SOCIAL STATUS OF WOMAN. By the Rev. T. G. CRIPPEN.

[*It will be perceived from several parts of the following Essay that the Theology contained in it is of a very orthodox and Conservative character.*

It is interesting to observe that the most rigid orthodoxy, far from being inconsistent with a desire to see women elevated in the social scale, actually furnishes some fresh and cogent arguments on their behalf.—THE EDITOR.]

I.—INTRODUCTORY.

FEW arguments in favour of mischievous error are so tenacious of life as those founded on misinterpretations of Holy Scripture. Though ten times confuted, they are brought forward again and again with unwavering assurance; and their pernicious effects are the greater that they appeal to the best feelings of the uninstructed portion of the community. That such arguments should have weight with good men, until their fallacy is exposed, is what might reasonably be expected; but it is indeed strange, yet not more strange than true, that men who care neither for God nor Gospel, and who contemn the plainest truths of the Bible, are accustomed with unwearying pertinacity to bring forward passages of Holy Writ, misinterpreted and misapplied, in defence of those errors and abuses in the maintenance of which their own pride or interest is concerned. Truly, "the devil can quote Scripture to his purpose."

We are led into these reflections by the assertion, so often made, that the testimony of Holy Scripture is in favour of the supremacy of the male sex over the female. In opposition to this, we shall endeavour to show, by the testimony of the sacred writings, that the two sexes, made alike in the image of God, are equal in His sight; and that this equality is only to be set aside when persons of divers sexes occupy such mutual relationships as involve the necessary precedence of one or the other, in which cases the man claims that position for which he is naturally qualified by his superior physical strength.

II.—THE CREATION AND STATE OF INNOCENCE.

Let us begin with the oldest account of the creation—that wonderful poem contained in Gen. i. 1, to ii. 3. The peculiar style of this venerable document, its stern simplicity, the paucity of its vocabulary, and that stately grandeur which constrained the heathen Longinus to regard it as the very noblest example of the truly sublime, all these lead us to the conclusion that we have here a revelation given by God to some one of the world's grey fathers, many ages before Moses, perhaps to some antediluvian patriarch. We here read that "God created man in His own image, in the image of God created He him; male and female created He them" (Gen. i. 27). The pronoun "him" is of course of the masculine gender; but the divine image is not thereby restricted to the male creature, for the plural pronoun "them" ('ōthâm) is also of the masculine gender, albeit expressly including the male and female. It is moreover remarkable that the word used for "man" is not 'ish, (Greek anēr, Latin vir,) denoting man as opposed to woman, but 'ádhâm, (Greek anthrōpos, Latin homo,) denoting human creature, whether male or female, as opposed to beast. 'Adhâm is indeed of the masculine gender, and has a cognate feminine, 'ădhâmâh; but this feminine does not signify "woman" (like 'ishâh from 'ish) but "the ground." And though 'ádhâm is used as a proper name for the father of the human race, being Anglicized into Adam, yet in Gen. v. 1, 2, we have the following instructive statement, "In the day that God created man ('âdhûm), in the likeness of God made He him, male and female created He them, and blessed them, *and called their name Adam ('ádhâm).*" From all which we may fairly conclude that the two sexes, equally possessing the image of the Creator, have a just claim to an equal status in creation, unless there be some limitation formally imposed by the Creator on one or the other.

We come next to the narrative contained in Gen. ii. 4, to iii. 26. This narrative is very unlike the former in language and style, albeit probably pre-Mosaic; and is variously regarded as a statement of actual occurrences, and as a myth embodying great truths in a kind of symbolic parable. In either case we have the following particulars brought before us as matters of fact:—(1.) The male human creature at first existing alone, a state of things which God accounted "not good;" (2.) Woman made in some such manner that she derived her origin from man, to be "a helper *as before* him," or "*like* him," *('ēzĕr k'nĕgdō)*; (3.) Marriage instituted, the ideal relation being one in which the man transfers to his wife some duty formerly claimed by his father and mother, and the husband and wife becoming " one flesh; " (4.) The entrance of sin into the world, the woman being beguiled into disobedience by a non-human deceiver, and in turn becoming a tempter; (5.) The man partaking in the sin of his wife, but without the extenuation of being deceived (*cf.* 1 Tim. ii. 14); (6.) The confession of sin by both, with this difference, that the man lays the blame on his wife, while the woman admits her weakness in being deceived; (7.) The promise of a deliverer, who should be in a peculiar manner "the seed of the woman" rather than of the man; (8.) The judgment of the woman, sorrow in child-bearing, "and thy desire shall be to thy husband, and he shall rule over thee;" (9.) The judgment of the man, "in the sweat of thy face shalt thou eat bread," &c. From these statements, which, whether the narrative be history or myth, we hold to be facts of divine revelation, we may fairly deduce an opinion as to the relative position of the sexes in the world as it is at present, *i.e.* infected with sin; and this position will be identical with that which they occupied before " The Fall," except so far as it is affected by the discriminating judgment passed on the transgressors.

In the state of innocence, Adam and Eve, being both of them created in the image of God, may fairly be presumed to have been equal, unless there is anything in the sacred history which implies inequality. If any such inequality is implied, it must be either in the prior existence of Adam, or in Eve's derivation from him, or in the purpose of her creation to be '*ēzĕr k'nĕgdō*, translated in the English Bible "a help meet for him." If Adam were superior to his wife because he was first formed, then there were creatures far superior to him upon the earth, the Mammoths, and the Ichthyosaurs before them, and greatest of all—because earliest of all—the semi-animate Lingulæ, whose organic remains are occasionally found amongst our Welsh slates. If this be absurd, equally absurd is it to argue Adam's superiority to Eve from his being first created; as to the social precedence among equals where one must needs be foremost, St. Paul's reference to the priority of Adam will be discussed hereafter. Again, if Adam were superior to Eve because she was in some manner formed from him, the dust of the earth must have been superior to Adam, because he was formed from it. Nay, a still more revolting inference must follow; Eve was formed from Adam by an act of Divine power; by a like act of Divine power was Adam formed from the dust; and by the power of the Most High did the Holy Child Jesus derive His humanity from the Virgin Mary without the intervention of a human father; if then the derivation of Eve from Adam by the power of God marked her as inferior to him, the manner of the incarnation in like manner marks the Lord Jesus as inferior to His mother. If this supposition is excluded from the category of blasphemies by its grotesque absurdity, the absurdity is transferable to the other supposition, from which it is legitimately deduced. As before, we still say nothing of the bearing which the manner of Eve's formation may have on the question of social precedence.

Once more, the appointment of woman to be a helper to man cannot be legitimately employed as an argument to prove her inferiority, since the very same word is used about God himself as is used about Eve. The well-known name Ebenezer is *'ĕbhĕn-'ĕzĕr,* "help-stone," in allusion to the help afforded by God to Israel, of which the stone in Mizpah (see 1 Sam. vii. 12) was set up as a memorial. Moreover, the word *k'nĕgdō* is understood by the ancient interpreters to imply likeness in Adam's helper to himself; the LXX. translate *kat'-auton* "according to himself," and *homoios auto,* "like to himself;" so the vulgate, *simile sibi* and *similis ejus,* "like to him." It is asserted by the opponents of female emancipation that we seek to confound the natural distinction of the sexes. So far is this from being the case, that we recognise in that distinction the very foundation of mutual helpfulness; but the distinction is that of unlikeness with an underlying resemblance which does not involve any superiority on either side. It is the likeness and unlikeness of a pair of hands or feet; the left hand is *'ĕzĕr k'nĕgdō* to the right; the right hand, by practice, usually (not invariably) acquires superior strength and dexterity, but no sane person would maintain that the left hand is naturally inferior.

Before passing to the consideration of the manner in which this social equality of the sexes is affected by the judgment passed on them after the Fall, we may glance at the original institution of marriage, which will not fail to cast some light on the matter in question. From the beginning it was ordained that "a man should leave his father and his mother, and cleave to his wife," the expression seeming to imply the transfer to the wife of some claims upon the man formerly held by his parents. The words are *'ish* and *'ishtō* (construct form of *'ishâh*), words which signify not the duty of each party in the marriage covenant to the other, but that of the husband to the wife. It would seem as if the inspired writer foresaw that men would not fail to claim the transference to themselves of all the affection and devotion of their wives, but would yet hold themselves absolved from any obligation to reciprocal duties; and that in view of such a state of society the common duty of both parties was set down as the special and peculiar duty of the husband.

However the terms of the marriage contract may be understood, the inferiority of woman cannot be deduced from the record of its institution.

III.—THE FALL, AND ITS CONSEQUENCES.

We come now to the entry of sin into the world, and its consequences. It cannot be denied that inferiority of intellectual power subjects a person to be the more readily deceived, but it is equally certain that it argues a lower moral tone to sin without being deceived than to be beguiled into transgression. Apart from the teachings of experience, we might suppose from the narrative of the Fall that Eve was intellectually inferior to Adam; and as this is constantly asserted by our opponents, we will admit it for the purpose of argument, though not by any means assenting to it as a fact. But if Eve were intellectually inferior to Adam, it follows that his fault had less extenuation than hers, and consequently Adam was morally inferior to Eve. The question is, whether the highest intellect with the lowest conscientiousness, or the highest moral with the lowest intellectual strength, has the best right to claim supremacy; or, since the intellect is occupied about knowledge, while the conscience is dominated by love, whether knowledge or love ranks the highest? Taken in the abstract, this question receives the same answer from Jews and Christians; the rabbins, regarding the Seraphim as the embodiment of love, set them before the Cherubim, to whom they attribute unlimited knowledge. To the same purpose writes the monkish author of that beautiful, albeit fantastic, poem, "In Urbe meâ, Hierusalem summâ."

> "Foremost of all, the blessed Seraphim
> There fervently, and ever more and more
> In loving burn, and still in burning love;
> But God is all their flame. The Cherub host
> *Stand next*, from whom is nothing hid, but all
> The depths of knowledge to their sight expand."

If it be said that Eve exhibited no great love or conscientiousness in her sin, she is certainly seen to advantage in her confession, humbly acknowledging both her sin and folly, while Adam ("just like a man," as we once heard a lady say) tries to throw the whole blame of the matter on his wife. If simplicity and honest penitence are better than presumption and cowardice, there is certainly nothing in the history of the Fall to justify the assumption by Adam of supremacy over Eve.

"But is there not such supremacy conferred by God, in the sentence passed on the transgressors?" "Yes," say savages, rabbins, philosophers, and theologians. "No," say we; at least, not in the sense in which supremacy is claimed by the opponents of our plans of female emancipation. The institution of the family is now fairly recognised. Children are now first mentioned, although none were yet born. Supposing the story to be strictly historical, we have sometimes thought that at the time of her first transgression Eve may have been *enciente*, and that Cain and Abel were twins, like Esau and Jacob. Now in the family, as in every other society, there must be a recognised head, having precedence, and exercising authority where authority is needed. But the first family consisted only of two persons, each subsequent addition being received in the form of a helpless infant. Sin having entered the world, the family of sinners would naturally be exposed to pain and danger; and since one of the family must rule, it was reasonable that he should rule who, by virtue of his greater physical strength, was best able to protect wife and children. Still, the rule conferred upon the husband and father is only that of precedence—or perhaps presidentship, and it is only the presence of evil in the heart of the man that converts his precedence into dominancy, his presidentship into despotism. Still, the possession of even the smallest degree of power by a wicked man is an irresistible temptation to its abuse; and the woman being in the transgression is restrained by a natural instinct from escaping by celibacy from the suffering inflicted by the abuser of his presidential rights —"Thy desire shall be to thy husband." If this view of the matter be correct, (and it is equally applicable to the narrative, whether the latter be regarded as history or myth,) the power of the husband to abuse his marital authority, and his disposition to do so, are alike the consequence of the guilt in which he is at least equally involved with his wife; and one would expect that the more virtuous a man became, the more willing he would be to free himself from such temptation, and to facilitate the re-establishment of that divine order of "equality limited only by marital precedence," which was marred by the intrusion of sin.

In the judgment passed on Adam and Eve, it is, we think, possible to discern a recognition of the dissimilarity of their guilt. Besides the disarrangement of the family relationship, which enables and tempts the man to become an oppressor, a peculiar burden is laid upon the woman: "In sorrow shalt thou bring forth children." The pain and danger of parturition to which woman is subject is certainly to a great degree exceptional amongst living creatures, and is a legitimate consequence of sin: but side by side with this comes a remarkable alleviation, in the promise that, "The seed of the woman (not the seed of the man) shall bruise the head of the serpent;" and it is surely not unreasonable to believe that Our Lord chose the woman, rather than the man, as the human instrument of His incarnation, in part, at least, to reprove the all but universal notion of her native inferiority. The curse laid on Adam is altogether different: "Cursed is the ground for thy sake; in sorrow shalt thou eat of it all the days of thy life; . . . . in the sweat of thy face shalt thou eat bread." Adam's burden is toilsome labour, as distinguished from mere work, and to his curse there is no such alleviation as is granted to Eve. It is further important to observe, by way of refutation of those who pretend that women are compensated for their quasi-servile condition by their exemption from masculine burdens, that the respective sentences of Adam and Eve are mutually exclusive; the man is not appointed to bear children, the woman is not ordained to physical toil; those who would doom her to the alternative of physical toil, or social and domestic Helotism, lay upon her a burden which God has not imposed.

The curse of Adam and Eve rests, and must rest, upon the world; toil for man, pain for woman, this is the sentence, and "Shall not the Judge of all the earth do right?" As our friend Kingsley says—

"Men must work and women must weep,"

And no political or social reforms can alter it. But the conversion of household precedence, and of that social precedence which seems naturally to follow from its establishment and recognition, into domestic tyranny and political subjugation, is not a part of the penalty inflicted by God for sin, but the perversion of a divine ordinance by the selfishness of persons whose conscience and will are depraved. This perversion may lawfully be resisted by all women, and should be disowned, and as far as possible remedied, by all virtuous and right-minded men.

Notwithstanding what has been thus far advanced, there are not a few persons who maintain that Eve's sin, either on account of its priority, or of her becoming a tempter in turn, was more heinous than that of Adam; and that God, in consideration of this, has imposed subjugation as an additional burden upon the female sex. Denying altogether the supposed greater heinousness of Eve's transgression, we will yet assume, for argument's sake, that it was so. Still, every man is as much a descendant of Eve as of Adam, and every woman as much a descendant of Adam as of Eve, and no woman is responsible for her sex, more than for her existence. How then can it be reconciled with divine justice that because, of the first couple of sinners, the female sinned more deeply than the male, therefore amongst the whole of their common sinful posterity the sins of the parents should be most heavily visited on the females, even though they may be more virtuous than the males? The only possible answer to this query is that which the Calvinist makes when one points out the horrible injustice that he ascribes to God, in supposing Him to relegate men to hell-fire by unconditional predestination; begging the whole question at issue, he triumphantly asks— "Who art thou that repliest against God?" Of course, if it were certain that God had done this or that, we must suppose that he acted not inconsistently with justice, how little soever we might be able to understand it; but when the question is whether God has done this or that, or not, it is surely legitimate to argue that He has not done, and will not do, anything of which the justice cannot readily be made apparent. Seeing then that the narrative of the Fall and subsequent judgment does not in express terms assign woman to social and political degradation, we may justly conclude that no such degradation is intended.

IV.—The Pre-Mosaic Period.

The next portion of the sacred narrative which gives any light on the question before us, is the account of Lamech and his two wives. It is not pretended that Lamech's polygamy is mentioned with approval, but that the instinct in man, which exhibits itself in polygamy, is a tacit witness to the inferiority of the female sex. We shall have occasion hereafter to discuss the recognition granted to polygamy in the divine law, and shall at present simply remark that amongst certain savage races in India, and amongst the Esquimaux, the abomination of polyandry prevails; if, therefore, the prevalence of polygamy amongst one portion of mankind proves the inferiority of woman, the prevalence of polyandry amongst another portion equally proves the inferiority of man. Each of these practices is alike a violation of the original institution of marriage; and inferences from either, as to the purpose of the Creator in regard to the relation of the two sexes, must be alike fallacious.

From the judgment passed on Adam and Eve after the Fall to the giving of the law by Moses, we have no divine enactment bearing on the mutual relationship of man and woman. But we find the upgrowth of customs which seem to proceed upon a regularly acknowledged principle, and of other customs which seem to proceed from abuse or perversion of principle. Of the first class are the recognition of the rights of primogeniture, and of the precedence of the male sex over the female otherwise than in the connubial relation; in the second class, we may put the assumption of unlimited power by the head of the family over the subordinate members thereof, male as well as female. The rise of all these customs may easily be accounted for. Headship in the family being a matter of necessity, and the family in its simplest form consisting of the husband and wife, with or without a dependent child or children, the possession of superior physical strength, and consequent power to afford protection, naturally designates the husband and father as president. On the demise of the father (unless life has been abridged by accident or disease), the children, now in the prime of life, would be better able to protect the mother than she to protect them; in like manner the sons would be the natural protectors of the daughters, and the eldest son of the younger. Hence the recognition of the eldest son's right to succeed to the family presidentship, with its duties and honours. But the family, being the simplest form of society, would naturally furnish a pattern for the other social organisations; and the instinct of uniformity would lead mankind everywhere to accord precedence to the elder over the younger, and to the male over the female. So far all was well; but, as we have already seen, the possession even of the smallest amount of authority by a wicked man is an irresistible temptation to its abuse. And in the early ages of the world moral decay was rapid, God was soon forgotten, idolatry became all but universal, might usurped the place of right, and in the time of Abraham we read that men were "wicked, and sinners before the Lord exceedingly" (Gen. xiii. 13). It was not therefore surprising that the patriarchal rule should have become an irresponsible tyranny, that slavery existed (Gen. xx. 14), that the father claimed a despotic right over the persons of his daughters (Gen. xix. 8), and the brother over his sister (Gen. xxiv. 51), that the parent made matrimonial arrangements for the son (Gen. xxiv. 1-6), that a few years later the daughter had come to be regarded as a piece of property to be disposed of by her father to the best advantage for himself (Gen. xxix. 17), and that unchastity was deemed a venial offence in man but a capital crime in woman (Gen. xxxviii. 15, 16, 24). All these phases of injustice are mentioned in Holy Scripture, and men eminent for goodness are represented as influenced in these respects by the public sentiment which prevailed around them. Yet the mention of these things, or any of them, without formal disapproval, does not imply divine approbation of any one of them, more than the similar mention of the barbarous cruelty of Amaziah in 2 Chronicles xxv. 11, 12.

V.—THE LAW OF MOSES.

We are now prepared to consider the light cast on the relative status of the sexes by the law of Moses: merely observing by way of introduction that God's way of setting wrong things right is usually by reform, not by revolution, leading men from a low standard of morality to a higher, step by step, as they are able to bear it; and that the indications of popular opinion which we have already noticed show that, prior to the giving of the law, women were commonly regarded as beings all but utterly destitute of civil rights. This state of things the law recognised, and recognised with a view to provide such an amount of relief as the then existing state of society rendered possible; and the wisdom of God is herein manifest, that instead of setting before mankind such an ideal of society as it was certain they would not appreciate, and therefore would not attempt to realise, He sought rather to educate them by little and little, until they should be prepared for a more complete revelation of His mind. This accounts for certain precepts which, Jesus tells us, were written "for the hardness of men's hearts," although, "from the beginning it was not so" (Matt. xix. 6).

The Mosaic law recognised and embodied the patriarchal system, but restrained its worst abuses. For example, domestic slavery was permitted, but there were a multitude of enactments to soften its rigour, and to secure to slaves a share of civil rights. In like manner the subjugation of woman which had grown up during the patriarchal ages was not brought to an end, but modified and rendered endurable. We have not space to review all the laws which regulated the status of the sexes under the Mosaic economy, but we may sum up their general tenour in this one statement, that wherever they effected any alteration in the customs of preceding ages, that alteration was in favour of the weaker sex, and tended, so far as it went, towards the obliteration of their social inferiority. A few examples only can be given, as illustrative of the general principle. The right of the father to bestow the daughter in marriage was still recognised, but he was forbidden to dispose of her in a dishonourable manner (see Lev. xix. 29); and on his death she does not seem to have come under the tutelage of her nearest male kindred, as formerly, but to have been free to dispose of herself (see Num. xxxvi. 6). Neither was it permitted to next of kin, who might happen to be of the male sex, to usurp the property of a man who left no son, if he had daughters to inherit it (see Num. xxvii. 8, 9). The authority of the husband over the wife was confirmed (see Num. vi. 8, &c.), but there is not the smallest evidence that he was permitted to confiscate her property; and we may safely determine that such was not the case, both from Isa. iv. 1, and from the commendation bestowed upon Abigail for disposing of a large quantity of valuable property in a fashion of which we may be sure her churlish husband would not approve (see 1 Sam. xxv. 18, &c.) It is uncertain whether the author of the "Character of a virtuous woman" in Prov. xxxi. was subject to the law of Moses; but if so, it is pretty evident that the married woman was allowed to transact business on her own account, a permission which has not yet been accorded by the enlightened (!) British legislation of the nineteenth century A.D. Divorce was permitted "For the hardness of men's hearts" (*cf.* Matt. xix. 8), but though permitted it was discouraged, the later prophets speaking against the practice in emphatic terms; "For the Lord, the God of Israel, saith that He hateth putting away" (Mal. ii. 16). There were also important limitations to the permission of divorce; the privilege granted to a husband thus to release himself *à vinculo matrimonii* was forfeited if he had seduced the woman before marriage, or if he had falsely accused her of unchastity (see Deut. xxii. 19, 29). Polygamy and concubinage were likewise allowed; but we have already seen that these practices do not *necessarily* imply the inferiority of the female sex. Still, there can be no doubt that they tend to the degradation of woman; and in view of this we find them generally discouraged, and allowed only under such restrictions as, if observed, would prevent many of the degrading effects which the practices in question commonly produce. It is remarkable that, as throughout the law of Moses, so also in the New Testament, polygamy and concubinage are dealt with in the same manner as slavery; none of them are prohibited in express terms, but all are discouraged, and the whole tendency of the education which Holy Scripture bestows upon mankind is to their gradual but complete extinction. This is instructive; for if it should be argued that the permission of polygamy under the Mosaic dispensation brands woman as an inferior creature, it must also follow that the permission of slavery inflicts a like brand of inferiority on the servile caste. If any of our opponents accept this position we will not discuss the matter with them further; domestic slavery and the subjugation of women have so much in common that it is fitting they should stand or fall together.

In the laws of Moses, respecting the punishment of unchastity, the equality of the sexes is more clearly recognized than in any other code with which we are acquainted. Adultery was impartially punished by the death of both the offenders. In case of seduction, the seducer was compelled to marry his victim, and was not permitted to rid himself of her by a divorce, even in a case where divorce would otherwise have been legitimate. The allowance of polygamy rendered it possible to enforce this enactment in every case. It may be remembered that in the last century the adoption of a similar piece of legislation in England was recommended by Rev. M. Madan; it is doubtful whether the howl of execration with which his book, "Thelyphthora," was assailed, arose more from honest aversion to polygamy, than from preference of the modern custom, which hunts the victim out of society, and allows her to sink into the grave or the street, and permits the criminal to air his gentility as before, and boast of his exploits. The Mosaic enactment was still further in the interest of the victim of seduction: if she had erred through ignorance of her deceiver being a married man, and was unwilling to accept the status of a second wife, it was only needful for her to induce her father to refuse his consent to such a marriage, and the seducer would be compelled to expiate his guilt by a heavy fine (see Exod. xxii. 16, 17, and Deut. xxii. 28, 29). It is true that the father, and not the victim, was to be the ultimate judge of the manner in which reparation should be made : but this was an instance, not of the peculiar subjection of the woman to the man, but the regular subjection of the junior members of the family to its head, which was a distinctive feature of the patriarchal system.

Such are the principal Mosaic enactments in regard to the relation of the two sexes; not one of them tends to the relegation of woman to a lower position than she held before, but all seem designed—so far as we can understand them—to raise her from the degradation to which she had previously been subjected, and enable her to approximate to that position which was assigned to her at the creation. And surely it will not be pretended that the Mosaic dispensation, which was in every other respect transitional and educational, was yet, so far as she is concerned, to be accounted final ! If the law, in giving place to the gospel, made way for a more complete realization of the mind of God concerning the mutual relations of his creatures, it is certainly reasonable to think that the restoration of woman to her true position, like every other portion of that great reformation, in which both law and gospel were intended to have a share, would only be completed under the latter. To the New Testament, therefore, we must look for the final determination of the relative status of the sexes.

Before doing this, however, we must refer to one historical incident under the Mosaic dispensation, which cuts up by the roots a whole thicket of arguments in continual use by our opponents. "Politics," say they, "are outside a woman's proper sphere of action; her place is at home, her kingdom the family." John Knox was more explicit; the substance of his notorious "Blast of a Trumpet against the Monstrous Regiment of Women" was simply this, " woman, by the ordinance of God, is inferior to man, therefore she ought not to rule over men ; " and the principle thus enunciated is still in very general acceptance. But what if we find a Scriptural account of a woman, a married woman, taking an active part in politics, and ruling over men with an authority which they willingly recognised? and what if all this is mentioned in such terms as plainly indicate the Divine approval of the arrangement? Surely if this be so, John Knox's Blast of a Trumpet will prove to be quite out of harmony with the voice of Revelation. Turn we then to Judges iv. 4, 5—"And Deborah, a prophetess, the wife of Lapidoth, she judged Israel at that time; and the children of Israel came up to her for judgment."

VI.—State of Society at the Christian Era.

Coming now to the teachings of the New Testament, we must remember that our Lord Jesus and His Apostles, like Moses, recognised the condition of the world as they found it; and that the Divine method of rectifying the evils of society is, as we have said before, reform, not revolution. At the time when Christianity was first promulgated the state of society among the Jews was substantially that established by Moses on the basis of the patriarchal system, but very considerably modified by the infiltration of Greek and Roman elements. In the Gentile nations amongst whom the Gospel was first proclaimed, the theory and practice of society were at variance with each other. Alike amongst Greeks and barbarians, the subjugation of woman was *in theory* absolute; though *in practice* this was far from being the case. Amongst the Romans patriarchal despotism had been developed to the utmost conceivable extent, the very life of wife and children being at the mercy of the husband and father; but the system had broken like an over-stretched bow, and the social liberty that ensued had degenerated into the wildest licentiousness. Everywhere it seemed as if woman, casting off the fetters with which she had been bound, had cast away with them the last vestige of modesty and virtue; so that the terrible satire of Juvenal was not unfounded—"It is said that once upon a time a chaste woman was seen in some remote village." In the midst of societies so characterized, the religion of the New Testament was first promulgated—that religion which was destined to be the grand liberator of the human race, and to afford a complete and final exposition of God's purpose concerning mankind. It might, therefore, be reasonably expected, not indeed that every social right which had been withheld from any person during the worst ages of tyranny would be secured by a formal grant, but only those rights which had not hitherto been claimed or conceded by society. On the other hand, it might be expected that any rights, or pretended rights, which had been claimed or exercised by any class of persons contrary to the will of God, would be formally restricted; and this, whether such rights had been held by virtue of a divine grant of a temporary character or were only claimed and permitted by the community in the midst of that licentious reaction which always follows the sudden overthrow of any form of despotism. Guided by this reasonable expectation, we will first enquire whether the New Testament restricts any of the social rights enjoyed by women under the law of Moses; we will see next, if there be any enactments which tend in the opposite direction and remove any of the social inequalities which under the Mosaic dispensation existed between the two sexes. Afterwards we will examine those passages which seem to make for the natural inferiority of woman, to see if that be their legitimate force, or if they be not rather intended as necessary safeguards against that licentiousness of freedom which at the time they were written had began so extensively to prevail; and lastly we will consider if there be not some direct statement as to the relative status of the sexes which ought to obtain in such a perfect of society as the religion of the New Testament is designed to bring about.

VII.—NEW TESTAMENT MODIFICATIONS OF THE MOSAIC LAW.

We have first to see if the New Testament restricts any of the social rights enjoyed by women under the law of Moses; in other words, if it removes any of those limitations which were imposed by that law on the ancient patriarchal despotism. We shall not be long occupied with this inquiry, for there is not a single statement from Matthew to Revelation that would relegate the Christian woman to a social position inferior to that held by the daughter of Israel. On the other hand, there are enactments which distinctly abrogate certain forms of supremacy formerly conceded to the male sex. In particular, divorce is absolutely forbidden except for adultery; that is, except in the case in which the faithless wife was, under the Mosaic economy, condemned to death. And though the divorced wife is prohibited from marrying again, while the emancipated husband appears to be left at liberty (see Matt. xix. 3-9), yet is this not to be regarded as an evidence of partiality to the man; for the adulteress was deemed worthy of death, and the commutation of her sentence into divorce and perpetual widowhood is really an extension to her of mercy previously unauthorised. And still the original penal enactment is unrepealed, so that there is nothing to prohibit the punishment of both the parties to the act of adultery with death, if it should seem expedient to the civil magistrate. And here we may remark that the Christian law concerning divorce is so simple, that it is amazing how any uncertainty could be entertained about it. The husband has a right to divorce his wife for adultery, and for no other cause; the divorced wife has no right to contract another marriage; but the husband, being innocent, has an implied permission to do so. So much may be learned from the passage in Matt. xix. already referred to; and the parallel case of infidelity on the part of the husband is elucidated in 1 Cor. vii. 10-15. The wife is forbidden to depart from her husband; "But if the unbelieving depart, let him depart; a brother or a sister is not under bondage in such cases." It is to be observed that St. Paul is particular to tell us that he is not here writing under divine inspiration, but simply giving his own opinion (see ver. 12); still, his opinion is the highest authority we have on the matter, and is therefore entitled to our entire respect. Belief in Christ, in St. Paul's epistles, never means mere assent to a creed, but that practical belief which we call Christian faith; but a man who possessed this Christian faith would be effectually restrained by it from deserting his wife; whoever, therefore, acts thus, must needs be accounted "unbelieving," or, "unfaithful." It is the opinion of St. Paul that the deserted wife is "not under bondage;" if this means anything, it means that she is at liberty to adopt such measures as may be necessary to dissolve the marriage, and contract another. In the matter of divorce, therefore, the two sexes are on an equality; except only that there does not appear to be any permission for the wife to obtain a dissolution of marriage on account of the husband's unchastity, unless he be also guilty of desertion. Yet this does not imply inferiority on the part of the woman, since it is manifest that unfaithfulness to the marriage covenant, though equally culpable in both parties, is productive of greater social evils on her part than on that of the man, and should, therefore, be more severely punished. It should, surely, be superfluous to observe that the English law, which permits the guilty person to marry after divorce, is altogether contrary to the spirit of the Bible.*

We have already stated that polygamy is not forbidden in express terms in any part of Holy Scripture; it is, however tacitly discouraged, even while allowed, under the Mosaic economy. But in the New Testament, though not formally, yet by implication, it is prohibited; and with reason, for though the permission of the practice does not necessarily imply the inferiority of woman, the practice itself tends to her degradation. The true ideal of marriage, the union of one man with one woman, is involved in 1 Cor. vii. 2, "Let every man have his own

---

* A distinguished advocate of female emancipation objects to the statement that unchastity in a wife is productive of greater social evils than the same crime committed by the husband. We willingly concede to the objector that an equal injury is inflicted in both cases upon the innocent spouse and on the partner and offspring of guilt. But the adultery of the wife commonly injures the legitimate family by introducing a spurious child, which does not occur when the husband is the offender. And although he *may* rob his legitimate children to maintain such as are illegitimate—on a sort of "honour among thieves" principle—and so inflict a similar injury to that which is wrought by an unfaithful wife, yet, in the majority of cases, this consequence will not ensue, because the partner of his crime is generally a common strumpet. It is the recognition of this fact that has found expression in the terms of contempt with which a man is assailed who condones the adultery of his wife; nearly all those terms contain allusions to the hedge-sparrow fostering the progeny of the cuckoo.

wife, and let every woman have her own husband;" and in the law already quoted against divorce (Matt. xix.) it is said that, " Whosoever shall put away his wife and shall marry another committeth adultery;" surely then, he is no less adulterer who takes a second wife without putting away the first. It is not, however, certain that a heathen polygamist is bound, upon his conversion, to put away all his wives but one; it may be plausibly argued that 1 Cor. vii. 10, 11, applies to this case: " Let not the wife depart from her husband; but if she depart, let her remain unmarried: and let not the husband put away his wife." But in any case polygamy is not to be entered into by a Christian, and the polygamist is disqualified for any and every office in the Church (see 1 Tim. iii. 2, 12).

Divorce and polygamy (of course including concubinage) being thus prohibited, the former expressly, the latter implicitly, the most active causes of female degradation under the Mosaic economy are removed. We will now recall to mind the ameliorating influences exercised by that economy at the time of its first institution, so that we may fairly understand the effect of the successive enactments in the direction of female emancipation which we have already had under review. Moses found the unmarried woman under the absolute authority of her father, or, in his absence, of her nearest male kindred. The law restricted the power of the father to giving her in marriage; and her subjection to him in this respect was not the mere subjection of woman to man, but of a junior member of the family to its patriarch —a subjection which she shared in common with her brothers; and, although this subjection remained, the law set her on an equality with her brothers upon the demise of the father, inasmuch as it did not transfer her—as did the olden custom—to their tutelage. Moses found the married woman under the absolute authority of her husband, and subject to all the evils arising from the unrestricted practice of polygamy and divorce. The law restrained and discouraged, though it did not forbid, these practices, and it was clearly understood by the Jews that the married woman had a right to possess and dispose of personal property, *a right which necessarily removed* HER *from the category of property*, to which she had been consigned under patriarchal despotism. Still, the authority of the husband was maintained, with the limitations just mentioned; and it could not fail that the possession of this authority, together with that habitual jealousy which is as characteristic of the Oriental as pride is of the Spaniard, or drunkenness of the Russian, would lead to a grievous amount of oppression. But the New Testament, by prohibiting polygamy and divorce, imposes further limitations on marital authority, and leaves the wife in just the same relation to her husband as she sustained in the earliest ages, before presidentship degenerated into despotism, and subordination into subjugation. The status of the *unmarried* woman is not affected by anything in the New Testament which we have thus far examined : but, indeed, the breaking up of the patriarchal system affects her in precisely the same manner as her brothers. Under the law of Moses, she was in exactly the same position as they, except in so far as she might be subjected to extra-legal oppression by masculine selfishness, and strength, and Oriental jealousy ; and now that the rule of the father over his family is only absolute during the age of childhood—a limitation which needed no formal expression, as the family despotism which prevailed of old had no divine authority—the emancipation of the unmarried woman, so far as Holy Scripture is concerned, is complete.

VIII.—Passages Alleged in Favour of the Subjection of Women.

We come now to examine those passages in the New Testament which seem to make for the natural inferiority of woman, and in so doing we shall first consider those which relate to the duties of married life, and then those which apply to womankind in general. Let it be remembered that amongst the Jews, Greeks, and barbarians, at the time when these passages were written, the possession of marital authority—whether with or without the limitations imposed by Moses—was continually affording to wicked men an irresistible temptation to oppression; while among the Romans the marital despotism that existed in theory had completely broken down in practice, carrying with it almost every vestige of modesty and virtue; and that Jew, Greek, and barbarian were all more or less influenced, for good or for evil, by the social condition, no less than by the laws of Rome.

The passages which assert the authority of the husband over the wife are these—Ephesians v. 22-5 and 33; Colossians iii. 18; Titus ii. 5; 1 Peter iii. 1-6; and it is worthy of note that in immediate connection with three of these the co-ordinate duty of the husband, to love, honour, and cherish his wife, is insisted upon with equal definiteness; while in the other we simply have " obedience to their own husbands " mentioned amongst a whole catalogue of duties which the aged women (or perhaps female elders in the church, *presbuterides*,) are to inculcate on their younger sisters. It would be quite legitimate to argue from this collocation, without at all justifying the unruly or rebellious wife, that the duties of obedience on the one side and love on the other are so far correlative, that the unloving and tyrannous husband forfeits all right to claim from his wife the fulfilment of her share in the contract. In every one of the passages referred to the same verb occurs, *hupotasesthai*, variously translated, " To obey, to be in subjection, to submit." In the active voice the word would signify " to put down, subdue, or reduce to order; " in the passive, "to be subdued or brought into subjection; " and in the middle or reflexive, " to submit oneself." Now, whenever this word occurs in relation to the duty of a wife to her husband it is in the middle voice, and ought to be translated accordingly. The duty which it imposes is not, therefore, to permit herself to be brought into a state of subjugation or servitude, but voluntarily to submit to the precedence of her husband in the family. This view of the matter is confirmed by the use of the very same word in Ephesians v. 21, " Submitting yourselves (this refers to the whole body of believers) one to another in the fear of God," a precept identical in substance with that in Phil. ii. 3, " In lowliness of mind let each esteem other better than themselves."

Can we now find any reason expressed in the New

Testament why the wife should render this submission to her husband? If not, we must still accept the divine command by which it is enjoined upon her, even if that acceptance should compel us to admit her natural inferiority. But it will certainly be gratifying if we can find an explanation of the command which will enable us to escape this necessity. Such a reason appears in connection with the very passage in which the duty of the wife to submit is most definitely asserted. In Ephesians v. 24, we read, " As the church is subject (better 'submits herself') to Christ, so let the wives [be] to their own husbands in everything." But on what ground does Christ claim the unreserved submission of the Church? Surely because " He loved it, and gave Himself for it, that He might sanctify and cleanse it." The sanctification and cleansing of the Church is in effect its deliverance from the greatest of all evils—sin, and the greatest of all dangers—the wrath of God, which sin must incur. So then Christ is Head of His Church by virtue of His being its Saviour and defender; and St. Paul says, " The husband is the head of the wife, *even as* (*hōs kai*) Christ is the head of the Church; and he is the Saviour of the body." The theologians generally apply the *He* to Christ, as Saviour of "the Church, which is His body;" but it is hard to conceive why St. Paul should introduce any such reference unless he meant to indicate a closer parallel between the relation of a wife to her husband and that of the Church to Christ than is found in the mere fact of each relationship being one of ruler and subject. Rather is the parallel to be exhibited thus: Christ is constituted Head of the Church, inasmuch as He gave Himself to be its Saviour and defender; and the husband is constituted head of the wife, inasmuch as he is appointed to be her protector in her bodily weakness. So then the submission of the wife to the husband is simply—as we intimated when discussing the sentence passed on Eve after the Fall—the price she pays for his protection.

The subordination of woman in marriage depends then, Holy Scripture being witness, merely upon her inferior bodily strength and consequent need of protection. And this is so far from being an evidence of actual inferiority when all things are considered that St. Peter bids the husband "give honour to the wife as to the weaker vessel," (1 Peter iii. 7,) as if her body, which is notoriously weaker than that of man, were simply the vessel in which the true image of God was contained. How complete is the contrast between St. Peter's estimate of what is due to "the weaker vessel" and the image of God that inhabits it, and the estimate formed by most men! It is to be feared that shame, rather than anything nobler, restrains them from expressing their thoughts in language such as R. Browning has put into the mouth of Count Guido Franceschini:—

> "Where's the bond obliges horse to man
> Like that which binds fast wife to husband? God
> Laid down the law, gave man the brawny arm
> And ball of fist, woman the beardless cheek
> And proper place to suffer in the side,
> Since it is he can strike, let her obey!"
> "*The Ring and the Book*."—xi. 1400, &c.

We have next those passages in which the female sex seems to be subordinated to the male, without reference to the marriage contract; or in which restrictions are imposed on women such as appear inconsistent with the doctrine of her social equality. The strongest of these is in 1 Cor. xi. 1-12, in which she is commanded to wear a covering upon her head when praying or prophesying. It cannot be denied that this paragraph fairly bristles with difficulties; but the difficulties are not by any means all on the side which opposes the traditional interpretation. If the veiling the head in the presence of men is enjoined on women as a token of subjection, it is not easy to conceive why a similar act should be forbidden to men when in the presence of God, before whom even the Seraphim cover their faces (see Isaiah vi. 2). Neither is there any perfectly satisfactory explanation amongst the many that have been proposed of verse 10, "For this cause ought the woman to have power on her head because of the angels." But let us remember the circumstances under which the paragraph was written. At Corinth, more than any other city of Greece, the morality of the female population was at the lowest ebb; how could it be otherwise, when we call to mind the abominations which were there associated with the worship of Aphrodite? The wearing of a veil was the distinguishing sign of a modest woman, as its absence was the sign of a courtesan, while shaving the head was part of the punishment of an adulteress. The veil was looked upon by both Greeks and Orientals as a token of subjection, and it would seem that the Christian ladies of Corinth, rejoicing in the emancipation they had received by the gospel, had cast it aside, at least in their meetings for worship. St. Paul perceives the reproach this was calculated to bring on the Church, and at once condemns it, reminding the Corinthian ladies that though they were *not an inferior or subject class,* yet *the precedence of the other sex* was a matter of divine order (verses 11, 12, with 8, 9,); and it would surely be no hardship for them to recognise this by resuming their veils " *dia tous angelous,*" (verse 10,) which Rosenmuller, Schrader, &c., explain not of "the angels," but of unbelievers who might be present, and might become "messengers" of evil report against the disciples. "See, then, (we may suppose the apostle to say, verses 5, 6,) what a report may be made concerning you; if in the Church you are seen to lay aside your veils like courtesans, you proclaim yourselves to be as bad as those adulteresses whose punishment is to be shaven." This explanation is at least as consistent as any other that has been proposed of this very difficult passage; and it affords an intelligible reason why St. Paul should refer to the priority of Adam's creation as illustrative and indicative of the precedence of man, and should immediately after demolish his fancied superiority by insisting on the mutual dependence of each sex on the other.

The other passages which are supposed to indicate the inferiority of woman are 1 Cor. xiv. 34 and 35, " Let your women keep silence in the churches, for it is not permitted unto them to speak, but to submit themselves (so the word ought to be translated), as also saith the law; and if they will learn anything, let them ask their husbands at home, for it is a shame for women to speak in the church;" and 1 Tim. ii. 11, " Let the women learn in quiet in all submission (*a.v.* incorrectly ' silence with all subjection ') but I suffer not a woman to teach, nor to usurp authority over the man, but to be in quietness (*a.v.* silence)." Had we nothing to guide us but the words just quoted, we might well hesitate before committing ourselves to the doctrine of the social equality of the sexes. But we have statements and directions which cannot be accepted as of divine authority without materially limiting the principles that seem at first sight to be there laid down. In Titus ii. 4, certain *presbuterides*, either " aged women " in general, or " female presbyters," are formally commissioned to *teach*; to teach those of their own sex, indeed, but in Acts xviii. 26, a woman, Priscilla, is mentioned in terms of approbation for uniting with her husband in teaching Apollos. Again, if the prohibition of women speaking in the church was absolute, it is hard to conceive why St. Paul did not formally forbid it when he was writing of the proprieties of public worship, why he *seems* to permit women to pray and prophesy (in 1 Cor. xi. 5, 6) if they wear a decent covering, and afterwards retracts that permission. But if the permission were retracted, how comes it to pass that we have no disapproval of the utterances of Philip's four daughters which did prophesy (Acts xxi. 9)? And what shall we say to the prediction of Joel, which was destined to find its accomplishment in the Church, " Your sons *and your daughters* shall prophesy?" (Acts ii. 17)? If under the Christian dispensation, women are absolutely forbidden to teach, or to speak in public assemblies, then these quotations are simply unintelligible; and, besides, the progress of society must have been backward rather than forward, since Deborah judged Israel under a palm tree, and Miriam led the choirs of the freed-women on the Red Sea shore.

The true explanation of the passages quoted above is very simple. We learn the meaning of that in Cor. xiv. 34, 35 from Origen; some of the Corinthian ladies, forgetful of that modest reserve which is certainly not a badge of inferiority, had fallen into a habit of interrupting the public exercises of worship, and, it should seem, of interposing questions. We are not accustomed to such interruptions in England, but we are informed by missionaries that, when preaching in India and China, they are often called upon in the midst of their discourses to explain hard sayings and answer objections. It would seem that this practice prevailed at Corinth, and if the interpellators were ladies, their proceedings would appear much more objectionable to the Greeks than even to us. It is therefore simply this impropriety that St. Paul rebukes, on the principle, so we understand it, that he lays down elsewhere, " give none offence, neither to the Jews nor to the Gentiles, nor to the Church of God " (1 Cor. x. 32). The passage in 1 Tim. is to be explained on the same principle. The word " quietness," wrongly translated, " silence," is opposed not to speech but to clamour, the whole life of a woman should be characterised by that modest quietness which is her most attractive charm. In accordance with this rule she may not "usurp authority over the man," as the word is rightly translated; but there is nothing to forbid her exercise of authority if it be conferred upon her, nothing like a general Salic Law applicable to the whole of Christendom. The prohibition of teaching by women must be understood in accordance with this principle; it cannot be that knowledge possessed by a woman may not be imparted to such as are willing to receive it, or that she may not endeavour, in such a manner as does not involve an abandonment of becoming modesty and quietness, to remove ignorance and error. In the light of the commendations bestowed on Priscilla, the teacher of Apollos, and of the spirit of prophecy promised by the prophet Joel to " my servants *and my handmaidens*" under the Christian dispensation (see Acts ii. 18), the intention of St. Paul can only be to restrain women from *setting themselves up* as persons commissioned to teach with authority.*

---

* Does it not appear somewhat inconsistent that those who think it unbecoming in women, on the score of modesty, to stand up in public for the purpose of communicating useful information, can yet see no impropriety in the public appearances of actresses, opera-singers, and ballet-dancers? Or does immodesty only begin when a woman, refusing to be a mere caterer for the amusement of men, endeavours to make them wiser or better?

IX.—OBJECTIONS AND REPLIES.

"But," it will be said, "by conceding precedence to the male sex, by admitting that submission and modesty are duties especially incumbent on the female, and by recognising her undeniable inferiority in physical strength, you practically withdraw your plea for the equality of the sexes." By no means. Physical strength is not the standard of true greatness, otherwise many a pugilist, many an acrobat, would be superior to the greatest philosophers. If relative personal excellences are to be compared, a very small degree of mental superiority will counterbalance a very large amount of mere physical deficiency. But it will be said that even on this principle the lack of physical strength places the weaker sex below the stronger, unless we are prepared to maintain the greater mental calibre of woman, which, our opponents say, is so far from being the fact that she is as much inferior intellectually as physically. We certainly do not claim for woman greater strength of intellect than is possessed by man; we are even willing to admit that the male and female minds have each their peculiar complexion, and are to some extent unlike, but we totally deny that one sex is by nature possessed of greater intellectual powers than the other. It is true the male intellect commonly attains a larger development, but we hold that this depends entirely on the fact that the two sexes have not, in general, equal educational advantages. If the minds of girls were directed to studies of a substantial character, instead of useless accomplishments, there would be as large a proportion of learned women as of learned men. But in the artificial state of society in which we live, it has come to pass that there is such a thing as "The Marriage Market;" in other words, the number of marriageable women is much greater than the number of men able and willing to marry; and the greater number of trades and professions are so monopolised by the (physically) stronger sex, that most women—the exceptions are very few—are compelled to look to marriage as a means of sustenance. And men, having thus the command of the market, and desiring to maintain their factitious predominance, have constantly discouraged solid education amongst women. Hence it comes to be accounted a proper thing for a woman with no taste for music painfully to acquire the power of executing a number of *fantasias, capriccios,* &c., " of a kind as quite impossible in Johnson's day as still they might be wished;" or for a woman who has no capacity even for appreciating high art, to spend months and years in learning to paint flowers such as never grew in Paradise, to draw costumes from French engravings, and to sketch landscapes on tinted backgrounds, which are admired by other victims of the same sort of " education," in spite of the most outrageous faults in perspective. But if a girl sets herself to obtain the privilege of an acquaintance with the writings of Moses, David, and Isaiah, of St. Paul and St. John, and the words of the Great Teacher Himself, in their original languages; if she seeks to cultivate her reasoning powers by the study of logic, and to correct her judgment by familiarity with the works of Plato and Aristotle, Bacon and Locke, Stewart and Hamilton, she is frowned upon as " unfeminine," and ridiculed as " a blue-stocking." Yet where women have broken through the artificialities of society they have not failed to leave their mark on the history of the world. One is tempted to ask if those who talk of the intellectual inferiority of women have ever met with the names of Hypatia amongst philosophers, Sappho and Elizabeth Browning among poets, Angelica Kaufmann and Rosa Bonheur among painters, Maria Agnesi Gaetana and Madame Lepaute among mathematicians, Madame Dacier amongst classical students, Zenobia, Isabella of Castile, and Maria Theresa among rulers, Joan of Arc among military commanders. But if it be still insisted that these are exceptional cases, and that the allusion to Eve, and not Adam, being deceived in 1 Timothy ii. 14, is intended as an inspired assertion of the intellectual inferiority of the physically weaker sex, we are willing —though stoutly denying both propositions—to grant to our opponents the benefit of them, such as it is. For if it be true, as we maintain, that woman is intellectually equal to man, yet her deficiency of physical power being granted, it is evident that her equality cannot be defended unless some element of excellence can be found in her in a greater degree than in the other sex, to compensate the admitted want of bodily strength. And if any such element can be found — which we have already intimated is not to be sought in the intellectual department of her being—is it not conceivable that it may be so far predominant as fully to counterbalance not only physical but also intellectual deficiency?

Now, it is admitted on all sides, that woman is capable of greater moral degradation than man; however vile a thoroughly bad man may become, it is possible for a totally depraved woman to become worse. But this very possibility of sinking to a lower depth of vice implies a counter-possibility. As the sweetest wine makes the sharpest vinegar, as the "dead fly" converts the perfume of the most fragrant ointment into the most repulsive stench, so it is the highest moral capacity that is capable of being perverted to the lowest moral degradation. And as the intellectual element in human nature is superior to the merely physical, so is the moral to the intellectual; and exalted virtue, associated with the lowest mental calibre and the most pitiable bodily weakness, is an infinitely nobler thing than the mightiest intellect, enshrined in the most perfect specimen of mere bodily strength and beauty, if goodness be wanting. The feeblest child, who is prepared in the presence of temptation resolutely to say—"How can I do this great wickedness, and sin against God?" is nobler, is more truly excellent in His sight than an ungodly man who may combine the strength of Samson with the wisdom of Solomon; and we boldly assert that the admitted deficiency of bodily strength and the mental inferiority, if it exists, are, as a rule, abundantly compensated in woman by a very substantial moral superiority. Her conscientiousness is more acute, her perceptions of duty more clear, her affections more intense, than those of a man. These facts are admitted by our opponents, only they deny that they constitute a claim to superiority, and, indeed, commonly profess to look upon them as tokens of feebleness. Hence unscrupulous boldness is deemed a more noble, a more "manly" thing than tenderness of conscience; shrewdness in perception of expediency is thought a more suitable quality for one who has to "get on in the world," than delicacy in perception of duty; intensity of affection is set down as "womanish" weakness. St. John, the disciple whom Jesus loved, who summed up his whole philosophy in the proposition "God is love, and whoso dwelleth in love dwelleth in God and God in him," and whose practical divinity was included in one maxim—"Little children, love one another," is accounted infinitely less of a hero than Nimrod, "the mighty hunter before the Lord." If this estimate of relative excellence be right, if the moral characteristics that are called "womanly" are really less pleasing in the sight of God, than those which are called "manly," we will at once withdraw our plea, and admit that woman is, indeed, a creature of a much lower order than man; but if conscientiousness be better than unscrupulousness, if an instinctive perception of right be better than a shrewd appreciation of expediency, if an unlimited capacity for loving be more Godlike than the like capacity for trading, then we are justified in maintaining that there is among women in general an amount of moral superiority that fully compensates their admitted physical and alleged intellectual subordination. It is not necessary to insist that this moral distinction is natural; for all the purposes of our argument, it may suffice that it actually exists. If it be not natural, but capable of being accounted for by the educational effects of the existing state of society, we are supplied with an argument more cogent than any we have advanced; for if this be so, it will follow that there was, indeed, originally an inequality in the sexes, woman being morally and intellectually equal to man, but physically inferior, and that man—by abandoning his moral equality, and departing more widely from the image of God, abdicated his supremacy and reduced himself to the lowest place. For certainly the loss of moral equality is of itself so degrading that it places him who has sustained it lower than if that equality had never been enjoyed.

We shall, perhaps, be assailed with another objection. It will be said, "You prove too much; if the female sex possesses such decided moral pre-eminence, no amount of physical or intellectual weakness can counterbalance it, and the woman is therefore not equal, but vastly superior to man." If it were necessary to choose between this position and that we are opposing, we should not hesitate in the matter. The poets, several of them, have accepted the alternative proposed by our objector. Old Lydgate advanced in earnest the position which Burns afterwards assumed in jest:—

> " Her 'prentice han' she tried on man,
> And then she made the lasses O ! "

But it is by no means necessary so to do. We do not assert that there are heights of virtue attainable by woman which are inaccessible to man; the moral superiority on which we insist, is just that which has been aptly described by a recent essayist:—" Faith, hope, and love, the vital principles of religion, are as natural to her as they are hard of attainment to man." And that such is the case has been not merely admitted, but asserted by our opponents, as if it made for their cause rather than ours.

A law was proposed, having for its object the suppression of a most degrading vice by means which would be completely effective, but which would involve such a degree of restraint on those who were not the victims of that vice, as supposes a larger amount of Christian self-denial than is possessed by most men. The *Times*, casting unmerited ridicule on the proposal, characterised its promoters as " Women and children and Sunday-school teachers." If, indeed, women and children and Sunday-school teachers are more willing than the rest of the community to submit to a vexatious restraint in the interest of public morality, the fact is at least a strange sort of evidence of their moral inferiority.

"How then," it will be asked, "do you harmonise your claim of personal equality, as between the two sexes, with your concession of precedence to man, and with your imposition of modesty and submission on woman, as duties especially proper to her sex?" We reply, by reverting to the family as the germ and model of all social arrangements. When the family is first constituted, the wife yields up her personal independence, that she may be " a help meet " for her husband.

In consideration of the help thus afforded him by her, he provides her maintenance; and it is mentioned, as a characteristic of a totally disordered state of society, that women should waive their lawful claim for such maintenance (*see* Isaiah iv. 1). Here we may remark in passing that the claim of the husband, enforcible under English Common Law, to confiscate the whole property of the wife as a condition of affording her that maintenance which she purchases by the surrender of her personal independence to become his helper, is nothing else but an assertion of robber's law, a practical confession by the stronger sex of being satisfied with—

> "The simple plan
> That they should take who have the power,
> And they should keep who can."

It is probable that the marriage contract would have remained in this form, maintenance afforded by the husband as the equivalent of help rendered by the wife, if mankind had continued in a state of innocence. But sin brought with it a sort of emancipation of the inferior creation from the supreme control of mankind, hence the human race — and especially those who are physically weaker—have need of protection. Of the parties to the marriage contract, the woman is the weaker; but the protection she requires, from the necessity of which she would not be relieved even by the possession of intellectual and moral superiority in a very high degree, suggests an addition to the contract; the husband shall be the protector, and, in consideration of his undertaking this office, the family headship shall be conceded to him, which involves submission on the part of the wife. And it is noteworthy that we do not find any injunction laid upon woman in Holy Scripture to render submission to man in general; she is only to " submit herself to *her own* husband " (Ephes. v. 22), and to avoid *usurpation of authority* over man (*see* 1 Tim. ii. 12). The disregard of this omission has led the opponents of female emancipation into a notion that every man in particular may rightfully claim precedence of all women in general; thus, in a debate on the rights of women to the Parliamentary franchise, we once heard it gravely alleged that no woman could have any such right so long as one man remained unenfranchised. Our worthy disputant would probably except criminals; but even so it was maintained that Florence Nightingale or Harriet Martineau could have no claim to any political right or privilege, while it was withheld from the most ignorant navvy or ploughman who was unconvicted of crime! A truly monstrous assertion, worthy only of an Oriental polygamist, or perhaps of John Knox. In short, we maintain that the submission of the wife to her husband, and, in like manner, of the sister to the brother, is the price she pays for protection, and is wholly independent of any consideration of personal superiority or inferiority; and that the precedence of the male sex obtains only when social relations are entered into, which necessarily involve precedence on one side or the other, in which case, the family forms the pattern to which other social arrangements are to be conformed.

One part of the objection still remains unanswered—that founded on the instinctive feeling which prescribes modesty and gentleness as virtues peculiarly feminine. This is more forcible in appearance than in reality, as will be manifest if the converse of the proposition be looked at. For surely immodesty and rudeness are not virtues in man more than in woman. In truth, the modesty and gentleness which are worthy the name of virtues are equally admirable in either sex. And if it be true—which we will not dispute—that a retiring habit and a willingness to take a subordinate place which would be undesirable in man are pleasing and attractive in woman, the fact may be easily accounted for by her physical weakness and consequent sense of dependence, and by the habit of society, which leads both sexes to expect superior knowledge and a more logical manner of thinking in man—a habit which arises from his monopoly of educational advantages. If proof be needed, it is not far to seek. Female emancipation is not, indeed, complete even in America; but there both sexes have equal facilities for acquiring knowledge, and the weaker is not kept in a state of unworthy dependence by unjust laws in regard to property, consequently American women have more self-reliance and less mock-modesty than those of

Europe, but it will not be said that they are inferior—comparing each class with the corresponding class amongst ourselves—in true modesty and gentleness.

X.—The Divine Ideal of Society.

We have been led into this digression by the necessity of meeting some obvious difficulties. We now return to the teachings of the New Testament, and have to consider, in accordance with the plan already laid down, if there be not some direct statement as to the relative status of the sexes which ought to obtain in such a perfect state of society as the religion of the New Testament is designed to bring about. We may first ask—What would be the leading feature in the constitution of such a society? And the natural answer will be, *the absolute and unresisted dominion of the Lord Jesus Christ.* "For He must reign, until He hath put all enemies under His feet" (1 Cor. xv. 25). If this were realised, there would be universal obedience to His two great commandments, whereof the first is supreme love to God, and the second, "Thou shalt love thy neighbour as thyself." Accordingly, all selfishness would be abolished, all monopolies would come to an end, all class distinctions, which God has not ordained, would be abrogated. This remark about class distinctions brings us directly to the point at issue; in the Christian Church, which is designed as a model of, and preparation for, the state of society we are describing, St. Paul tells us, "There is neither Jew nor Greek, there is neither bond nor free, *there is neither male nor female,* for ye are all one in Christ Jesus" (Gal. iii. 28). In other words, as in the kingdom of Christ the temporary pre-eminence of the Jew over the Gentile is abolished, and the enslavement of one man by another is no longer to be endured, so must the dominancy of one sex over the other come to an end; and in the ideal state, in which sin is to be totally destroyed, even the marital precedence which was founded on the need of a protector—a need which was only felt after the fall—will no longer have place. To the same effect is a traditional saying of our Lord's, preserved by one of the early Fathers. The Lord being asked when the kingdom of God should come, replied, "When the male shall be as the female, and the female as the male, and neither male nor female."

The world is not as yet prepared for so complete an inversion of its established customs as is here shadowed forth. But the testimony of Holy Scripture as to the relative status which the two sexes ought to occupy in the world *as it is* is clear and forcible. " That the two sexes, made alike in the image of God, are equal in His sight; and that this equality is only to be set aside when persons of divers sexes occupy such mutual relationships as involve the necessary precedence of one or the other, in which case the man claims that position to which he is evidently designated by his greater physical strength." In accordance with this principle we have a right to demand:—

(1.) The concession to women of the same political rights and privileges as are enjoyed by men, subject to the same conditions.

(2.) The removal of all laws, whether enacted by Parliament or by trades-unions, whereby women are restrained from the exercise of any trades or professions for which they are naturally qualified.

(3.) The abrogation of all those laws respecting property, the effect of which is to reduce married women to a state of artificial dependence on their husbands.

(4.) The revisal of the laws concerning marriage and divorce, and concerning the punishment of unchastity, so that the two sexes shall be treated with perfect impartiality in these respects.

(5.) The extension to women of the same facilities for education as are enjoyed by men, including admission not only to the teaching bestowed in the universities, but also to participation in their honours and emoluments.*

---

* When arguments fail, the partisans of existing social monopolies have an unfailing resource in the assertion that, if these just demands were conceded, women would be the worse for it; that they would lose those graces which are peculiarly feminine, without acquiring the corresponding masculine virtues, and would, consequently, become personally inferior to what they are at present. If this be true, it must follow that feminine graces are likely to abound chiefly where the despotism of the male sex is completest—say in Turkey, or among the Hottentots, and to be wanting where a nearer approach has been made to equality, as in America or Russia. But this is notoriously the reverse of truth; and the pretence of our opponents is strikingly

We do not expect soon to obtain all, or the greater part, of these reforms. Abuses die hard, and none harder than monopolies. But we take courage from the history of the past, and from faith in the justice of our cause. We shall win slowly, but we shall win. A hundred and eighty years have passed since the Toleration Act; ever since then religious disabilities have been dealt with piece by piece, and equality is not secured even yet. Nearly fifty years intervened between the first attack upon the slave trade, and the final abolition of slavery in the British colonies. Not four years have yet elapsed since Mr. J. S. Mill first enunciated the doctrine for which we are contending in the House of Commons, on which occasion his motion for recognising the political equality of the sexes was supported by a larger minority than supported the first resolution against the slave trade. And since then there has been continuous progress; some of the reforms for which we ask have been partially conceded, the complete attainment of others appears at hand. The rest will not be easily won; prejudice, covetousness, the natural conservatism of those who think their own interests are concerned in the maintenance of existing wrong, and even the apathy, or ignorance, or dread of appearing " unfeminine " in asking for those rights which they feel to be unjustly withheld, into which, perhaps, the majority of women have been educated, all these will co-operate in delaying our victory. But the ultimate issue is not doubtful : *magna est veritas, et prevalebit;* our cause is the cause of truth, and therefore, of God, and He will conduct it on to victory.

> " The world's old,
> But the old world waits the time to be renewed,
> Towards which new hearts in individual growth
> Must quicken, and increase to multitude
> In new dynasties of the race of men;
> Developed whence, shall grow spontaneously
> New churches, new œconomies, new laws
> Admitting freedom, new societies
> Excluding falsehood. HE shall make all new."

---

suggestive of a jest that is said to have been popular in Rome, when Decius was persecuting the Christians—" That the martyrs ought to be very much obliged to their persecutors, for shortening their journey to Paradise."

Art. II.—GENTLEWOMEN AND SELF-HELP.

EARLY in May a large number of ladies and gentlemen assembled at Stafford House, by invitation of the Duchess of Sutherland, to hear an explanation of the objects of the " Gentlewomen's Self-Help Institute."
The Earl of Shaftesbury took the chair, and Mr. S. Morley, M.P., Dr. Cumming, Mr. M'Garel, and Sir R. Anstruther, spoke in favour of the institution.
The following concise explanation of its objects is taken from the printed circular of the society.

OBJECT.—The promoters of this institution seek to place within the reach of educated ladies, who may have been reduced from easy circumstances to narrow means, an opportunity of turning their natural or acquired abilities to account. There are, unhappily, numerous cases in which ladies—widows or daughters of clergymen, barristers, military and naval officers, and professional men, gently and carefully reared—suddenly find themselves, by the death of their natural protectors, reduced to destitution. To no other class can such a condition be more terrible—none can, from previous circumstances, be generally more helpless, and, at the same time, none can shrink more sensitively from the slights and miseries that attend poverty and dependence. It is in the hope of placing means of "self-help" within the reach of this class that this institution has been established.
METHODS.—Rooms have been opened at the premises, Bessborough Gardens, for the reception and sale of articles, the production of ladies in reduced circumstances. Free lessons in photographic colouring, and other branches of Art, are also given at the institution. (A very considerable number of pupils have taken advantage of this opportunity of instruction, and several ladies are now, through its means, earning a comfortable livelihood.)
The *sale-room* for the disposal of ladies' handiwork has been extensively made use of, and it is now crowded with a great variety of articles of every description—oil paintings, drawings, modelled wax-work, guipure and other lace, wool-work, embroidery, baby-clothes, and plain work of all sorts.

It is difficult to imagine objects more benevolent, and at the same time less ambitious, than the above "programme" sets forth. Gentlewomen, ordinarily, have been trained to no remunerative employment, and on the death of their fathers find themselves destitute. In many instances their parents, doubtless, intended them to marry, and taught them such accomplishments as would be likely to attract husbands; but fate was not propitious, the husbands were not attracted, or though attracted, were repelled by a dislike to portionless brides. In other instances the parents would perhaps have been glad to give their daughters such an education as should enable them to earn a respectable livelihood, but found insurmountable obstacles in the way. In all cases, whether the parents were to blame or not, it is pretty certain the daughters were not. They stayed at home, added to their parents' cheerfulness by their society, nursed them in sickness and old age, and are now left in middle life destitute and helpless.

The Gentlewomen's Self-Help Institute offers them a means of turning their accomplishments to some account, and enables them to sell their work to better advantage than usual, as the shopkeeper's profit is saved. The work done is, perhaps, not always of use, but even when the article purchased is of no value, and is taken by the purchaser merely as an excuse for giving money without hurting the feelings of the recipient, it is better the money should be given in return for work, than simply as charity, for the fabrication of the article sold has filled up for the maker many a long, weary hour, which would otherwise have been passed in idleness and despondency. It might have been thought that such a simple benevolent plan would escape opposition, and the following ill-natured sneers which appeared in the *Pall Mall Gazette* the day after the meeting must have been generally read with surprise:—

> Without in any way wishing to damp the ardour of those who, with the best intentions, seek to relieve the necessities of distressed gentlewomen, we may, perhaps, be permitted to ask those who met at Stafford House on Wednesday, whether it would not be possible to hit upon some scheme for bettering the condition of their *protégés* less likely to lead to disappointment than that embodied in the objects of the institution as explained at the meeting. According to Mr. S. Morley, the Gentlewomen's Self-help Institute is founded for the reception and sale of articles produced by ladies in straitened circumstances. These articles, Mr. Morley stated, consist of oil paintings, drawings, modelled

waxwork, tinted photographs, guipure and other descriptions of lace, wool-work, embroidery, baby-clothes, and plain needlework. The great difficulty, he said, was to find customers. This is indeed a serious difficulty, and any man of business could inform Mr. Morley and his fellow philanthropists that it is a difficulty not likely to be overcome unless there is a scarcity in the ordinary markets of the articles on sale at the Institute, and such a demand for them that the public will rush to the Institute for the purpose of obtaining them; or unless by going to the Institute the articles (for which there must be a constant demand) can be obtained at a lower price than in other quarters. Then, again, the man of common sense would tell Mr. Morley that people who as a matter of business require oil paintings, drawings, modelled waxwork, tinted photographs, &c., are but few in number compared with distressed gentlewomen, and generally prefer purchasing such articles at those establishments where the manufacture and sale of them are a spécialité. The frequenters of the Institute will, therefore, probably be confined to the charitable, who might just as well leave their money there as carry off articles they do not really require, and which can only prove encumbrances; but, again, the distressed gentlewomen far outnumber the charitable, who are unlikely to come in such numbers and leave such contributions as will support all the penniless ladies in the United Kingdom. This may be a painful view to take of the subject, but it is none the less the true one, and no real friend of a distressed gentlewoman could advise her to depend on such a plan as that enunciated on Wednesday for earning a livelihood—at the best it could only by chance give her a few shillings, and leave her in the same position as before. What is really required for distressed gentlewomen, and, indeed, for everybody who is distressed, is a market for such labour as they are capable of performing. If a gentlewoman can do nothing but tint photographs she will probably remain distressed to the end of her days—if, on the other hand, she is not above competing with those who are not gentlewomen, such as nurses, cooks, ladies' maids, and housekeepers, she ought to have, and probably would have, an advantage over the uneducated which would ensure her the comfortable home they have no difficulty in finding. The great and benevolent ladies who take such an interest in her welfare will best show their benevolence by offering such situations to their distressed and educated sisters, and treating them when in their service with that consideration to which they are entitled so long as they perform their duties satisfactorily. Both parties must put their pride in their pockets —the opulent gentlewoman must not be ashamed to be on a footing of intimacy with her servant, and the distressed gentlewoman must not be ashamed of earning her bread by faithful service. There will also be this advantage, the high sense of honour which as a rule influences the conduct of those who have "seen better days" will prevent ladies holding responsible situations in the households of the wealthy from receiving those perquisites which are given by dishonest tradesmen to servants who will consent to rob their employers. In many little ways the lady servant will detect and expose the rascality which it is to be feared prevails to a great extent in the dealings carried on through the medium of the ignorant and unscrupulous. Such, sentiment apart, is the real state of the case, and until all sentiment is eliminated from the discussion, and it is treated as a mere matter of business and common sense, we shall never solve the problem of how to provide for distressed gentlewomen.

The solution thus offered of the problem of how to provide for distressed gentlewomen is both absurd and cruel. Middle-aged gentlewomen cannot be turned into servants, as they possess neither the strength nor skill necessary for the purpose. A distressed gentlewoman may become a housekeeper, and no doubt many do; but to be a lady's maid, a knowledge of hairdressing and dressmaking is necessary, and a lady of forty or fifty could not possibly turn herself into an apprentice to a milliner, not to mention that there are already many more women anxious to be engaged as ladies' maids than can obtain situations. Cooking may be learned at any age, but it is a hard trade, requiring an exceptional amount of health and strength even in a young woman.

Some time ago complaints were heard that a number of middle-aged Government clerks had been dismissed, and it was asked how they were to live. No one was ridiculous enough to suggest to these men that they should become cooks and valets, yet the absurdity is no greater in one case than in the other. The heartlessness of the advice is however even worse than its uselessness, and if the world had not grown callous to the sufferings of women such advice could never have been given. Let us just change the sex of the persons to whom the advice is offered, and then its extraordinary selfishness will become more apparent. "If a gentleman can do nothing but copy letters he will probably remain distressed to the end of his days. If on the other hand he is not above competing with those who are not gentlemen, such as tailors, cooks, valets, and butlers, he ought to have, and probably would have, an advantage over the uneducated, which would ensure him the comfortable home they have no difficulty in finding. The great and benevolent noblemen who take such an interest in his welfare, will best show their interest by offering such situations to their distressed brothers, and treating them when in their service with that consideration to which they are entitled, so long as they perform their duties satisfactorily. Both parties must put their pride in their pockets." If the daughters of naval and military officers, clergymen, &c., may become ladies' maids, why should not a younger son's younger son put his pride in his pocket, get a situation as valet to his noble relative the Earl, black his boots and clean his hunting gear? Why, indeed! It is an odd thing to say, but it really does seem as if a great many writers (and speakers too) were not aware that women are human beings, and suppose them not to possess a particle of human feeling.

We are of course ready to acknowledge that these distressed gentlewomen ought not to exist; they ought to have been taught some business in their youth, and to be self-supporting members of society; but as they were not taught, and as they unhappily do exist; the question is what to do with them; and we do not think a better answer can be given to the question, than is afforded by the " Self-Help Institute," at 20, Bessborough Gardens, and by the " Association for the Sale of Work by Ladies of Limited Means," at 47, Great Portland Street, yet it is undeniable that these societies are quite unequal to the task they endeavour to perform, and that in spite of these efforts, numbers of poor gentlewomen drag on in extreme poverty and discomfort.

We now come to consider what is to be done to prevent a fresh generation of young girls from being brought up to become equally useless. The one only way to prevent them from following in the footsteps of their elders is to give them a good education, and then to remove every obstacle, whether social or legal, which prevents women from engaging in remunerative employments.

Here, however, we meet with great difficulties. So strong is the prejudice against permitting women to enjoy these advantages that Mr. Bouverie, speaking in the House of Commons as the organ of the Government, actually stated on the 12th of May that one of his objections—it appeared to be his chief objection—to giving women the franchise was, that it would lead to their admission into several lucrative and respectable professions, which are now closed to them; and, strange to say, he held that this admission into new employments would be an injury to women, and would tend to degrade them! He said, " It is avowed that we are to become a nation of Amazons, that we are to have women barristers, attorneys, doctors, and, for aught I know, bishops. (Much laughter.) I have here a clever little book, written with great eloquence, power, earnestness, and honesty of purpose. It is entitled, ' Woman's Rights,' and is written by a lady named Caroline H. Downe. It was published in America, and I believe the writer is either a Canadian or an Englishwoman. In it I find these passages:—

> When society strikes out from the Statute-book all distinctions of sex, and admits she is a person capable of thinking and acting for herself, she will lay the foundation of a new civilization (p. 27). The result of a great deal of reading of a great many law books is only this, that we are more firmly convinced than ever that the most necessary reform is a simple erasure from the Statute-book of whatever recognises distinctions of sex (p. 64). In the laws which regard single women, we object, then —1. To the withholding of the elective franchise. 2. To the law's preference of males, and the issue of males in the division of estates. 3. We object to the estimate of woman which the law sustains, which shuts her out from all public employment, for many branches of which she is better fitted than man (p. 66). After women have gone on for some twenty years electing members of Parliament, nobody will be surprised to find some women sitting in that body. But, objects somebody, " If that ever happens we shall have women on juries, women pleading at the bar, women as attorneys, and so on."

" She then adds, ' And this is exactly what we want.' I venture to think that the objects thus avowed are such as should not receive the sanction of this House, because if they were realised they would upset all the domestic relations of life. My hon. friend and the other advocates of this Bill, say their object is to raise women. After all the arguments I have heard on the subject, and the best reflection I have been able to give it, my opinion is that the result of the Bill would be to degrade women."

After making due allowance for exaggeration, it must be confessed that there is a great deal of truth in what Mr. Bouverie says. If women had political influence enough to cause the removal of all legal and educational obstacles, it is probable they would enter many new professions. The change, though gradual, would be great. After the lapse of a good many years, it is probable that a considerable number of women might be found acting as physicians to their own sex, and it is quite possible that some would become architects, and others practice the law as solicitors, while with the removal of all educational disadvantages, the number of female writers and artists would be greatly augmented and the merit of their productions be much increased. All this is true, but we do not see wherein the degradation to women consists.

It is, on the contrary, evident that these changes would elevate them by increasing the number of self-supporting workers, and diminishing the number of poor helpless gentlewomen. The female artist who paints pictures for the Exhibition of the Royal Academy, or for the Society of Painters in Water Colours, stands socially higher than the lady who sends pictures for sale to the "Gentlewoman's Self-Help Institution." The woman clerk who is paid for copying law papers stands higher than the lady who makes wax flowers, or does worsted work to sell to the charitable. The woman-doctor who ministers to the wants of her own sex, and by her skill earns a fortune or a competence, stands highest of all.

Many of the poor ladies who are now struggling to maintain themselves by the aid of the Self-Help Institution, and of other kindred societies, would have followed some of these paths to independence had they been open to them. The duty of benevolent people in the matter seems clear enough. First, to help the present generation of poor gentlewomen, by purchasing their work, and thus alleviating as far as possible the miseries of their position. Secondly, to remove the obstacles which now prevent young gentlewomen from engaging in remunerative employments. If Mr. Bouverie is right, and we think he is, in saying that these obstacles will be removed when women obtain the franchise, the benevolent ought to use their utmost endeavours to obtain the franchise for women, that the obstacles may be removed without delay.

ART. III.—PUBLIC OPINION ON QUESTIONS CONCERNING WOMEN.

WANT of space compels us to omit much valuable matter under this head.

The *Times, Standard, Pall Mall, Morning Post, Telegraph,* and *Saturday Review,* have all written more or less strongly against Women's Suffrage.

As far as we know the *Daily News,* the *Economist,* and the *Echo* are the only London newspapers which have written in its favour.

The article in the *Daily News,* May 14, is given below.

By a majority of 126—220 Noes to 94 Ayes—the House of Commons has refused to go into Committee on the Women's Disabilities Bill, which is therefore lost. From the list of the minority we miss the names of Mr. Stansfeld, Sir J. D. Coleridge, Mr. Dowse (Solicitor-General for Ireland), Mr. Young (the Lord-Advocate), and Lord Otho Fitzgerald, who voted for the second reading of the Bill on the 6th of May, but on the 12th gave up to party what they owed to womankind. Mr. Bouverie led the Opposition in a speech cleverly enough directed to current prejudice. His argument was what may be called the argument from the Harem, or the Harem Scare'em argument. An intelligent Turk would find the perfect expression of his own mind in the language of the Member for Kilmarnock. He would denounce the admission of women into society, just as Mr. Bouverie denounces their proposed admission to the Parliamentary suffrage, as "fraught with serious consequences to all our social and domestic relations, and with danger to all that renders those relations happy." It is said by the Member for Kilmarnock, that the great majority of women do not desire the suffrage. To the great majority of men are without the suffrage, and do not desire it. But it has been thought that the status of a householder is the true condition of the franchise in England; and the separation of representation from taxation, of burthens from privileges, and of duties from rights, if justifiable at all, must rest for its defence on something better than the semi-barbarous sentimentalities of which Mr. Bouverie made himself the organ. That right honourable gentleman declares that it has never been his lot to fall in with one sensible woman who desired the franchise. Sensible women, perhaps, do not seek the conversation and society of Mr. Bouverie. This may be his misfortune, and not his fault. At any rate, it is clear that Miss Martineau, Miss Florence Nightingale, Mrs. Grote, and Mrs. Somerville do not possess the advantage of his improving and agreeable acquaintance. His objection, that it is the tendency of the Bill to make women into men by Act of Parliament, proceeds on the assumption that women are women only by the Common or Statute Law of England, and that to repeal either would be to annul nature. It might just as well be urged that the rose is a rose, and the oak an oak, only by virtue of the gardener's care. The freer the course open to women as to men the more genuinely will their true nature develop itself. Their unfitness for the rough and coarse work of politics is alleged. But politics are rough and coarse only in rough and coarse hands, and it is desirable that they should become more refined and gentle. In proportion as women have entered into the pursuits of ordinary life, they have not become less womanly, but those pursuits have become more humane. There is no reason to think that what is true in literature, in art, and in society, would be untrue in politics. We venture to think that a good deal of the language used by Lord Elcho, Lord Garlies, and even by Mr. Bouverie himself, would have been softened and improved if it had been spoken under the restraints of courtesy and breeding, which that influence which they desire to keep out of politics has a tendency to foster. As to Mr. Gladstone, his speech was a matter of course. The hour has not come, and therefore the man is not ready. He will answer his own remarks a year, two years, or three years hence. His attitude now with respect to the political disabilities of women is just what it was with respect to Free Trade immediately before he assented to the Repeal of the Corn Laws, to Household Suffrage in 1866, to the Ballot a year ago, to the Irish Church Establishment not long since, and to the repeal of University and College tests, and the legalisation of marriage with a deceased wife's sister, at a still more recent period. The list of subjects on which the Prime Minister has changed his mind, burning what he once adored, and adoring what he once burned, might be lengthened. It would be alarming, if it were not idle, to imagine that a career of brilliant, useful, and sincere inconsistency with the relics of a Toryism of inheritance and education, is henceforth to be stereotyped into rigid immobility. Mr. Gladstone is sometimes accused of seeing political truth and justice only in the light of a large majority and an impending victory. Of course, this lack of independent discernment, and failure to judge promptly of questions on their merits, is a defect of intellectual character. But it is in some respects a source of political strength. A party leader is the better as a party leader for not being right too soon, if he can avoid the not less serious danger of being right too late. If Mr. Gladstone is never before the time, he is never long after it. His conversions are usually simultaneous with those of the great body of the nation. When a political truth has to be thought out in the study, or propagated in society, the work is for others. When legislative form needs to be given to matured public opinion and determined popular purpose, no statesman of this generation has anything like the capacity which Mr. Gladstone possesses for the work. The qualities of an intellectual pioneer are scarcely compatible with those of a party chief. It would be fruitless and absurd to complain that the Prime Minister does not unite irreconcilable gifts. It would be equally unreasonable to be discouraged by his hostility, at any given moment, to a particular reform.

An excellent article by Mrs. Fawcett has appeared in the *Fortnightly Review*, on the Disabilities of Women. Many country papers have had articles in favour of women's suffrage.

On the Married Women's Property Bill, the *Times*, *Daily News*, *Telegraph*, *Echo*, and *Spectator* have written in favour. The *Pall Mall Gazette* has written against it.

On the Higher Education of Girls, the *Contemporary Review* contains an excellent article by Miss Smedley. The *Spectator* has had several articles and notices on the same subject especially relating to endowments.

Miss Pechey's grievance at Edinburgh has called forth more than one good article in the *Times* on the Medical Education of Women, also from the *Spectator*, and two or three Scotch papers.

Remarks favourable to the appointment of women as Poor Law Guardians have appeared in the *Echo* and *Spectator*. On the Boarding out of Pauper Children, excellent articles have appeared in the *Times* and a great number of country papers.

Art. IV.—REVIEWS OF BOOKS.

Texts on Woman's Normal Position. Edinburgh: John Maclaen. 1870.

THE title of this small tract explains itself. A few words of judicious comment are added to the texts.

The writer commences by saying—

The events of the day have led me to link together a few texts, to show the position God intended woman to occupy in the world; in contrast to that into which she has been constrained by custom, and forced by the laws of man. I would draw attention to the fact of the *oneness* of man and woman in creation and redemption; and that an indignity cannot be offered to woman, without debasing mankind, and casting contempt on the humanity of Christ.

This is the book of the generation of *Adam.* In the day that God created man in the likeness of God made he him.

Male and female created he *them* and *blessed them,* and called *their* name *Adam* in the day when *they* were created.

And God said, Let us make man in our image, after our likeness; and let *them* have *dominion* over the fish of the sea, and over the fowl of the air, and over the cattle, and over all the earth, and over every creeping thing that creepeth upon the earth.

So God created *man* in his own image, in the image of God created he *him*; male and female created he *them.* And God blessed them : and God said unto *them,* be fruitful, and multiply, and replenish the earth, and *subdue* it; and have *dominion* over the fish of the sea, and so on.

It was in *man's dual* nature that man had *dominion* given *them.*

Further on he remarks—

A disregard of this truth—like every other disregard of God's will and design, has led to much error. Destroy the unity of man and woman, and you destroy the one federal headship; and that would involve the necessity of man and woman having separate Saviours. May it not have been through losing sight of this unity, that the heresy of worshipping the Virgin arose?

We often hear it said that some course of action may be right in itself, but that it is not " womanly." If it was generally remembered that Christ is the one " Exemplar," both for men and women, the remark would not be made by Christians. If Christ is not an example to women as well as to men there ought to be a female exemplar, and it is in this character that Roman Catholic writers sometimes speak of the blessed Virgin.

We heartily recommend this tract to our readers, both for their own perusal and for distribution.

Le Droit des Femmes. Par Alfred Assolant, Paris. Armand Anger.

M. ASSOLANT's book was written two years ago, but

as it is probable that few of our readers have seen it, their attention ought to be called towards it. The book consists of a series of clever sketches illustrative of the state of society in France, which would, M. Assolant believes, be much improved by giving women their proper position. The titles of some of the sketches are— " The Widow," " The Governess," " The Bachelor," " Johanna," " Choice of a Wife," &c., &c.

The Bachelor is capitally described, the gaiety of his youth, the comfortable egotism of his middle-life, and the desolation of his old age.

" Johanna," is a charming, sadly-charming sketch of a young girl, amiable, well-born, and handsome, but poor, who from adverse circumstances turns into an old maid, and dies at fifty-three of sheer weariness of life from having nothing to do.

" The Wife," is also a good sketch. She is not a bad woman, married, as people in France are married, by the arrangement of the parents, to a man who is not bad either. After five years of marriage she makes the following reflection—" My husband is not a fool ; I might perhaps even have loved him ; but why did they make us marry before we knew each other." Of all bad customs M. Assolant considers the custom of arranging marriages the worst, and the custom prevalent in Protestant countries of freedom of choice in marriage the best.

The book is free from the coarseness, so common with French writers, but retains their peculiar liveliness.

[Want of space obliges us to omit the rest of the Reviews.]

Art. V.—EVENTS OF THE QUARTER.

WOMEN'S SUFFRAGE.

GREAT changes of fortune have been experienced of late by the cause of Women's Suffrage. Early in May, the second reading of Mr. Jacob Bright's motion for removing women's disabilities was carried in the House of Commons by a majority of thirty-three, but a few days later the motion for going into Committee on the Bill was defeated by a majority of 126.

The different result is said to be chiefly due to the strong opposition of Mr. Gladstone, though there may have been, and probably were, other causes.

We give an abridgment of the two debates.

On the 4th of May, Mr. Jacob Bright moved the second reading of the Bill. He said that if the Bill passed into law, women householders, paying rates, would have votes for the election of members of Parliament for boroughs, and women in counties, who had houses rated at 12*l.* a year, would have votes for county members. To show the proportion in which women would be enfranchised, he said that in Bath there was on the burgess roll one woman to rather more than three men; this was the largest proportion of women householders in any town in England. The smallest proportion was in Walsall, where there was only one woman householder to twenty-two men. In several other boroughs the proportion was about one to seven. There was therefore no danger that the number of women voters would swamp the men voters. Parliament applied a certain test, and gave votes to all men who could submit to that test, though they were thieves, drunkards, or returned criminals, but denied them to women, however much property or intelligence they might possess. Men wished for the franchise that they might have control over the expenditure of the taxes they paid, and also because exclusion was like a mark of inferiority. Was there any reason which men urged for possessing the franchise which did not apply with equal force to women? It might be asked what advantage it would be to women to possess votes. Let them consider the law with regard to married women. The married woman had not the control of any portion of her property, nor the possession of one farthing of her earnings. Her husband, however unintelligent and worthless, had the absolute control of her and her money. The House was probably unanimous as to the justice of this claim, but there was a great difference between acknowledging an evil and finding a remedy. The Married Women's Property Bill had three times received the sanction of the House and been twice before a Select Committee; but he would be an imprudent man who would undertake to say when it would become law. That was not the way in which they treated the classes who had the franchise. What was the position of a woman who lost her husband? If he died intestate the law protected her, and gave her a certain portion of the income of his property. If he did not die intestate she was left to his justice and mercy. He did not deny that the majority of women were treated with fairness in that respect, but many cases might be cited of the contrary. He merely pointed to these inequalities, and reminded the House that they had been made by a section of the community, because the other section was entirely without influence. It required ten times the provocation a man required before a woman could obtain a divorce. A woman had no control over her children after they were, seven years of age. The husband might take them from her. It was painful to see the difficulties which were thrown in the way of women obtaining the higher education. Women and men might be associated in the theatre and opera, but a difference was made in the lecture-room. At the present moment there was an admirable free school in Manchester; it took male children out of the gutter, while the girls were left in the street. This was the first proposal for the extension of the suffrage which was free from party conflicts and the passions that arose out of them. When made by Mr. Mill in 1867 it received very general support. Five who supported it were now members of the Government, but that did not exhaust the members of the Government who were in its favour. He had no doubt the leader of the Opposition, had he been present, would have supported the Bill. In April, 1866, the right hon. member for Bucks said, "I have always been of opinion that if there is to be universal suffrage women have as much right to a vote as men. A woman having property ought to have a vote in a county in which she may have manorial courts, and sometimes act as a churchwarden." (Hear, hear.) But whatever claim he had to support on the other side of the House, he had a still stronger claim on the great Liberal party to which he had the honour to belong. He did not ask for liberality, but for the barest justice. If justice did not require that every individual should vote, it did require that every class should be represented in that House. He was told that women were unfit to be enfranchised, but they never would be fit till they had the franchise and were invested with its responsibility. On the other side of the Atlantic 4,000,000 negroes had recently been enfranchised, and nobody would deny that the peace and prosperity of the Southern States were better secured by that measure. He was astonished to hear it stated that women were unfit for the franchise when he considered the number of women who were engaged in literature, at the head of educational establishments, managing farms and factories, controlling various industries throughout the country. (Hear, hear.) As a proof of their intelligence he might refer to the history of the agitation which had produced this Bill, and the various committees conducting it. Considering the small means at their disposal, never had a question made such rapid progress in so short a space of time. He was told by some of his political friends that if this Bill were passed the Government would be handed over to the Conservative party in the very crisis of the country's fate. (A laugh.) Well, he derived consolation from the fact that this country had sometimes even survived a Conservative administration. ("Hear," and a laugh.) If there was any meaning in an argument of that kind it was this, that if the country were properly and justly represented, the Liberal party should be sitting on the other side of the House. (A laugh.) He did not believe a word of it. He undertook to say there would be no change in the balance of parties. But there would be a change from the moment women obtained the franchise in the way in which subjects in which they were interested were treated by the House. It was sometimes said that women ought not to be political; it might as well be said that grass should not be green, and if they excluded a sufficiency of air and light and moisture, it would not long be so. With their daily Press, the ablest, most interesting, and cheapest in the world, falling like snow-flakes on their houses, how could they prevent women being political? To say that women should not be political was to say that they should take no care of their children and no interest in the greatness and progress of their country. (Hear, hear.) They were presumed not to know that there was a gallery behind that screen (a laugh), but he always noticed that when any hon. member was about to deliver what he considered an important speech, some of the female members of his family came down to listen to him. (A laugh.) If females deteriorated as political knowledge became general among them, the families of members of Parliament must be deplorably ignorant. (Hear.) But he had never observed that deterioration; on the contrary, he had found all the more force and vivacity and intellectual flavour than was to be found elsewhere. (Hear, hear.) But it was said women would not use the franchise if they had it. Since the Municipal Franchise Bill passed women had the power of local voting, and they used it, in the neighbourhood with which he was connected, much in the same proportion as men. This Bill would not compel women to vote; many men even had votes and did not use them. Women now voted in corporate and non-corporate towns. In non-corporate towns and parishes they voted, under the Sturges Bourn's Act, according to the property on which they were rated. A woman might thus have as many as six votes while a man had only one; but—here was the anomaly—when they came to the Parliamentary election the man had one vote, but the woman, of however large property, had none. So also, in the municipal towns, women were admitted to vote; they went to the poll and voted once a year, and these municipal elections had become as completely political as any Parliamentary election could possibly be. He did not know why, having given women municipal votes, they should deny them the Parliamentary franchise. Lord Cairns on this subject had said:—

"An unmarried woman could dispose of her property and deal with it in any way she thought proper. He did not know why she should not have a voice in saying how it should be lighted and watched, and generally in controlling the municipal expenditure to which that property contributed."

If that was right with regard to municipal expenditure he did not see why the same reasoning should not apply to Parliamentary expenditure. He was told that the Government were to stand neutral on this question. Unfortunately, it was characteristic of all governments to be so engrossed in attending to the wants of the powerful that they could seldom give consideration to the claims of the weak. (Hear.) However, there was one thing on which it was pleasing to reflect. Nobody in that House was more open to conviction than the first Minister of the Crown, and when once convinced no one was more resolute in carrying out his convictions. (Hear, hear.) There was a very general movement in favour of this Bill in almost every part of the three kingdoms. Many petitions had already been presented this Session in its support, with more than 100,000 signatures. He hoped when their children came to read the story of their country's fame they would find it written that the British Parliament was the first great Legislative Assembly in the world which, in conferring the franchise, recognised no distinction of strong or weak, male or female, rich or poor. (Hear, hear.) He concluded by moving the second reading of the Bill.

Colonel Sykes, in supporting the Bill, said he looked on the question as a simple practical one. It resolved itself into a matter of money. What entitled a man to vote for a member of Parliament? The payment of rates. It was a mere question of money and had nothing to do with sex. The number of petitions showed there was a pretty extensive feeling in the country in favour of the Bill. Women had had votes for the twenty-four directors of the East India Company who had to govern 200,000,000 of human beings. Women were just as capable of exercising the franchise as men, and had as good a right to exercise it.

Mr. Scourfield was quite ready to admit that women possessed high qualities, but the question was, did women wish to have this privilege conferred upon them. He had asked the question of many women, and the answer was, that they would rather not have it. Every one knew how petitions were got up. Dr. Johnson had said of women's preaching, that it is like a dog dancing on his hind legs, it is not well done, but we are astonished to find it done at all. Women would not perform political duties well, though they were admirable in private life. If voting papers were used at elections the Bill would be possible, but it was monstrous to ask women to go to the poll. He concluded by moving the previous question.

Mr. Fowler, in seconding the motion, said he had shown he sympathised with women by the steps he had taken to amend the law, but he could not require them to embark in political life. It was a privilege to be free from the obligation of voting. If women were endowed with the right to vote, there was no reason why they should not be elected to sit in the House. He denied that unrepresented classes were treated with injustice or neglect. If single women were to have votes, why not married ones too? He felt things were safer as they were.

Sir C. Dilke said, in reply to the objection that women could not go to the poll, that women already went to the municipal poll, and upon the statement that women did not appeal against their position, he remarked that the women of Turkey or India would be surprised at any movement to improve their condition. As to the admission of women into Parliament that was a question for constituencies. There was no need to make a law to prevent men of ninety years of age from being elected; the electors would settle that. Opposition to the Bill was really founded on a belief in the incapacity of women, but if a woman was capable of being queen it could hardly be contended she was unfit for a vote.

Mr. Beresford Hope said it was unfair to infer that because no petitions were presented by women against the Bill that therefore they were favourable to it. To most women the act of petitioning was objectionable. If unmarried women of property had votes, married women with separate property ought to have votes too; yet the supporters of the Bill were not sufficiently consistent to advocate the principle to that extent. If women shared men's political privileges, they must share their burdens, and sit on juries. He believed if they enfranchised women that in questions where sentiment was opposed to political economy they would fail to get as calm, business-like, and judicial legislation as they did at present.

Dr. Playfair said he wished to take women out of the category of minors, lunatics, idiots, and criminals. It was unwise that so much property as that possessed by women should be unrepresented. The world had benefitted much by the sympathies of women. He would mention only three names to show that— Miss Florence Nightingale, Miss Martineau, and Miss Burdett Coutts. (Hear, hear.) It was said the education of women did not fit them for taking part in politics, but whose fault was that? He would promise hon. gentlemen who were anxious for the education of women, that they would soon find an increased impulse given to that question if they passed the Bill before the House. Other questions would also be pressed on them, for instance, the case of the sick poor. Women it was said did not want the franchise. It was true that women had not pulled down the Park palings, but at least 100,000 had demanded the suffrage in a constitutional way. Italy, Austria, Sweden, and some of the United States, had already given the political suffrage to women more or less completely. There were movements everywhere among us in this direction. Even the Universities, in a halting, timid way, were opening their advantages and honours to women. It was because this Bill appealed to our sense of national justice that he supported it.

Mr. Jenkinson gave his cordial support to the Bill, not on the ground of the rights of women, but on the ground of the rights of property. Women managed their property just as well as men, and in some instances better. Why should Miss Burdett Coutts be denied the right of voting?

Mr. Muntz asked why a ratepayer should be prevented from voting on account of sex. He would give votes to women ratepayers, but not to all women. Women now were made to perform very onerous public duties, and were very unfairly treated about them. He knew an old lady of seventy-one who had been appointed to the office of overseer.

Sir H. Croft said no lady among his constituents had sent him a petition, so he concluded none of them wished for votes. He did not like women lecturers. He agreed with *Punch* that "those who are wanting women's rights are wanting women's charms." (A laugh.)

Mr. Bruce said the Government had not had time to consider the question as it deserved. He should, on that ground, ask for delay. With regard to the manner of voting, were women to be exposed to the rough usage of an election? If they gave women the right to vote for the election of Members of Parliament, how could they refuse them the right, if otherwise qualified, of sitting in that House? (Hear, hear.) He was sure there were many members prepared to support the second reading who would not wish to go further, and that was a good ground for delay. It was for these reasons that he was not able to give his personal support to the Bill, at the same time that he was desirous of having it understood that neither personally, nor as a member of the Government, was he giving any opinion upon its merits.

Mr. Jacob Bright, in replying, stated that he had just received a telegram that the Manchester Town Council had decided to petition Parliament in favour of the Bill by a majority of forty-two to twelve. (Hear, hear.)

The House then divided on the previous question:—

For putting the question - - - - 124
Against - - - - - - - 91
Majority - - - - - —33

The result was received with loud cheers.

The Bill was then read a second time, and the committee fixed for Wednesday next.

On the 12th of May, on the order for going into Committee on the Women's Disabilities Bill—

Mr. Bouverie rose amid cheers to move that the Bill be committed that day six months. He said he looked on the Bill as of the utmost importance. It threatened danger to all our social relations. In many localities women would hold the balance between rival candidates. The measure would be a curse to women, and the great bulk of them knew it. Several hon. members had been entreated to oppose the Bill by their wives. How could a candidate bring himself into the notice of women electors? To address them at a public meeting would be ridiculous. He would be obliged to canvass personally widows and single women. Women ought not to be subjected to anything of the kind. It would be odious to them. Their lives would be rendered intolerable to them. Women are unfit to vote whether they possess property or not. If a wife possessed separate property she would have a vote. If she voted with her husband he would in fact have two votes; if she voted against him there would be discord. It would be impossible to prevent women from entering the House of Commons. They might even sit on the Treasury benches. (Laughter.) Women ought not to be taken down from their pedestal and made to enter into competition with men. If they got votes they might become doctors and lawyers, perhaps even bishops. (Much laughter.) The writer of a book on women's rights says, that she wishes everything to be erased from the Statute Book which recognises the distinction of sex. Women are not fitted for rough work, and are prevented by law from working in mines. To allow women to engage in any kind of work, political or otherwise, would be to degrade them. They already possess great indirect political influence, and ought to be content with indirect influence. To show how great this influence is, Mr. Bouverie related the following anecdote—"I well recollect a gentleman, formerly an hon. member of this House, telling me that on one occasion he went down to a pleasant borough in the west of England, where he was utterly unknown, which he was anxious to represent in Parliament. Immediately on his arrival he announced that he was unmarried, that he possessed a good fortune, and that he proposed, if elected, to marry a lady of the borough. (A laugh.) The consequence was he was returned triumphantly. (Hear, and a laugh.) Well, the hon. member sat upon these benches for some years, but unfortunately he did not keep his promise, and the result was that when he again went down to his borough on the occasion of the next general election, they would not even look at him; he had not the slightest chance and he never sat again in this House. (A laugh.) That is a proof of the great indirect influence which the ladies exert in political affairs, and that influence I, for one, am most anxious to preserve to them."* Mr. Bouverie concluded by moving that the House form itself into a Committee that day six months.

Lord Elcho, in seconding the motion, remarked that the concession was only asked for by a few strong-minded ladies.

Sir R. Anstruther said that in his opinion women were quite as competent to pass judgment on social questions as men. As to the horrors attending elections he should not have supposed that the hon. member for Kilmarnock would terrify ladies greatly if he did call upon them to ask for their votes. (Laughter.) He would also point out that under the measures just introduced by the Government, elections would be made much less turbulent, so that the most timid ladies or gentlemen need not be deterred from recording their votes. It was evident from the petitions presented that a great many women did wish for greater political

---

* It is surprising that Mr. Bouverie did not see how insulting this story is to women. It means that the women of that borough used their influence to get the candidate returned, in the hope that he would marry some one of them, or it means nothing. If women have any influence, the man who told that anecdote ought not to sit in the House of Commons again after the next election.

power than they now possessed. With regard to the medical profession, he thought women were peculiarly well fitted for it, and that it would be advantageous to the State if there were many female practitioners. (Hear and laughter.) He directed the attention of the House to the observations of an American judge who, though he had been opposed to women acting as jurors, yet admitted that they had conducted themselves in an admirable manner in that capacity. He did not believe that women's votes would materially strengthen the Conservative benches.

Lord Garlies said he represented sixteen parishes, and half of them had gone mad on the subject of women's rights. It would be to his advantage to support the Bill, but he should not do so, as he was convinced that the majority of women did not desire a masculine privilege.

Mr. Newdegate said there was a great distinction between voting at municipal elections and Parliamentary ones. He did not think the hon. member for Manchester had rightly understood the remarks of the right hon. member for Buckinghamshire on the subject. Proposals similar to this were always advocated by persons of ultra-democratic views, and he could not lend himself to them.

Mr. Gladstone, after explaining why the Government had not opposed the Bill on the second reading, said, that in his opinion it would be a great mistake to proceed with the Bill. It would be better to wait until turbulent proceedings at elections were abolished. If women are competent to vote, married women ought to vote as well as single ones. Joint ownership is recognised in trade. Why not recognise joint ownership in marriage, and allow both a man and his wife to vote in respect of property which is of sufficient value to qualify them both? In Italy, widows and single women who possess the qualification exercise the franchise through the medium of a relative whom they appoint for the purpose, thus avoiding many objections. But the real issue is much broader. The question is, whether there is a real desire for this measure. He could not recognise that there was such a demand as would justify the uprooting of the old landmarks of society. Mr. Gladstone concluded with these words—" I am perfectly content to give my adhesion, not only to the proposal, but also to the reasoning of my right hon. friend the member for Kilmarnock,* and I shall cheerfully follow him into the lobby."

Mr. Jacob Bright said that during the present session petitions with 130,000 signatures had been presented in support of the measure. The municipal franchise had been given to women without their being admitted to town councils. Nobody had a higher sense of justice than the Prime Minister; and he would, therefore call his attention to one argument. There were two kinds of vote—the local vote and the imperial vote; women now have the local vote universally; but it was of comparatively small

---

* Mr. Bouverie.

importance to them, for, as no distinction was made between men and women, the men, in protecting themselves, protected women too. Parliament, however, legislated for men and for women separately; it constantly imposed inequalities upon women in regard to property, social matters, and many most important questions. It legislated in one direction for men, and in another for women. Thus, while the local vote was of comparatively small importance to women, the imperial vote was of great importance to them. His opponents said that one-seventh portion of the occupiers and owners of property in the country were to be for ever excluded from the political franchise. Why were they to be excluded? No rational reason had been given for their exclusion, beyond the fact that they were women. Representation always meant protection; protection was more necessary for the weak than for the strong; and he appealed to a Parliament elected by household suffrage to make household suffrage a reality.

The House divided with the following result:—

For going into Committee 94
Against 220
Majority ... ... —126

The motion to go into Committee was therefore negatived, and the Bill lost.

DIVISION LIST.

The following members (126, including tellers) voted on May 4th in favour of the second reading of Mr. Jacob Bright's Bill to give the Parliamentary franchise to women:—

Allen, W. S.
Amphlett, R. P.
Anstruther, Sir R.
Baines, Edward
Bass, Arthur
Bateson, Sir Thomas
Bazley, Sir Thomas
Birley, Hugh
Brand, Hon. Robert
Brewer, Dr.
Brodrick, Hon. William
Brown, Alexander H.
Callan, Phillip
Campbell, Henry
Carter, Mr. Alderman
Charley, William T.
Cholmeley, Captain
Coleridge, Sir J. D.
Cowen, Joseph
Cubitt, George

Dalglish, Robert
D'Arcy, M.P.
Dawson, Robert P.
Delahunty, James
Denman, Hon. George
Dickinson, S. S.
Dixon, George
Digby, Kenelm T.
Dillwyn, Lewis L.
Dimsdale, Robert
Downing, M'Carthy
Dowse, Richard
Eastwick, Ed. B.
Edwardes, Hon. Col. William
Edwards, Henry
Elphinstone, Sir J. D. H.
Fawcett, Henry
Figgins, James
Fitzgerald, Right Hon. Lord Otho A.

Fitzmaurice, Lord E.
Fletcher, Isaac
French, Right Hon. Colonel
Gavin, Major
Goldney, Gabriel
Goldsmid, Sir F. H.
Gourley, Edward T.
Grant, Colonel Hon. J.
Gray, Lieut.-Colonel
Gray, Sir John
Guest, Arthur E.
Hadfield, George
Herbert, Hon. Auberon E. W.
Herbert, Henry A.
Hibbert, John T.
Hick, John
Hill, Alexander S.
Hoare, Sir H. A.
Hodgkinson, G.
Hutt, Rt. Hon. Sir W.
Illingworth, Alfred
Jenkinson, Sir G. S.
Johnston, William
Johnstone, Sir H.
Jones, John
Keown, William
King, Hon. P. J. L.
Kinnaird, Hon. A. F.
Langton, W. Gore
Lawson, Sir Wilfrid
Lewis, John D.
Lewis, J. Harvey
Liddell, Hon. H. G.
Lloyd, Sir T. D.
Lush, Dr.
M'Combie, William
Macfie, R. A.
M'Lagan, Peter
M'Laren, Duncan
Maguire, John F.
Maitland, Sir Alexander
Mellor, Thomas W.
Melly, George
Miller, John
Morley, Samuel

Mundella, A. J.
Muntz, Philip H.
Noel, Hon. G. J.
Platt, John
Playfair, Lyon
Plimsoll, Samuel
Pollard-Urquhart, William
Potter, Thomas B.
Powell, Walter
Power, John Talbot
Reed, Charles
Richard, Henry
Richards, Evan M.
Robertson, David
Robertson, Elisha S.
Rylands, Peter
Samuelson, Bernhard
Sartoris, Edward J.
Shaw, William
Sherriff, A. C.
Sidebottom, James
Simon, Mr. Serjeant
Simons, William B.
Sinclair, Sir John G. Tollemache
Smith, John B.
Smith, Eustace
Stacpoole, W.
Stansfeld, Rt. Hon. J.
Stevenson, J. C.
Sykes, Colonel W. H.
Talbot, Christopher R. M.
Taylor, Peter A.
Trelawny, Sir J. S.
Villiers, Right Hon. C. Pelham
West, Henry W.
Wheelhouse, W. S. J.
Whitworth, Thomas
Williams, Watkin
Wingfield, Sir C.
Young, Adolph W.

TELLERS.

Bright, Jacob
Dilke, Sir Charles

The following (ninety-three, including tellers) voted against the Bill:—

Amory, John H.
Arkwright, Richard

Ayrton, Rt. Hon. Acton Smee
Baker, Richard B. Wingfield

Barttelot, Colonel
Beaumont, H. F.
Beaumont, W. B.
Bingham, Lord
Bowring, Edgar A.
Brassey, H. A.
Bright, Richard
Brinckman, Captain
Bruce, Right Hon. H. Austin
Buxton, Charles
Candlish, John
Cartwright, Fairfax
Cartwright, W. C.
Clay, James
Craufurd, E. H. J.
Crawford, R. W.
Crichton, Viscount
Croft, Sir Herbert
Cross, Richard A.
Dalrymple, Donald
Dalrymple, Charles
Davenport, W. B.
Denison, Christopher B.
Dent, John Dent
Dyke, William Hart
Egerton, Hon. A. F.
Fielden, Joshua
Finnie, William
Foljambe, F. J. S.
Fowler, William
Gladstone, W. H.
Glyn, Hon. G. G.
Gore, J. Ralph O.
Gower, Hon. E. F. L.
Grieve, James J.
Guest, Montague J.
Hamilton, Lord C.
Hamilton, Lord C. J.
Hamilton, Marquis of
Hamilton, Lord G.
Henley, Right Hon. J.
Henley, Lord
Howes, Edward
Hyde, Lord
James, Henry

Kavanagh, A. M'M.
Kekewich, S. T.
Knatchbull Hugessen, E. H.
Lawrence, Sir J. C.
Leatham, E. A.
Lennox, Lord G. G.
Locke, John
Mackintosh, E. W.
Maxwell, W. H.
Milles, Hon. G. W.
Mitchell, T. A.
Mitford, W. T.
Monk, Charles James
Mowbray, Rt. Hon. J. Robert
Newport, Viscount
Nicol, James Dyce.
O'Brien, Sir Patrick
Pease, Jos. W.
Pell, Albert
Philips, R. N.
Phipps, Charles Paul
Potter, Edmund
Raikes, H. Cecil
Ramsden, Sir J. W.
Ridley, M. White
Russell, Arthur
Salt, Thomas
Seeley, Charles
Selwin Ibbetson, Sir Henry J.
Smith, Abel
Stapleton, John
Strutt, Hon. Henry
Tollemache, John
Tollemache, Hon. Frederick J.
Tracy, Hon. C. R. D. Hanbury
Walker, Major G. G.
Walpole, Rt. Hon. Spencer H.
Waterhouse, Samuel
Whalley, G. H.
Whitwell, John
Williamson, Sir H.
Woods, Henry

TELLERS.

Scourfield, J. H.
Hope, Beresford A. J.

The following members (ninety-six, including tellers) voted last night to go into committee on Mr. Jacob Bright's Bill to give the Parliamentary franchise to women:—

Record of Events.

Amphlett, Richard P.
Bagwell, John
Baines, Edward
Bass, Arthur
Bateson, Sir Thomas
Bazley, Sir T.
Beach, W. W. Bramston
Beaumont, Somerset A.
Birley, Hugh
Brewer, Dr.
Brise, Colonel Ruggles
Brown, Alexander H.
Bruce, Right Hon. Lord E.
Cameron, Donald
Campbell, Henry
Chadwick, David
Charley, William Thomas
Cowen, Joseph
Cowper-Temple, Rt. Hon. W.
Dalglish, Robert
Delahunty, James
Dixon, George
Digby, Kenelm Thomas
Dilke, Sir Charles W.
Dimsdale, Robert
Dodds, Joseph
Eastwick, Edward B.
Edwards, Henry
Elliot, George
Ewing, Archibald Orr
Fawcett, Henry
Figgins, James
Fitzmaurice, Lord E.
Fortescue, Hon. D. F.
Fowler, Robert N.
Gavin, Major
Goldsmid, Sir Francis H.
Gourley, Edward T.
Gray, Sir John
Guest, Arthur E.
Gurney, Right Hon. Russell
Herbert, Hon. A. E. W.
Hibbert, John T.
Hill, Alexander Staveley
Hodgkinson, Grosvenor
Holmesdale, Viscount
Howard, James
Illingworth, Alfred
Jenkinson, Sir George S.
Jones, John
Kinnaird, Hon. A. F.
Knight, F. Winn
Langton, W. Gore
Lawson, Sir Wilfrid
Lea, Thomas
Lewis, John Harvey
Liddell, Hon. H. G.
Lopes, Sir Massey
Lowther, James
Lush, Dr.
Lusk, Andrew
M'Lagan, Peter
M'Laren, Duncan
Maguire, John Francis
Mellor, Thomas W.
Melley, George
Miall, Edward
Miller, John
Montagu, Right Hon. Lord R.
Morrison, Walter
Mundella, Anthony J.
Noel, Hon. Gerard J.
Playfair, Lyon
Pollard-Urquhart, William
Powell, Walter
Power, John Talbot
Robertson, David
Robinson, Elisha Smith
Round, James
Rylands, Peter
Shaw, Richard
Sheriff, Alexander C.
Simonds, William B.
Sinclair, Sir John G. T.
Stacpoole, William
Stevenson, James C.
Talbot, Christopher R. M.
Taylor, Right Hon. Colonel
Taylor, Peter Alfred
Wedderburn, Sir David
Wheelhouse, W. S. J.
Whitworth, Thomas
Wingfield, Sir Charles
Wyndham, Hon. Percy

TELLERS.
Mr. Jacob Bright
Sir Robert Anstruther

188 Record of Events.

The following (222, including tellers) voted against going into committee:—

Acland, Thomas Dyke
Adam, William Patrick
Adderley, Right Hon. Sir C.
Agar-Ellis, Hon. L. G. F.
Amcotts, Colonel W. C.
Annesley, Hon. Colonel H.
Anson, Hon. A. H. A.
Archdall, Captain M.
Arkwright, Richard
Armitstead, George
Ayrton, Right Hon. A. S.
Aytoun, Roger Sinclair
Backhouse, Edmund
Barnett, Henry
Barrington, Viscount
Barry, Arthur H. Smith
Barttelot, Colonel
Beach, Sir Michael H.
Beaumont, H. F.
Beaumont, Captain Frederick
Bowmont, Marquis of
Bentall, Edward H.
Bingham, Lord
Blennerhassett, Sir R.
Bolckow, Henry F. W.
Bonham-Carter, John
Bowring, Edgar A.
Brassey, T.
Bright, R.
Brinckman, Captain
Bristowe, Samuel Boteler
Broadley, William H. H.
Brocklehurst, William C.
Brogden, Alexander
Bruce, Lord C.
Bruce, Right Hon. H. Austin
Bruce, Sir H. Hervey
Bruen, Henry
Bury, Viscount
Butler-Johnstone, H. A.
Cadogan, Hon. F. W.
Candlish, John
Cardwell, Right Hon. E.
Carnegie, Hon. Charles
Cartwright, Fairfax
Cartwright, William C.
Castlerosse, Viscount
Cavendish, Lord F. C.
Cavendish, Lord G.
Cawley, Charles E.
Cecil, Lord E. H. B. G.
Chambers, Thomas
Chaplin, Henry
Clive, Colonel Edward
Clowes, Samuel William
Cogan, Right Hon. W. H. F.
Colthurst, Sir George C.
Craufurd, Edward H. J.
Crawford, Robert Wygram
Croft, Sir Herbert G. D.
Cross, Richard A.
Dalrymple, Donald
Dalrymple, Charles
Davenport, William B.
Davies, Richard
Davison, John Robert
Dease, Edmund
De Grey, Hon. Thomas
De La Poer, Edmond
Dodson, John George
Duff, Mount E. Grant
Duff, Robert William
Eaton, Henry William
Egerton, Hon. A. F.
Egerton, Captain Hon. F.
Elcho, Lord
Enfield, Viscount
Erskine, Admiral J. E.
Esmonde, Sir John
Eykyn, Roger
Finnie, William
FitzGerald, Right Hon. Lord Otho A.
Fitzwilliam, Hon. H. W.
Foster, William Henry
Fothergill, Richard
Fowler, William
Garlies, Lord
Gladstone, Right Hon. W. E.
Gladstone, William Henry
Glyn, Hon. George G.
Gore, J. Ralph Ormsby
Gower, Hon. E. F. L.
Goschen, Right Hon. G. J.
Graves, Samuel Robert
Grieve, James Johnstone
Greville, Hon. Captain
Grey, Right Hon. Sir G.

Grosvenor, H. Norman
Grosvenor, Captain R. W.
Grove, Thomas Fraser
Hamilton, Lord Claud
Hamilton, Lord Claud J.
Hamilton, Lord George
Hamilton, John G. C.
Hammer, Sir John
Harcourt, W. G. G. V. Vernon
Hardy, John
Hartington, Marquis of
Hay, Sir J. C. D.
Headlam, Right Hon. T. E.
Henley, Lord
Henry, John Snowdon
Hervey, Lord A. H. C.
Hodgson, W. Nicholson
Holland, Samuel
Holms, John
Hope, A. J. B. B.
Hornby, E. Kenworthy
Hoskyns, C. Wren
Howard, Hon. C. W. G.
Hyde, Lord
Ingram, Hugo F. M.
James, Henry
Jessel, George
Johnston, Andrew
Kavanagh, A. Mac M.
Kay-Shuttleworth, U. J.
Kennaway, John Henry
Kirk, William
Knox, Hon. Colonel Stuart
Lacon, Sir E. H. K.
Laird, John
Lancaster, John
Lawrence, Sir James C.
Lawrence, William
Lindsay, Colonel R. Loyd
Lowe, Right Hon. Robert
Lowther, William
Lyttleton, Hon. C. G.
M'Arthur, William
Mackintosh, Eneas W.
Martin, Phil. Wykeham
Matthews, Henry
Milbank, Frederick Aclom
Milles, Hon. George W.
Mills, Charles Henry
Milton, Viscount
Monk, Charles James
Monsell, Right Hon. William
Montgomery, Sir G. G.
Morgan, C. Octavius
Newdegate, C. N.
Newport, Viscount
Nicol, James Dyce
O'Conor, Denis Maurice
O'Conor Don, The
Ogilvy, Sir John
Onslow, Guildford
O'Reilly-Dease, Matthew
Paget, Richard Horner
Palmer, John Hinde
Palmer, Sir Roundell
Parker, Lieut.-Colonel W.
Parry, Love Jones
Pease, Joseph Whitwell
Peel, Arthur Wellesley
Pell, Albert
Pemberton, E. L.
Percy, Earl
Philips, R. Needham
Phipps, Charles Paul
Portman, Hon. William H. B.
Potter, Edmund
Price, William Philip
Raikes, Henry Cecil
Rathbone, William
Ridley, Matthew White
Rothschild, N. M. de
Royston, Viscount
Russell, Arthur
Sandon, Viscount
Saunderson, Edward
Scourfield, John Henry
Seely, Charles
Seymour, Alfred
Seymour, Hugh de Grey
Shirley, Sewallis Evelyn
Smith, Abel
Smith, Frederick C.
Smith, Rowland
Smith, Samuel George
Stanley, Hon. Frederick
Stone, William Henry
Stuart, Colonel
Sturt, Henry Gerard
Sturt, Lieut.-Colonel Napier
Sykes, Christopher
Talbot, John Gilbert
Talbot, Hon. R. A. J.

Tollemache, Hon. F. J.
Torrens, W. T. M'C.
Tracy, Hon. C. R. D. H.
Trevelyan, George O.
Turner, Charles
Turnor, Edmund
Verner, William
Vivian, Henry Hussey
Vivian, Arthur P.
Walker, Major G.
Walsh, Hon. A.
Walter, John

Wells, William
Whitbread, Samuel
Whitwell, John
Williamson, Sir H.
Wilmot, Henry
Wise, Henry C.
Woods, Henry
Wynn, Charles W. W.
Young, G.

TELLERS.
Mr. Bouverie and
Mr. Brand

PAIRS.

FOR.
Trelawny, Sir J.
Gilpin, Charles
Cubitt, George
Potter, T. B.
Morley, Samuel
Brand, H. R.
Hoare, Sir H.
Smith, J. B.
Johnston, William
Villiers, C. P.
Fagan, Captain
Gregory, G. B.
Herbert, H. A.
West, H. W.
Keown, W.
White, James
Hick, John
M'Combie, William
Downing, M'Carthy
Dickinson, S. S.
Brodrick, William
Hughes, T.

AGAINST.
Hardcastle, J. A.
St. Aubyn, J.
Adair, Hugh E.
Mowbray, J. R.
Bective, Lord
Du Pre, C. G.
Rebow, Gurdon
Neville-Grenville, R.
Heygate, Sir F.
Cholmeley, Sir M.
Lewis, J. D.
Barclay, A. C.
Clay, James
Gregory, W. H.
Dick, F.
Dawson-Damer, S.
Finch, E. H.
Maxwell, W. H.
Salamons, Sir D.
Leslie, C. P.
Amory, J. H.
Scott, Lord H.

LONDON NATIONAL SOCIETY FOR WOMEN'S SUFFRAGE.

ON Saturday, May 21, a meeting of the above Society was held at Aubrey House, Notting Hill, to discuss the future course of action of the Society. There were present by invitation, Sir C. Dilke, M.P., Sir Wilfrid Lawson, M.P., Mr. Jacob Bright, M.P., Mr. McLaren, M.P., Mr. P. A. Taylor, M.P., Mr. Eastwick, M.P., and Dr. Lyon Playfair, M.P. Also, as members of the other Committees, Mrs. McLaren, and Mrs. and Miss Wigham, from the Edinburgh Committee, Mrs. Jacob

Bright and Miss Becker from Manchester, and Miss Estlin from the Bristol Committee.* There were also present, Mr. T. Hare, Professor Hunter, Mr. Boyd Kinnear, Mrs. W. Burbury, and Mr. and Mrs. Pennington. The London Committee was represented by Mrs. F. Hill, Mrs. R. Martineau, Mrs. Westlake, Mrs. Brewer, Miss Hare, Mrs. Fawcett, Miss Keary, Mrs. Kinnear, Mrs. Taylor, and Miss C. Biggs.

Mr. Jacob Bright, M.P., was voted into the Chair.

The Secretary read letters from Lord and Lady Amberley and from Mr. Mill suggesting that the work to be carried on by the central committees should be the establishment of branch associations in other boroughs, and if possible, also for the counties, and this was held to be the general opinion of the meeting.

After some observations, Mr. Bright, M.P., said that there was no ground for despondency at the defeat of the Women's Disabilities Bill in the House of Commons, on Thursday, May 12. At two o'clock in the morning ninety-four members had voted for us, in spite of a furious whip of the Government. The late discussions in the House had advanced the measure from a theoretical to a practical basis. The press was paying the subject serious attention; the *Times* had had three articles. In the interests of the cause the Bill ought to be brought in next session, as we shall only then really know how we stand in the opinion of the House and the country. This Bill as it stood would enfranchise more persons than Gladstone's proposed Bill of 1866, or Disraeli's of '67. He proposed that the Disabilities Bill be introduced again next Session.

To the question if he would again take charge of it, Mr. Bright pledged himself to do so if the feeling of the Committees remained the same.

The thanks of the meeting were then given to the three hon. gentlemen who had taken charge of the Bill this Session, and the meeting closed.

At a previous meeting of the Committee, it was decided that an active sub-committee should be formed to meet

---

* Miss A. Robertson, of Dublin, was invited to attend to represent the movement in Ireland, but was unable to do so.

fortnightly to transact the business of the Society. Mr. Thomas Hare, Mrs. Burbury, Mr. James Macdonell, and Professor W. Hunter, were invited to be on it. The London Executive Committee now stands as follows:—

Mrs. Brewer.	Mrs. Boyd Kinnear.
Mrs. Donkin.	Mrs. Lucas.
Mrs. H. Fawcett.	Mrs. F. Malleson.
Miss Hare.	Mrs. Stansfeld.
Mrs. F. Hill.	Mrs. Westlake.
Miss E. Keary.	

Hon. Secs. and Treasurers.

Mrs. P. A. Taylor.	Miss C. A. Biggs.

Sub-Committee.

Mrs. Burbury.	Professor Hunter.
Miss Biggs.	Mr. James Macdonell.
Mrs. Fawcett.	Mrs. Taylor.
Mr. Thos. Hare.	

Friends to the movement of "Women's Suffrage," in London and the country, are earnestly invited by the Committee to communicate with the Secretaries at Aubrey House, Notting Hill.

On the 14th of May, the following letter from Mrs. P. A. Taylor appeared in the *Pall Mall Gazette*:—

The division in the House of Commons on Thursday, on the Women's Disabilities Bill might give a false impression as to the numerical strength of its supporters. Fifty-nine members who voted in favour of the Bill on the 4th of May were absent from the division on the 12th of May. The number of members, therefore, who have recorded their votes in our favour is 155. The division on the second reading had taken every one by surprise, and had, perhaps, unduly excited the hopes of those most interested in the success of the Bill. The triumph of May 4 is nullified by the defeat of May 12; but the defeat will only incite us to renewed energy. We do not mean to succumb. Before the next session of Parliament we shall confidently hope it will be in our power to prove to our opponents that the women of England earnestly desire the franchise. Over 130,000 men and women have signed the petitions which have been presented this year. Before the introduction of the Bill in 1871, we trust we shall have thrice, and more than thrice, that number. From every borough must a petition be presented, that no hostile member may solace himself with the plea that his constituency was either opposed or indifferent to the franchise.

On the 25th, the following correspondence appeared in the *Times*:—

Sir,—Having the permission of the writer to publish the subjoined note from a member of Parliament assigning his reason for voting against the Women's Disabilities Bill, I beg that you will give it a place in your columns.

It was written in reply to one reminding him that he had, both during his canvass and since his election, positively promised to vote for such a measure, and asking why, notwithstanding these pledges, his name appears in the list of Mr. Bouverie's majority against going into committee on the Women's Disabilities Bill.

How far the motives so frankly avowed by the hon. member for Carnarvonshire may have influenced other members of the Liberal party to vote against a measure of enfranchisement it is, of course, impossible to conjecture; but, since they were strong enough in one instance to cause the violation of distinct pledges, it is not unreasonable to imagine that they may have prevailed with others not so bound. Perhaps they may afford some explanation of the determined though tardy opposition of the Government, and of the apparently capricious rejection by the House of Commons, of a measure the principle of which had been accepted after a full debate on the second reading.

Both friends and opponents of the Bill will, doubtless, agree that, in a question of justice regarding them, women have a right to expect that the votes of members of the Legislature should be given on the merits of the case, and not out of party considerations.

Yours respectfully,
Lydia E. Becker.
Manchester, May 24.

House of Commons, May 18.

Dear Madam,—In the county I represent, Carnarvonshire, the women are all Liberal in politics and Nonconformists in religion—that is, the vast majority of them; and this may be said of all North Wales.

On the other hand, in England, and particularly in boroughs, such as Bath, women are Conservative, under great clerical influence, which always tends to fetter freedom of thought. I reluctantly, for these reasons, voted (against my own interests) to prevent women being made capable of doing what I consider political wrong in many places—viz., voting against the Liberal party.

Yours faithfully,
Miss Becker.
Love Jones Parry.

MEETINGS AND LECTURES ON THE ELECTORAL DISABILITIES OF WOMEN.

On April 18, a very large and influential meeting was held in Dublin, to hear a lecture on the Electoral

Disabilities of Women, delivered by Mrs. Fawcett, wife of Professor Fawcett, M.P. for Brighton. The Molesworth Hall was crowded in all parts by a most attentive and fashionable audience. Among those on the platform were—Sir Robert Kane, F.R.S., who was the Chairman, Lady Kane, Sir John Gray, M.P., and Lady Gray, Sir James Power, Bart., and Lady Power, the Misses Robertson, Lady Wilde, the Right Hon. Sir Joseph Napier, Sir John Burrington, D.L., the Provost of Trinity College and Mrs. Lloyd, John Talbot Power, Esq., M.P., the Archdeacon of Dublin and Mrs. Lee, Professors Webb, Shaw, Dixon, and Ingram, Fellows of Trinity College, John Francis Waller, Esq., LL.D., the Right Honourable Sir Maziere Brady, Bart., the Rev. Dr. Tisdall, &c., &c.

Mrs. Fawcett's lecture was the same of which we have previously spoken as having been delivered at Brighton.

A vote of thanks to her was proposed at the conclusion of the lecture by Miss Anne Isabella Robertson, under whose auspices the meeting was arranged, and who was received with warm applause. In the course of her speech Miss Robertson observed that she felt much gratification in testifying to the great intelligence of the people of Dublin upon the subject of the enfranchisement of women, stating that she had spoken to many thousands of the inhabitants of Dublin on the question, separately and individually in their own houses, and was therefore able to speak from her own experience. After London and Manchester, Dublin had sent more signatures to petitions in favour of women's suffrage last session than any other place in the United Kingdom. At the last meeting of the London Women's Suffrage Society, held on March 26, Mr. Jacob Bright alluded to this fact, so gratifying to Dublin. John Francis Waller, Esq., LL.D., seconded Miss Robertson's vote of thanks to Mrs. Fawcett, and upon the motion of the Rev. John Mahaffy, F.T.C.D., seconded by Professor Shaw, a petition in favour of the Bill for removing the Electoral Disabilities of Women, was adopted by the meeting. Sir Joseph Napier having been called to the second chair by Sir John Gray, M.P., the proceedings terminated, the meeting having been most successful in its manifestation of approval. A remarkable feature of this meeting was, that persons of such opposite political and religious opinions took part in it. Every daily morning and evening paper in Dublin gave full and favourable reports of the proceedings.

Mrs. Fawcett has also lectured at Greenwich to a large audience.

On May 25, Lady Amberley delivered a lecture to a large audience at Stroud. We hope that it will be published at length, and as it would be quite impossible to do it justice in an abridgment, we shall not attempt it. The main object of the lecture was to point out that it was the duty of women in happy circumstances to try to improve the laws, that they might be able to ameliorate the condition of less fortunate women. A short extract is all we can give—

> Too often we are told by women, "I should be no better off if I had my own property or a vote," or, "I like trusting to myself better than to rights," or, "what do women want with colleges; why cannot they be happy and quiet at home?" or again, "I should hate to be a doctor or a lawyer; women are not fit for it; they had better look after their husbands and children." The people who argue in this way fail to perceive that in so doing they are only asserting their own happiness or their own comfort, and are entirely forgetting the thousands, I might say, millions of women, who are alone in the world, who have neither parents, nor home, nor friends, nor fortune of their own, and who are driven to seek these for themselves, or to die. . . . . It is not for you I urge any change, if you feel no need for it, though the fact of your indifference argues your need of enfranchisement. But though you and I may be happy, it is no reason not to urge it on behalf of the millions of women in England and America, who are not living in this blissful state of comfort and content. We are apt to forget that the Priest and the Levite who looked and passed by on the other side, are not the examples we would wish to follow; let us look then at these sores and see if we cannot aid in binding them up.

At one of the meetings of the Discussion Society, held in Conduit Street, early in June, a paper was read by a gentleman, recommending that women should elect 150 representatives, who should sit in the House of Lords. A lady present quickly demonstrated the absurdity of the proposal. Whether it was intended seriously by the writer, or whether it was meant as a joke, we are unable to say.

Mrs. Crawshay, of Cyfarthfa Castle, has given a lecture at Merthyr Tydvil, from which we give the following extract:—

In answer, then, to those who object to the effect on woman that voting will have, and that it will unfit her for home duties, I reply, "I think it better for the surplus time of woman to be applied to the consideration how to mend the wickedness and miseries of the world than in striving to mar the human form divine in her own person in the way she now does." And having now told you why I think the possession of a vote will tend to ennoble women's characters, I will add that through them I hope to see a higher standard of morality introduced into the world. And I fancy few of those present to-night will consider the course of all events so pure and noble that we can afford to throw aside the help of at least half the human intellect as a thing not worth having.

Miss Taylour has given lectures at Aberdeen, Peterhead, Inverness, Blairgowrie, Alyth, and Dundee. Each of these lectures resulted in a petition being sent to Parliament.

All these ladies have done good by their lectures, and more lecturers are much wanted. The requisites for lecturing successfully, are a good address, a knowledge of the subject, and an unimpeachable character.

A lecture on "Woman's Place in Creation," was given last October, at Nelson, New Zealand, by Joseph Giles, Esq., Resident Magistrate. He advocated the admission of women to a share of whatever educational advantages might hereafter be bestowed on young men when the time should come for founding universities in that country.

ELECTION INTELLIGENCE.

"On Saturday night, the Working Men's Liberal Committee met Mr. Moffatt at the Justice-room, at the Town-hall, Ryde, for the purpose of hearing his opinions on the various political topics of the day. Among other things the propriety of giving votes to single women and widows was discussed. It was urged that as they possessed the property qualifications of the members of the sterner sex they ought to possess electoral privileges. Mr. Moffatt asked his questioner what he would do in the case of married women who had property independently of their husbands, should they have votes? He was answered in the affirmative. Mr. Moffatt observed, that in that case this question arose ' Why should one married lady have a vote and not another?' It was manifestly unfair. On the whole, the question was in so crude and unsettled a state that he must decline pledging himself on it."—*Times*, June 7th.

Mr. Moffatt was defeated by thirty-five votes.

We do not know the opinions of Mr. Baillie Cochrane, the successful candidate, on women's suffrage.

We have much pleasure in recording the formation of a Branch Suffrage Society in Glasgow. It was organised on March 4, and in less than a month sent up petitions with more than 3000 signatures.

GLASGOW BRANCH OF THE NATIONAL SOCIETY FOR WOMEN'S SUFFRAGE.

President :—Mrs. John Smith.

Miss Anderson.	Mrs. Glasford.
Miss Catherine Anderson.	Miss Macrae.
Miss Elizabeth Anderson.	Mrs. David Russell.
Mrs. Bell.	Mrs. Frances Smith.
Mrs. Charles Bell.	Miss Kate Smith.
Miss Cochrane.	Mrs. Stewart.

Secretary :—Mrs. Neilson, 42, Dalhousie Street.

Treasurer :—Mrs. Harvey.

The first meeting of the Stroud Women's Suffrage Society was held on the 16th June. It was resolved that the Society was formed to extend the suffrage to women possessing the same qualifications as male voters, and that the Society shall confine its attention solely to that object. Miss A. Evans was appointed Local Secretary.

The following is a list of petitions presented this session in favour of women's suffrage :—

REPORTS OF THE SELECT COMMITTEE OF THE HOUSE OF COMMONS ON PUBLIC PETITIONS—SESSION 1870.

FOR EXTENSION OF ELECTIVE FRANCHISE TO WOMEN.

*The petitions marked thus ¶ have the addresses of some or all of the petitioners affixed. The petitions marked * are signed officially.*

Feb. 10.	¶ Inhabitants of Taunton and vicinity *(Mr. Barclay)*	51
„ 11.	Inhabitants of Kingstown, county of Dublin *(Mr. Pim)*	13
„ 11.	Inhabitants of Blackrock, county of Dublin *(Mr. Pim)*	3
„ 11.	Inhabitants of Williamstown, county of Dublin *(Mr. Pim)*	3
„ 11.	Inhabitants of the county of Longford *(Mr. Pim)*...	2
„ 11.	Inhabitants of Booterstown, county of Dublin *(Mr. Pim)*	5
„ 11.	Inhabitants of Dublin *(Mr. Pim)*	129
„ 14.	*Inhabitants of Newcastle-on-Tyne in public meeting assembled. Signed, James Morrison, chairman *(Mr. Cowen)*	1
„ 24.	Inhabitants of Normanton, Yorkshire *(Mr. Hadfield)*	14
„ 24.	*Inhabitants of Barnsley, Yorkshire, in public meeting assembled; B. Deake, chairman *(Mr. Hadfield)*	1
„ 24.	*Inhabitants of Sheffield, Yorkshire, in public meeting assembled; E. Priest, chairman *(Mr. Hadfield)*	1
„ 28.	¶Inhabitants of Salford *(Mr. Charley)*	127
„ 28.	¶Inhabitants of Edinburgh *(Mr. M'Laren)* ...	1,020
„ 28.	Inhabitants of Hull, in public meeting assembled; T. Minto, chairman *(Mr. Norwood)*	1
March 10.	Inhabitants of Halstead *(Dr. Brewer)*... ...	121
„ 14.	*Inhabitants of Edinburgh, in meeting assembled; D. M'Laren chairman *(Mr. Miller)* ...	1
„ 22.	Isabella Hughes, 30, Broad-street, Aberdeen *(Colonel Sykes)*	1
„ 22.	Ann Reid, 25, Marywell-street, Aberdeen *(Colonel Sykes)*...	1
„ 22.	Margaret M'Donald, 26, Dee-street, Aberdeen *(Colonel Sykes)*	1
„ 23.	¶Inhabitants of Dumfries *(Sir Wilfrid Lawson)*	904
„ 23.	Inhabitants of Shetland *(Mr. M'Laren)* ...	45
„ 24.	*Inhabitants of Trowbridge, Wilts, in public meeting assembled; D. Lucas, chairman *(Sir George Jenkinson)*	1
„ 25.	Inhabitants of Leeds and neighbourhood *(Mr. Carter)*	178
„ 28.	Women householders of Aberdeen; 113 petitions *(Colonel Sykes)*	113

March 28.	Ann Gordon, and others, Aberdeen (*Col. Sykes*)	12
„ 29.	Inhabitants of Paignton, county of Devon (*Mr. Solicitor-General*)	19
April 5.	Inhabitants of Rawtenstall, county of Lancaster (*Mr. Holt*)	254
„ 12.	¶Inhabitants of Roscommon, and others (*Mr. Pim*)	21
„ 27.	Women householders of Aberdeen ; 32 Petitions (*Colonel Sykes*)	32
„ 28.	Mary Thomson, Paris Lodge, Old Aberdeen (*Col. Sykes*)	1
May 2.	*Inhabitants of Bradford-on-Avon, in public meeting assembled ; John Thomas Linom, chairman (*Lord Charles Bruce*)	1
„ 2.	*Inhabitants of Market Lavington, county of Wilts, in public meeting assembled ; Samuel Saunders, chairman (*Lord Charles Bruce*)	1
„ 2.	Diana Jamieson, Aberdeen (*Colonel Sykes*)	1
„ 2.	Inhabitants of Putney and other places (*Mr. Broderick*)	47
„ 2.	Inhabitants of Capel, Ockley, and other places (*Mr. Onslow*)	68
„ 4.	Mary M'Leish, 7, Cornwall-street, Edinburgh (*Mr. M'Laren*)	1
„ 4.	Inhabitants of Buckingham (*Mr. Taylor*)	5

Total number of Petitions 180—Signatures 3,200

REPORTS OF THE SELECT COMMITTEE OF THE HOUSE OF COMMONS ON PUBLIC PETITIONS—SESSION 1870.

WOMEN'S DISABILITIES BILL—In favour.

The petitions marked thus ¶ have the addresses of some or all of the petitioners affixed. The petitions marked * are signed officially.

Feb. 17.	¶ Inhabitants of Manchester (*Mr. Bazley*)	815
„	—¶ Chorlton-on-Medlock, Manchester (*Mr. Birley*)	600
„	—¶ Salford (*Mr. Cawley*)	500
„	—¶ Salford (*Mr. Cawley*)	588
„	—¶ Scarborough (*Sir Harcourt Johnstone*)	828
„	— Church Coniston (*Colonel Wilson Patten*)	99
„	—¶ Lancaster (*Mr. Frederick Stanley*)	71
Feb. 18.	Inhabitants of Ardwick, Manchester (*Mr. Jacob Bright*) [APP. 61]	716
„	* Inhabitants of New Mills, Stockport, in public meeting assembled; John Pollitt, chairman (*Mr. John Benjamin Smith*)	1
„	— High Wycombe (*Mr. Taylor*)	14
Feb. 21.	*Inhabitants of Newcastle-upon-Tyne, in public meeting assembled; W. Armstrong, chairman (*Mr. Cowen*)	1
„	—* Riddings, near Alfreton, in public meeting assembled; A. Butler, chairman (*Mr. Cowen*)	1
„	—* Crook, Durham, in public meeting assembled; T. Brown, chairman (*Mr. Cowen*)	1
„	—* Alnwick, in public meeting assembled; W. Wright, chairman (*Mr. Cowen*)	1
„	— Knutsford (*Mr. Wilbraham Egerton*)	2
„	— Pinner, in the county of Middlesex (*Viscount Enfield*) [APP. 85]	129
„	—¶ Oxford (*Mr. Vernon Harcourt*)	41
„	— Monmouth (*Mr. Taylor*)	15
„	—* Crewe, in public meeting assembled; J. Eaton, chairman (*Mr. John Tollemache*)	1
Feb. 22.	¶ Inhabitants of the borough of Salford (*Mr. Cawley*)	503
„	— Bolton, Lancashire (*Mr. Hick*)	220
„	—¶ Bristol	1,067
Feb. 23.	*Inhabitants of Bacup, Lancashire, in public meeting assembled; J. Holland, chairman (*Mr. Holt*)	1
„	— Rawtenstall, in the county of Lancaster (*Mr. Holt*)	213
„	—¶ Chelsea	2,832
Feb. 24.	¶ Inhabitants of Bolton (*Colonel Gray*)	303
„	—¶ „ (*Colonel Gray*)	26
„	—¶ Hastings (*Mr. Kay-Shuttleworth*)	120
„	E. Slatter, Battle, Sussex, and others (*Mr. Taylor*)	180
Feb. 25.	Inhabitants of Bath (*Mr. Donald Dalrymple*)	105
„	— „ (*Mr. Donald Dalrymple*)	170
„	— Hendon, Middlesex (*Viscount Enfield*)	218

Feb.	25.	Inhabitants of Harrow, Middlesex (*Viscount Enfield*)	100
,,	25.	Inhabitants of Budleigh, Salterton, Devon (*Mr. Thos. Hughes*)	25
,,	25.	Inhabitants of Church Coniston, Lancashire (*Mr. Frederick Stanley*)	102
,,	28.	¶Inhabitants of Newton Saint Loe, Corston, and other places (*Major Allen*) ... ' ...	64
,,	28.	*Inhabitants of Oldham, Lancashire, in public meeting assembled; Thos. Haigh, chairman (*Mr. Hibbert*) ...	1
,,	28.	Inhabitants of Ambleside and other places (*Mr. William Lowther*)	72
,,	28.	¶Inhabitants of Cheltenham (*Mr. Henry Samuelson*)	62
,,	28.	¶Inhabitants of Stockport (*Mr. John Benjamin Smith*)	46
,,	28.	¶Inhabitants of Beverley (*Mr. Taylor*) ..	646
,,	28.	Inhabitants of Leominster	85
March	1.	¶Inhabitants of Manchester (*Mr. Jacob Bright*)	508
,	1.	¶Inhabitants of Marylebone (*Mr. Thos. Chambers*)	2,363
,,	1.	¶Inhabitants of Tower Hamlets	1,779
,,	1.	¶Inhabitants of Hackney	2,560
,,	2.	Inhabitants of Ancoats, Manchester (*Mr. Birley*)	410
,,	3.	Inhabitants of Hertfordshire (*Mr. H. Cowper*) ...	40
,,	3.	Inhabitants of Inch, Wigtownshire (*Ld. Garlies*)	120
,,	3.	Inhabitants of Preston and other places (*Mr. Hermon*)	60
,,	3.	Inhabitants of Glenridding and other places (*Mr. William Lowther*)	53
,,	4.	¶Inhabitants of Macclesfield (*Mr. Chadwick*) ...	136
,,	4.	¶Inhabitants of Durham (*Mr. Henderson*) ...	495
,,	7.	Inhabitants of Budleigh, Salterton (*Mr. Kekewich*)	39
,,	7.	¶Inhabitants of Tottenham (*Mr. Taylor*) ...	11
,,	8.	¶Inhabitants of Cheetham Hill, county of Lancaster (*Mr. Henry*)	49
,,	8.	¶Inhabitants of Nottingham (*Mr. Auberon Herbert*)	1,440
,,	8.	¶Inhabitants of Ashton-under-Lyne (*Mr. Mellor*)	1,004
,,	8.	¶Inhabitants of Oldham (*Mr. Platt*)	157
,,	9.	Inhabitants of Coventry (*Mr. Taylor*) ...	18
,,	9.	Inhabitants of Peterborough	1,563
,,	10.	¶Inhabitants of Manchester (*Mr. Birley*) ...	552
,,	10.	¶Inhabitants of Rusholme, Lancashire (*Mr. Algernon Egerton*)	109
,,	10.	¶Inhabitants of Oldham (*Mr. Hibbert*) ...	518
,,	10.	¶Inhabitants of Stockport (*Mr. Tipping*) ...	202
,,	11.	Inhabitants of Rugby, in public meeting assembled; James Littlemore, chairman (*Mr. Davenport*)	1
,,	11.	Inhabitants of Stockport (*Mr. John Smith*) ...	92
,,	11.	Inhabitants of South Shields, in public meeting assembled; John Strachan, mayor, chairman (*Mr. Stevenson*)	1
,,	14.	Inhabitants of Teignmouth and other places (*Mr. Bowring*)	124

March 14.	¶Inhabitants of Strangeways, Manchester (*Mr. Jacob Bright*)	166
,, 14.	Inhabitants of Dinas y Mowddy, Merionethshire (*Mr. Holland*)	43
,, 14.	Inhabitants of Endon, Stoke-upon-Trent (*Mr. Melly*)	22
,, 14.	Inhabitants of Mossley (*Viscount Milton*)	177
,, 14.	Inhabitants of Blandford Forum (*Mr. Portman*)	43
,, 14.	Inhabitants of Penzance, West Cornwall (*Mr. St. Aubyn*)	73
,, 15.	Inhabitants of Bourton-on-the-Hill, county of Gloucester (*Mr. Holford*)	77
,, 15.	Inhabitants of Moreton-in-the-Marsh, county of Gloucester (*Mr. Holford*)	23
,, 15.	Inhabitants of Hawkshead (*Mr. Fred. Stanley*)	55
,, 15.	¶Inhabitants of Monk Coniston (*Mr. Frederick Stanley*)	63
,, 15.	*Inhabitants of Upper Largwith, in public meeting assembled ; Alfred T. Blythe, chairman (*Mr. Taylor*)	1
,, 15.	*Inhabitants of Stacksteads, Manchester, in public meeting assembled ; James Cox, chairman (*Mr. Taylor*)	1
,,	Inhabitants of Brighton	1,001
,, 16.	Inhabitants of Thetford (*Sir William Bagge*)	58
,, 16.	Inhabitants of Salford (*Mr. Charley*)	503
,, 16.	¶Inhabitants of Deal (*Mr. Knatchbull-Hugessen*	71
,, 16.	¶Inhabitants of King's Lynn, county of Norfolk (*Mr. Taylor*)	730
,, 16.	Inhabitants of Chester (*Mr. John Tollemache*)	53
,, 16.	¶Inhabitants of Finsbury (*Mr. W. M. Torrens*)	2,584
,, 17.	Inhabitants of Liverpool (*Mr. Rathbone*)	500
,, 17.	Inhabitants of Hackney (*Mr. Reed*)	2,419
,, 17.	Inhabitants of Merthyr Tydvil (*Mr. Christopher Talbot*)	331
,, 17.	¶Inhabitants of Leswalt, county of Wigtown	94
,, 17.	Inhabitants of Portpatrick	86
,, 17.	Inhabitants of Southwark	2,187
,, 18.	Inhabitants of St. George's Ward, Manchester (*Sir Thomas Bazley*)	504
,, 18.	Inhabitants of Westminster (*Capt. Grosvenor*)	2,123
,, 18.	Inhabitants of Birkenhead (*Mr. Laird*)	72
,, 18.	¶Inhabitants of Edinburgh (*Mr. M'Laren*)	531
,, 18.	Members of the Executive of the Holbeck Reform Association ; J. Denton, president, and others (*Mr. Miall*)	3
,, 18.	Inhabitants of Dewsbury (*Mr. Serjeant Simon*)	142
,, 18.	Inhabitants of Stranraer (*The Lord Advocate*)	859
,, 21.	Inhabitants of Newburgh, county of Fife (*Sir Robert Anstruther*)	88
,, 21.	¶John Harrison and others, 52, Stanhope-street, W.C. (*Dr. Brewer*)	202
,, 21.	¶James Ralph and others (*Dr. Brewer*)	49
,, 21.	Inhabitants of Devizes (*Sir George Jenkinson*)	399
,, 21.	Inhabitants of Perth, in public meeting assembled ; E. M. Lennie, chairman (*Mr. Kinnaird*)	1

March 21.	¶Inhabitants of Perth (*Mr. Kinnaird*)	...	437
,,	22. Inhabitants of North Wootton, county of Norfolk (*Sir William Bagge*)	...	17
,,	22. Inhabitants of New Luce, county of Wigtown (*Sir John Hay*)	...	110
,,	22. Inhabitants of Glenluce (*Sir John Hay*)	...	342
,,	22. Inhabitants of Lawrey (*Mr. Frederick Stanley*)	...	45
,,	22. ¶Inhabitants of Edinburgh	...	1,005
,,	23. ¶Inhabitants of Salford (*Mr. Charley*)	...	518
,,	24. Inhabitants of Newton Stewart, county of Wigtown (*Lord Garlies*)	...	46
,,	24. Inhabitants of Lambeth (*Sir James Lawrence*)	..	2,428
,,	24. ¶Inhabitants of New Wortley, Leeds, and district (*Mr. Wheelhouse*)	...	507
,,	25. ¶Inhabitants of Holbeck (*Mr. Carter*)	...	512
,,	25. ¶Inhabitants of Edgbaston (*Mr. Dixon*)	...	806
,,	25. ¶Inhabitants of Tunbridge Wells (*Mr. Mills*)	...	362
,,	25. ¶Inhabitants of Bristol (*Mr. Morley*)	...	1,072
,,	28. ¶Inhabitants of Weetwood, county of York (*Mr. Baines*)	...	512
,,	28. ¶Inhabitants of Northampton (*Lord Henley*)	...	1,008
,,	28. Inhabitants of Gateshead (*Mr. Hutt*)	...	24
,,	28. *Inhabitants of Aberdeen, in public meeting assembled; Alexander Bain, Professor of Logic, University of Aberdeen, chairman (*Colonel Sykes*)	...	1
,,	28. ¶Inhabitants of Shrewsbury (*Mr. Taylor*)	...	249
,,	28. ¶Inhabitants of York (*Mr. Taylor*)	...	34
,,	28. ¶Inhabitants of Wolverhampton (*Mr. Villiers*)		43
,,	29. ¶Inhabitants of Saint Michael's Ward, Manchester (*Mr. Jacob Bright*)	...	441
,,	29. Inhabitants of Collegiate Ward, Manchester (*Mr. Jacob Bright*)	...	307
,,	29. Inhabitants of Chelsea (*Sir Charles Dilke*)	...	2,106
,,	29. *Inhabitants of Dalkeith, in public meeting assembled; William Thomson, chairman (*Sir Alexander Maitland*)	...	1
,,	29. Inhabitants of Denbigh (*Mr. Watkin Williams*)	..	111
,,	29. Inhabitants of Rhyl	...	18
,,	29. Inhabitants of Saint Asaph	...	43
,,	29 Inhabitants of Rugby	...	301
,,	30. ¶Inhabitants of Edinburgh (*Mr. M'Laren*)	...	1,003
,,	30. Inhabitants of Lichfield	...	394
,,	31. Inhabitants of Evesham (*Colonel Bourne*)	...	16
,,	31. ¶Inhabitants of Medlock Street Ward, Manchester (*Mr. Jacob Bright*)	...	502
,,	31. William T. Wood and others (*Sir Charles Dilke*)		3
,,	31. Inhabitants of Coupar Angus (*Mr. Parker*)	...	143
,,	31. *Lord Provost, Magistrates, and Council of Edinburgh (*Mr. M'Laren*)	...	1
,,	31. Inhabitants of Carmarthen (*Colonel Stepney*)	...	166
April	1. ¶Inhabitants of Salford (*Mr. Cawley*)	...	129
,,	1. ¶Inhabitants of Salford (*Mr. Cawley*)	...	377
,,	1. Fanny Rogers and others (*Sir John Ramsden*)	...	16
,,	4. Inhabitants of Dysart (*Mr. Aytoun*)	...	69

April	4.	Inhabitants of Flixton, county of Lancaster (*Mr. Algernon Egerton*)	16
„	4.	¶Inhabitants of Cupar (*Mr. Ellice*)	121
„	4.	¶Inhabitants of Sheffield (*Mr. Hadfield*)	2,375
„	4.	¶Inhabitants of Portobello (*Mr. Macfie*)	633
„	4.	Inhabitants of Alnwick (*Mr. Ridley*)	35
„	4.	Inhabitants of Ludlow (*Mr. Taylor*)	17
„	4.	*Inhabitants of Kentish Town; John Pearce, chairman (*Mr. Taylor*)	1
„	4.	¶Inhabitants of Sheffield	1,517
„	5.	Inhabitants of Salford (*Mr. Charley*)	529
„	5.	Inhabitants of Tenterden, Mid Kent (*Mr. Hart Dyke*)	35
„	5.	Inhabitants of Calne (*Lord Edmond Fitzmaurice*)	39
„	5.	Inhabitants of Finsbury (*Mr. Lusk*)	1,615
„	5.	Inhabitants of Camberwell and Walworth (*Mr. M'Arthur*)	16
„	5.	Inhabitants of Lambeth (*Mr. M'Arthur*)	2,184
„	5.	Inhabitants of Blairgowrie (*Mr. Parker*)	233
„	7.	¶Inhabitants of Macclesfield (*Mr. Brocklehurst*)	107
„	7.	¶Inhabitants of Middlesex (*Viscount Enfield*)	572
„	7.	¶Inhabitants of Brighton (*Mr. White*)	1,064
„	8.	¶Inhabitants of Oxford Ward, Manchester (*Mr. Jacob Bright*)	409
„	8.	¶Inhabitants of Saint Michael's Ward, Manchester (*Mr. Jacob Bright*)	561
„	8.	Inhabitants of Renfrew, in public meeting assembled; Andrew Brown, chairman (*Mr. Secretary Bruce*)	1
„	8.	Inhabitants of Peterhead (*Mr. Grant Duff*)	193
„	8.	Inhabitants of Chatham (*Mr. Otway*)	306
„	8.	Inhabitants of Dublin (*Mr. Pim*)	1,013
„	8.	¶Inhabitants of Glasgow	1,734
„	8.	¶Inhabitants of Windsor	1,855
„	11.	¶Inhabitants of Forfar (*Mr. Baxter*)	243
„	11.	Inhabitants of Knaresborough (*Mr. Illingworth*)	299
„	11.	Inhabitants of Marylebone (*Mr. Harvey Lewis*)	2,025
„	11.	*Inhabitants of Galashiels, in public meeting assembled; Thomas Clapperton Bailie, chairman (*Mr. Trevelyan*)	1
„	12.	¶Inhabitants of Loughborough (*Dr. Brewer*)	78
„	12.	¶Inhabitants of Dublin (*Mr. Pim*)	2
„	12.	Inhabitants of Monkstown (*Mr. Pim*)	23
„	12.	¶Inhabitants of Bray (*Mr. Pim*)	21
„	12.	¶Inhabitants of Tipperary (*Mr. Pim*)	20
„	12.	¶Inhabitants of Cavan (*Mr. Pim*)	13
„	12.	Inhabitants of Bantry (*Mr. Pim*)	20
„	12.	¶Inhabitants of Wexford (*Mr. Pim*)	14
„	12.	¶Inhabitants of Down (*Mr. Pim*)	20
„	12.	¶Inhabitants of Hackney (*Mr. Taylor*)	3,248
„	25.	¶Inhabitants of Kirkcaldy (*Mr. Aytoun*)	176
„	25.	¶Inhabitants of Montrose (*Mr. Baxter*)	336
„	25.	*Inhabitants of Greenwich, in public meeting assembled; J. Stuart Mill, chairman (*Mr. William Ewart Gladstone*)	1
„	25.	¶Inhabitants of London (*Mr. Goschen*)	1,015

April 25. Inhabitants of Tetsworth, county of Oxford (*Mr. Henley*) ... 266
„ 25. ¶Inhabitants of Birmingham (*Mr. Muntz*)... 650
„ 25. ¶Inhabitants of Lincoln (*Mr. Seely*) ... 558
„ 25. Inhabitants of Saint Columb, county of Cornwall (*Sir John Trelawny*) ... 16
„ 25. Inhabitants of Brimscombe (*Mr. Winterbotham*)... 44
„ 25. Inhabitants of Helston, county of Cornwall (*Mr. Adolphus Young*) ... 24
„ 26. ¶Inhabitants of Chesterfield (*Mr. Michael Bass*) ... 263
„ 26. ¶Inhabitants of Renfrew (*Mr. Pleydell Bouverie*)... 152
„ 26. Inhabitants of Renfrew (*Mr. Pleydell Bouverie*) ... 2
„ 26. ¶Inhabitants of Stroud (*Mr. Dickinson*) ... 73
„ 26. Inhabitants of Edgware and Little Stanmore, county of Middlesex (*Viscount Enfield*) ... 60
„ 26. Inhabitants of Great Stanmore, county of Middlesex (*Viscount Enfield*) ... 5
„ 26. Inhabitants of Gosport (*Mr. Taylor*) ... 12
„ 26. ¶Inhabitants of Huntingdon (*Mr. Taylor*)... 16
„ 26. ¶Inhabitants of Dumfries (*Major Walker*)... 407
„ 27. Inhabitants of Marlborough (*Lord Ernest Bruce*).. 139
„ 27. ¶Inhabitants of South Queensferry (*Mr. Campbell*) 156
„ 27. ¶Inhabitants of Bath (*Mr. Donald Dalrymple*) ... 723
„ 27. ¶Inhabitants of Bath (*Mr. Donald Dalrymple*) ... 163
„ 27. ¶Inhabitants of Altrincham and Bowdon (*Mr. Wilbraham Egerton*) ... 235
„ 27. Inhabitants of Knutsford (*Mr. Wilbraham Egerton*) 100
„ 27. ¶Inhabitants of Finsbury (*Mr. Lusk*) ... 1,598
„ 27. ¶Inhabitants of Folkestone (*Mr. Taylor*) ... 39
„ 27. Inhabitants of Carperby, Bedale (*Mr. Taylor*) ... 74
„ 27. *Inhabitants of Selkirk, in public meeting assembled; J. Johnston, chairman (*Mr. Trevelyan*) 1
„ 28. ¶Inhabitants of Arbroath (*Mr. Baxter*) ... 263
„ 28. ¶Inhabitants of Newcastle-upon-Tyne (*Mr. Cowen*) 532
„ 28. Inhabitants of Retford (*Mr. Foljambe*) ... 203
„ 28. Inhabitants of Bedford (*Mr. James Howard*) ... 121
„ 28. Inhabitants of New Malton (*Mr. Thomas Hughes*) 242
„ 28. Inhabitants of Northallerton (*Mr. Hutton*) ... 194
„ 28. Inhabitants of Worcester (*Mr. Laslett*) ... 554
„ 28. Inhabitants of Exeter (*Sir Massey Lopes*) ... 59
„ 28. ¶Inhabitants of Plymouth (*Mr. Morrison*) ... 102
„ 28. Inhabitants of Westbury (*Mr. Phipps*) ... 30
„ 28. Inhabitants of Portsmouth (*Mr. Stone*) ... 108
„ 28. Inhabitants of Aberdeen (*Colonel Sykes*)... 258
„ 28. Inhabitants of Middlesborough ... 806
„ 28. Inhabitants of Glasgow ... 2,337
„ 29. ¶Inhabitants of Saint John's Ward, Manchester (*Mr. Jacob Bright*) ... 232
„ 29. ¶Inhabitants of Ingatestone, county of Essex (*Dr. Brewer*) ... 160
„ 29. ¶Inhabitants of Yapton (*Dr. Brewer*) ... 149
„ 29. *Inhabitants of Stirling, in public meeting assembled; David Yellowlees, chairman (*Mr. Campbell*)... 1
„ 29. ¶Inhabitants of Stirling (*Mr. Campbell*) ... 240

April 29.	*Inhabitants of Paisley, in public meeting assembled; David Murray, chairman (*Mr. Crum-Ewing*)	1
„ 29.	¶Inhabitants of Paisley (*Mr. Crum-Ewing*)	276
„ 29.	¶Inhabitants of Huddersfield (*Mr. Leatham*)	325
„ 29.	*Inhabitants of Coupar Angus; William Marshall, chairman (*Mr. Parker*)	1
„ 29.	¶Inhabitants of Westminster (*Mr. Taylor*)	1,529
May 2.	*Inhabitants of Dundee, in public meeting assembled; D. Cork, chairman (*Mr. Armistead*)	1
„ 2.	Inhabitants of Derby (*Mr. Michael Bass*)	34
„ 2.	Inhabitants of Waterford (*Mr. Delahunty*)	40
„ 2.	¶H. Evelyn and others (*Sir Charles Dilke*)	2,865
„ 2.	¶Inhabitants of Hartlepool (*Mr. Dimsdale*)	454
„ 2.	Inhabitants of Bridge of Allan (*Admiral Erskine*)	116
„ 2.	Inhabitants of Dumfries (*Mr. Jardine*)	419
„ 2.	Inhabitants of Marylebone (*Mr. Harvey Lewis*)	1,220
„ 2.	¶Inhabitants of Rathmines and neighbourhood (*Mr. Pim*)	140
„ 2.	Inhabitants of Kingstown (*Mr. Pim*)	20
„ 2.	¶Inhabitants of South Shields (*Mr. Stevenson*)	463
„ 2.	Women householders of Aberdeen; 27 petitions (*Colonel Sykes*)	27
„ 2.	¶Inhabitants of Aberdeen (*Colonel Sykes*)	63
„ 2.	Inhabitants of Chelsea	2,565
„ 3.	Inhabitants of Exeter (*Mr. Bowring*)	56
„ 3.	Reverend W. Sharp, Altham Vicarage, and others (*Mr. Jacob Bright*)	32
„ 3.	¶Inhabitants of Chorlton-upon-Medlock (*Mr. Jacob Bright*)	100
„ 3.	¶Inhabitants of Manchester (*Mr. Jacob Bright*)	145
„ 3.	Inhabitants of Gainsborough (*Sir Montague Cholmeley*)	212
„ 3.	Inhabitants of Kintore (*Mr. Grant Duff*)	79
„ 3.	Inhabitants of Nantwich (*Sir Philip Grey Egerton*)	16
„ 3.	Anne Barrington, Beddale, Parnelscroft, Congleton (*Mr. Wilbraham Egerton*)	1
„ 3.	Elizabeth Clarke Wolstenholme, Moody Hall, Congleton (*Mr. Wilbraham Egerton*)	1
„ 3.	Inhabitants of Anstruther (*Mr. Ellice*)	95
„ 3.	Inhabitants of Banbury (*Mr. Henley*)	33
„ 3.	Sarah Mitford and others (*Mr. Gore Langton*)	86
„ 3.	Inhabitants of Grimsby (*Sir Wilfrid Lawson*)	75
„ 3.	Inhabitants of Petersfield (*Sir Wilfrid Lawson*)	91
„ 3.	Isabella Garland, Aberdeen (*Mr. M'Combie*)	1
„ 3.	*Inhabitants of Inverness in public meeting assembled; J. Mackenzie, M.D., provost and chairman (*Mr. Mackintosh*)	1
„ 3.	Mary Thomas, 13, Buckingham Vale, Clifton, Bristol (*Mr. Morley*)	1
„ 3.	Louisa Leonard (*Mr. Morley*)	1
„ 3.	¶Inhabitants of Guildford (*Mr. Onslow*)	39
„ 3.	Inhabitants of Alyth, county of Perth (*Mr. Parker*)	8
„ 4.	¶Inhabitants of Manchester (*Mr. Birley*)	1,512
„ 4.	¶Inhabitants of Dublin (*Mr. Bowring*)	211
„ 4.	Inhabitants of Magherafelt (*Mr. Bowring*)	24

May	4. *Inhabitants of Dublin, in public meeting assembled; Robert Kane, Knight, F.R.S. (*Mr. Bowring*)...	1
„	4. Sarah Mary Maguire, 51, Westland Row, Dublin (*Mr. Bowring*)	1
„	4. Elizabeth Clare, 43, Caffee-street, Dublin (*Mr. Bowring*)	1
„	4. Caroline Cadosch, 28, Lincoln Place, Dublin (*Mr. Bowring*)	1
„	4. ¶Inhabitants of Hastings (*Mr. Thomas Brassy*) ...	60
„	4. Inhabitants of Heaton Chapel, and others, Levenshulme (*Mr. Jacob Bright*)	67
„	4. Inhabitants of Barnstaple (*Mr. Jacob Bright*) ...	47
„	4. Inhabitants of Framlingham (*Mr. Jacob Bright*) ...	89
„	4. Inhabitants of Manchester (*Mr. Jacob Bright*) ...	468
„	4. Inhabitants of Worsley (*Mr. Jacob Bright*) ...	35
„	4. Inhabitants of Sale and Timperley (*Mr. Jacob Bright*)...	189
„	4. Inhabitants of Middleton and Tonge, county of Lancaster (*Mr. Jacob Bright*)...	77
„	4. Inhabitants of Darlington (*Mr. Jacob Bright*) ...	6
„	4. Mary Clodd, Framlingham, county of Suffolk (*Mr. Jacob Bright*)	1
„	4. Inhabitants of Weymouth (*Mr. Jacob Bright*) ...	70
„	4. ¶Inhabitants of Wilmslow (*Mr. Brooks*)	103
„	4. ¶Inhabitants of Leeds (*Mr. Alderman Carter*) ...	717
„	4. Members of the Holbeck Liberal Registration Committee, Leeds (*Mr. Carter*)	39
„	4. Inhabitants of Leeds (*Mr. Carter*)	196
„	4. Inhabitants of Ilkley (*Mr. Carter*)	83
„	4. Members of the Women's Club and Institute, 77, Newman-street, London (*Mr. Thos. Chambers*)	71
„	4. ¶Inhabitants of Salford (*Mr. Charley*)	1,042
„	4. ¶Inhabitants of Glasgow (*Mr. Dalglish*)	3,497
„	4. Inhabitants of Tiverton (*Mr. Denman*)	116
„	4. ¶Inhabitants of Edgbaston (*Mr. Dixon*)	782
„	4. ¶Inhabitants of Stretford (*Mr. Algernon Egerton*) ..	164
„	4. ¶Inhabitants of Hull (*Mr. Fawcett*)	86
„	4. Inhabitants of Haywards Heath (*Mr. Fawcett*) ...	55
„	4. Inhabitants of Norwich (*Mr. Fawcett*)	104
„	4. Inhabitants of Monaghan and other places (*Mr. Ion Trant Hamilton*)	22
„	4. Inhabitants of Glasthule (*Mr. Ion Trant Hamilton*)	30
„	4. Inhabitants of Dalkey (*Mr. Ion Trant Hamilton*) ...	2
„	4. Inhabitants of Sandycove, county of Dublin (*Mr. Ion Trant Hamilton*)	25
„	4. Inhabitants of Kingstown, county of Dublin (*Mr. Ion Trant Hamilton*)	60
„	4. Inhabitants of Dalkey, county of Dublin (*Mr. Ion Trant Hamilton*)...	25
„	4. Inhabitants of Dundrum, county of Dublin (*Mr. Ion Trant Hamilton*)	20
„	4. Elizabeth Debitt, Leslie Avenue, Dalkey, county of Dublin (*Mr. Ion Trant Hamilton*)	1
„	4. Eliza Langan, 11, Sussex-street, Kingstown, county of Dublin (*Mr. Ion Trant Hamilton*) ...	1

May 4.	Mary Weston, Cross Avenue, Blackrock, county of Dublin (*Mr. Ion Trant Hamilton*) ...	1
„ 4.	¶Inhabitants of Newark (*Mr. Hodgkinson*)	140
„ 4.	Inhabitants of Thirsk (*Mr. Illingworth*) ...	194
„ 4.	¶Inhabitants of Salisbury (*Dr. Lush*) ...	128
„ 4.	¶Inhabitants of Nairn (*Mr. Mackintosh*)...	30
„ 4.	¶Inhabitants of Edinburgh (*Mr. M'Laren*)	3,168
„ 4.	Inhabitants of Leith (*Mr. M'Laren*)	40
„ 4.	Inhabitants of Stirling (*Mr. M'Laren*) ...	24
„ 4.	Inhabitants of Helensburgh (*Mr. M'Laren*)	20
„ 4.	¶Inhabitants of Perthshire (*Mr. M'Laren*)	64
„ 4.	Mary Burton, Silverton Bank, Silverton (*Sir Alex. Maitland*) ...	1
„ 4.	Inhabitants of Stapleton (*Mr. Morley*) ...	27
„ 4.	Catherine Norris, Clifton Park House, Clifton, Bristol (*Mr. Morley*) ...	1
„ 4.	Inhabitants of Glastonbury (*Mr. Neville-Grenville*)	43
„ 4.	Inhabitants of Wells, county of Somerset (*Mr. Neville-Grenville*) ...	20
„ 4.	Inhabitants of Street (*Mr. Neville-Grenville*)	148
„ 4.	Inhabitants of Kelso (*Mr. Robertson*) ...	428
„ 4.	Elizabeth Cobb, Congleton (*Mr. Hastings Russell*)...	1
„ 4.	Inhabitants of Canterbury (*Mr. Taylor*) ...	94
„ 4.	¶Inhabitants of Hertford (*Mr. Taylor*) ...	185
„ 4.	Inhabitants of Weymouth (*Mr. Taylor*) ...	3
„ 4.	¶Inhabitants of Sunderland (*Mr. Taylor*)	31
„ 4.	Inhabitants of Liverpool (*Mr. Turner*) ...	498
„ 5.	¶Inhabitants of Brechin (*Mr. Baxter*) ...	172
„ 5.	¶Inhabitants of Manchester (*Sir Thomas Bazley*)...	1,500
„ 5.	*Mayor, Aldermen, and Citizens of Manchester (*Sir Thomas Bazley*) ...	Seal.
„ 5.	*Inhabitants of Barrhead, in public meeting assembled; John Heys, chairman (*Mr. Sec. Bruce*)..	1
„ 5.	Inhabitants of Sheffield (*Mr. Cawley*) ...	1,194
„ 5.	¶Members and Friends of the Edinburgh Branch of the National Secular Society (*Mr. Miller*)...	16
„ 5.	¶Inhabitants of Bristol and neighbourhood (*Mr. Morley*)...	335
„ 5.	Inhabitants of Congleton (*Mr. Winterbotham*)	182
„ 9.	¶Inhabitants of Dundee (*Mr. Armitstead*)	458
„ 9.	Inhabitants of Garstang (*Colonel Wilson Patten*)	11
„ 9.	¶Inhabitants of Tavistock (*Mr. Arthur Russell*)	80
„ 10.	¶Inhabitants of Gloucester (*Mr. William Philip Price*)...	126
„ 10.	¶Inhabitants of London (*Mr. Taylor*) ...	112
„ 6.	Mary Ann Estlin, Hereford House, Durdham Down, Bristol (*Mr. Morley*) ...	1
„ 11.	Inhabitants of Melrose (*Marquis of Bowmont*)	5
„ 11.	¶Inhabitants of London (*Mr. Goschen*) ...	943
„ 11.	¶Inhabitants of Dundee (*Mr. M'Laren*) ...	147
„ 11.	Women householders of Edinburgh; 4 petitions (*Mr. M'Laren*) ...	5
„ 11.	Inhabitants of Seaforth and Waterloo, county of Lancaster (*Mr. Turner*) ...	166
„ 12.	Alexina C. Eker, county of Fife (*Sir Robert Anstruther*) ...	1

May 12. *Members of the Kilmarnock Reform League;
Andrew Ingle, chairman (*Mr. Pleydell Bouverie*) ... 1
,, 12. Catherine Love (*Mr. Pleydell Bouverie*) 1
,, 12. *Inhabitants of Kilmarnock in public meeting assembled ; Alexander Webster, chairman (*Mr. Pleydell Bouverie*) 1
,, 12. Janet Campbell (*Mr. Pleydell Bouverie*) 1
,, 12. Eliza Flint, Watford (*Mr. Henry Robert Brand*) ... 1
,, 12. Mary Ann Holbrook, Lower Vale, Hendon, county of Middlesex (*Viscount Enfield*) 1
,, 12. Jane E. Taylour (*Lord Garlies*)... 1
,, 12. Rose Ann Hall, Burton-on-the-Hill, county of Gloucester (*Mr. Holford*) 1
,, 12. Women householders of Edinburgh ; 14 petitions (*Mr. M'Laren*) 15
,, 12. Women householders of Edinburgh ; 12 petitions (*Mr. Miller*) 12
,, 12. Matilda Adriana Chaplin, 35, Blandford Square, London (*Mr. Taylor*) 1
,, 12. Joseph Allen and others (*Mr. Taylor*) 157
,, 12. Marion P. Aird, of Kilmarnock (*Sir D. Wedderburn*) 1
,, 13. Inhabitants of Rutherglen (*Mr. Pleydell Bouverie*)... 431
,, 13. ¶Inhabitants of Salford (*Mr. Charley*) 470
,, 13. Inhabitants of Saint Ives (*Mr. Maguire*)... ... 18
,, 13. Inhabitants of Newcastleton (*Mr. M'Laren*) ... 85
,, 16. Emma Mary Nicoll, Copt Hall, Hendon, county of Middlesex (*Viscount Enfield*) 1
,, 17. Inhabitants of Southampton (*Mr. Fawcett*) ... 66
,, 18. H. Sidgwick, Cambridge, and others (*Mr. Jacob Bright*) 7
,, 18. ¶Inhabitants of Manchester (*Mr. Jacob Bright*) ... 701
,, 18. ¶Inhabitants of Manchester (*Mr. Jacob Bright*) ... 327
,, 19. ¶Inhabitants of Teignmouth (*Mr. Thomas Cave*) ... 105
,, 20. Inhabitants of Cork (*Mr. Pim*) 30

Total number of Petitions 435— Signatures 130,463

SUMMARY.

	No. of Petitions signed officially or under seal.	Total No of Petitions.	No. of Signatures.
For Extension of the Elective Franchise to Women [2, 99]	8	180	3,200
Women's Disabilities Bill—In favour [61, 85]	31	435	130,463
	39	615	133,663

MARRIED WOMEN'S PROPERTY BILL.

On May the 18th, Mr. Russell Gurney proposed the second reading of his Bill (No. 1).

He carefully explained how unsuited settlements were to the case of small properties, and of married women earning wages. He said that in Rochdale a large co-operative society existed in which there were 7000 members, including a number of married women, who held shares in their own name. Frequently the husbands endeavoured to get the amount secured by those shares, but the Committee, which consisted altogether of working men, always resisted this course, and threw such obstacles in the way that in no one case had the law been resorted to. (Hear, hear.) Public feeling would, therefore, go along with the proposed legislation.

Mr. Raikes said, he would not oppose the second reading of the Bill, but proposed that his own Bill should also be read a second time so that both plans might be considered together in committee. He said that the motives of those who supported his right hon. and learned friend were to get a recognition of the equality of the sexes. The House was asked to distrust the identity of interest between a man and his wife. The law they were asked to pass was humiliating to Englishmen, and detrimental to the best interests of Englishwomen.

Mr. Jessel supported Mr. Russell Gurney's Bill. Mr. Charley preferred Mr. Raikes's Bill. Mr. S. Hill did the same. Mr. Hermon preferred Mr. Gurney's.

Mr. Mundella hoped the House would support Mr. Gurney's Bill. The Solicitor-General congratulated his right hon. friend on the great advance which the subject had made. He, for his part, regarded the question not as a poor woman's question, or a woman's question, but as a simple matter of justice, because the law of England as it now stood allowed A to take B's property without B's consent. Such a state of things was contrary to equity, and should not be permitted to continue. Upon the very broadest grounds he hoped they would direct that the measure should be read a second time, for in his opinion no reasons had been given why they should hesitate to do so.

The Bill was then read a second time, amidst cheers.

MARRIED WOMEN'S PROPERTY (No. 2) BILL.

Mr. C. Raikes moved the second reading of this Bill, and hoped that the House would accept the motion.

Mr. Jacob Bright moved that the measure should be read a second time that day six months.

For the second reading	46
Against	208
Majority	162

The Bill was accordingly lost.

Mr. Russell Gurney's Bill passed through Committee a few days' later, and was afterwards read a third time. It will be introduced into the House of Lords very shortly, probably before this *Review* is published.*

A great number of petitions have already been presented to the Lords in favour of the Bill.

The following members (forty-eight, including tellers) voted in favour of the second reading of Mr. Raikes's Married Women's Property Bill:—

Arkwright, Richard
Bentinck, George C.
Burrell, Sir Percy
Charley, William T.
Clive, Col. Hon. G. W.
Crichton, Viscount
Cross, Richard A.
Cubitt, George
Dimsdale, Robert
Du Pre, C. George
Eaton, Henry William
Egerton, Sir Phil. Grey
Egerton, Hon. William
Feilden, Hen. Master
Fielden, Joshua
Fowler, Robert N.
Gore, J. Ralph Ormsby
Gore, Wm. Richard Ormsby
Graves, Samuel Robert
Greene, Edward
Hamilton, Ion Trant
Henry, John Snowdon
Hick, John
Hodgson, W. Nicholson
Holford, Robert Stayner
Holmesdale, Viscount
Hope, Alexander J. B. B.
Laird, John
Lowther, William
Mackintosh, Eneas William
M'Lagan, Peter
Morgan, C. Octavius
Morgan, Hon. Major
Read, Clare Sewell
Scourfield, John Henry
Selwin-Ibbetson, Sir H. J.
Smith, Rowland
Smith, William Henry
Starkie, John Pierce C.
Sykes, Christopher
Talbot, Chris. R. M.
Talbot, John Gilbert
Taylor, Right Hon. Colonel
Walpole, Hon. Frederic
Whalley, G. Hammond
Winn, Rowland

TELLERS.

Mr. Raikes
Mr. Staveley Hill

The following (210, including tellers) voted against the Bill:—

Adam, William P.
Adderley, Right Hon. Sir C.
Amphlett, Richard P.
Armitstead, George
Aytoun, Roger Sinclair
Backhouse, Edmund
Bailey, Sir Joseph R.
Baines, Edward
Barclay, Alexander C.
Barttelot, Colonel
Bass, Arthur
Bazley, Sir Thomas
Beach, W. W. Bramston
Beaumont, W. B.
Beaumont, Captain F.
Bonham-Carter, John
Bouverie, Right Hon. E. P.
Bowring, Edgar A.
Brady, John
Brewer, Dr.
Brinckman, Captain
Brocklehurst, William C.

---

* See Postscript.

Brodrick, Hon. William
Brogden, Alexander
Brown, Alexander H.
Bruce, Right Hon. H. A.
Butler-Johnstone, H. A.
Cadogan, Hon. Frederick W.
Cameron, Donald
Candlish, John
Carter, Mr. Alderman
Cavendish, Lord F. C.
Cavendish, Lord G.
Chadwick, David
Chambers, Thomas
Chaplin, Henry
Clive, Colonel Edward
Cole, Colonel Hon. Henry
Colebrooke, Sir T. E.
Coleridge, Sir John D.
Cowen, Joseph
Craufurd, Edward H.
Crawford, Robert W.
Dalrymple, Donald
Dalrymple, Charles
Davenport, William B.
Davie, Sir H. R. F.
Davison, John Robert
Denman, Hon. George
Dickinson, Sebastian S.
Dixon, George
Digby, Kenelm Thomas
Dilke, Sir Charles W.
Dodds, Joseph
Duff, Mount E. Grant
Eastwick, Edward B.
Egerton, Captain Hon. F.
Enfield, Viscount
Esmonde, Sir John
Ewing, H. Ewing Crum
Ewing, Archibald Orr
Eykyn, Roger
Fawcett, Henry
Fellowes, Edward
Figgins, James
Finnie, William
Fitzwilliam, Hon C. W. W.
Fletcher, Isaac
Foljambe, Francis J. S.
Forde, Colonel
Forster, Right Hon. William E.
Fortescue, Hon. D. F.
Fowler, William

Galway, Viscount
Gilpin Charles
Glyn, Hon. George G.
Goldsmid, Sir F. H.
Gourley, Edward T.
Grant, Colonel Hon. J.
Grieve, James Johnstone
Gregory, William H.
Grosvenor, Hon. Norman
Grosvenor, Captain R. W.
Hadfield, George
Hamilton, Lord George
Harcourt, W. G. G. V. V.
Hardcastle, Joseph A.
Hardy, John S.
Hartington, Marquis of
Headlam, Right Hon. T. E.
Henley, Right Hon. J. W.
Henley, Lord
Herbert, Hon. A. E. W.
Hermon, Edward
Hibbert, J. Tomlinson
Hodgkinson, Grosvenor
Holms, John
Hoskyns, Chandos Wren
Howard, Hon. C. W. G.
Hutt, Right Hon. Sir W.
Ingram, Hugo F. M.
James, Henry
Jessel, George
Johnston, Andrew
Jones, John
Kavanagh, A. MacM.
Kay-Shuttleworth, U. J.
Kennaway, John Henry
Kirk, William
Knightley, Sir Reginald
Lacon, Sir Edmund H. K.
Lancaster, John
Lawrence, William
Lawson, Sir Wilfrid
Leatham, Edward Aldam
Lefevre, G. J. Shaw
Lewis, John D.
Lewis, John Harvey
Liddell, Hon. H. G.
Lindsay, Colonel R. L.
Loch, George
Lowe, Right Hon. R.
Lusk, Andrew
Lyttelton, Hon. C. G.

M'Arthur, William
M'Clure, Thomas
M'Combie, William
M'Laren, Duncan
Marling, Samuel S.
Martin, Philip W.
Mellor, Thomas W.
Melly, George
Meyrick, Thomas
Miall, Edward
Miller, John
Milton, Viscount
Monk, Charles J.
Montgomery, Sir G. G.
Morley, Samuel
Morrison, Walter
Mundella, Anthony J.
Muntz, Philip Henry
O'Conor, Denis M.
Ogilvy, Sir John
O'Neill, Hon. Edward
O'Reilly, Myles William
Parker, Charles Stuart
Pim, Jonathan
Platt, John
Playfair, Lyon
Portman, Hon. W. H. B.
Potter, Edmund
Potter, Thomas Bayley
Powell, Walter
Price, William P.
Rathbone, William
Reed, Charles
Ridley, Matthew White
Robertson, David
Roden, William S.
Russell, Arthur
Russell, Hastings
Rylands, Peter
St. Aubyn, John
Samuda, Joseph D'A.
Samuelson, Bernhard
Saunderson, Edward
Seely, Charles

Seely, Charles
Seymour, Alfred
Shaw, Richard
Sherriff, Alexander C.
Simon, Mr. Serjeant
Smith, Frederick C.
Smith, John Benjamin
Smith, Eustace
Smith, Samuel George
Stacpoole, William
Stansfeld, Right Hon. J.
Stapleton, John
Stepney, Colonel
Strutt, Hon. Henry
Stuart, Colonel
Sykes, Colonel William Henry
Taylor, Peter Alfred
Tollemache, Hon. Frederick
Trelawny, Sir John
Trevelyan, George Otto
Trevor, Lord A. E. Hill
Turnor, Edmund
Villiers, Right Hon. C. P.
Vivian, Henry Hussey
Walker, Major George G.
Waters, George
Wedderburn, Sir David
Weguelin, Thomas M.
Welby, William E.
Wethered, Thomas O.
Whitbread, Samuel
Whitwell, John
Whitworth, Thomas
Williams, Charles H.
Williams, Watkin
Wingfield, Sir Charles
Woods, Henry
Wyndham, Hon. Percy
Wynn, Charles W. W.
Young, Adolphus W.

TELLERS.

Mr. Jacob Bright.
Mr. Russell Gurney.

The following petitions have been presented on the Married Women's Property Bill:

MARRIED WOMEN'S PROPERTY BILL

(Mr. Russell Gurney's)—*In Favour.*

Feb.	17.	Inhabitants of Flixton (*Mr. Algernon Egerton*)...	30
,,	18.	Inhabitants of Bradford (*Mr. Miall*)	94
,,	18.	Inhabitants of Rochdale (*Mr. Thomas Potter*)...	495
,,	21.	Inhabitants of Hendon, Middlesex (*Viscount Enfield*)	110
,,	21.	Inhabitants of Harrow Middlesex (*Viscount Enfield*)	130
,,	21.	Margaret Mills and others (*Mr. Russell Gurney*).	200
,,	21.	Arthur Hobhouse and others	104
,,	22.	Inhabitants of Glenridding (*Mr. Wm. Lowther*)	65
,,	22.	David Robertson and others (*Mr. Wells*) ...	60
,,	24.	Inhabitants of Nottingham (*Mr. Seely*) ...	102
,,	25.	Inhabitants of Prestwich, Lancashire (*Mr. Algernon Egerton*)	89
,,	28.	Inhabitants of Corston, Newton St. Loe, and other places near Bristol (*Major Allen*) ...	62
,,	28.	Inhabitants of Hawkshead (*Colonel Wilson Patten*)	77
March	1.	Inhabitants of Stockport, Manchester, and other places (*Mr. Jacob Bright*)	223
,,	1.	Inhabitants of Manchester (*Mr. Jacob Bright*)...	230
,,	1.	Inhabitants of Church Coniston (*Colonel Wilson Patten*)	102
,,	2.	Inhabitants of All Saints' Ward, Manchester (*Mr. Birley*)	506
,,	7.	Men of Rawtenstall, county of Lancaster (*Mr. Holt*)	142
,,	7.	Inhabitants of Budleigh Salterton (*Mr. Kekewich*)	38
,,	7.	¶Camberwell and other places (*Sir James Lawrence*)	85
,,	7.	¶Lancaster (*Mr. Frederick Stanley*)	76
,,	7.	¶Women of Rawtenstall, county of Lancaster (*Mr. Starkie*)	201
,,	8.	¶Inhabitants of Peterborough (*Mr. Whalley*)	92
,,	9.	¶Inhabitants of Manchester (*Mr. Jacob Bright*).	153
,,	10.	¶Inhabitants of Wootton, Norfolk (*Sir William Bagge*)	41
,,	10.	¶Inhabitants of Waterford	110
,,	14.	¶John Jones Brine and others (*Mr. Bowring*) ...	103
,,	14.	¶Inhabitants of Weston-Super-Mare, Somerset (*Mr. Richard Bright*)	37
,,	14.	¶Inhabitants of Bolton, Lancashire (*Col. Gray*).	561
,,	14.	Inhabitants of Spetisbury, in the county of Dorset (*Mr. Portman*)	77
,,	14.	Inhabitants of Blandford Forum, in the county of Dorset (*Mr. Portman*)...	111
,,	14.	Inhabitants of Charlton Marshall, in the county of Dorset	84

March 15.	Inhabitants of Bath (*Mr. Donald Dalrymple*) ...	401
„ 15.	Mary Hornby and others (*Mr. Frederick Stanley*).	100
„ 16.	¶Inhabitants of Liverpool (*Mr. Dyke*)... ...	265
„ 17.	¶Inhabitants of Manchester (*Mr. Birley*) ...	507
„ 17.	¶Inhabitants of Manchester (*Mr. Jacob Bright*).	1,150
„ 17.	Inhabitants of Watford, Herts (*Mr. Gurney*) ...	39
„ 17.	Inhabitants of Chipperfield (*Mr. Gurney*) ...	23
„ 18.	*Members of the Holbeck Reform Association; Joseph Denton, president, and others ...	3
„ 21.	Inhabitants of Great Stanmore, county of Middlesex (*Mr. Gurney*)	6
„ 21.	Inhabitants of Hendon, county of Middlesex (*Mr. Gurney*)	151
„ 21.	Inhabitants of Pontesbury, county of Salop (*Mr. Gurney*)	25
„ 21.	Women residing in Boston Spa (*Mr. Gurney*) ...	57
„ 21.	Inhabitants of Margate, county of Kent (*Mr. Jessel*)	116
„ 21.	¶Inhabitants of Dover, county of Kent (*Mr. Jessel*)...	82
„ 21.	Inhabitants of Street (*Mr. Neville-Grenville*) ...	263
„ 21.	Inhabitants of Tavistock, county of Devon ...	147
„ 22.	Inhabitants of Ambleside (*Earl of Bective*) ...	58
„ 22.	¶Inhabitants of Haward's Heath (*Mr. Fawcett*)	77
„ 22.	Inhabitants of Liverpool (*Mr. Graves*) ...	208
„ 22.	Inhabitants of Youghal (*Mr. Montague Guest*) ...	16
„ 22.	Inhabitants of Bradford-on-Avon (*Sir George Jenkinson*)	56
„ 22.	Inhabitants of Ballymena (*Mr. M'Clure*) ...	439
„ 22.	Inhabitants of Newport, county of Monmouth (*Mr Octavius Morgan*)	15
„ 22.	¶Inhabitants of Rathmines (*Mr. Pim*) ...	176
„ 22.	Inhabitants of Kingstown (*Mr. Pim*)	27
„ 22.	Inhabitants of Leskinfere (*Mr. Pim*)	7
„ 22.	Inhabitants of Hawkeshead (*Mr. Frederick Stanley*)	55
„ 22.	Inhabitants of Bootle, county of Cumberland (*Mr. Frederick Stanley*)	56
„ 22.	John Topping and others (*Mr. Frederick Stanley*)	56
„ 22.	Inhabitants of Leamington (*Mr. Wise*) ...	489
„ 23.	¶Inhabitants of Headingley (*Mr. Baines*) ...	1,056
„ 23.	Inhabitants of Leeds (*Mr. Baines*)	1,058
„ 23.	Inhabitants of Winscombe, county of Somerset (*Mr. Jacob Bright*)	68
„ 23.	Inhabitants of Glastonbury (*Mr. Jacob Bright*)...	100
„ 23.	¶Inhabitants of Manchester (*Mr. Jacob Bright*).	15
„ 23.	Inhabitants of Manchester (*Mr. Jacob Bright*)...	1,080
„ 23.	Inhabitants of Manchester (*Mr. Jacob Bright*)...	715
„ 23.	Inhabitants of Cambridge (*Mr. Jacob Bright*) ...	22
„ 23.	Inhabitants of Broughton (*Mr. Jacob Bright*) ...	31
„ 23.	Inhabitants of Winscombe (*Mr. Jacob Bright*)...	63
„ 23.	Inhabitants of Glastonbury (*Mr. Jacob Bright*)...	93
„ 23.	Inhabitants of Cambridge (*Mr. Jacob Bright*) ...	16
„ 23.	Inhabitants of Alderley Edge (*Mr. Jacob Bright*)	164
„ 23.	Inhabitants of Manchester (*Mr. Jacob Bright*)...	13
„ 23.	Inhabitants of Cheddar (*Mr. Jacob Bright*) ...	75

March 23.	Inhabitants of Freshford, county of Somerset (*Mr. Richard Bright*)	20
,, 23.	Inhabitants of Cheddar, county of Somerset (*Mr. Richard Bright*)	15
,, 23.	¶Inhabitants of Bath (*Mr. Donald Dalrymple*)...	462
,, 23.	Inhabitants of Bath (*Mr. Donald Dalrymple*) ...	500
,, 23.	¶Inhabitants of Islington (*Mr. Gurney*) ...	519
,, 23.	Inhabitants of Worsley (*Mr. Gurney*) ...	47
,, 23.	Inhabitants of Tunbridge (*Mr. Gurney*) ...	85
,, 23.	Harriet Martineau, The Knoll, Ambleside (*Mr. Gurney*)	1
,, 23.	Inhabitants of Bushey Heath (*Mr. Gurney*) ...	29
,, 23.	Inhabitants of Royston (*Mr. Gurney*)... ...	50
,, 23.	Inhabitants of Tiverton (*Mr. Gurney*) ...	93
,, 23.	Inhabitants of Wandsworth (*Mr. Gurney*) ...	25
,, 23.	Inhabitants of Middleton, county of Lancaster (*Mr. Gurney*)	121
,, 23.	Inhabitants of Framlingham, county of Suffolk *Mr. Gurney*	56
,, 23.	¶Inhabitants of Tiverton (*Mr. Gurney*) ...	81
,, 23.	Inhabitants of Tunbridge (*Mr. Gurney*) ...	62
,, 23.	Inhabitants of Royston (*Mr. Gurney*)... ...	81
,, 23.	Inhabitants of Harrow (*Mr. Gurney*)	86
,, 23.	¶Sheldon Amos and others (*Mr. Jessel*) ...	377
,, 23.	Inhabitants of Bridgwater (*Mr. Gore Langton*)...	153
,, 23.	Inhabitants of Bridgwater (*Mr. Gore Langton*)...	129
,, 23.	¶Inhabitants of Southwark (*Mr. Locke*) ...	2,988
,, 23.	¶Inhabitants of Westminster (*Mr. Shaw Lefevre*)	2,422
,, 23.	Inhabitants of Dinas-y-Mowddy, county of Merioneth (*Mr. Shaw Lefevre*)	43
,, 23.	¶Inhabitants of Barnsbury (*Mr. Shaw Lefevre*)...	28
,, 23.	Inhabitants of Bourton-on-the-Hill, county of Gloucester (*Mr. Shaw Lefevre*)	28
,, 23.	Inhabitants of Carmarthen (*Mr. Shaw Lefevre*)...	181
,, 23.	Inhabitants of Moreton-in-the-Marsh, county of Gloucester (*Mr. Shaw Lefevre*)	24
,, 23.	¶Louisa E. Buckwald and others (*Mr. Shaw Lefevre*)	73
,, 23.	¶Inhabitants of Belfast (*Mr. M'Clure*) ...	950
,, 23.	Inhabitants of Burslem and other places (*Mr. Melly*)	40
,, 23.	Inhabitants of Bristol (*Mr. Morley*)	894
,, 23.	Inhabitants of Bristol (*Mr. Morley*)	296
,, 23.	¶Inhabitants of Bantry (*Mr. Pim*)	23
,, 23.	Inhabitants of Howth, county of Dublin (*Mr. Pim*)	6
,, 23.	Inhabitants of Dublin (*Mr. Pim*)	2
,, 23.	¶Inhabitants of Dublin (*Mr. Pim*)	316
,, 23.	Inhabitants of Donabate and others (*Mr. Pim*)...	9
,, 23.	Inhabitants of Tipperary (*Mr. Pim*)	21
,, 23.	¶Inhabitants of Blackrock, county of Dublin (*Mr. Pim*)	21
,, 23.	Inhabitants of Dublin (*Mr. Pim*)	2
,, 23.	¶Inhabitants of Phibsborough (*Mr. Pim*) ...	5
,, 23.	Inhabitants of Blackrock (*Mr. Pim*)	3
,, 23.	¶Inhabitants of Wexford (*Mr. Pim*)	20

March 23.	Inhabitants of Malahide, county of Dublin (*Mr. Pim*)	11
„	23. ¶Inhabitants of Dublin (*Mr. Pim*)	2
„	23. ¶Inhabitants of Phibsborough, county of Dublin (*Mr. Pim*)	27
„	23. ¶Inhabitants of Blackrock, county of Dublin (*Mr. Pim*)	27
„	23. ¶Inhabitants of Dublin (*Mr. Pim*)	211
„	23. Inhabitants of Donabate (*Mr. Pim*)	7
„	23. ¶Inhabitants of Dublin (*Mr. Pim*)	3
„	23. Anne Isabella Robertson, Saint James Place, Blackrock (*Mr. Pim*)	1
„	23. Ann Lindsay, 182, Great Britain-Street, Dublin (*Mr. Pim*)...	1
„	23. ¶Inhabitants of Queen's County (*Mr. Pim*) ...	20
„	23. Inhabitants of Pendlebury and neighbourhood (*Dr. Playfair*)	68
„	23. Inhabitants of Chester (*Mr. Raikes*)	630
„	23. Inhabitants of Cheltenham (*Mr. Henry Samuelson*)	191
„	23. Board of Guardians of the Kendal Union; James Cropper, chairman (*Mr Whitwell*)	1
„	23. Guardians of the Kendal Union; James Cropper, chairman (*Mr. Whitwell*)...	1
„	23. ¶Inhabitants of Bath	673
„	24. Inhabitants of Freshford, county of Somerset (*Major Allen*)	20
„	24. Inhabitants of Alderley Edge (*Mr. Jacob Bright*)	163
„	24. Inhabitants of Cheltenham (*Mr Jacob Bright*) ...	35
„	24. ¶Inhabitants of Cambridge (*Mr. Jacob Bright*)...	45
„	24. ¶Inhabitants of Manchester (*Mr. Jacob Bright*)	43
„	24. ¶Inhabitants of Cheetham Hill (*Mr. Jacob Bright*)	45
„	24. Inhabitants of Walness and Rockley Pendleton (*Mr Jacob Bright*)	33
„	24. ¶Inhabitants of Cheltenham (*Mr. Jacob Bright*)	25
„	24. ¶Inhabitants of Chelsea (*Sir Charles Dilke*) ...	636
„	24. Inhabitants of Birmingham (*Mr. Dixon*) ...	748
„	24. Inhabitants of Monk Coniston (*Marquis of Hartington*)	65
„	24. Inhabitants of Trowbridge (*Sir George Jenkinson*)	70
„	24. Inhabitants of Trowbridge (*Sir George Jenkinson*)	60
„	24. ¶Inhabitants of Lambeth (*Sir James Lawrence*)	4,264
„	24. ¶Inhabitants of West End, Edinburgh (*Mr. M'Laren*)	131
„	24. ¶Inhabitants of Edinburgh (*Mr. M'Laren*) ...	26
„	24. ¶Inhabitants of Morningside (*Mr. M'Laren*) ...	133
„	24. ¶Inhabitants of Edinburgh (*Mr. M'Laren*) ...	149
„	24. Inhabitants of Sheffield (*Mr. Mundella*) ...	49
„	24. ¶Inhabitants of Nottingham (*Mr. Seeley*) ...	679
„	24. ¶Inhabitants of Nottingham (*Mr. Seeley*) ...	379
„	24. ¶Inhabitants of Leicester (*Mr. Taylor*) ...	37
„	24. ¶Inhabitants of Leicester (*Mr. Taylor*) ...	37
„	25. Inhabitants of Leek (*Sir Edward Buller*) ...	25
„	25. ¶Inhabitants of Brighton (*Mr. Fawcett*) ...	152
„	25. ¶Inhabitants of York (*Mr. James Lowther*) ...	78
„	25. ¶Inhabitants of York (*Mr. James Lowther*) ...	77
„	25. Members of the Burnley Reform Club ...	80

March	22.	Inhabitants of Box, Wiltshire (*Sir G. Jenkinson*)	42
,,	28.	Members of the Law Amendment Society; E. Pears, general secretary (*Mr. Gurney*)	1
,,	28.	¶Inhabitants of Salisbury (*Dr. Lush*)...	79
,,	29.	Inhabitants of Paignton (*Mr. Solicitor General*)	25
,,	29.	Inhabitants of Aldborough ...	39
,,	29.	Inhabitants of Roscommon, and others	17
,,	31.	British Subjects resident in Lisbon (*Sir Charles Dilke*)...	3
April	4.	Inhabitants of Capel Ockley and other places (*Mr. Briscoe*)	136
,,	8.	Inhabitants of Swansea (*Mr. Dillwyn*)	171
,,	8.	Inhabitants of Swansea (*Mr. Dillwyn*)	105
,,	12.	*Scottish Trade Protection Society (*Mr. M'Laren*)	2
,,	27.	A. Sidgwick, M.A., Rugby, and others (*Mr. Gurney*)	18
,,	28.	Inhabitants of Southport (*Mr. Cross*)...	173
,,	28.	¶Inhabitants of Frome (*Mr. Thomas Hughes*) ...	190
,,	28.	Members and Friends of the Edinburgh Branch of the National Secular Society (*Mr. Miller*).	68
May	2.	¶Inhabitants of Scarborough (*Mr. Dent*)	314
,,	2.	¶Inhabitants of Kingstown (*Mr. Pim*)	42
,,	3.	¶Inhabitants of Putney and other places (*Mr. Broderick*)	52
,,	4.	¶Inhabitants of Huddersfield (*Mr. Russell Gurney*)	28
,,	11.	¶Inhabitants of Rock Ferry, county of Chester (*Mr. Laird*)	408
,,	11.	Inhabitants of Melrose (*Sir David Wedderburn*).	36
,,	12.	Inhabitants of Darlington (*Mr. Backhouse*)	172
,,	16.	¶Inhabitants of Rochdale (*Mr. Thomas Potter*)..	590
,,	17.	¶Inhabitants of Marylebone (*Mr. Thos. Chambers*)	327
,,	17.	Inhabitants of Tiverton (*Mr. Denman*)	62
,,	17.	Inhabitants of Tiverton (*Mr. Jessel*) ...	169
,,	17.	¶Inhabitants of Hythe, County of Kent (*Mr. Jessel*)	136
,,	18.	Eliza S. Oldham and others (*Mr. Jacob Bright*)..	52
,,	18.	Margaret P. Mills and others (*Mr. Jacob Bright*).	96
,,	18.	Inhabitants of Dublin (*Mr. Pim*)	1,025
,,	18.	Inhabitants of Glasthule, county of Dublin (*Mr. Pim*)	23
,,	18.	Inhabitants of Monkstown, county of Dublin (*Mr. Pim*)	61
,,	18.	Inhabitants of Kingstown county of Dublin (*Mr. Pim*)	62
,,	18.	Inhabitants of Sandcove, county of Dublin (*Mr. Pim*)	50
,,	18.	Inhabitants of Dalkey, county of Dublin (*Mr. Pim*)	22
,,	18.	Inhabitants of County of Cavan and others (*Mr. Pim*)	21
,,	18.	Inhabitants of Bray, county of Wicklow (*Mr. Pim*)	26
,,	18.	Helen Carter, of Friars' Hall, Melrose (*Sir David Wedderburn*)	1
,,	18.	¶Charles R. Drysdale and others	110
,,	18.	Inhabitants of Watlington and other places in Oxfordshire	51
,,	18.	Inhabitants of Coventry	68
,,	19.	¶Inhabitants of Teignmouth (*Mr. Thomas Cave*)	150
,,	19.	¶Inhabitants of Tranmere, county of Chester (*Mr. Laird*)	95

May	19.	¶Helen Anderson and others *(Sir Wilfrid Lawson)*	150
,,	19.	¶Inhabitants of Devizes *(Sir John Lubbock)* ...	262
,,	19.	Inhabitants of Edinburgh *(Mr. M'Laren)* ...	58
,,	20.	Inhabitants of Cork *(Mr. Pim)*	36

Total number of Petitions, 212; Signatures ... 41,620

MARRIED WOMEN'S PROPERTY (No. 2) BILL
(Mr. Raikes')—*Against.*

March	11.	Inhabitants of Monk Coniston *(Mr. Frederick Stanley)*...	58
,,	14.	Inhabitants of Hawkeshead	57
,,	15.	Mary Beever and others *(Mr. Frederick Stanley)* ...	209
,,	17.	Inhabitants of Hertfordshire *(Mr. Gurney)*	9
,,	18.	Members of the Executive of the Holbeck Reform Association *(Mr. Baines)*	3
,,	21.	Inhabitants of Corston *(Mr. Richard Bright)*	35
,,	21.	Inhabitants of Pontesbury, county of Salop *(Mr. Gurney)*	21
,,	21.	Inhabitants of Boston Spa, Yorkshire *(Mr. Gurney)* ...	59
,,	21.	Inhabitants of Street *(Mr. Neville-Grenville)*	296
,,	21.	Inhabitants of Tavistock *(Mr. Arthur Russell)*.. ...	168
,,	22.	Inhabitants of Bradford-on-Avon *(Lord Charles Bruce)*..	55
,,	22.	Inhabitants of Box *(Lord Charles Bruce)* ...	42
,,	22.	¶Inhabitants of Rathmines *(Mr. Pim)*...	65
,,	22.	Inhabitants of Leskinfere *(Mr. Pim)*	7
,,	28.	¶Inhabitants of Scarborough and others *(Mr. Dent)* ...	101
,,	28.	Inhabitants of Salisbury *(Dr. Lush)*	70
,,	29.	N. Garrett and others	35
April	12.	Inhabitants of Cambridge *(Mr. Lefevre)*	20
,,	27.	A Sidgwick, M.A., Rugby, and others *(Mr. Gurney)* ...	18
,,	28.	¶Inhabitants of Southport and Kirkdale *(Mr. Cross)* ...	161
,,	28.	¶Inhabitants of Frome *(Mr. Thomas Hughes)*	138
May	3.	Inhabitants of Huddersfield *(Mr. Leatham)*	24
,,	6.	Ann Shaw, the Firs, Elstree, county of Herts *(Mr. Robert Brand)*	1
,,	11.	Inhabitants of Melrose *(Sir David Wedderburn)* ...	29
,,	17.	Inhabitants of Tiverton *(Mr. Denman)*	48
,,	18.	Inhabitants of Shepherds Bush *(Mr. Gurney)*... ...	345
,,	18.	Inhabitants of Dalkey, county of Dublin *(Mr. Pim)*...	31
,,	18.	Inhabitants of Kingstown, county of Dublin *(Mr. Pim)*...	61
,,	18.	Inhabitants of Monkstown, county of Dublin *(Mr. Pim)*.	43
,,	18.	Inhabitants of Glasthule, county of Dublin *(Mr. Pim)* ...	41
,,	18.	Inhabitants of Sandy Cove, county of Dublin *(Mr. Pim)*.	36
,,	18.	Inhabitants of Bantry, Ireland, and other places *(Mr. Pim)*	22
,,	18.	Inhabitants of Dublin *(Mr. Pim)*	1,015
,,	19.	Inhabitants of Edgbaston *(Mr. Muntz)*	56

Total number of Petitions, 34; Signatures ... 3,379

MARRIED WOMEN'S PROPERTY (No. 2) BILL
(Mr. Raikes')—*Against;*
And **MARRIED WOMEN'S PROPERTY (No. 1) BILL**
(Mr. Gurney's)—*In favour.*

March	22.	Inhabitants of Salford *(Mr. Charley)*	1,001
,,	22.	Women of Rawtenstall, county of Lancaster *(Mr. Holt)*...	121
,,	23.	Members of the Executive Committee for Amending the Law with respect to the Property of Married Women *(Mr. Jacob Bright)*	9
,,	23.	Men of Rawtenstall, county of Lancaster *(Mr. Starkie)* ...	69

Total number of Petitions, 4—Signatures ... 1,200

SUMMARY.

	No. of Petitions signed Officially or under seal.	Total No. of Petitions.	No. of Signatures.
Married Women's Property Bill (Mr. Gurney's) In favour	3	212	41,620
Married Women's Property Bill (Mr. Raikes')— Against	—	34	3,379
Married Women's Property Bill (No. 2, Mr. Raikes')—Against; and Married Women's Property Bill (No. 1, Mr. Gurney's)—in favour	—	4	1,200
Total	3	250	46,199

The Petitions marked thus ¶ have the Addresses of some or all of the Petitioners affixed.
The Petitions marked thus * are signed officially.

In the above list, five petitions from Ireland in favour of the principle of the Bill have been omitted, viz., from Dublin with 134 signatures, Kingston 15, Booterstown 5, Williamstown 3, Longford , all presented by Mr. Pim, February 11.

Miss A. Robertson, of Dublin, requests us to say that the 42 petitions sent through her, gave the addresses of those who signed, even to the number of the street.

EDUCATION AND EMPLOYMENT.

The *Spectator* of June 4 contains some interesting information.

It is with the most lively satisfaction that we see from a report of one of the very ablest of the Assistant Commissioners for Endowed Schools, Mr. J. G. Fitch, sent to the Bristol Committee for promoting the application of a fair proportion of the educational endowments of the country to the education of girls, that the three Commissioners under the Endowed Schools' Act are setting themselves seriously to work to organise efficient and cheap middle-class schools for girls no less than for boys; and if not as yet schools of the very highest grade—the grade which is intended to prepare for the universities—yet of the two inferior grades, that which is intended to teach girls who are not to leave school before sixteen or seventeen, and that which is intended to teach girls who are to be kept at school only up to fourteen or fifteen. Mr. Fitch's letter, published in the *Bristol Daily Post*, of May 30, contains both the most satisfactory evidence of the deliberate intention of the Commissioners, and an admirable *résumé* of the objects to be aimed at in organising the new middle-class girls' schools. We cannot pretend to condense its recommendations here. We will only say that in the higher schools, the schools for girls remaining till seventeen, the object is to give a solid education in Latin, two modern languages, history, geography, arithmetic, the elements of geometry and algebra, English literature, drawing, vocal music, and needlework, for a sum varying from 6*l.* to 10*l.* for day scholars, and from 35*l.* to 60*l.* for boarders : and that in the lower schools, those intended for girls who leave at fourteen or fifteen, the object is to teach thoroughly arithmetic, English, French, drawing, needlework, and vocal music, in addition to all that is taught in the higher classes of primary schools, together with some practical instruction in household economy for the boarders, for a sum varying from 4*l.* to 6*l.* for day scholars, and 18*l.* to 25*l.* for boarders. The endowments would chiefly be used in providing scholarships to be competed for by girls from the primary schools, or from the general public, for use in the schools of the lower grade, and by girls from the lower middle-class schools for use in those of the higher grade, and in adding to the salaries of the mistresses of such schools so as to give them a certain independence. How immense is the demand for education of this substantial sort for girls, Mr. Fitch shows, by mentioning that in Birmingham, where four schools of the kind, containing on an average 160 scholars each, and all quite full, have just been established out of the surplus revenues of the King Edward's Grammar School, there were no less than 501 names of girls registered as applying for admission, and all compelled to wait for vacancies. Whether women want votes or not, there can be no manner of doubt that parents of all classes are eager enough to give their girls education.

The following is a list of the ladies who passed the recent general examination for women held by the London University:—

Honours division: Mary Deborah Albright, private tuition; Emma Mabel Case, private study; Laura Gertrude Eaton, Ladies' College, Cheltenham; Jane Ellen Harrison, Ladies' College, Cheltenham; Emma Kate Woodward, North London Collegiate School for Ladies. First division: Mary Anne Belcher, Hillersdon House and Ladies' College, Cheltenham; Katharine Margaret Cadwallader, Ladies' College, Cheltenham; Margaret Jane Nimmo, Bedford College; Sarah Sophia Purton, Ladies' College, Cheltenham.

At a Meeting of the General Council of the University of Edinburgh, held on April 19, Professor Masson moved:—

That, as the present arrangements for the medical instruction of women in the University impose great and unnecessary inconveniences on the women who are students and also on professors, and may, if continued, even nullify the resolution of the University, admitting women to the study of medicine, the General Council recommend to the University Court that women desiring to study medicine be admitted to the medical classes as other students are, and on the same terms, except in cases where the Court may see special reasons why the instruction should be separate.

His motion was seconded by Professor Balfour. Professor Laycock moved as an amendment that Professor Masson's motion be not adopted. Professor Christian seconded the amendment. Professors Calderwood and Crum-Brown supported the motion. On a division, the amendment was carried by fifty-eight to forty-seven.

From the "Lancet," June 18th, 1870.

"In great haste I write you a few lines touching the medical event of the day—to wit, the reception of Miss Garrett as an M.D. of the Paris Faculty, which has just this instant taken place, and in which I had the pleasure of assisting. I say it is an event, because it is, I believe, the first time that a lady has graduated at the Paris Faculty since its foundation; and Miss Garrett is justly proud that it has been given to an English lady to establish the precedent. I must be brief, and can only now refer to the main points of the ceremony. Several ladies, friends and relatives of Miss Garrett, were in attendance, and had graciously been admitted for this once into the *salle des Etats*. Miss Garrett wore the traditional gown and bands hitherto reserved on such occasions for the ruder sex, and I must say that, in this attire, she presented a most pleasing appearance. Her friends must have been highly gratified to hear how her judges congratulated her on her success, and to see what sympathy and respect were shown to her by all present on the occasion. The hall was literally crowded with students, and, on Miss Garrett's crossing the courtyard to leave the school, I observed with pleasure that almost all the students gallantly bowed to their lady *confrere*. All the judges, on complimenting Miss Garrett, more or less expressed liberal opinions on the subject of lady doctors, and one Professor, M. Broca, was especially energetic and enthusiastic. Altogether there was really an air of *fête* about the Faculty this day; everybody was to some extent under the influence of the novelty and importance of the proceedings.

"*Paris, June* 15*th,* 1870."

It is stated that the Russian Government has announced that women will hereafter be admitted to medical schools and to medical practice.

The following question and answer appeared in the report of the debates in the House of Commons of June 16:—

WOMEN ON EDUCATIONAL BOARDS.

Mr. Taylor asked the Vice-President of the Committee of Council on Education whether by the use of the words "he" and "his" in the clauses of the Elementary Education Bill relating to local boards he intended to exclude women from sitting on such boards.

Mr. W. E. Forster, in reply to the question of the hon. member, had to state that the words "he" and "his" were not used with the view of excluding women from the local boards of education, but because the use of those words was the best way to include them. (Hear, and a laugh.) He was not at all surprised at hon. members laughing, but the reason why "he" meant " she " in this case was that Lord Brougham's Act, 14 Vict. c. 21, enacted that in all Acts words importing the masculine gender should be taken to include and mean the feminine gender, unless the contrary was specifically declared. So far from being anxious to exclude women from these boards, he looked forward to their assistance in some cases being most valuable. (Hear, hear.)

The sixth meeting of the Female Medical Society was held on May 25, the Earl of Shaftesbury in the chair. The secretary, Dr. Edmunds, read the report, which stated that eighty-seven ladies had availed themselves of the teaching of the Society, of whom the greater number intended to become midwives. Two were now practising in connection with the Birmingham Lying-in Hospital. Two past students, Mrs. Thorne and Miss M. Chaplin, had gone to Edinburgh, and were studying for the degree of M.D.

AUBREY INSTITUTE, NOTTING HILL, LONDON.

WE had the satisfaction last year of noticing in our pages the growth and progress of this very useful institution, and are glad to hear that it continues to advance in its laudable career, and is becoming a subject of growing interest in its neighbourhood.

The classes for instruction, embracing French, Latin, singing and drawing, history, arithmetic, geography, grammar, and composition, are well attended by pupils of both sexes, and the ladies and gentlemen who conduct them work with continuous and praiseworthy zeal, while the elementary classes are making steady advances under the tuition of a lady permanently engaged, and well qualified for the task.

On Sunday afternoons and evenings a reading-room, well-supplied with books and papers, is open to the pupils and their friends, an extensive lending library is also available, and lectures are occasionally given on Saturday evenings to the pupils and public. Among the gentlemen who have kindly given their services as lecturers, we may mention Mr. M. D. Conway, Dr. Hodgson, LL.D., and Herr Hoffman, on the Kinder-Garten.

As showing the interest taken in the work by the pupils themselves, we may mention an entertainment of vocal music, readings, and recitations, given on Saturday, May 28, by the elder members of the classes (the musical performances being presided over by Mrs. Boyd Kinnear). The rooms were lent by Mr. P. A. Taylor, M.P., and Mrs. Taylor, the liberal founders and supporters of the institution, and the chair was taken by the former.

Recognising in the progress of this foundation the growing desire of the people for something higher and better than the schools hitherto accessible to them have offered, we heartily wish it continued success, and trust it may be an example for imitation in other districts of London which are in need of such assistance.

At the annual meeting of the supporters of the Queen's Institute, Dublin, the Marquis of Kildare presided, and a very satisfactory report was read. The porcelain painting studio had eight ladies in it, painting for Mr. Kerr, and altogether fifty-eight ladies had been taught the art. During the winter thirty classes were at work. The number of pupils at present was 336. During the last eight years there have been 175 women trained in book-keeping, in the telegraph 111, in law writing 117, and many more in other ways.

The Steam Navigation Company at Odessa has decided to employ women in the sale of passenger-tickets.

The Queen has intimated her intention to offer in competition to the female artists of all nations a prize of 40*l.* for the best fan, painted or carved, by a lady under twenty-five years of age. The fan must be exhibited at the International Exhibition of next year.

Early in April, Miss E. Faithfull gave a very effective lecture, at Devonport, on the Employment of Women.

The Female Printers' Union, of New York City, now numbers about fifty members. The total number of women type-setters in that city is 150.

At the annual festivity, held at Notre Dame des Arts (the superior technical school for girls at Paris), amongst a great number of distinguished persons there were present, Madame Ollivier, the wife of the Prime Minister, and the Countess Walewski. The music and paintings of the pupils were much admired.

o

POOR LAW.

BOARDING-OUT OF PAUPER CHILDREN.

A DEPUTATION of ladies had, on the 3rd of May, an interview with the Right Hon. the President of the Poor Law Board, at his official residence, on the subject of boarding out pauper children: The ladies were—Mrs. Archer, Miss Frances Anne Cropper, Miss Hill, Miss Louisa Boucherett, Miss Frances Power Cobbe, Miss Joanna Hill, Mrs. Hansard, Mrs. Agnes Moore. The Rev. S. Hansard, Mr. George Moore, and Mr. Archer accompanied the deputation.

Mrs. Archer presented Mr. Goschen with the following memorial—" 1. That the system of educating orphan and deserted pauper children, and more especially girls, in large schools—massing several hundreds together under the same roof—be, as far as possible, discontinued, as its results have been unsatisfactory, and much money has been thereby wasted. 2. That the ladies who are desirous to help in the better education of such pauper children be legally empowered to do so. 3. That for this purpose a law be passed to allow ladies to co-operate with the Poor Law authorities in the charge of pauper children, and to be made responsible for them in the same way as a guardian or trustee is for his ward. 4. We also would respectfully propose: (*a*) That children entrusted by Poor Law guardians to ladies residing in a different Poor Law union or district, should not thereby cease to belong to their own union, but retain a claim upon it in case of becoming incapable of self-support, so that they should not become a burthen upon the district to which they have been sent. (*b*) That the ladies should bind themselves to the board of guardians who hand over children to them to superintend the children's education, training, and clothing, to send them to public worship and school, to select suitable foster-parents for them, with whom they may board and lodge, and to see carefully to their mental and bodily welfare, to report to the guardians of their union half-yearly, and to submit the children to any official inspection which the guardians may think desirable. (*c*) That boards of guardians should pay such sums as may be agreed upon for the maintenance and education of each child, and, in case of a child's death, should defray funeral expenses, and should receive again any child whom the ladies may, upon sufficient grounds, apply to them to take back. 5. Lastly, we beg your honourable board to consider that our endeavours may be the means of rescuing thousands of children from an unnatural, sad, useless, and unhealthy life, and of adding a large number of useful servants and able working people to the community."

Several of the ladies addressed the President of the Poor Law Board in support of the memorial.

Mr. Goschen said that in Scotland, where the system was in vogue to a very great extent, it was almost entirely based upon children being removed from the towns to the country.

Miss Hill observed that it was very desirable that the local authorities, if not the central authorities, should deal with the ladies who undertook the responsibility.

Mr. Goschen remarked that the matter would have to be considered with very great care, because there used to be a system which was called "farming," which could not now be allowed. It would never do that cottagers should look upon it as a source of profit. They had been enquiring into the system in Scotland, and there the evidence was that the children were kindly treated, that they afterwards joined the general population—what he supposed the ladies desired—(Yes, yes)—and so prevent what was called "pauper taint." (Hear, hear.) That object was realised in Scotland to a very great extent. But the evidence on the other hand showed that, as regards accommodation, in many respects the children were in a very bad state. They were not in a worse condition than the general poor population, but scarcely such as a Government department could sanction. This was really at the root of the whole question. It would be too much to expect that the cottagers should treat these children better than their own; but many of these children were treated in a way that, if it were known, and a reporter got hold of it, would make a very fine paragraph in a sensational newspaper. If the public were told how half of the children lived in the cottages it would look like a very sad story, and one which no one could approve of. It was clear there was very great difficulty respecting the sleeping accommodation, and the reports they had from Scotland on that part of the subject were not satisfactory. If this plan were adopted, and three or four cases of cruelty were heard of, or anything of the kind, there would be a re-action in the public mind, and the system would have to be abandoned. He was favourable to the proposal if he could see his way clearly to the machinery by which it was to be done. There was an objection raised to the system by a certain number of gentlemen who took an interest in education.

Mr. Hansard thought that, with an Educational Bill, this objection would be met.

Mr. Goschen said he did not hold the objection. If they did not surround the system with sufficient safeguards, great difficulties would arise.

Two or three of the deputation pointed out that the active supervision of the ladies was a very great safeguard.

Mr. Goschen might frankly say that one of the great advantages of the system in the country as compared with it in the towns was that the children were much more under the eye——

Miss Hill: I have heard that the town is much superior, because the children are so much more under observation. (A laugh.)

Mr. Goschen: I confess I do not share that view. Supposing it was in London, who was to be entrusted?
The Ladies (together): The ladies!
The Gentlemen: Hear, hear.
Mr. Goschen: Yes; but they only visit periodically. In the country you practically know the character of the people much better.
Miss. Hill: I should have thought so myself, if I had not been assured to the contrary.
Mr. Goschen: If we make a change in the law we must do it with the confidence that it would be as likely to succeed in England as in Scotland.
During a conversation as to the best method of inspection, which the deputation quite agreed with the right hon. gentleman must be thoroughly efficient, the ladies said they should desire to work with inspectors of the Poor Law Board and not with relieving officers.
Miss Boucherett: I never knew a relieving officer find out anything wrong about children I have placed out. Some of them seem to have mole's eyes. (Laughter, and "Hear, hear.")
Mr. Goschen: I am quite sure ladies' eyes are much sharper than those of relieving officers. (The ladies bowed in acknowledgment of the compliment.) I can only say I do not regard the difficulties as insuperable, but the question requires much consideration.
Mrs. Archer thanked the right hon. gentleman for his courtesy in granting the interview, and the deputation retired.

WOMEN AS POOR LAW GUARDIANS.

MISS BURDETT COUTTS was nominated for a seat on the Board of Guardians of the west ward of Bethnal Green by Mr. Atkins, who is, we believe, a working man. There were nine candidates for that ward and only six could be elected. Miss Coutts stood fifth on the list at the poll, beating Mr. Nicholson 108 votes. Mr. Howard, the clerk, however, in casting up the votes took no notice of the votes given for the lady, considering her to be disqualified by sex. Mr. Nicholson was therefore given the seat which Miss Coutts would otherwise have had. Mr. Atkins appealed to the Poor Law Board. They however decline to interfere, and suggest that the case should be brought before the Court of Queen's Bench. This would involve some expense, and it is feared Mr. Atkins will be unable to pursue the matter further.

THE EMIGRATION OF PAUPER CHILDREN.

A MEETING was held June 17, at the rooms of the

National Association for the Promotion of Social Science, for the purpose of considering the proposal of Miss Rye, that she should be allowed to take orphans and deserted pauper girls of the age of from seven to twelve, from the London workhouse schools and other workhouse schools throughout the country, to Canada, where they would be placed (under proper legal protection) till eighteen years of age in respectable families. The Earl of Shaftesbury presided. Miss Rye read a paper in which she stated that her proposal was to take out children of the class in question to Canada, and place them, under due specific regulations, in the custody of old and established families in that country, who would train them up in a proper manner, and render them, before they had completed their term of apprenticeship, at eighteen years of age, thoroughly competent in every respect to make their way in the world. She had already on her books 200 families in Canada who were ready and willing to receive such children; and when the authorities at the unions were willing to give them up in that way, she would distribute them among those families. The stipulation on which she parted with them was that, whatever age the child who was bound might be, the people receiving her should educate, clothe, and feed her, and see that she attended a place of worship on Sunday, and Sunday school, if possible, till she was fifteen years of age; from fifteen to seventeen the family taking the girl covenanted to give her three dollars a month wages, with a rise to four dollars during the last year of her apprenticeship. Miss Rye said that of the children she took out in October last, fifty were orphans given up to her care by the select vestry of Liverpool, and that body had been so well satisfied with the manner in which she had disposed of them, that they had just voted her a second party of fifty children to take out in the same manner, together with the money for their expenses at the rate of 10*l.* a head, which was much less than the rate at which they could be kept in this country. A resolution in support of Miss Rye's proposal was adopted by the meeting.

MISCELLANEOUS.

WOMEN ON JURIES.—Judge How gives the following account of the conduct of the female jury in Wyoming:—

With all my prejudices against the policy, I am under conscientious obligations to say that these women acquitted themselves with such dignity, decorum, propriety of conduct, and intelligence as to win the admiration of every fair-minded citizen of Wyoming. They were careful, painstaking, intelligent and conscientious. They were firm and resolute for the right as established by the law and the testimony. Their verdicts were right, and after three or four criminal trials the lawyers engaged in defending persons accused of crime began to avail themselves of the right of peremptory challenge to get rid of the women jurors, who were too much in favour of enforcing the laws and punishing crime to suit the interests of their clients! After the grand jury had been in session two days, the dance-house keepers, gamblers, and *demi monde* fled out of the city in dismay, to escape the indictment of women grand jurors! In short, I have never, in twenty-five years of constant experience in the courts of the country, seen a more faithful, intelligent, and resolutely honest grand and petit jury, than these.

The judge concludes with these words—

The universal judgment of every intelligent and fair minded man present was, and is, that the experiment was a success.

At the Portsmouth Quarter Sessions, the *Law Times* remarks, some of the female burgesses were summoned upon the jury in pursuance of the provisions of the Municipal Corporation Act, which requires that "persons" upon the burgess roll shall be impanelled to serve on juries at the quarter sessions for the borough. It was, however, decided by the recorder (Mr. Serjeant Cox), that, inasmuch as the Act of 1868, which admits women to the municipal franchise, declares that words importing the masculine gender shall be held to include the feminine gender, was expressly limited to the purposes of voting at municipal elections, female burgesses could not be required to serve on juries.

CALL TO THE BAR.—Miss L. Burkalow was admitted to the Bar of Missouri on the 25th of March (Lady Day). She was a student of the St. Louis law school.—*Times*, April 13.

WHY WOMEN'S SUFFRAGE IS WANTED.—A woman named Ellen Wallis, aged 27, was yesterday committed for trial, on a charge of attempting to murder her two children. For some years she had lived with a commercial traveller named John Chapman, and had passed as his wife. A year ago, according to her statement, he began to abuse her, and told her he had another wife living. A few weeks since he left her with an allowance of 10s. a week for herself and the two children. On Sunday morning he called at her house, and took out one of the children. She was not then at home, but when she returned she took the other child, aged six months, and followed him to one of the piers on the Thames. A witness thus details the conversation. She began to reproach him with not having told her that he was a married man. He said, "Take the children home," and she replied, "No, I will throw them into the river." He answered, "What are the children to me?" and the prisoner then said, "The children are yours; I will throw them into the river and myself after them." "Do it, do it," said Chapman. Taking the children in her arms, she then jumped into the water, from which all three were rescued with difficulty. The woman is committed for trial, and the law will deal with her. There is no law to deal with John Chapman. Public opinion may form its own estimate of his position with regard to the affair, and how far punishment always lights on the right shoulders.—*Echo.*

The number of signatures to petitions against the Contagious Diseases Acts is 453,089.

At length there is a ladies' newspaper in India. It is called *The Woman of Bengal,* is published at Calcutta, in Bengali, and is edited by a Hindoo lady.

Ten native Christian women are studying medicine in connection with the American missions in India. The Government of India has made a small grant in aid of the enterprise.

INTERNATIONAL WOMEN'S ASSOCIATION.

The first meeting of this Society was held on the 27th of March last, when Madame Marie Goegg, the President, pronounced an eloquent discourse. The Secretary, Madame Gandillon, read the report. It stated that the Association was formerly inaugurated July 26, 1868, at

Geneva. A great sensation was caused by its establishment. Many newspapers wrote about it, and it was much talked of.

Various petitions were sent by the Committee to various governments and public bodies with little or no success, until in November, 1869, a petition was presented to the Italian parliament, asking that lay schools for girls might be taken under the protection of the government. A real success followed this step, and the Minister of Instruction took into consideration several pamphlets and books published in different countries, on the education of girls.

The Society is also endeavouring to found a college for girls. Madame Goegg started a newspaper in March, 1869, *Le Journal des Femmes*, which has since been incorporated with M. Leon Richel's newspaper, *Le Droit des Femmes*.

Letters were read from several ladies in different countries regretting their inability to attend, and expressing sympathy with the movement.

The receipts since the formation of the Society amounted to 975 francs, about 40*l*.

The *Woman's Journal* of Boston, U.S., a well conducted and truly admirable publication, makes the following remarks with regard to the accusation which has been brought against the movement, of being hostile to the marriage relation and of advocating divorce at will.

So far from woman suffrage meaning license it means exactly the contrary. If woman's suffrage means anything, it means greater purity and perpetuity in the marriage relations. It means legislation for the interests of woman. Free love is not for the interest of man or woman, but its consequences are far more fatal to women than to men. Freedom of divorce for trifling causes is cruelly unjust to women. The wife and mother is in no condition to earn her subsistence by labour. She does it at a terrible disadvantage.

The *Revolution*, also an American publication, has changed hands. It has hitherto been a clever and amusing, but somewhat eccentric newspaper, advocating women's rights, together with a good many "isms," amongst others—*Fenianism!* In its early days it was widely distributed in England and did some harm to the cause here by these eccentricities. We hope that under its new owner it will continue equally amusing, but that she will be more careful to avoid "isms," at least if it is to be distributed in England.

POSTSCRIPT.

MARRIED WOMAN'S PROPERTY BILL.

On June 21 Lord Cairns moved the second reading of this Bill, and explained its provisions in a short speech. Lord Penzance said the Bill went too far, and that an extension of the Protection Order System was all that was required. Lord Westbury said the passing of the present Bill was out of the question. He recommended that a new Bill with reasonable provisions should be drawn.

Lord Romilly hoped such a course would not be pursued, as it would stop legislation for a year. Lord Shaftesbury hoped that a wife's earnings from intellectual work would be secured to her, as well as her earnings from manual labour. The disappointment felt by working women when the Bill did not pass last year was extreme. He did not approve of the Bill with regard to property, but only as far as regarded earnings.

The Lord Chancellor supported the second reading of the Bill; he thought it a good Bill on the whole, and that a few alterations would make it all that was desirable.

Lord Lyveden recommended that the Bill be referred to a select committee.

The Duke of Cleveland thought the Bill ought to be considerably modified, and recommended that legislation should, for the present, be confined to the first part of the Bill.

Lord Cairns thought Lord Penzance inconsistent in opposing the Bill, as he had himself moved the second reading of it last year. He defended the Bill. His concluding words were—

All he desired to do was to secure that wherever property had been acquired by a married woman by virtue of her own industry, be it either bodily or mental, she was entitled to the property so acquired to her separate use, just as if it were settled in the Court of Chancery to her separate use. That he considered the principle of the Bill. Some of the provisions of the Bill he thought unnecessary.

Lord Westbury was quite content with the assurance of his noble and learned friend with regard to the principle of the Bill. It was limited to the settlement of property acquired by the woman's own labour, mental and bodily.

The Bill was read a second time and referred to a select committee.

An admirable article appeared in the *Times* next day, containing the following remarks :—

The change in the law would at once give a better position to every woman, and not merely to the woman who is sufficiently provoked and sufficiently strong-minded to take an unusual and most hostile proceeding against her husband. It would not supersede marriage settlements, for the settlement is as much to protect the woman from herself as from her husband; but it would in thousands of households give greater moral influence to the wife, and tend to the happiness and prosperity of both her husband and herself. Indeed, the right of women to the possession and disposal of property being admitted, we cannot believe, until it is shown by arguments stronger than any used in the House of Lords last night, that the ceremony of marriage ought to "act on a woman like a conviction for felony." and reduce a person of independent fortune into a dependent on the bounty of another.

THE ENGLISHWOMAN'S REVIEW

(NEW SERIES.)

No. IV.—OCTOBER, 1870.

ART. I.—MARRIED WOMEN'S PROPERTY.

THE following is the text of the Married Women's Property Act, passed last Session:—

An Act to amend the Law relating to the Property of Married Women. [*9th August,* 1870.]

Whereas it is desirable to amend the law of property and contract with respect to married women:

Be it enacted by the Queen's most Excellent Majesty, by and with the advice and consent of the Lords Spiritual and Temporal, and Commons, in this present Parliament assembled, and by the authority of the same, as follows:—

1. The wages and earnings of any married woman acquired or gained by her after the passing of this Act in any employment, occupation, or trade in which she is engaged or which she carries on separately from her husband, and also any money or property so acquired by her through the exercise of any literary, artistic, or scientific skill, and all investments of such wages, earnings, money, or property, shall be deemed and taken to be property held and settled to her separate use, independent of any husband to whom she may be married, and her receipts alone shall be a good discharge for such wages, earnings, money, and property.

2. Notwithstanding any provision to the contrary in the Act of the tenth year of George the Fourth, chapter twenty-four, enabling the Commissioners for the Reduction of the National Debt to grant life annuities and

P

annuities for terms of years, or in the Acts relating to savings banks and post office savings banks, any deposit hereafter made and any annuity granted by the said Commissioners under any of the said Acts in the name of a married woman, or in the name of a woman who may marry after such deposit or grant, shall be deemed to be the separate property of such woman, and the same shall be accounted for and paid to her as if she were an unmarried woman ; provided that if any such deposit is made by, or such annuity granted to, a married woman by means of moneys of her husband without his consent, the Court may, upon an application under section nine of this Act, order such deposit or annuity or any part thereof to be paid to the husband.

3. Any married woman, or any woman about to be married, may apply to the Governor and Company of the Bank of England, or to the Governor and Company of the Bank of Ireland, by a form to be provided by the governor of each of the said banks and company for that purpose, that any sum forming part of the public stocks and funds, and not being less than twenty pounds, to which the woman so applying is entitled, or which she is about to acquire, may be transferred to or made to stand in the books of the governor and company to whom such application is made in the name or intended name of the woman as a married woman entitled to her separate use, and on such sum being entered in the books of the said governor and company accordingly, the same shall be deemed to be the separate property of such woman, and shall be transferred and the dividends paid as if she were an unmarried woman ; provided that if any such investment in the funds is made by a married woman by means of moneys of her husband without his consent, the Court may, upon an application under section nine of this Act, order such investment, and the dividends thereof, or any part thereof, to be transferred and paid to the husband.

4. Any married woman, or any woman about to be married, may apply in writing to the directors or managers of any incorporated or joint stock company that any fully paid up shares, or any debenture or debenture stock, or any stock of such company, to the holding of which no liability is attached, and to which the woman

so applying is entitled, may be registered in the books of the said company in the name or intended name of the woman as a married woman entitled to her separate use, and it shall be the duty of such directors or managers to register such shares or stock accordingly, and the same upon being so registered shall be deemed to be the separate property of such woman, and shall be transferred and the dividends and profits paid as if she were an unmarried woman; provided that if any such investment as last mentioned is made by a married woman by means of moneys of her husband without his consent, the Court may, upon an application under section nine of this Act, order such investment, and the dividends and profits thereon, or any part thereof, to be transferred and paid to the husband.

5. Any married woman, or any woman about to be married, may apply in writing to the committee of management of any industrial and provident society, or to the trustees of any friendly society, benefit building society, or loan society, duly registered, certified, or enrolled under the Acts relating to such societies respectively, that any share, benefit, debenture, right, or claim whatsoever in, to, or upon the funds of such society, to the holding of which share, benefit, or debenture, no liability is attached, and to which the woman so applying is entitled, may be entered in the books of the society in the name or intended name of the woman, as a married woman entitled to her separate use; and it shall be the duty of such committee or trustees to cause the same to be so entered, and thereupon such share, benefit, debenture, right, or claim, shall be deemed to be the separate property of such woman, and shall be transferable and payable with all dividends and profits thereon as if she were an unmarried woman; provided that if any such share, benefit, debenture, right, or claim, has been obtained by a married woman by means of moneys of her husband without his consent, the Court may, upon an application under section nine of this Act, order the same and the dividends and profits thereon, or any part thereof, to be transferred and paid to the husband.

6. Nothing hereinbefore contained in reference to moneys deposited in or annuities granted by savings

banks or moneys invested in the funds or in shares or stock of any company shall, as against creditors of the husband, give validity to any deposit or investment of moneys of the husband made in fraud of such creditors, and any moneys so deposited or invested may be followed as if this Act had not passed.

7. Where any woman married after the passing of this Act shall, during her marriage, become entitled to any personal property as next of kin, or one of the next of kin of an intestate, or to any sum of money not exceeding two hundred pounds under any deed or will, such property shall, subject and without prejudice to the trusts of any settlement affecting the same, belong to the woman for her separate use, and her receipts alone shall be a good discharge for the same.

8. Where any freehold, copyhold, or customaryhold property shall descend upon any woman married after the passing of this Act as heiress or co-heiress of an intestate, the rents and profits of such property shall, subject and without prejudice to the trusts of any settlement affecting the same, belong to such woman for her separate use, and her receipts alone shall be a good discharge for the same.

9. In any question between husband and wife as to property declared by this Act to be the separate property of the wife, either party may apply by summons or motion in a summary way either to the Court of Chancery in England or Ireland according as such property is in England or Ireland, or in England (irrespective of the value of the property) the judge of the County Court of the district in which either party resides, and thereupon the judge may make such order, direct such inquiry, and award such costs, as he shall think fit; provided that any order made by such judge shall be subject to appeal in the same manner as the order of the same judge made in a pending suit or on an equitable plaint would have been, and the judge may, if either party so require, hear the application in his private room.

10. A married woman may effect a policy of insurance upon her own life or the life of her husband for her separate use, and the same and all benefit thereof, if expressed on the face of it to be so effected, shall enure

accordingly, and the contract in such policy shall be as valid as if made with an unmarried woman.

A policy of insurance effected by any married man on his own life, and expressed upon the face of it to be for the benefit of his wife or of his wife and children, or any of them, shall enure and be deemed a trust for the benefit of his wife for her separate use, and of his children, or any of them, according to the interest so expressed, and shall not, so long as any object of the trust remains, be subject to the control of the husband or to his creditors, or form part of his estate. When the sum secured by the policy becomes payable, or at any time previously, a trustee thereof may be appointed by the Court of Chancery in England or in Ireland according as the policy of insurance was effected in England or in Ireland, or in England by the judge of the County Court of the district, or in Ireland by the chairman of the Civil Bill Court of the division of the county, in which the insurance office is situated, and the receipt of such trustee shall be a good discharge to the office. If it shall be proved that the policy was effected and premiums paid by the husband with intent to defraud his creditors, they shall be entitled to receive out of the sum secured an amount equal to the premiums so paid.

11. A married woman may maintain an action in her own name for the recovery of any wages, earnings, money, and property by this Act declared to be her separate property, or of any property belonging to her before marriage, and which her husband shall, by writing under his hand, have agreed with her shall belong to her after marriage as her separate property, and she shall have in her own name the same remedies, both civil and criminal, against all persons whomsoever for the protection and security of such wages, earnings, money, and property, and of any chattels or other property purchased or obtained by means thereof for her own use, as if such wages, earnings, money, chattels, and property belonged to her as an unmarried woman; and in any indictment or other proceeding it shall be sufficient to allege such wages, earnings, money, chattels, and property to be her property.

12. A husband shall not, by reason of any marriage

which shall take place after this Act has come into operation, be liable for the debts of his wife contracted before marriage, but the wife shall be liable to be sued for, and any property belonging to her for her separate use shall be liable to satisfy, such debts as if she had continued unmarried.

13. Where in England the husband of any woman having separate property becomes chargeable to any union or parish, the justices having jurisdiction in such union or parish may, in petty sessions assembled, upon application of the guardians of the poor, issue a summons against the wife, and make and enforce such order against her for the maintenance of her husband as by the thirty-third section of "The Poor Law Amendment Act, 1868," they may now make and enforce against a husband for the maintenance of his wife who becomes chargeable to any union or parish. Where in Ireland relief is given under the provisions of the Acts relating to the relief of the destitute poor to the husband of any woman having separate property, the cost price of such relief is hereby declared to be a loan from the guardians of the union in which the same shall be given, and shall be recoverable from such woman as if she were a femme sole by such and the same actions and proceedings as money lent.

14. A married woman having separate property shall be subject to all such liability for the maintenance of her children as a widow is now by law subject to for the maintenance of her children: Provided always, that nothing in this Act shall relieve her husband from any liability at present imposed upon him by law to maintain her children.

15. This Act shall come into operation at the time of the passing of this Act.

16. This Act shall not extend to Scotland.

17. This Act may be cited as the "Married Women's Property Act, 1870."

The most satisfactory clauses in this Act are the first and second, and it is to be regretted that the principle which runs through them does not extend into other clauses. It is a happiness to think that the poor wives and mothers who are forced to maintain their families by working in cotton factories and elsewhere, will no longer be met at the factory gate on pay days by their husbands, and compelled to give up a portion of their earnings. Drunken husbands and fathers will still be able to spend the whole of their wages on their own gratification, but they will no longer be able to possess themselves of any portion of their wives' earnings. Whatever the wife and mother earns may now be spent, without deduction, for the benefit of the family. This is a great victory.

Clause 2 will also prove a blessing to working women, particularly to maid-servants. We well remember when the regulations of the Post Office Savings Bank were published, with what shame for our country we read the rule which enabled a man to draw out his wife's savings made before marriage. No thoughtful person could read that clause without sorrow, for it fed the arrogance and selfishness of every bad man, and brought humiliation on every woman. Let us thank God that this cause of demoralisation to the population has been removed.

We are sometimes told that women, by agitating about their rights, will cause the laws regarding them to be made still harsher. The enactment of these clauses shows the contrary. Those who have carried on the agitation now see the first fruits of their labour, and may rejoice at the termination of no small amount of misery.

The 500*l.* or so which has been spent in obtaining this change in the law will prevent more distress than ten times the amount spent every year in charity would relieve, for a permanent improvement has been made in the condition of women and children, in the country generally, and especially in the great towns and the manufacturing districts.

No unqualified praise can be given to the other clauses, though their general tendency is favourable to women. Some of them demand special remark. It should be observed that clauses 7 and 8 only apply to women married after the passing of the Act. These clauses contain a singular anomaly. If a father, uncle, or other relative or friend, carefully leaves his real property by will to his married daughter, or niece, or friend, it will *not* become hers, but will go to her husband, though if he make no will, it will become hers if she is the next of kin. The same rule holds good with regard to personal property of more than 200*l.* value. The relative will defeat his own intention by making a will. This curious arrangement is justified on the ground that if a relative wished his property to go to the wife rather than the husband, he could leave it for her " sole and separate use," in which case it really would become hers. It might be argued in reply, that if he wished it to go to the husband rather than to the wife, he could so leave it by will. It is not an unreasonable assumption that a testator wishes his property to go to the person whom he names in his will. Among the general public the meaning of the words "sole and separate use," are not understood. They seem to imply that the property thus left is to be expended solely on the wife and could not be used for the benefit of the husband and children. It is not likely therefore that an ordinary man or woman, unlearned in the law, would leave more than a very small sum to a married woman, for what would seem to be a narrow and selfish object.

Clause 11 is more important than it appears to be from the marginal note. It provides, that any property belonging to a woman, will remain hers if her husband before marriage has agreed in writing to its so remaining. Thus, if a woman when engaged to be married makes a list of things that belong to her, and her intended husband writes at the bottom that these articles are to be his future wife's separate property, they will remain her own; so at least we understand. We think that a house, a shop, furniture, jewels, a watch, a sewing machine, or anything else might be secured in this manner.

It would, however, perhaps be necessary that the list should be in the husband's handwriting.*

Clause 12 declares that a husband shall not be liable

---

* One defect in the Act is that it requires a lawyer to interpret it, and in an Act intended for the benefit of the *poor* this is a great fault. We give what we believe to be the true interpretation of clause 11, but it would be rash to act upon our opinion without consulting a lawyer.

for his wife's debts contracted before marriage. The wife will be liable for them, and any separate property she may possess will be liable to satisfy them. It is certainly right that where a wife keeps her property she should be liable for her debts, but where a wife's property was not placed before marriage in any of the investments mentioned in the Act, or though so placed was not secured to the wife, and has therefore been taken possession of by the husband, it seems hard that she should remain liable for her debts, the means of payment having been taken from her.

The Act is a great improvement on the law it has displaced, but had not the Bill been much altered in the House of Lords, the improvement would have been far greater. It is incorrect to speak of it as "Mr. Russell Gurney's Bill," its character being quite different from that of the Bill introduced by that gentleman. The first five clauses of the Bill as sent up from the House of Commons were expunged by the Lords.

These clauses will sufficiently show the character and intention of the Bill passed by the House of Commons.

1. A married woman shall be capable of holding, acquiring, alienating, devising, and bequeathing real and personal estate, of contracting, and of suing and being sued, as if she were a feme sole.

Provided, that nothing herein contained shall empower a married woman to dispose otherwise than by will of any freehold or copyhold hereditaments, or any money subject to be invested in the purchase of freehold or copyhold hereditaments, or any future or reversionary interest, whether vested or contingent, in personalty, or to release or extinguish any power which may be vested in her in regard to such freehold or copyhold hereditaments, money, or personal estate, but the power of disposition otherwise than by will now vested in married women over all such hereditaments and other property shall remain the same as if this Act had not passed.

2. No judgment founded upon a contract made or act done by a woman during coverture, or execution thereon, shall bind or affect any property except such personal estate (if any) as she may be possessed of or entitled to for a present interest during her coverture.

3. Every woman who marries after this Act has come into operation, shall, notwithstanding her coverture, have and hold all real and personal property, whether belonging to her before marriage or acquired by her in any way after marriage, free

from the debts and obligations of her husband, and from his control or disposition, in all respects as if she had continued unmarried.

4. Every woman married before this Act has come into operation shall, notwithstanding her coverture, have and hold all the real and personal estate, her right to which shall arise after this Act shall have come into operation, free from the debts and obligations of her husband, and from his control or disposition, in all respects as if she had continued unmarried; but nothing herein contained shall exempt any such property from the operation of any settlement or covenant to which it would have been subject if this Act had not passed, or shall prejudice any rights or interest to which her husband or any person claiming through him may be entitled at the date at which this Act comes into operation.

5. The earnings of a married woman in any trade or other occupation carried on by her as a principal separately from her husband shall be deemed to be her property acquired after marriage.

Mr. Russell Gurney's Bill asserted the principle that married women were as capable of holding property as unmarried ones, though it limited their right under certain circumstances. The present Act is a compromise between the old Common Law and Mr. Gurney's Bill, and contains no principle at all. Some of the hardships which arose under the old law will be removed, but others will remain. Perhaps one reason why the House of Lords showed such hostility to Mr. Gurney's Bill is that they have but little knowledge of those hardships. It is, therefore, the more to be regretted that the Select Committee of Lords should have *refused to hear evidence,* and have met only twice to consider the subject. The Select Committee of the House of Commons met several times, and heard voluminous evidence before it reported in favour of Mr. Gurney's Bill; we may believe without prejudice that the Committee which heard evidence and took time to consider the subject arrived at a juster conclusion than the Committee, which declined to hear evidence and decided hastily.

But although women have no cause for gratitude towards the Lords as a body, several individuals among them behaved with much kindness in endeavouring, sometimes with success, to obtain the introduction of clauses for the better protection of wives' property, or the modification of other clauses that were unfavourable to wives. The part taken by the various lords is tolerably well shown in the reports of the debates, given in "Events."

A bad part of the Act is its tendency to produce family discord.

Mr. Gurney's Bill, which allowed a married woman to keep her property just as other people are allowed to keep theirs would not have produced that effect; for if a man knows before he marries, that his wife's property will continue to belong to her, just as his own property will continue to belong to himself, he must be of a very unreasonable disposition if he quarrels about it, and it is quite impossible that there should be any disappointment on his part. But if he believe that his wife's property will belong to himself, and then finds that she has prudently ordered her money in the funds and her shares in the railroad to be registered in her own name, as her separate property, according to clauses 3 and 4, it is probable that he will be extremely disappointed and angry.

The present law contains no principle.

It does not pronounce whether it is right or wrong for a married woman to possess property. A confiding woman will not secure any property to herself. A prudent woman can secure all, or nearly all, she possesses.

The confiding woman may be robbed by a dishonest, or ruined by a foolish husband, while the prudent woman runs the risk of giving mortal offence to a proud and sensitive man, who may regard her natural desire to retain her own property as arguing distrust of him. A good deal is left to chance. To give the property to the wife if it comes to her from an intestate, and to the husband if left to her by will, leaves the ownership of the property to be decided by luck, almost as much as if it had been directed that the husband and wife were to appear before the Court of Chancery and there solemnly to "toss up" for it.

In spite, however, of the shortcomings of the Bill as amended by the Lords, we are glad it was not rejected by the Commons, for while it relieves some suffering, it has broken down the false principles of the old Common Law and opened the way for further improvements.

In the course of the next year or two the defects of the present law will become conspicuous, and we have no doubt that then Mr. Russell Gurney, Mr. Shaw Lefevre, or some other member of the House of Commons, will reintroduce the original Bill, which will be carried through the Lords with less difficulty than if the present Act had been rejected by the Commons.

Art. II.—FRENCHWOMEN AND THE WAR.

Some extracts from the *Droits des Femmes*, a French weekly newspaper, will be found interesting, as they show the tone assumed by the women's rights party in France with regard to the war.

On the 13th of July, the eve of the declaration of war, the editor writes:—

> While I write news is being brought in every hour. The most disquieting rumours follow quickly upon assurances of peace. For my part I believe in war. If you ask me why, I reply— "Because the government chooses to have it so." . . If Prussia were to give full satisfaction to the French Government on the Spanish question, it would not suffice. The object is to humiliate the King of Prussia. . . These questions of "*amour propre*" do not concern us. The two nations are friendly at bottom, and questions of dynastic interest ought to be postponed to national interests. War may be agreeable to kings; it is not agreeable to the peoples. Mothers of families write to us from all sides to ask what is to be done. . . Let voices be raised everywhere against the war. If anything can ward off war it will be a general cry from all France. Let us protest in the name of humanity against this pastime of princes, which causes the blood of the people to flow. . . And here women have not only the right to interfere, it is their duty to do so. Let them protest. This is what they can do. Who will dare to say now that politics do not concern wives and mothers?
>
> When politics bring such consequences they concern everybody. The protest of women ought to be placed by the side of the protest of working men. Let it come. We will publish it.

The following week the *Droits des Femmes* says :—

Our appeal has been heard. Numerous and energetic protests against the war have been sent us. All are written and signed by women. . . We acknowledge their receipt, but do not publish them, for events have passed so quickly that it is no longer time. It is too late!

In another article in the same issue the editor exhorts women to volunteer to assist the wounded.

Money and gifts in kind will be received at the office and transmitted by the editor, but this is not all. It is not enough to give one's mite or to pick lint; what is wanted are hands. There are the wounded to attend, the sick to nurse, the dying to comfort, not only in the hospitals, but on the field of battle. They tell you, oh women! that you bear none of the burdens of war. It is one of the great arguments brought against you when you ask for equal rights with men. Show now that you know how to take your share of dangerous duties!

It is no question of approving of the war, but of mitigating the evils of war.

You will have to save even those who are now called "the enemies of France."

Forward, then, women! Forward, volunteers of charity! Remember the mothers whose sons will be dying. On whichever side they fall, the wounded are your brothers.

These extracts show how averse many women in France were to the war, before it broke out.

If women had had political power might they not have prevented it?

The Emperor went to war because he wanted to please the people; he was growing unpopular, and thought that a war would restore his popularity, and if the war had been successful, no doubt he would have been right; but to go to war would not have been the way to gain popularity with women, even had the war been successful, if the readers of the *Droits* may be regarded as representing the feelings of Frenchwomen generally. Our moral is— give women all over Europe political power, and a great peaceful influence will thus be created, which will immediately tend to diminish the frequency of wars, and may ultimately put an end to war altogether.

Art. III.—A CASE OF WIFE STARVING.

The following story so well illustrates the deficiencies of the law with regard to the maintenance of wives that we reprint it from the *Devonport Independent*.

INQUEST AT PLYMOUTH.—CENSURE OF A RELIEVING OFFICER.

An inquest was held by Mr. T. C. Brian, coroner, on Saturday, at the Queen's Arms Hotel, North Road, Plymouth, on the body of a woman residing at 6, Ashley Place, named Bella Nelson, whose husband, a Dane, is a bandsman on board H.M.S. *Royal Adelaide*. It appeared from the evidence that the poor woman was very far advanced in a decline, and was in a state of pitiable destitution. Her husband, against whom no complaint was made for unkindness or unattendance to the deceased, was in the receipt of 8s. per week, with some ship's provisions, which, if turned into money, would produce about 2s. 4d. more, making in all 2l. 1s. 4d. per month. Out of this sum he had to maintain the sickly wife and two step-children. In order to meet the wants of his family, and procure nourishment for the dying woman, the greater part of the wearing apparel and furniture had been pledged, and she was left with nothing but a few rags to lie upon, and a ragged petticoat to cover her.

The surgeon of the district, Mr. John McWilliams Graham, deposed that he was first called to visit her on Monday, August 1, and he then found her in a very emaciated condition, and in the last stage of consumption. The bed, and everything she was lying on, were in a dreadful state, the room in fact was quite poverty stricken. He left her some medicine to ease her cough and two days afterwards he called again, because it struck him on the first occasion that she was very much in need of an increased amount of nourishing food. He then made inquiries as to her condition, and the poor woman herself told him that her husband had spent his every farthing upon her, and that they had nothing more. She expressed a desire to have some mutton, and he left an order for it to be delivered to the relieving officer. Had that order been complied with, he should afterwards have ordered wine and other nourishment, but when he found that it had not been complied with, he told the deceased that he could do no more for her as he should like to have done, because the guardians gave him no power to compel the relieving officer to execute his orders.

The Coroner said the probability was that if she had had proper nourishing things she might have been living now.

A Case of Wife Starving.

A juror to Mr. Graham: Have you ever given orders in similar cases before this that have not been attended to?

Mr. Graham: Yes, hundreds, and the notes have either been torn up or thrown away. At any rate, they have been taken no notice of.

Mr. Mayell: That is rather strong language.

Mr. Graham: It is true, nevertheless. That is where we have so much trouble.

Mr. Matthews: Have you before this ever known any serious consequences to arise through this non-attention to your orders?

Mr. Graham: No, because I have always taken the trouble to see about it.

Mr. Matthews: Why did you not see about it in this case?

Mr. Graham: I have got tired of doing so.

Mr. Mayell, the relieving officer, was next examined. He said he had ascertained that the husband was in the receipt of between 3*l*. and 4*l*. per month, and that it was his duty to have come to him. If he had done so he should have attended to the case; he, however, gave the girl (daughter) an order thinking that something serious might happen while the father was away. Two days afterwards the girl came to him with an order from the surgeon for some meat, and he then told her if her father would come to him he would attend to the case, but he had never said that if she brought 100 orders she would get nothing. In some cases where similar orders have been given he had gone to see the people, and they said they did not want meat, but medicine.

Mr. Graham: That does not apply to my district?

Mr. Mayell: Yes, sir, it applies to your district.

Mr. Graham: I defy you to mention a single case.

The Coroner: Don't you think that after the order had been given it was your duty to inquire into the case?

Mr. Mayell: I think it was the duty of the husband to come to me.

The Coroner: You have stated that people have expressed their indignation to you at having had a doctor's order for meat given them. Can you specify one single case?

Mr. Mayell: I cannot at this moment, but I might do so were I at home.

This was the whole of the evidence, and

Mr. Matthews, on behalf of Mr. Mayell, reminded the jury that if all orders given by the doctors were executed without inquiry on the part of the relieving officers, the number of cases would be increased by hundreds, and the rates would have to bear the burthen. The only possible measure of fault he could find with Mr. Mayell was that, having received the order, he might have gone himself to see the woman, but then he was told that the father was a bandsman and came home every evening, and no doubt he considered it to be the duty of the man to come to him.

The Coroner, in summing up the evidence to the jury, remarked that had Mr. Mayell visited the woman himself, the probability was that he would have executed the doctor's order; at any rate he would have been in a better position to judge as to whether it was a proper case for relief. Here was a very anomalous state of things which could not work beneficially for the public; it was an illustration of how it could not. A medical officer deemed certain things necessary for a person dangerously ill, and gave an order for the relieving officer, who refused to execute it. Was not that a mockery? (Hear, hear.) Was there not something wrong about the mode of acting? If Mr. Mayell was not under any obligation to obey such an order, why was Mr. Graham empowered to give it? (Mr. Mayell: It is not an order, only a recommendation.) Well, granted that it was only a recommendation, why should the doctor have the power to give it if the relieving officer had it at his option to refuse to execute it? Whatever the result of the present inquiry was, he sincerely hoped that it would lead to a better state of things in future; that when a medical man thought a poor person was entitled to necessaries his wishes should be carried out, and that the public would hear no more of such cases.

The jury returned as their verdict that the deceased died from natural causes, but they blamed the husband for not making a personal application on behalf of his wife to the relieving officer, and censured Mr. Mayell for not complying with the order of the medical man, or at least for not going personally to inquire into the case.

The inquiry lasted upwards of three hours.

At a subsequent meeting of the guardians, the relieving officer, Mr. Mayell, called the attention of the Board to the censure pronounced against him by the jury, for the purpose of justifying himself:—

Mr. Mayell said he could prove that there was no destitution in the case, as the husband of the woman was in receipt of 16s. 11d. per week. He had been on board H.M.S. *Royal Adelaide* and inquired for himself. (Hear, hear, and cries of "bravo.") Suppose the woman had received relief she would only have got 3s. per week for herself, and 1s. 6d. for her child. At the inquest it was stated that the husband of the woman was in receipt of only 8s. per week; this was untrue. He had bitterly to complain of the conduct of the Coroner towards him, in summing up the facts of the case to the jury. He had acted in the most prejudiced manner. He had also to complain of the conduct of Mr. Williamson, one of the guardians, for the manner that gentleman had acted towards him. Had it not been for Mr. Williamson no inquest would have been held, and no charge made against him.

The Clerk said that he had ascertained from the boatswain of H.M.S. *Royal Adelaide*, that the husband of the woman Nelson received 16s. 11d. per week, instead of 8s. (Hear, hear.)

Mr. Williamson said that he had furnished the coroner with the facts of the case laid before the jury at the inquest, for which the Coroner publicly thanked him. He considered he had done his duty, and did not even now regret what he had done. If a man had 50,000*l*. a year, and was to desert his wife, the Board were bound to relieve her if she applied to them for relief, and then sue the husband. He therefore did not think that the fact of the woman Nelson's husband, being in receipt of 16*s*. per week, was anything to do with his wife if she applied for relief. In conclusion, he said, he thought it was Mr. Mayell's duty to have relieved the woman, and that he had not done his duty in not doing so.

After a long discussion a resolution was carried by a large majority "that the Board are satisfied with the information given concerning the case."

This appears to be equivalent to a vote of approbation of the relieving officer's conduct.

The *Plymouth Independent* makes the following remarks on the case:—

There were several points in the recent case of alleged starvation at Plymouth which are of public importance, and which it is necessary should be speedily and effectually settled. That any relieving officer should possess the power to contemptuously neglect and destroy the order of a medical officer when he directs that food or nourishment shall be administered to a suffering pauper, seems, on the face of it, to be a monstrous anomaly. In this instance, it was stated that the relieving officer "tore up" the order, and that such a course is by no means unfrequent with him and others in the town in a similar position. In fact, one surgeon stated in evidence that "hundreds of orders which he had issued had been destroyed by the relieving officer, who had refused to act upon them!" If the relieving officer is better able to judge scientifically of the condition of persons when they are ill, and if he knows what is good for them better than a medical man, what is the good of the parish electing medical men at all? It is a waste of money—an extravagant expenditure of the rates for which the guardians ought to be called to account. But the fact is that relieving officers ought to be bound to carry out the orders of a medical man; and it is no less than unwarrantable assumption and impertinence which can induce a man to "tear up" such an order and disregard it as in this case. The surgeon was paid by the parish to give food or medicine when required to persons who were too poor to procure it themselves; the medical man acted to the best of his ability, and, doubtless, did so with as keen a conscience as the relieving officer possessed; and, moreover, he was responsible for his own actions. The relieving officer was not responsible for what the surgeon did; and, therefore, to "tear up" the order for food when it was presented to him was an amount of assumption which is intolerable. Besides, it turned out that the woman for whom the food was ordered absolutely required it; the want of nourishment hastened her death, and the relieving officer was deservedly censured. If relieving officers are permitted such a power as this, it will assuredly lead to serious results; and even now, in regard to this officer, he having "destroyed hundreds of orders," it is impossible to say what suffering and misery has gone unrelieved. The fact that the woman's husband was in receipt of wages sufficient to maintain his wife is not to the purpose. The point was, was the dying woman in poverty, did she require nourishment, and was she unable to procure it, and did she apply for assistance? If so, that assistance ought to have been granted her. But with the surgeon's order—based upon his professional and scientific knowledge, for the devotion of which to the poor the parish pays him—there was no alternative left open to the relieving officer. If he had proof that the surgeon was acting wrongly, he could have complained, and the surgeon would have had to answer for himself. But it so happened that the surgeon did perfectly right, proving the incapacity of the relieving officer to decide against the medical man in such cases. A severe effort has been made by one or two men to save the rates in Plymouth: the object is a good one undoubtedly, but rather than such means as this should be adopted to accomplish it, it would be better that the rates were never decreased, and the ratepayers will to a man concur in this feeling. Every right-thinking person must feel that Mr. Williamson courageously performed a good service, and that he is entitled to the thanks of the public.

It must not be supposed that such cases are rare. They are common. My attention having been attracted to the subject by a case that occurred in my own neighbourhood, I watched the newspapers for similar instances, and in two years collected four cases of wives on whom inquests were held, and who died from want of food, which their husbands omitted to supply them with, though having the means of so doing. I also collected three cases of wives who, to shorten their sufferings from famine, attempted to kill themselves, but were prevented from so doing and taken before a magistrate. I have had these stories reprinted and will send them to any one who wishes to see them. I do not suppose that a tenth part of the cases that occur ever appear in the newspapers, and I had the opportunity of seeing only a limited number of local newspapers, so that my collection is most imperfect, and represents, probably, not 1 per cent. of the cases that really occur.

Mr. Williamson points out the course that guardians ought to pursue when a man neglects to supply his wife with the necessaries of life, *i.e.*, they should send food to the wife and prosecute the husband.

There is, however, a great difficulty to be overcome before a prosecution can be made successfully. The magistrate is almost always unwilling to send a man to prison for this offence, for he generally entertains a strong suspicion that the guardians are acting harshly towards him. Some excuse is, therefore, found for letting him off, and the parish simply loses the expenses of the prosecution. Prosecutions are, consequently, rare, and the plan followed by guardians generally, is to order the relieving officer to supply the wife with necessaries in illness, where the husband does not earn enough to supply her himself, but to refuse relief when he earns good wages.

The doctor simply orders relief when the woman requires it, without considering the man's circumstances. The relieving officer, however, ignores the order whenever the husband is well off. It often happens that the husband when he finds nothing can be got from the parish, takes compassion on his wife and feeds her; but sometimes he does not, and then she dies. Now and then an inquest is held, and the relieving officer is blamed. When this happens the guardians meet and declare themselves perfectly satisfied with his conduct and the matter ends. It is only in exceptional cases, however, that even thus much notice is taken. It must often happen that the disorder from which the wife was suffering gets the credit of her death, when, in fact, starvation was the real cause. There is no one to tell. Children dare not complain of their father, and neighbours, even if they know the woman has died of want, do not like to interfere, and so, unless the parish doctor is extraordinarily attentive and zealous he gives a certificate that she died of disease; the woman is buried and nothing is said.

It is evident that a change in the law is required, and after long study of the subject, I venture to make the following suggestion:—

When the parish surgeon has ordered necessaries for a sick wife, and the relieving officer is of opinion that the husband is able to supply her with them himself, the magistrate should be empowered to make an order on the husband, in proportion to his wages, for as many shillings a week as he thinks right, for the maintenance of his wife and of any children who may be too young to maintain themselves. The money to be paid to the relieving officer, who should supply the family with an equivalent in food and other necessaries. Magistrates would not be unwilling to make this order. As long as the husband continued to pay the money he would remain unmolested, but if he ceased to pay, a warrant or summons should be issued against him, and he should be brought before the magistrate.

As the order would have been made for no larger an amount than the magistrate himself thought right, he would probably feel no reluctance to punish the man, as it would be clear to his mind that no harshness had been shown.

If a man's wages were not large, the extra comforts required by a sick person, such as meat and wine, should be supplied at the expense of the parish, and the husband should be required to pay only for ordinary necessaries.

Now that a wife is entitled to keep her own earnings it would be necessary to apply the same rule to wives in case of a husband's falling ill, and his wife refusing to supply him with food though able to do so.

The probability is that very few husbands or wives would have to be committed to prison for neglecting to obey the order. They would feel that punishment would be certain to follow disobedience, and consequently they would obey.

Art. IV.—PUBLIC OPINION ON QUESTIONS CONCERNING WOMEN.

THE LORDS AND THE MARRIED WOMEN'S PROPERTY BILL.

An immense preponderance of public opinion disapproves of the alterations which the Lords have made in this Act.

Public Opinion.

Times, June 22.*

As might have been expected, the Law Lords exhibited their usual ingenious diversity of opinion in the matter of the Married Women's Property Bill last night. The measure has passed the Commons, where it has been preferred by a large majority to a rival measure less thorough in its principle, and less complete in the remedy it affords. Last year the House of Commons examined the subject by means of a Select Committee, and it can hardly be denied that the Bill now sent up to the Lords represents a maturely formed opinion. . . . . The change in the law would at once give a better position to every woman, and not merely to the woman who is sufficiently provoked and sufficiently strong-minded to take an unusual and most hostile proceeding against her husband. It would not supersede marriage settlements, for the settlement is as much to protect the woman from herself as from her husband; but it would, in thousands of households, give greater moral influence to the wife, and tend to the happiness and prosperity of both her husband and herself. Indeed, the right of women to the possession of and disposal of property being admitted, we cannot believe, until it is shown by arguments stronger than any used in the House of Lords last night, that the ceremony of marriage ought to "act on a woman like a conviction for felony," and reduce a person of independent fortune into a dependent on the bounty of another.

Spectator, June 25.

The Lords are trying to improve the Married Women's Property Bill out of the world. As it has passed the House of Commons by large majorities, and is desired by a great majority of Her Majesty's subjects—namely, by all women, and by all men in whom habit has not stifled the original instinct of justice—the Peers have not thrown it out on the second reading, but have only sent it up to a Select Committee, with orders to recast it until it shall affect only the very poor, and shall have no clear principle in it whatever. They refuse altogether to acknowledge that a married woman has as inherent a right to own property as a single one; they have resolved to continue the oppression under which marriage operates as a conviction for felony; they have decided that confiscation, so shocking a crime when committed by the State against a landlord, is no crime at all when committed by a husband against his wife; but just to quiet clamour, and get rid of "painful cases," they have agreed that if the wife, while a wife, contrives to earn anything, she may keep the control of it. . . . . We earnestly trust that the Members who have passed this Bill will allow it to drop sooner than admit any amendment whatever which interferes with its grand principle—that a woman's right to her own, now fully admitted

---

* This article, and one or two others, was written before the Act, now law, was cast in its present form, but it is still quite applicable.

by the law, which gives to Miss Burdett Coutts exactly the rights it gives to her coachman, is no more forfeited by marriage than a man's. No change in the law short of that can be of any real value, for no change short of it will relieve women from their present position as lawful subjects of permitted plunder. Their property is either theirs or it is not. If it is not, the Legislature has no right to give it them; if it is, it has no right to take it away on the mere charge of being women. . . . .

There is one argument against the Bill which was faintly pressed in the Peers, and is very operative in society, and that is the religious one—that separate rights of property are opposed to the unity which the Christian, no less than the English, law desires to establish between the husband and wife; but the Lords have themselves destroyed this argument. They have repeatedly passed laws intended to enable the wives of the rich to retain their separate rights, and are even now, as Lord Shaftesbury confesses, willing to abandon that principle entirely as regards the poor, by giving every woman control over her own earnings. The Earl of Shaftesbury and Lord Hatherley, each in his way a perfect representative of English religious feeling, both expatiated on the great hardship which fell on industrious women when their husbands swept away their savings, but under the unity idea he has surely as much right to them as to the property the wife may have inherited. Jane Smith goes out "charing," earns ten shillings a week, and saves up five for her child. John Smith waits till she has twenty shillings, and then, as her husband, comes and sweeps it away. That, say the Peers, is an iniquity which ought to be prevented. Jane's mother, however, dies, and leaves her five battered spoons, worth four weeks' savings, and John when he drinks up that is within his divine right. Was ever such nonsense talked in a Legislature composed of laymen? However, we do not wish to make much of that. We are not to-day trying to fight the battles of the poor, or to establish any sentimental case whatever: we admit to the full that heaps of women will misuse their new power; we doubt very greatly whether it will not produce new kinds of evils among the poor, even if it remedies the old—the husband in default of a legal mode of oppression trying an illegal one—our single contention is that a woman has as much moral claim to her own as a man, and does not forfeit her right by marriage, and that the Legislature in decreeing such forfeiture formally sanctions a violent wrong, openly legalizes a theft.

The same, August 6.

The Lords' version of the Married Women's Property Bill has been accepted by the Commons, and may be considered passed. The new Bill would in a clumsy sort of way protect women's earnings, if the poor ever read Bills, and even their property acquired after marriage, but its principle is fundamentally wrong. It re-sanctions the English practice by which marriage is made an excuse for confiscation, and a woman who marries is treated as an infant or a lunatic, incompetent to use, bequeath, or hold her own money. We regret the passing of the Bill, because English Philistinism never can understand a grievance which does not appear in the Law Courts, but we do not believe that the only "Woman's Right" upon which the sex is united can be long refused.

Economist.

If the Lords succeed in limiting the operation of the Bill to the protection of a married woman's earnings or wages, and in striking out the part which enables a married woman to hold property exactly as if she were unmarried, they will have succeeded, to our mind, in postponing the recognition of a very gross blunder of principle by preventing the logical application of the right principle to one of the most ordinary of all the inferences which flow from it. If a married woman is to be incapable of holding the principal of a sum left to her, she ought to be incapable also of receiving the interest to her separate use. If she is to be refused the right to spend her own fortune, she ought to be refused the right to spend her own wages. Their Lordships seem to us as illogical in retaining the part of the Bill they wish to retain, as they are irrational in rejecting the part of the Bill they propose to reject.

Law Journal.

SEPARATE ESTATE.—If the new edition of the Married Women's Property Bill, prepared by the Select Committee of the House of Lords, passes into law, the result as to what property of the wife will be in the disposition of the husband, and what will be held to the separate use of the wife, will be very curious. We will endeavour to classify the various kinds of property which may come to a married woman according to the new law under these two heads. The following species of property will be held to the separate use of the wife, and be free from the control of the husband and of his creditors :—(1.) Wages and earnings of the woman acquired in any employment, occupation, or trade carried on separately from the husband. (2.) Money or property acquired by her through the exercise of any literary, artistic, or scientific skill. (3.) All investments of such wages, earnings, money, or property. (4.) Deposits in savings banks in the name of the woman. (5.) Public stocks and funds standing in the books of the Bank of England in the name of the woman. (6.) Paid-up shares in a joint-stock company registered in the name of the woman. (7.) Shares in any friendly society registered in the name of the woman. (8.) Personal property devolving on her as next of kin to an intestate. (9.) Rents and profits of real property descending to her as heiress upon an intestacy. (10.) Policy of insurance effected by her in her own name or by her husband in her name for her use. The following species of property coming to the wife be in the disposition of the husband in the manner and to the extent existing under the present law :—
(1.) Wearing apparel, jewels, ornaments, furniture, plate, instru-

ments of trade, and other goods and chattels not acquired by her own labour, or devolving on her upon an intestacy, and including money, shares, stocks, &c., acquired by her by donation, *inter vivos*, or under any testamentary disposition. (2.) Real estate devised to her by a simple devise. Among other anomalies presented by this legislation this may be noted, that a husband will be unable to plunder his wife of the fruits of her industry, but he will be able to prevent her starting in any handicraft or trade by seizing on or disposing of any instruments or stock necessary for use in such handicraft or trade, even if these be given to her by a person other than himself. In revenge she may, under section 10, indict him for stealing from her any property secured to her by the Bill.

Echo.

There is, we must admit, something deeply impressive in seeing such an acknowledged pillar of English domestic morality, such a paragon of good old-fashioned piety as Lord Westbury, standing forth to plead for the "domestic rule which had lasted in England for a thousand years!" We are compelled to reflect on how much of the solid character of our national virtues, and the purity of our English homes, must be traceable to the prototypes of Lord Westbury, who have "kept the king's conscience" from the days of Alfred to our own, and how becoming it is for a man of his venerable reputation to stand up as the champion *pro aris et focis*.

Pall Mall Gazette, July 12.

The House of Commons will find some little difficulty in recognising their old acquaintance, the Married Women's Property Bill, on its return from its temporary absence in the House of Lords. In the short interval which has elapsed since it was sent across the lobby it has been subjected to a process of transformation almost as complete as it certainly was summary. The Select Committee to whom it was referred did not think it requisite to meet on more than two occasions. On the first they settled their course of procedure, and on the second they agreed to their report. The result of their deliberations is that with the exception of the preamble the measure has been entirely recast. About one half of the clauses of which it originally consisted have been altogether expunged, and we are glad to see that among them are those which were at once the most characteristic and the most objectionable. Only the more sanguine, possibly only the female portion of Mr. Russell Gurney's supporters, could have expected any other kind of termination to the labours of the Select Committee. To all the rest it must have appeared at the least improbable that a measure combining in so marked a degree some of the weakest points of hysterical discontent with some of the worst features of amateur legislation should have passed muster before a tribunal of which Lord Westbury, Lord Penzance, and Lord Cairns were members. . . . .

In order to benefit a confessedly insignificant minority of

married women it seems hardly worth while to revolutionise the domestic economy of every household in the kingdom. The means proposed are out of all proportion to the end in view, and will inevitably be productive of far more evil than they are adapted to counteract. In a healthy condition of society the support of the family must be the care of the husband, and if the wife engages in any occupation beyond those duties which specially belong to her situation, it should be in aiding and in conjunction with him. It is surprising how deeply the current of popular sentiments become tinged by the influence of laws, and the influence of this Bill, if it gets into the Statute-book, will tend directly to infuse a spirit of isolated avarice in every woman who comes within its purview. It will teach them to separate their interests from those of their husbands, and to see in the persons whom they should regard as their helpmates only rival competitors for gain. And, beyond this, the general tone of public morality could not be otherwise than lowered by its operation, since it would open up novel facilities for fraud, without establishing any fresh checks on its perpetration. It is at present difficult to prevent post-nuptial settlements from being perverted to dishonourable uses by debtors, and under this Bill creditors would literally have no chance at all of helping themselves against a conspiracy between husband and wife. On these among other grounds we base our opposition to the Married Women's Property Bill, which, although less mischievous than it was, is still an eminently mischievous measure.

The *Post* cannot see in the Bill, as it now stands, any ground for Mr. Russell Gurney's lamentations. It wholly changes the wife's legal status. . . . But, subject to these restrictions, the Bill gives to married women all and more than the rights of spinsterhood. Whether it will work well is a question which time alone can answer.

Saturday Review, August 6.

The Married Women's Property Bill, as amended by the House of Lords, resembles an old coat which has been repaired by the addition of a new body and new sleeves. This child, says Mr. Russell Gurney, is not my child, but it is a good-looking child, and I adopt it. The Bill as it went up to the Lords contained seventeen clauses, besides the clauses which occur in all Bills, and it returns with only three of these seventeen clauses uncancelled, while twelve new clauses have been introduced. The House of Commons has substantially accepted this transformation of its own work, and legislation on this subject is likely to be completed under the guidance of practical sagacity. . . . Respectfully condoling with Miss Becker and her friends on their disappointment, we must nevertheless congratulate the country on possessing a House of Lords which had the wisdom to amend this Bill, and a House of Commons which had the wisdom to accept the amendments made in it. There are, doubtless, many members of the House of Commons who voted for this Bill, and are glad that it did not pass as it went from them. Philosophy in the British Parliament is still happily mitigated by common sense.

The *Daily News* and (we believe) the *Telegraph*, also the *Manchester Examiner*, and several country newspapers have written against the amendments made by the Lords.

COLLEGE EDUCATION FOR WOMEN.

An admirable article has appeared on this subject in the *Contemporary Review*, by Miss Emily Shirreff.

Certain objections that I have urged strongly myself* against any public education for girls, and which might seem to tell against the college, rested on wholly different grounds from those glanced at above; and owing to the change of the times, they have less weight than they once had. They considered school education in relation to the after career; and looking upon domestic life as the one destiny of women, everything that might foster a habit of looking out of home for help or excitement seemed unwise. On the one hand, it appeared cruel to expose girls to the effects of rivalry and to the possible contagion of ambition; and, on the other, there seemed more hope of forming the habit of pursuing study for the mere love of knowledge and desire after higher and higher grades of self-culture, if early studies had never known the stimulus of companionship or emulation. The reasoning still seems perfectly just, but circumstances have changed, and are changing yet more. No lives are so retired now as the lives of most women formerly were. Ferment and excitement are everywhere. And if, indeed, women are on the eve of gaining an altogether freer position, if they are to be allowed to make their own way in the world, so that the gifted and ambitious may find a scope if they will, and those ill-favoured by fortune shall no longer depend solely on the labour of men, or be ruined by their neglect, then the restrictions that were wise before lose their value, and it may be as well to let girls learn early, as boys do, the art of living among their equals. Doubtless far the larger number of women will remain within the circle of home-life as before; but home-life will itself feel the reaction of the changes outside. We see it even now. Few women yet have taken a share in the work of the world—thousands have been stirred. Even in those frivolous circles that seem impervious to all the influences which affect rational humanity, the very

---

* Intellectual Education.

faults that have called down so much censure of late years upon women may be only another form of the same spirit that manifests itself, in more earnest minds, in greater boldness of opinion and more active energy than young women have ever shown before. A breath of freedom has passed through the air they live in, and the confined regions adapted to another state of things will suit them no longer. . . . .

What degree of mental power use and culture would develop in women, whether men would find them dangerous rivals in any of the higher fields of intellect, and how far society may be benefited by the addition of their labour, are questions upon which it would be very useless to speculate, and which are quite beyond my purpose. In our present state of society a large and an increasing number of women are forced to depend on their own resources; and on whomsoever rests the blame of that state of things which has made marriage more difficult and its conditions more onerous, and has thus driven women from the old sheltered paths, it is evidently a fearful injustice to let the penalty fall wholly upon them, by denying them the means of meeting the new difficulties. There has been satire enough directed, justly and unjustly, against women for marrying for a position or a maintenance; and miserable and degrading has been the system, which was, however, in great measure forced upon them. Now, if they would shake off this reproach, parents should be made to feel that, when they cannot insure their daughters an independence, they are bound to educate them, as they would their sons, to provide one for themselves; and women may justly expect that society should throw no conventional hindrance in their way, that no path shall be closed against them by law or by any legally-protected monopoly. This is the point which it is desirable earnestly to press, and which women might well be content to urge almost exclusively. Nature and time may be trusted to adjust the balance of doubtful claims, and to solve doubtful questions. Even supposing that women must fail, as many predict, they may at least, in justice, claim the right to achieve the failure, since they are determined on the risk.

Daily Telegraph, September 3.

Without venturing upon the delicate ground of woman's rights, or debating the vexed question whether "woman is not undeveloped man, but diverse," we may yet point with satisfaction to the widening and multiplying spheres of woman's work as a satisfactory sign of our times. Of the success attained by female writers it is not necessary to speak; yet it is worth while to remark that such success has generally been attained, not in consequence, but almost in spite, of previous training and preparation. The tendency of female education has been to qualify its recipients for the Gynæceum rather than for the arena of active life, or for judicious competition with men. A change has set in; and, as a matter of course, the tide will carry some of our strong-minded ladies into a very opposite extreme indeed. With that ulterior probability we are not at present concerned. A reaction will occur, which will doubtless result in the attainment of the "golden mean." Of all the straws, however, that show which way the wind is blowing, one of the most unmistakable has been quietly brought under our notice during the past week. For some years the University of Cambridge has undertaken the examination of girls and women on the same plan as that of boys and young men at the "local" or "middle-class" examinations; and this year the sister University has modified the scheme in a way calculated still more to equalise the position of the sexes in intellectual matters. In the statute of the University of Oxford, as amended by the Convocation of December 9, 1869, "*De Examinatione Candidatorum qui non sunt de corpore Universitatis,*" occur the following significant words: "*Liceat delegatis puellas inter candidatos adnumerare,*" which we translate,—though no longer "for the benefit of the ladies,"—"Let the delegates have power to enroll girls among the candidates." .... Yes, the authorities of the University of Oxford have recognised the existence of ladies, not only as creatures designed by Providence to render Fellowships vacant by their matrimonial devices, but actually as beings to be examined, classified, and possibly "plucked." The ladies are literally "*adnumeratæ inter candidatos*" in the division lists of the Oxford Middle-class Examinations for this year—so much so, indeed, that there is nothing on the face of the class-list to give one a clue to the sex of the candidate, except when the successful tutor is set down as a lady, or the educational establishment is specified as a "Ladies' College." The candidates themselves are simply garnished with initials; so that one can only infer from accompanying circumstances that M. may stand for Mary instead of Matthew or Marmaduke, or that P. means Priscilla or Pauline, and not Peter.

Advancing, with such a slender clue alone to guide us, into the intricate mazes of the division lists, we find that twenty-nine senior and seventeen junior competitors, whose names appear this year among the successful, were presumably "*puellæ inter candidatos adnumeratæ.*" Happily there is nothing to enlighten us whether any young ladies were among the "plucked." We will chivalrously conclude that there were none. The most casual inspection of the list of ladies, which we have diligently extracted for our own edification, leads us to conclude that the air of Ramsgate must be as favourable to the intellectual faculties as we know it to be to the physical frame. No fewer than seven of the successful seniors and eight of the juniors have passed at this centre. Cheltenham stands next in order of success, and the metropolis shows very small indeed. The supplementary tables inform us that the young ladies naturally selected such subjects as French and German, music and drawing; a very large proportion satisfied the examiners in the rudiments of faith and religion; many "took up" mathematics with success; and a few aspired to subjects hitherto deemed yet more masculine, such as Latin and physics. It may not be generally known, but it falls in with our present purpose to mention, that this experiment of grouping boys and girls together for examination in scientific subjects was successfully tried last year at the London Institution. One professor delivered a course of lectures on physical geography, and was followed, during two succeeding sessions, by professors of equal note, who lectured to mixed audiences of boys and girls on chemistry and botany. At the conclusion of each series there was an examination of such candidates as thought proper to present themselves, and we had, in that case too, the feature of "*puellæ inter candidatos adnumeratæ*," with a corresponding average of success on the part of the female portion. The experiment of the separate examination of girls was tried by the University of Cambridge so long ago as the year 1866, and the report of the Syndicate for that year closes with the following summary of results: " I conducted the girls' examination in London. Everything went on quite as regularly and quietly as at any examination at which I have been present. The girls seemed to take a great interest in it, and worked at their papers in a very businesslike way, and for the whole time allotted to them. I was quite struck with the easy way in which they bore the stress of the examination. I could not detect any flagging of interest in it, or any sign of weariness, or any ill effect upon them whatever." It may fairly be assumed that the growing success of these separate examinations has led to the present amalgamation, and also to the grouping of the candidates in one list.

Now, that fact represents a vast social change; it marks a prodigious step in advance of former generations. The great question is, whether it is a change for the better, a step in the right direction. Will the time come, when, as Sydney Smith says, a lady will neglect her infant for a quadratic equation ? Will a nervous young gentleman ask a lady to dance a quadrille, when she may possibly assail him with a Greek quotation, or will he venture to propose for the hand of a fair "Associate in Arts of the University of Oxford ?" Time alone will show. It would seem, indeed, that, if kept within judicious limits, such a movement is likely to equalise the sexes, and to make the wife more thoroughly the companion of the husband than she was in the old-fashioned days when "the accomplishments" were deemed the acme of a woman's ambition. . . . . In the meantime, we cannot but congratulate both the young ladies and their teachers on the honourable places attained in the recent examination, the first where male and female students and instructors have had an opportunity of testing their relative powers. One lady stands in the second class of the seniors, and one occupies the same distinguished position among the juniors. There may be more; and we would gallantly presume that there are some blushing unseen in the first class. But here we are again met with a difficulty as regards the teachers similar to that which results from the fact of letting the students' names be entered with initials only. Unless we have "Mrs." or "Miss" prefixed to the teacher's name, or are helped by the specification of "Ladies' College," we cannot tell whether the title we are reading is that of a male or a female professor; and, from long though ungallant custom, we infer the masculine gender. May we suggest to the University authorities that for the future they print the Christian names of candidates in full; and to the heads of ladies' colleges or private female coaches, that they also subscribe their names at length? By those means we shall be enabled, in subsequent examinations, to do even-handed justice to the honourable positions that they will assuredly attain—an endeavour which may now possibly have been frustrated by the fact that some lady's name which really stood higher up in the division list than we have specified was veiled under treacherous initials. It has frequently been affirmed that women were the best, if not the only, proper teachers in elementary education; and the present results convince us that the higher branches, even in subjects not usually assigned to their sex, may be successfully conducted by them. Hence, in a kindred spirit with that displayed by the University of Oxford, we henceforth enter on our Statute book the sentence, "*Liceat feminas inter professores adnumerare.*" It sounds a little Hibernian to say so, but we are literally glad to recognise ladies among the schoolmasters.

THE ENGLISH REVOLUTION.

PROFESSOR SEELEY has written two articles in *Macmillan*, for August and September, on the English Revolution of the 19th century. This revolution he considers to consist in the destruction of monopolies, a task, for the performance of which Parliament is peculiarly well constructed. This gradual revolution will, he thinks, continue until no monopolies remain.

Doubtless we shall find, sooner or later, that there are other tasks in politics besides this useful one of removing monopolies. If it were not so, we might, perhaps, expect politics to be speedily exhausted. So few monopolies remain to be devoured that, unless our monopolivorous monster can learn to change his diet, he will be in danger of starving. He seems already to be beginning his final meal. It promises, indeed, to be a long one. To remove from our laws and social institutions every trace of the ascendency of the male sex—this is no light undertaking. But when it is accomplished, when the male monopoly has gone the way of the Protestant one, of the boroughmongering one, of the Protectionist one, of the Anglican one, of the denominational one, what task of this sort will remain to occupy us? It is hard to conceive.

But ages overlap each other. Perhaps before the last monopoly has entirely disappeared, new forces will have begun to work, a different chapter in politics will open upon us, politicians will be busy with a different class of problems, and will have learnt new phrases and new catchwords. When this has happened, and from the middle of another age they look back upon ours, I believe it will assume a unity which it wears to few of us. To them, not less plainly than the 16th century was the age of abolition of Popery, and the 17th the age of emancipation from the yoke of Prerogative, it will appear that the 19th century brought the age of the abolition of monopolies.

BOARDING OUT OF ORPHAN PAUPER CHILDREN.

Times.

IF our readers can spare a brief attention from the stirring events of war to quiet details of peace, they will find to-day a subject well worth their notice in the Circular of the Poor Law Board on the system of boarding-out pauper children. . . . . The children of paupers, they are liable to become themselves paupers, and the parents of paupers. We are in danger of rearing in our workhouse schools the future inmates of our workhouses. Few tendencies are so much a matter of birth and education as pauperism. Any money is economically spent, and any care is prudently bestowed, in so training children to leave the workhouse that they may never return to it.

After saying that district schools often train pauper children exceedingly well, the *Times* continues:—

There can be no question, however, that the healthiest education for a pauper child is one which resembles as closely as possible the natural training of home. A child without father or mother, and free from the ordinary discipline of domestic life, is in as unnatural a condition as a bird in a cage. It breathes an unnatural moral atmosphere, and is destitute of the influences most essential to the development of its mind and heart. Men have never yet thoroughly understood that human beings cannot receive a healthy development when placed in unnatural circumstances. The world has never been without ingenious schemes for making men and women live in some artificial system designed to be superior to the homely order in which they find themselves. Children, as they are more susceptible, are more liable to suffer from such mismanagement, and a large orphanage, or workhouse schools, is, at the best, a necessary evil. But if these little ones have no fathers and mothers, cannot we revert to the time-honoured institution of foster parents? There must be numbers of poor families, with a small number of children of their own, who would gladly take charge of one or two foundlings, if they were duly paid. There are, of course, great possibilities of abuse in such arrangements. After some recent horrible disclosures, the dangers are too familiar to us. But there must be people who would do their duty by children entrusted to their care, and it ought to be possible to guard against abuse by proper supervision.

The latter qualification is, indeed, the point from which Mr. Goschen has started in the sanction now, for the first time, granted by the Poor Law Board to this system. "A great portion of the public, and especially ladies," have displayed a practical readiness to lend their personal assistance in securing a due supervision of these proposed foster homes. In short, a remarkable amount of voluntary agency is offered to the Poor Law authorities for this purpose, and Mr. Goschen is wisely of opinion "that it would be a serious loss to the public interest if means could not be found to utilize such services." He has prepared, accordingly, a general order, soon to be published, by which boards of guardians will be enabled "to enter into arrangements with committees duly authorised." Legal difficulties which hindered the removal of children from urban Unions to country homes have been overcome. Minute inquiries, the results of which were last session laid before Parliament, have indicated the chief precautions which will be necessary, and these will be enforced in the regulations shortly to be published. The field is, therefore, fairly open for a new and valuable exercise of personal charity. It is possible that the requirements which the Poor Law Board will think it necessary to enforce may be of indirect advantage, by forcing certain obligations of health and decency on the attention of poor families; but, at all events,. those who have initiated this movement will have the opportunity they have desired of showing the possibility of giving to pauper children the best kind of education open to an orphan. Everything depends on the manner in which such a system is worked, and for this we must now look partly to the guardians, and partly to the ladies and gentlemen whose generous importunity has at length overcome the scruples of the Poor Law Board. We do not expect to find that Mr. Goschen's confidence has been misplaced.

Almost all the other newspapers write in the same spirit.

The *Contemporary Review* for September contains a powerful article on "The Family System for Workhouse Children," by Florence Hill; and the *Cornhill* for the same month a very charming one on "Little Paupers," said to be by Miss Thackeray.

Public opinion has clearly been won over to the Boarding-out System.

Art. V.—REVIEWS OF BOOKS.

Industrial Employment of Women in the Middle and Lower Ranks. By John Duguid Milne, Advocate, Aberdeen. London: Longmans, Green, & Co. 1870.

The first edition of this book was published anonymously thirteen years ago, under the title of "The Industrial and Social Position of Women." In the preface to the new edition the author says, that he has made little change in the text beyond adding some extracts from the returns of the last census, and that he could not " omit to notice the remarkable advance that has taken place, during these years, in public opinion and in legislation, on the relative position of the sexes—an advance that has surpassed my expectation."

To this advance few have contributed more than Mr. Milne himself, for, during these years of struggle, this book has been the hand-book of the promoters of the movement—the main source from which both facts and arguments have been drawn in support of the woman's cause.

Mr. Milne believes that industry has a most beneficial influence on the character; thus, the exclusion of women of the middle classes from remunerative employment not only plunges them into poverty, but prevents them from benefitting by the moral discipline of work. He believes their exclusion from industry to have also the bad effect of increasing the mental separation between the sexes.

Men are brought up to work, women to be idle; hence arises a complete difference of pursuits and experience, and, consequently, a want of sympathy with and influence over each other.

In the higher ranks, where neither men nor women engage in industry, and amusement is the chief pursuit, women have, he thinks, more influence, and are less looked down upon, than in the middle ranks, for the amusements of the men are, to a great extent, shared in by the women; and, in the lower ranks, where work is

R

the lot of both sexes, women are also more on a footing of equality with men.

The mental separation between the sexes enfeebles the influence of women over men, and the want of the beneficial effects of industry on the female character renders even the feeble influence that remains less salutary than it would otherwise be; hence arise many evils, especially the lack of public spirit, which can scarcely exist unless it is general and shared by women as well as men.

Patriotism, public spirit, are sympathetic sentiments, and will not thrive unless shared in by those we esteem and love. They must be felt at home; must be nourished by domestic warmth: must be shared in by woman; otherwise private interest will soon swallow them up. . . . . The times may be peaceful, but in them there is still much to do, and much to suffer, in the cause of truth, of justice, and of patriotism.

But, for the reason we have explained, women are unable to take part, or to feel much interest, in these things. Public life is, in modern days, a growth from industrial life, in like manner as in ancient times it was a growth from warlike relations. Politics, political rights, political influence, are now inseparably connected with business; it is on business, on our means of livelihood, on our future prospects, that our public honesty or dishonesty most directly tells; public movements either spring from, or have for their object to act upon, the industrial condition of society; our public conduct is continually modified by industrial experience and industrial interest; the character of the people, their intelligence, and their comfort depend in a great degree on their industrial occupations and industrial relations. It is impossible, therefore, for woman—so long as excluded from industry—to take a part or feel an interest in political and social movements, or to influence public opinion, national virtue, or national progress.

And if woman know little of the public duties of modern life, it cannot be expected that the virtues of public life should be valued within our families, or should have a habitual hold on national character. A desire for the public good has, therefore, no very prominent place among our national sentiments. Our patriotism regards more the material interest of ourselves and of our families; if life and property be secure, we care for little else.

By the exclusion of woman from participation in public opinion and in public sentiment, not only is the growth of patriotism checked in the mind of man, not only is society deprived of the full benefit of a masculine spirit (devoted to national honour and good), but our patriotism, our public spirit, such as they are, show a manifest want of those feminine characteristics flowing from the softer influence of woman. It is remarkable that benevolent movements, having for their object to ameliorate the condition of the working classes, have emanated chiefly from the higher ranks, where the influence of woman is stronger.

The material, as well as the moral, effects of the exclusion of women from industrial pursuits, are taken into consideration by Mr. Milne, also the right of a husband over the property of his wife, and the political status of women. The last chapters are devoted to the consideration of the intellectual capacity of women. We cannot recommend this book too strongly to our readers.

Difference of Sex as a Topic of Jurisprudence and Legislation. By Sheldon Amos, M.A., Professor of Jurisprudence at University College. London: Longmans, Green, & Co. 1870.

WE wish we could agree with the whole of this clever *brochure*. Short, clearly expressed, and printed in large type, it is an attractive work, and contains so much that is good and true that we regret one cardinal error should be found there, which makes it impossible for us to recommend it for general distribution. The author is in favour of allowing divorce at the wish of either of the parties, trusting entirely to moral agencies of all sorts to render such divorces as unfrequent as possible. Those who recommend this course cannot have considered the consequences that would ensue among the working classes. We believe that bad results would follow among all classes, but the results among the poor would be especially disastrous. Professor Amos says that the State has no moral claim to insist on more than "securing publicity for the act of marriage, and that of divorce, and that suitable provision be made for the guardianship and support of children in the several cases calling for it."

This object of securing support for the children of a divorced wife is, however, the point that would be certain to fail the moment divorce at will was permitted. Let us take the case (not an imaginary one) of an agricultural labourer who is heartily tired of his wife, with whom, however, he has no fault to find. He meets the daughter of a neighbour, carrying a heavy load, and offers to take it home for her; the offer is accepted, an acquaintance springs up. He becomes strongly attached to the girl, who, however, is perfectly respectable, and, perhaps because she knows marriage to be impossible, merely regards him as a friend. After a time she discourages his attentions, and, his landlord wanting his cottage for some one else, he has to remove to a distance, and the girl marries another man. If the man could have divorced his wife he would have done so, for he openly regretted his marriage. He would then have married the girl he admired, leaving his first wife with five little children to support. The law would have attempted to compel him to support them. He would have been ordered to pay so many shillings a week for their maintenance, and the 15s. a week he earned would have been divided between two households. What poverty and misery would thus be caused.

No doubt there is unhappiness now in the man's house. He weary of his wife, and she vexed and angry with him. Such cases are probably common; but the misery caused by divorces at will would be ten times greater than the misery caused by the present system. The country would be full of divorced wives with starving families. It is not enough for the advocates of divorce to say that the State will enforce the maintenance of the children, they must show by what means this can be done. It seems captious to pick out, for animadversion, the one defect of a work which is, in all other respects, admirable; but there is a notion in the world that if women had political power they would be in favour of divorce at will; we believe this to be a mistake, and, whether it is or not, we wish to show our own colours.

We conclude with an extract from another part of the book, and it will, perhaps, be thought that Professor Amos has himself explained in the passage the reason why some eminent men have taken, on this point, what most women will consider a mistaken view.

The conclusion is that it is for the highest and best interests of all—men and women alike—that upon every one of the urgent problems of the day, whether presented in the family, the State, or the brotherhood of nations, the mind of both sexes, and not of one only, be equally turned. Neither sex can see truly unless illuminated by the supplementary light contributed by the other;

neither can feel truly unless quickened and steadied by the reciprocating sympathy of the other. Where law obtrudes its presence, and affects to separate what is eternally joined together, artificial disunion forthwith takes the place of a living moral co-operation. Admit and encourage such moral co-operation to the full by law, by the elevation of "public opinion," by the formation in private circles of generous and intelligent sentiments, and a new creation will displace the grating memories of the effete and turbid old. The men of the future will be greater as men, the women as women, than the men and women of the past; while the true fields in which men and women severally can most ably, usefully, and happily labour will manifest themselves with a clearness to which the definitions of lawgivers bear about as much resemblance as the cavern torch-light to the mid-day sun.

Pauperism and Self-Help. By Charles Lamport. "Sessional Proceedings of the National Association for the Promotion of Social Science." No. 20. April 14, 1870. Published at the office of the Association, 1 Adam Street, Adelphi, London, W.C.

WE are surprised that this paper has met with so little attention. If it had been read in the winter, when the annually recurring distress turns the thoughts of the public towards the subject of pauperism, it would, perhaps, have received more notice. We believe it to be a very valuable contribution to Social Science, and that the plan for checking pauperism sketched out in its pages will ultimately be adopted, though half a century may elapse previously.

The Poor Law is at present both too severe and too indulgent. The industrious labourer, who has paid poor rates all his life, is sent, when superannuated, to the workhouse; there he meets the habitual tramp, also superannuated, and the two men receive precisely the same treatment. One has contributed to the poor rates a sum which would, perhaps, nearly suffice to maintain him in comfort for his remaining years. The other has contributed nothing; yet now they stand on the same social level, and are both branded as *paupers*.

This anomaly Mr. Lamport would abolish by treating able-bodied habitual vagrants so sharply as to deter people from adopting vagrancy as a profession. He proposes to hand them over to the police, and to make them work, and work hard, in return for subsistence. Those who are already old and infirm must, of course, be admitted into the workhouse and be treated as before; but young men would be driven out of the trade, and thus the supply of old ones would be cut off for the future.

To the industrious poor he would give the option of paying a slightly higher scale of poor rate, which should entitle the contributor and his wife, when sick or old, to a sufficient out-door allowance. The labourer who pays no more than the compulsory poor rate would go, as at present, to the workhouse, when too old to work, and, in case of temporary illness, before he became superannuated, would receive the same relief he does now.

The merit of the plan is that it would offer a great encouragement to sobriety, and afford a safe and profitable investment for a poor man's savings. At present a labourer's savings do him so little good that there is not sufficient inducement to save. If a labourer were to lay by a sixpence or even a shilling a week the sum would not be enough, at the end of thirty or forty years, to provide for his own old age, and that of his wife, in comfort, but by an extra payment of less than sixpence a week he could, if Mr. Lamport's calculation be correct, secure for himself and his wife a comfortable, retiring pension, when overtaken by old age and infirmity.

The inducement to save is now so trifling that the few pence which in many cases might be saved every week are spent in beer; but the advantages of the small extra payment to the rates would be so great and so apparent, as to enable many a man to resist the temptations of the beershop.

The men who paid the extra voluntary rate would form an aristocracy in every village—an aristocracy of industry and sobriety. It may, however, be said that benefit clubs already offer the same advantages. They do indeed offer them, but as the element of security is wanting, the advantages are too often only offered, not given.

Besides, the man who subscribes to a benefit club pays twice over; once to the poor rates, from which he will receive no benefit, unless the club breaks; he pays perhaps sixpence a week to his club, and threepence or fourpence to the rates; under Mr. Lamport's system he would pay threepence or fourpence in ordinary rates, and twopence or threepence to the extra rates. He would thus pay threepence or fourpence a week less than he now does, and his weekly allowance in old age would be absolutely safe.

We recommend our readers to send fourpence in postage stamps to Mr. Robinson, clerk to the Social Science Association, for the number which contains Mr. Lamport's paper, and to study the details of the plan for themselves.

The Americans at Home; Pen-and-Ink Sketches of American Men, Manners, and Institutions. By David Macrae. Edmonston & Douglas, Edinburgh. 1870.

A DELIGHTFUL book. The account of the Emancipated Blacks is especially interesting.

THE *Food Journal* always contains useful information about eating and drinking.

Art. VI.—EVENTS OF THE QUARTER.

THE GOVERNMENT OF FRANCE.

THE Empress of the French was a steady friend to the education and employment of women. It was at her desire that M. Duruy established lectures for ladies in Paris and other large towns, and technical schools for girls in country districts. These lectures have had but small success, being opposed by the priests. This opposition had not the effect of causing the Empress to withdraw her support. In spite of the angry pamphlets of Bishop Dupanloup, of the remonstrances of all the bishops (except the Archbishop of Paris), and of the disapprobation of the Pope himself, the Empress continued to support the lectures, and her two nieces to attend them.

We do not know what success the technical schools have had, but we fear they have not been generally established. Frenchwomen have two formidable enemies

—the priesthood, which objects to their receiving education, and working men, who object to their obtaining employment.

The Empress did her utmost to help them, and was about to establish a Female School of Medicine in Paris, when the war broke out. There can be little doubt that the admission of women to medical degrees, by the Paris Faculty of Medicine, was due to her influence.

That this powerful influence has ceased to operate on behalf of women in France is a cause for regret. A friend to women is, however, among the members of the Provisional Government. M. Jules Simon, the Minister of Education, is the author of "L'Ouvrière," perhaps the best book written in France on the condition of working women. If the present government should continue in office, there can be no doubt that he will do what he can in their favour, but the extent of his power will probably be but small.

MARRIED WOMEN'S PROPERTY.

The Select Committee of the House of Lords on the Married Women's Property Bill consisted of the following Peers:—

The Lord President, the Duke of Buckingham and Chandos, Earl of Shaftesbury, Earl of Airlie, Earl of Carnarvon, Earl of Morley, Earl of Lichfield, Bishop of Gloucester and Wells, Lord Dinevor, Lord Stanley of Alderley, Lord Clandeboye, Lord Westbury, Lord Romilly, Lord Cairns (in the chair), and Lord Penzance.

The Select Committee met twice, and declined to hear evidence. At the second meeting, the Bill, with amendments, nearly as it stands now, was read in draft. A discussion took place on Clause 3, as to whether a woman about to be married should be able to secure her money in the funds as her separate property, by writing to the Governors of the Bank of England, or whether it should be necessary for her intended husband to write also. The following Lords were in favour of omitting the words "intended husband:"—Earl of Shaftesbury, Earl of Airlie, Earl of Morley, and Lord Romilly. All the others present were in favour of letting them stand. It was therefore decided that a woman about to be married could not preserve her property to herself without the consent of her intended husband. The words were, however, taken out subsequently, probably by the House of Lords in Committee, though no mention of the transaction appeared in the report of the debate in the newspapers.

On July 18th, the House of Lords considered the order to go into Committee on the Bill.

Lord Cairns explained the alterations made by the Select Committee.

Lord Penzance said the Bill, as it now stood, was of a practical, workable character.

Lord Shaftesbury said he wished the Bill had secured all savings from earnings made before marriage. Many young women possessed articles of value, such as jewellery and clothes, had invested their savings in a sewing-machine or a mangle, yet these were not secured to them by the Bill, and would become the property of the husband immediately after marriage.

The House then went into Committee.

On Clause 1,

Lord Lyttelton suggested that it be made retrospective in its character.

Lord Cairns said that would be in violation of the principles which guided the legislation in such cases as this. To make this Bill retrospective would be to take from many men what they now believed to be their property.

The Lord Chancellor said the Bill had been much improved in the Select Committee, and he believed, when its provisions came to be understood, women would be quick to take advantage of it. A woman might protect any property other than that provided for in the Bill by appointing a trustee.

The clause was agreed to.

On Clause 2,

Lord Houghton remarked that this and the next two clauses were founded on a total absence of principle. Married women were obliged by them to invest their money in one of four different ways—as a deposit in a savings bank, as a Government annuity, in the funds, or in a joint-stock company, or not have those savings protected by law for their separate use. The noble and learned lord said they could appoint a trustee, but any one who knew anything of the habits of the women whom it was proposed by this Bill to serve would know that such a thing as a trustee never entered their heads. What was needed was some simple process by which property of all kinds acquired by a married woman could be secured to her separate use. He knew of an instance in which a widow married, bringing to her second husband the property of her first, and this second husband died, having willed the property away from the woman and her children.

Lord Cairns could not admit that the clause was devoid of principle; the property of a married woman could not be secured to her unless the law provided in what manner it should be invested.

The clause was agreed to.

On Clause 4,

The Marquis of Salisbury pointed out an omission in the wording of the Act with regard to partly paid-up shares.

Lord Cairns said he would attend to it.

Earl Powis inquired whether a married woman would have a right to vote at meetings of the company in respect of her shares?

Lord Cairns said she would have a right to vote if the shares stood upon the register in her name.

The clause, as amended, was agreed to.

The Earl of Morley moved the following new clause after Clause 4:—

"Any married woman, or any woman about to be married and her intended husband, may apply, in writing, to the committee of management of any industrial and provident society, or to the trustees of any friendly society, benefit building society, or loan society, duly registered, certified, or enrolled under the Acts relating to such societies respectively, that any share, benefit, debenture, right, or claim whatsoever in, to, or upon the funds of such society, to which the person or persons so applying is or are entitled, may be entered in the books of the society in the name of the woman as a married woman, entitled to her separate use; and it shall be the duty of such committee or trustees to cause the same to be so entered, and thereupon such share, benefit, debenture, right, or claim shall be deemed to be the separate property of such woman, and shall be transferable and payable, with all dividends and profits thereon, as if she were an unmarried woman; provided, that if any such share, benefit, debenture, right, or claim has been obtained by a married woman by means of moneys of her husband without his consent, the Court may, upon an application under Section 8 of this Act, order the same and the dividends and profits thereon, or any part thereof, to be transferred and paid to the husband."

The clause was agreed to, as was Clause 5.

On Clause 6,

Lord Houghton moved to insert the following amendment in line 3, "or any sum of money under 200*l.* which she may receive as legatee." The Court of Chancery was in the habit of apportioning all legacies to the wife above 200*l.* between the husband and wife. He thought the Bill should do the same thing for the poor woman that the Court of Chancery did for the rich woman.

Lord Penzance thought the noble lord was about to proceed further than the Court of Chancery, because, instead of apportioning the legacy between the husband and the wife, he proposed to give it altogether to the latter.

Lord Houghton withdrew his amendment, and proposed to bring it forward on the report.

The Lord Chancellor hoped the noble and learned lord would consider this question.

The clause was agreed to.

The remaining clauses were agreed to, and, on the suggestion of Lord Penzance, the date at which the Act is to come into operation was fixed as the 1st of November next, instead of the 1st January, 1871. The Bill, as amended, was then reported to the House.

House of Lords, Thursday, July 21, 1870.

On the bringing up of the report of amendments upon this Bill,

Lord Brougham observed that the Bill entirely excluded from its operation the savings of single women acquired before the passing of the Act. He therefore begged to propose the following amendment :—In Clause 1, page 1, line 7, after the word "earnings," leave out "married," and in line 8 leave out "after the passing of this Act." He further begged to move the following proviso :—" Provided always that this Act shall not apply to any wages earned before the passing of this Act by any woman married before the passing of this Act."

Lord Cairns thought that the Bill would not be improved either in composition or in meaning by the words proposed. If the amendment were adopted it would be necessary to trace to its origin every sum of money or portion of property possessed by a woman before her marriage. With the view of meeting an objection urged by his noble friend (the Earl of Shaftesbury) on a former occasion, he proposed to introduce in the 11th clause an amendment which would enable a man and woman on their marriage to agree as to what chattels should be considered the separate property of the woman. This might be done by a few words on the back of the marriage lines or on any other piece of paper.

The amendment proposed by Lord Brougham was then negatived without a division.

In Clause 7, which provides that where any woman married after the passing of this Bill shall, during her marriage, become entitled to any personal property as next of kin or one of the next of kin of an intestate, such property shall, subject and without prejudice to the trusts of any settlement affecting the same, belong to the woman for her separate use, and her receipts alone shall be a good discharge for the same.

Lord Romilly proposed, after the word "intestate," to insert the words "or to any sum of money not exceeding 200l. under any deed or will."

Lord Cairns, having regard to the provisions of the other clauses, as well as those of Clause 7, thought the words proposed by his noble and learned friend were unnecessary.

After a few words from the Lord Chancellor,

Their lordships divided on the question that the

words proposed by Lord Romilly be inserted in clause 7, and there voted—

    Content 29
    Not content 17
    Majority . . . . . −12

Contents—29.

Hatherley, L. (L. Chancellor).
Lansdowne, M.
Normanby, M.
Airlie, E.
Camperdown, E.
De Grey and Ripon, E.
Fortescue, E. [Teller.]
Granville, E.
Kimberley, E.
Lichfield, E.
Morley, E.
Shaftesbury, E.
Sydney, V.
Exeter, Bp.
Gloucester and Bristol, Bp.
Manchester, Bp.
Balinhard, L. (E. Southesk.)
Boyle, L. (E. Cork and Orrery.)
Brougham and Vaux, L.
Camoys, L.
Clandeboye, L. (L. Dufferin and Clandeboye.)
Lawrence, L.
Lurgan, L.
Lyttelton, L.
Romilly, L. [Teller.]
Saye and Sele, L.
Sundridge, L. (D. Argyll.)
Talbot de Malahide, L.
Vernon, L.

Non-contents—17.

Cleveland, D.
Richmond, D.
Salisbury, M. [Teller.]
Beauchamp, E.
Nelson, E. [Teller.]
Romney, E.
Stradbroke, E.
Halifax, V.
Cairns, L.
Colchester, L.
Egerton, L.
Fitzwalter, L.
Lyveden, L.
Northwick, L.
Redesdale, L.
Stanley of Alderley, L.
Wrottesley, L.

The words proposed by Lord Romilly were therefore inserted.

Certain verbal amendments having been made in Clause 8, the report was then received.

House of Commons, August 3.

On the consideration of the Lords' Amendments to this Bill,

Mr. Russell Gurney said that he had to call the attention of the House to the alterations, he wished he could say the amendments, made in the Married Women's Property Bill in the House of Lords. The Bill, in fact, as it had come down from the other House was a new

Bill, and framed upon a different principle from that
which left this House. This House had proceeded upon
the belief that the law by which a woman forfeited her
property by the act of marriage was a bad law, and that
great evils sprang from it, affecting, though in very
different degrees, both rich and poor, and had proposed
to remedy these evils by its repeal. In the other House,
the existence of these evils, especially as affecting the
working-classes, was fully admitted; but, instead of re-
pealing the law, they had proposed to apply specific remedies for the more glaring of the evils, and he fully and
gratefully admitted that as far as related to the working-
classes, who formed the most numerous and most helpless
class of the sufferers under the present law, the Bill
would, in its present form, afford real, though not complete relief. He did not, indeed, think that that relief
was afforded in the best form, and he feared that it
would be found to be attended with greater danger of
producing family discord than would the Bill which he
had himself introduced. He did not, however, hesitate
to advise the House to accept the Bill, as at that period
of the session it would be vain to propose any substantial
amendments. He should therefore merely propose some
verbal amendments which were necessary in some of the
clauses; and as the Bill was now to have effect only in
the case of marriages contracted subsequently to the
passing of the Act, he should propose that it should come
into immediate operation. He must, however, say that
legislation on this subject could not end with this Bill,
as there would yet remain much to be remedied, and
principles were admitted in the Bill in its present form,
which, unless it were to be contended that bad husbands
were to be found only amongst the poor, must lead to a
fuller and more complete measure.

Mr. Dickinson expressed his regret that the House of
Lords had not accepted the simple and just principle on
which the Bill as framed by the Commons was founded.
He thought that, as the Bill as framed by the Lords
effected a great improvement in the existing law, it would
be wise to accede to their amendments, and he hoped
that before long the principle for which they contended
would be acknowledged, and the law so altered as to

secure to married women the right to their own property and earnings as fully as to men.

Some verbal amendments were then made to the Lords' amendments on the motion of Mr. Russell Gurney, also that the Act should come into operation as soon as it received the Royal Assent; and on the motion of the Solicitor-General for Ireland, the Bill was made to apply to Ireland as well as to England.

On August 9th the Bill received the Royal Assent.

The following letters appeared, soon after the passing of the Act, in the *Times* and *Echo* :—

Sir,—Will you permit us, through your columns, to address an appeal to those favourable to the amendment of the law with regard to the property of married women?

While we gladly admit that the Act of last session provides an immediate remedy for some of the most common and palpable evils arising out of the Common Law, and that, having regard to the number of women whose position is favourably affected by it, it is a real and great gain, we regret that our legislators should have abandoned the vital principle of the original measure, and have retained the general rule of confiscation of a wife's property by the simple act of marriage.

We object further to the present Act because the protection it offers is wholly inadequate to meet the needs of the case; because it applies the complicated rules and decisions of the Equity Courts respecting the separate estate of a wife to sums of the most trifling amount; because it frees a husband from liability for his wife's debts contracted before marriage, whilst retaining the principle of confiscation of property owned before marriage; because in most of its provisions relating to property it requires a formal process of application on the part of a woman as regards each separate portion of her estate; and because, though professedly designed to benefit the poorest class of women, it is unintelligible without the aid of a lawyer. The marginal notes appended to the Act are calculated to mislead the public as to its real purport.

On these grounds, though we regard the Act as an important concession to the growing sentiment of justice, we decline to accept it as even a temporary settlement of the question. We have therefore decided to keep our organisation intact and in working order, and to continue to press the subject on public attention, in the hope that at a very early period a complete measure may be brought forward with a fair chance of success.

We ask our friends to contribute liberally towards the sum of 150*l*., which we wish to raise at once, so that we may not only meet existing liabilities, but be prepared to act with vigour at the first favourable crisis. Cheques and post-office orders, payable to Lydia E. Becker, Manchester.

The total sum we have received during our three years' agitation is 312*l*. 9*s*., and though we have been compelled to incur liabilities greatly in excess of that amount, we venture to affirm that few political agitations of equal importance have been conducted at so little cost. We therefore appeal with confidence to our friends for further support.

We are, Sir, yours respectfully,
ELIZABETH C. WOLSTENHOLME,
Moody Hall, Congleton.
LYDIA E. BECKER, *Hon. Treasurer*,
28, Jackson Row, Albert Square, Manchester.

Sir,—As this Act will, doubtless, be referred to by many persons, including many of the fair sex, may I warn them, through your valuable columns, not to be guided by the marginal notes of the Act, but to read the Act itself?

The marginal notes—through some oversight, I presume—are calculated seriously to mislead the public, and I would especially instance those to the important sections Nos. 7 and 8.

The marginal note to No. 7 is as follows:—"Personal property coming to a married woman to be her own;" from which one would naturally infer that all personal property of any amount was included, whereas, on reading the section itself, it will be found only to relate to certain property not exceeding 200*l*.

Again, the marginal note to section 8 is—"Freehold property coming to a married woman to be her own," whereas the Act merely gives her the rents and profits of the property for her separate use.

I would also point out that the first five sections of the Act, relating to the earnings and other property of women in savings-banks, the public funds, and joint-stock companies, apply to all women married or about to be married at the time of the passing of the Act—viz., the 9th inst., whereas the 7th and 8th sections, before referred to, only apply to women married after the passing of the Act.

I have the honour to be, Sir, your obedient servant,
A LONDON SOLICITOR.
London, E.C., Aug. 19.

We do not give the marginal notes with the Act, as a false explanation is worse than none; but we place them here. If compared with the clauses the discrepancies will appear, and they are a good specimen of the carelessness with which the Act has been treated. (1.) Earnings of married women to be deemed their own property; (2.) Deposits in a saving's bank, by a married woman, to be deemed her separate property; (3.) As to a married woman's property in the funds; (4.) As to a married woman's property in a Joint-Stock Company; (5.) As to a married woman's property in a society; (6.) Deposit of monies in fraud of creditor's invalid; (7.) Personal property coming to a married woman to be her own; (8.) Freehold property coming to a married woman to be her own; (9.) How questions as to ownership of property to be settled; (10.) Married women may effect policy of insurance. As to insurance of a husband for the benefit of his wife; (11.) Married women may maintain an action; (12.) Husband not liable on his wife's contracts before marriage; (13.) Married woman to be liable to the parish for maintenance of her husband; (14.) Married woman to be liable to the parish for maintenance of her children; (15.) Commencement of Act; (16.) Act not to extend to Scotland; (17.) Short title.

Although the Act ought to have come into operation on the 9th of August, no new regulations, with regard to the money of married women in post-office saving's banks, had been received up to the time of sending these pages to press.

The number of petitions presented to the House of Lords in favour of Mr. Russell Gurney's Bill is thought by Miss Wolstenholme to be larger than the number sent to the House of Commons, but no official record is kept of petitions presented to the Lords.

We forgot to say that the Act extends to Ireland.

EDUCATION AND EMPLOYMENT.

AT THE OXFORD LOCAL EXAMINATION division lists for the present year:—338 senior and 667 junior candidates out of 480 senior and 1173 juniors satisfied the examiners. The candidates included nearly fifty girls in each class.

UNIVERSITY OF LONDON.—The following ladies have passed examinations for special certificates of higher proficiency:—

French.—Emma Kate Woodward, educated at the North London Collegiate School for Ladies.

German.—Emma Kate Woodward, educated at the North London Collegiate School for Ladies.

Mathematics and Mechanical Philosophy.—Susannah Wood, educated at the Ladies' College, Cheltenham.

Natural Philosophy and Chemistry.—Eliza Orme, educated by Private study.

Harmony and Counterpoint.—Sarah Jane Moody, educated by Private tuition.

LECTURES FOR WOMEN.—EXHIBITIONS, &c.—The Committee have issued the following scheme of Lectures for the academical year 1870-71. They will be delivered generally speaking, twice a week within the period of University residence, between the hours of two and five in the afternoon:—

English History, by Professor Seeley.—[This course is only announced, at present, for the October Term, and the number of Lectures is not yet determined.]

English Literature, by W. G. Clark, M.A., Vice-Master of Trinity College, and others.—[It is proposed to give a series of short courses on different departments of English Literature. They will be delivered once a week, during the October Term certainly, and if possible during the whole academical year: commencing with a course on "Shakespeare and the Elizabethan Dramatists," by Mr. Clark.]

English Language and Literature, by W. W. Skeat, M.A., Lecturer and late Fellow of Christ's College.—[These Lectures will be on special books. For the October Term Mr. Skeat has chosen "Chaucer's Knight's Tale."]

Latin, by J. E. B. Mayor, M.A., Fellow and Lecturer of St. John's College, and A. Holmes, M.A., Fellow and Lecturer of Clare College. [Elementary Lectures.]

Greek, by J. Peile, M.A., Fellow and Assistant Tutor of Christ's College.

German, by W. C. Green, M.A., late Fellow of King's College.

French, by M. Boquel.

Algebra and the Principles of Arithmetic, by Professor Cayley.

Practical Arithmetic, by J. F. Moulton, B.A., Fellow and Assistant Tutor of Christ's College.

Geometry and Elements of Physics treated Historically, by W. K. Clifford, B.A., Fellow and Assistant Tutor of Trinity College.

Logic, by J. Venn, M.A., Fellow and Lecturer of Gonville and Caius College.

Political Economy, by A. Marshall, M.A., Fellow and Lecturer St. John's College.

Geology, by T. G. Bonney, B.D., Fellow and Tutor of St. John's College.
Chemistry, by P. T. Main, M.A., Fellow and Lecturer of St. John's College.—[Botany, by Professor Babington, will be substituted for Geology in the Eastern Term.]
Harmony and Thorough Bass, by G. M. Garrett, Mus. D., Organist of St. John's College.
Theory of Sound in its application to Music popularly and experimentally treated, by S. Taylor, M.A., late Fellow of Trinity College.

The Committee further announce the following Exhibitions:—

(1.) One Exhibition of 40*l.* per annum for two years, to be given to one of the Senior Candidates in the Cambridge Local Examinations January 1871, according to the report of the Examiners.
Attendance at two courses of Lectures in every Term will be required as a condition of receiving the Exhibition in each year. [Given by Mr. Mill and Miss Taylor:]
(2.) One Exhibition of 20*l.* for one year together with free admission to three courses of Lectures in each Term: and
(3.) One Exhibition of 10*l.* for one year. [Given by Mrs. Adams.]
These two will be given to two of the Candidates in the Cambridge Examination for Women, July 1870, according to the report of the Examiners.
Attendance at two courses of Lectures during each of two terms at least will be required as a condition of receiving either of these Exhibitions,

THE NUMBER of pupils at the Women's College, Hitchin, has already outgrown the accommodation, so that it is necessary to erect iron rooms for the new comers.

LECTURES IN LONDON.—Six courses of lectures have been delivered during the past session by Professors of University College; those of Latin, English Literature, French Literature, and Geometry, at St. George's Hall, Langham Place, and those of Experimental Physics and Chemistry in the Physical and Chemical Lecture Rooms at University College.
The numbers were:—English Literature, 104; Geometry, 57; Latin, 51; French Literature, 39; Experimental Physics, 24; Chemistry, 19; making a total of 294, as against 163 (with two classes) last session.

The attendance was regular, and the classes received a large accession after Christmas.

Of the Lectures on Latin Literature, in which everything was done by the Professor, there is nothing to report, except that they appeared to be received with interest and attention. In the Grammar Class three or four students regularly brought exercises, which were well done, and many others were willing to answer questions put to them in the course of the lecture. The instruction was given as much as possible in the catechetical method, and in the latter part of the course the students were occupied during the whole hour in rendering into Latin, translations of easy passages of Cæsar. There was no want of interest, or diligence, or intelligence, and there appeared to exist a real demand for such instruction as was given in the class. Nevertheless, the numbers were not satisfactory. It deserves to be considered whether a later hour would not be more convenient, as suiting the case of ladies whose mornings are spent in teaching.—J. R. SEELEY.

The course of English Literature consisted of thirty-six lectures. The subject was the Literature of the last 200 years. The proportion of students who sent in notes for revision, essays, and questions for answers, was greater than in the preceding session, and the class seemed to consist almost exclusively of steady workers, not of ladies to whom such courses of lectures are but a new kind of amusement.—HENRY MALEY.

The subject of my course of lectures was the history of French Literature from the time of Richelieu down to about 1840, with special attention to some of the principal authors. I dwelt chiefly upon the works of Corneille, Racine, Moliere, Boileau, Lafontaine, Voltaire, J. J. Rousseau, Montesquieu, Chateaubriand, Stael, Lamartine, and Victor Hugo; but I presented the history of literature as a whole, and in comparison with the history of other countries.

My audience not only understood well, but had a marked preference for the critical and philosophical part of the course; the fact being that my class was chiefly composed of ladies of high culture, whose wish was evidently for further progress, not in French only, but also in general notions of History and Literature. The attendance was very regular; the papers sent in showed rapid progress, the questions I was asked and the letters I received were evidences of a lively wish for further development of intellectual powers.—CH. CASSAL.

The twenty-four Lectures on the Elements of Plane Geometry, embraced the properties of straight lines, angles, tri-angles, parallelograms, and rectilineal figures; the fundamental properties of the circle, of chords, secants and tangents thereto; and the course concluded with theorems on the equivalence and quadrature of rectilineal figures. Upwards of sixty exercises, many of which were difficult ones, were proposed. More than one-third of the class solved these exercises habitually, and their written solutions, many of them of great merit, were revised and returned to the writers. Without exaggeration, I may say, that I never had the privilege of directing the studies of a more attentive class, nor had I ever greater reason to be satisfied with the progress of students commencing their study of the subject.—T. A. HIRST.

The course of instruction in Experimental Physics, consisted of thirty-six Lectures, of which twenty-three were upon Dynamics and the rest upon Heat. The number of pupils was twenty-four, of whom, however, four attended only part of the course. After most of the Lectures, exercises were given out—usually, numerical problems—to be worked by the class. Answers to these were always given in by a considerable number of students, and were returned to them by the Professor with corrections or remarks. The evidence of diligent work and of corresponding progress on the part of the class was very satisfactory.

The course of instruction, in the Chemical class, conducted by Professor Williamson, was partly theoretical, partly practical, experiments being performed in the laboratory by members of the class in accordance with the directions of the Professor.

THE SCHEME of an Endowed School for girls has been published by the Endowed Schools' Commission. It is to be situated in Westminster, in the parish of St. John, and to be called the Grey Coat Hospital. The object is to provide education for children who remain at school till fourteen years of age, or thereabouts—*i. e.* for the lower middle class, small shopkeepers, and superior artizans. The governors are to consist of twenty persons, three ex officio, the Dean, and the Members of Parliament for Westminster; seven nominated by various City authorities; and ten co-optative—*i. e.* chosen by the governors. Half of the co-optative governors must be women, and women may be selected as nominated governors. The Day School is intended to hold 300 pupils, the Boarding School 120 pupils. The head mistress of the Day School is to receive 80*l.* per annum, and a fee from each pupil of not less than 10*s.* a year, and not more than 30*s.*, as the governors shall decide. Even at the lowest fees the income will be very large if the school attains to the numbers intended. The Boarding School mistress will receive 100*l.* a year, and a fee of not less than 1*l.* from each pupil, or more than 2*l.* yearly.

The tuition fees are to be for the Day School not more than 4*l.* a year, or less than 2*l.* In the Boarding School not more than 5*l.* or less than 3*l.* The entrance fee not to exceed a guinea.

We hope the lowest fee will be adopted by the governors in respect of the Day School, as parents are always unwilling to spend as much on the education of daughters as on that of sons. No pupil is to remain after fifteen years of age. The school is to be Church of England, but parents may exempt their children from attendance at prayers or religious instruction. The following secular subjects are to be taught :—reading and spelling ; writing ; arithmetic ; English grammar and composition ; outlines of geography, political and physical ; outlines of English history ; English literature ; drawing ; vocal music ; needlework ; domestic economy, and the laws of health ; at least one branch of natural science ; at least one modern European language.

Pupils may be received without payment of fees as a reward for remarkable proficiency and Exhibitions may be established to enable pupils, after leaving the school, to continue their education at any college or place for the higher education of women.

As many assistant teachers will be employed as may be required, and they will be appointed by the head mistresses.

NORTH LONDON COLLEGIATE SCHOOL. The twentieth annual distribution of prizes to the pupils of this school took place on Thursday last, in St. George's Hall, Langham Place. The Marquess Camden in the chair, supported by Mr. Harvey Lewis, M.P., Dr. Storrar, the Revs. A. W. Thorold, T. Pelham Dale, C. Lee, H. Sinden, S. Buss, T. Temple, Dr. Williams, Dr. Drury, J. Payne, Esq., F.C.P. ; Mrs. Laing, Mrs. Dale, Mrs. Thorold, Mrs. Storrar, and others.

After an introductory speech by the Chairman, in which he expressed the pleasure he had in presiding at a meeting so calculated to aid in the advancement of female education, the Report was read by the Rev. S. Buss. The Report stated that there were 208 pupils in attendance, that Miss E. L. Greatbatch had obtained a prize at the London Institution, that Miss E. K. Woodward had passed the Senior Cambridge Local Examination with second-class honours, she had obtained the Reid Scholarship at Bedford College, and a second scholarship at the College for Women, Hitchin. Seventeen pupils had passed the Cambridge Local Examinations, six with honours. Fifteen had passed the Examination at the College of Preceptors, and one had gained the Natural History Prize. After speeches by Mr. Harvey Lewis, M.P., Rev. A. W. Thorold, vicar of St. Pancras; and the Rev. T. Pelham Dale, the Report was adopted, and the prizes were distributed to the successful competitors. Dr. Storrar, Chairman of Convocation of the University of London, and the Rev. Dr. Williams, moved a vote of thanks to the Chair, and the proceedings terminated by the pupils singing the national anthem.

A BODY OF TRUSTEES have arranged with Miss Buss to acquire the property now held by her in the North London Collegiate School for Girls, 12 to 14, Camden Street; and have also taken commodious premises in the Camden Road. In these premises they propose to carry on the schools, both under the management of Miss Buss, who will be head mistress of the upper school, and visitor superintendent of the lower.

MRS. LEGGETT, widow of an Indian officer, has entered, and is pursuing her studies, as medical student in Dr. Steevens's Hospital, Dublin. She attends the usual courses of lectures, and takes her place in the dissecting room, and is much respected by the professors and students.

THE SWEDISH newspapers publish in their official columns a Royal resolution, granting to Swedish women the right to practise medicine, after passing the examination exacted from students. A special course will be created for them in the Carolin Institute, at the end of this quarter.—*Pall Mall,* August 17.

THE LADIES have had the laugh on their side this summer in Pennsylvania. The editor of the leading medical journal in Philadelphia, professor of surgery at the Medical College, offered a prize for the best series of articles on clinical practice. A set of remarkably able papers were immediately sent in, and appeared in his journal, signed "M. M. W." Meanwhile, side by side with these articles appeared the learned Professor's own leaders, inveighing against the recent admission of women to medical instruction in Philadelphia, and setting forth the incapacity of the sex for such studies. When the prize for the papers on clinical practice came to be awarded, the doctor unhesitatingly gave it to the unknown " M. M. W."; and Mrs. Margaret M. Webster modestly put forward her right to them and to the reward. The editor (as the French say) executed himself with manly gallantry. He fairly confessed his defeat in his own columns, and admitted that a woman had proved her ability to compete with men, and that in future, professional questions must be settled as between man and man on grounds of merit alone.—*Echo.*

THE LECTURERS of Surgeons' Hall, Edinburgh, have thrown open the lectures at their school to students of both sexes without any restriction whatever. The experiment of mixed classes will, therefore, at last be fairly tried, and we shall learn whether British medical students are, as alleged, so much more brutal than those of Switzerland and America.—*Spectator*, July 16.

THE REV. C. H. JOHNSTONE, Inspector of Schools, in his report for last year, speaks in favour of the system of mixed schools. Much has been said, he observes, as to the undesirability of mixing boys and girls together, as to the acquaintances which the girls may form, and as to the coarse habits and manners which they may contract; but he does not believe that the school is answerable for such things. If they occur, it is in places where they would have occurred without the so-called facilities of school life, in places where a low tone of manners and morals prevail, and where the school is naturally found reflecting the general character of the people, but not infecting, rather being infected by, the surrounding population. The managers of the best mixed schools report that the greatest good results from the mixed system. The boys become in measure softened, and learn the practical lesson of consideration for others. The girls acquire confidence, and by the natural stimulus of rivalry are quickened in their studies. In all places where these schools would ordinarily be found the children are already acquainted with each other; they mingle at their homes and in their play; and it appears the wiser plan to allow this natural and healthy intercourse to be continued in their school, rather than to obtrude the ideas of separation and of difference by treating each sex as though they would corrupt the other. Perhaps the mixed-school system might be of advantage to the youth of London. It might soften their manners, cure them of bad language and of their stone-throwing propensities. There is no doubt they want something; but whether it is the society of ladies or a good thrashing we are unable to say—the former might do them good, the latter would certainly do them no harm.—*Pall Mall*, August 12.

MISS HATFIELD, of Northampton, Massachusetts, has done more for the higher education of her sex than all the ladies and gentlemen of England together have been able to accomplish in the vale of Hitchin. She has left 300,000 dollars to found a first-rate college for women. Other American women are busy, not merely in "opening doors" for further employment, but in pressing through them. In Boston a new firm of conveyancers has been established under the title of E. G. Stevens and Daughter, Miss Mary Stevens being her father's partner in the business.—*Echo*.

WORKMEN'S INTERNATIONAL EXHIBITION.—There are some excellent examples of engraved glass sent by the Society for Promoting the Employment of Women, and giving evidence of skilful hands as well as of artistic spirit. Messrs. Blews and Sons, of Birmingham, exhibit specimens of ecclesiastical carving that are excellent, both in design and workmanship, and some of the best of them have been executed by a woman, Mrs. Dewson, who deserves all the honour that the publicity of the exhibition can confer on her. Miss Allen's wax models of flax, cotton, and other plants, are of finished execution and true to nature.—*Times*, August 23.

THE SUFFRAGE.

THE following petitions were presented towards the end of the Session:—

June 9. Inhabitants of Tower Hamlets (*by Mr. Ayrton*) 842
* „ 9. Members of Executive Committee of the Leeds Reform League; J. Shepherd, chairman (*by Mr. Carter*) 1
*July 28. Inhabitants of Halifax in public meeting assembled; J. P. Dickin, chairman (*by Mr. Rylands*) 1

The total number presented during the Session is:—Petitions 621, of which 42 were under Seal (*i.e.*, signed by a chairman, and representing a public meeting), and signatures 134,561.

Public meetings, in favour of giving the franchise to women, have been held at Buxton, the Rev. J. T. Cooper, Nonconformist minister, in the chair; at Hebden Bridge, Yorkshire, where the meeting was addressed by Miss Craigen. A private meeting was held at Wigan, Miss Becker presiding, when a Suffrage Committee was formed in connection with the Manchester Society, consisting of—

Miss Davies.	Mrs. Ryley.
Mrs. Dawson.	Miss Ryley.
Mrs. Drew.	Miss Constance Ryley.

Secretary, Mrs. Leech, Fair View, Pemberton.
Treasurer, Miss M. A. Brown, 22, Dicconson-street.

Another has been formed at Southampton, consisting of—

Mrs. Cosens.	Mrs. Jackson.
Mrs. Dixon.	Rev. E. Kell.
Miss Hardiman.	Mr. Pearce.
Mr. Hardiman.	Mrs. Sharpe.
Miss Hart.	Miss Waymont.

Secretary, Mrs. Sawyer, Clayfield House, Avenue.

The Receipts of the London Society during the past year have been 469*l*. 9*s*. 6*d*.; the Expenditure, 432*l*. 17*s*. 7*s*.; remains in hand, 36*l*. 11*s*. 11*d*. We are requested to state that the publications of this Society can be obtained from Trübner, Paternoster Row.

A LETTER on Woman's Suffrage has appeared in rather a singular publication—the Journal of the Society for the Prevention of Cruelty, called *The Animal World*. The editor having "improved the occasion" of the formation of the Ladies' Humane Committee by writing a sermon against Women's Suffrage, Miss Cobbe sent him the following letter, which was duly published in the September number:—

Sir,—Permit me to remonstrate against the tone of an article in your last number, headed, "Our Ladies' Humane-Education Committee." The writer urges a good work, on what seems to me exceedingly bad grounds. He wishes to stir women to exert themselves in impressing humane ideas on children, and proceeds to offer this astonishing argument why they should do so: "Perhaps, in view of the tendencies of the age, it would be well, apart from the objects of the association, and on political and social grounds alone, to provide women with suitable work, and thus deprive energetic ladies of their most popular argument, 'We are idle, and seek employment. We have ability, but no field of action. Why should the State lose our services?'"

Women have already, it seems to me, since the world began, endeavoured to train their young to compassion, both for human sufferers and for those harmless brutes which nearly all women love and nearly all men delight to destroy. Their efforts, however, never being backed by the possession of any direct legislative power, have done but half the good they might have effected, and so at last women turn round and say, "Give us the right as well as the will to soften this hard world. Let not every ruffian costermonger who tortures his ass, and kills his wife, have a voice in making the laws of our country, while no woman's vote can be registered on the side of mercy and tenderness." Such being the state of the case, I ask, sir, whether such women have not cause for astonishment when they find the professed organ of humanity going far out of its well-marked track on purpose to condemn their demand, and suggesting their adopting "humane education" as quite a novel pursuit, and one desirable, "apart from the objects of the association," in nullifying their argument for employment?

I cannot but think that, had the writer of the article in question laboured as earnestly and for as many years as some "energetic ladies" have done to amend the condition of paupers, to obtain proper relief for the sick, and to protect animals from their masculine tormentors, he would understand how the more such objects are dear to women's hearts, the more they must necessarily desire the natural and direct means of promoting them through Parliamentary representation.

Frances Power Cobbe.

The editor also made a graceful apology.

SOCIAL SCIENCE AT NEWCASTLE.

The Ladies' Conference, held in connection with the Social Science Congress, seems to have been much more successful this year than last. Lady Bowring presided, and a large number of ladies attended. Lady Bowring read an eloquent address, after which the following ladies read papers, or, in some cases, had them read for them by the Secretary, Miss Adams:—Miss Isabella Tod, of Belfast, on "University Examination for Women;" Miss Porter, on "The Education of Girls;" Miss Wolstenholme, on the "Married Women's Property Act;" Mrs. Meredith, on "Righteous Baby Farming;" Miss Jessie Boucherett (not present), on "The Use Women would probably make of the Franchise." All the papers seemed to excite interest, and an animated discussion took place after each had been read.

We reprint from the *Newcastle Daily Chronicle* Miss Wolstenholme's Paper on the "Married Women's Property Act," as follows :—

Most of the ladies present are no doubt well aware that the Married Women's Property Act of last session, is *not* the measure advocated by the Association, and familiar to us under the name of "Mr. Russell Gurney's Bill." As it may not, however, be fully understood how wide is the difference between the two measures, and how far the Act of last session is from satisfying the claims of justice and expediency, as indeed I have reason to know that many, even of those most interested, do not understand to what the change in the law really amounts, I ask your indulgence whilst I try, as briefly as may be, to explain the original state of the law, the changes we proposed, and the changes which have been effected. As you all know very well, the broad general effect of the action of the Common Law was to take all property from the wife and vest it in the husband. Practically, the Court of Chancery had abrogated the rule of the Common Law in a great variety of cases effecting those who came under the protection of that court, whilst the rich almost universally made a private law to themselves by the intervention of settlements and trusteeships. These expedients all showed that the educated part of the community was gradually outgrowing that rude and barbarous stage to which alone a law so unjust could fitly belong. To the members of the Law Amendment Society it is due that thirteen years ago an attempt was first made in England to bring the law itself into harmony with the dictates of justice and expediency. A measure designed to effect this was then brought into the House of Commons, but went no further than the second reading. Public opinion was apparently not ripe for so considerable a reform, and all that was then gained was the insertion of certain clauses in the Divorce Act by which it was hoped to effect some slight improvement in the condition of wives deserted by their husbands. These provisions, in the shape of protection orders to be granted by magistrates, were, however, so cumbrous and so little adequate to the needs of the case, that they were practically inoperative. Public sentiment continued steadily to advance in the direction pointed out by these friends of justice, and the proved advantages of legislation similar to that proposed in the United States and in some of the British colonies and dependencies encouraged them to a further effort, and at length, in 1868, a Bill was introduced into the House of Commons by Mr. Shaw Lefevre, embodying the principle of simple justice. It is the measure, brought forward again in the session of 1869 by Mr. Russell Gurney, for which the Peers have substituted a changeling of their own. Mr. Russell Gurney's Bill proposed to set aside the rule of forfeiture, and provided that a married woman should retain all rights over her own property just as if she had remained unmarried. The essence of the Bill lay in its first clause, and most of the other clauses were applications of, or corollaries from, this first clause. No doubt the Bill, as it finally left the Select Committee of the House of Commons, contained some provisions inconsistent with its general principle (such as Clause 2, the provision preventing a married woman from disposing in any way, *inter vivos*, of real property without the consent of her husband); but though these exceptions were important in character, they would in practice have been too few to interfere with the general beneficial effect of the measure. It was, therefore, in spite of these limitations, a truly great measure, if we have regard to its indirect as well as to its direct effects, one of the greatest measures of this century. It would have given the sanction of law to that greatest of all the social advances which are now being made, the elevation of a wife from the legal status of a slave, without personal or property rights, to the status of an equal friend and yoke-fellow companion. There were many tokens that English public opinion was prepared for this advance—an advance already practically made by all who recognise the deeper and more spiritual side of the marriage relation—even the House of Commons having, by overwhelming majorities, repeatedly signified its approval of Mr. Gurney's measure. But some of the Lords, as the debate on the second reading, and the subsequent fortunes of the Bill plainly show, had not risen to the level of Mr. Gurney's great and simple principle. I need not criticise the Lords' debate. The promoters of the Bill were accused of revolutionary notions, and dreadful pictures of what must happen, if once wives were legally free to deal at their own discretion with their own property, were drawn by the prolific fancy of Lord Westbury, who, however, did not think it worth while to remind us that all husbands have the full power and legal right to do these very shocking things which he fears wives are inclined to do, and that every woman, whose friends have the prudence to insert the four magical words "to her separate use" in any deed or bequest for her advantage, also possesses this power, of the abuse of which, however, by wives, we have not

heard very much. Lord Cairns, who had taken charge of the
Bill, gave way and referred it to a Select Committee, with the
understanding that it was to be considerably modified. The
Select Committee dealt with the Bill in the most trenchant
manner. It came from their hands an absolutely new measure.
How completely this was the case may be judged from the fact
that fourteen clauses of Mr. Gurney's Bill had been struck out,
that twelve new clauses had been inserted, and that every clause
that was retained, except the formal clauses 19 and 20, had been
modified. The Bill was a new Bill, not simply in form, but in
substance. The very soul and essence of the original Bill had
been spirited away. It was no longer a great measure of social
reform, preventing injustice which might ripen into material
injury, but a measure of protection, retaining the old unjust
principle, and applying partial remedies for some of its worst
abuses. In one point, however, the Act does mark a real and
great advance. The Act came into force on the 9th of last
August, the day on which it received the Royal assent. From
that date, whatever a married woman " earns separately from her
husband," is legally and absolutely her own—to invest and dispose
of as she pleases. It is not, perhaps, a thing in itself to be de-
precated that the hardest working bees of the social hive should
be the first to be benefitted, and it is a great gain that such cases
as that of Susannah Palmer should be henceforth impossible.
It is a further gain to have got rid for ever of the absurd ineffec-
tiveness of protection orders, and of all talk about compulsory
marriage settlements, such as those proposed by Mr. Raikes in
the Bill which the House of Commons decisively rejected. The
Act provides that all wages and earnings gained by any married
woman, after the passing of this Act, in any occupation or trade,
" separate from her husband," or through the exercise of any
literary, artistic, or scientific skill, and all investments of money
so gained, shall be held to be settled to her separate use. By
this contrivance the Lords hoped to exempt all property of this
kind from the operation of the Common Law. Mr. Gurney's Bill
did this in a much simpler and more effective manner, and avoided
as to all property, however acquired, the disagreeable suggestion
of divided family interests conveyed by the ugly phrase "to her
separate use." Even the first clause of the Act gives rise to
many painful anomalies. A woman already married is protected
as to all she earns from the date of the passing of the Act, but
a woman who marries ten years hence must forfeit all earnings
and savings she has made *ad interim*, unless she deposits them in
a savings bank, which will not take more than 200*l*. in all. If
she has made her deposit in an ordinary bank she forfeits it.
Suppose a married woman painted a picture, or wrote a novel—
the money she received for it, paid to her credit at her banker's,
would be her separate property, free from her husband's control.
But suppose an unmarried woman did the same, and married the
very next day, the money would become her husband's. Whether
money earned before marriage, but not received till after mar-

riage, would be the husband's or the wife's, is a neat question for the lawyers. In fact, the attempt to set up a distinction between earnings and property otherwise acquired, and to make this distinction the basis of special legislation for women, has shown most conclusively how impossible it is to legislate wisely unless we base our legislation upon clearly defined principles. When Lord Brougham proposed an amendment, the effect of which would have been to protect earnings before marriage, it was rejected on the ground that it would make it necessary, in the case of a woman about to be married, to trace the origin of her claim to everything she then owned, in order to guard against protecting that which was not savings from earnings. And yet under the Act, any woman who claims property under Clause 1, may be put into the County Court, and called upon to prove that such property was really the result of savings and earnings. Again, though a married woman may earn wages in many departments of industry independently of her husband, it will be difficult for her to begin to trade separately from her husband without independent capital, which yet the Act only allows her to own under special limitations. And, as the good custom of the City of London as to women-traders does not prevail all over England, how far can a married woman be a "separate" trader? The question was put under the new Act. The Manchester magistrates decided last week that they could not renew a beerhouse license to a woman who had married, though they could transfer it to her husband. The Act gives very little help to women in the matter of property, as distinguished from earnings. Any property of whatever amount inherited by a married woman under an intestacy becomes absolutely her own, and any gift or bequest not exceeding 200*l.* may also remain hers. If a father therefore dies without a will, his married daughter's share of the property, whatever its amount, will be securely hers; if he leaves her by will 200*l.* or under, it will also be hers: but if he bequeathes her 250*l.* or 2000*l.*, it will pass to her husband, unless the words "to her separate use" be inserted. The lawyers can, perhaps, tell us whether if her father left her 2000*l.* without the protection of the four all-potent words, she would still be entitled under the terms of the Act to 200*l.* out of her 2000*l.* legacy? The Act has been well called a "permissive" measure in its provisions concerning property. It only protects certain kinds of property, and these only in the event of a married woman, or a woman about to be married, going through certain formal processes of application with regard to each separate bit of such property. The public stocks and funds, and fully paid up shares of certain kinds of companies, have been carefully selected by the peers as the only suitable investments for women. Land, houses, shares not fully paid up, are, it appears, regarded as altogether unsuitable, since no protection is provided for these. Women have been very often puzzled to select fitting investment. How will they be perplexed now when they have to consider not only the value and security of the investment itself, but also whether it is one of those specially protected by the Married Women's Property Act? By a later clause of the Act, it is provided that any property belonging to a woman before marriage, and which her husband shall, by writing under his hand, have agreed with her shall belong to her after marriage as her separate property, shall be so held. So that if a woman about to be married makes a careful inventory of her household goods, and gets her intended husband to express in writing his pleasure that they shall remain hers, they will continue her property. Whatever she omits from her inventory becomes his. Whether if the inventory should be forgotten to be made, or omitted to be signed, till after the marriage, it would then have any legal value, is a question which appears to have been left to the County Courts to decide. Clause 12 takes away the liability of any husband married after the passing of the Act for any debts of his wife contracted before marriage, and provides that she "shall be liable to be sued for, and any property belonging to her for her separate use shall be liable to satisfy such debts as if she had continued unmarried." Who is to be liable in case the wife has no "separate property?" The Act does not specify. This clause will scarcely satisfy creditors, and illustrates afresh the impossibility of fitting fragments of a measure based upon a clearly intelligible principle, into a measure from which that principle has been carefully eliminated. Such are the provisions of an Act which is professedly a poor woman's measure, and one which ought, therefore, to have been simple enough to be mastered without the help of a lawyer. But it is not possible to legislate simply and consistently except upon the one only just and equitable principle, that of the absolute equality of husband and wife as to rights of ownership. "The vice of the English Common Law rule," to quote Professor Amos, "which transfers all the wife's most important rights of ownership to the husband, is that, whereas it adds no advantage to either party where a marriage is wholly perfect, just so far as a marriage falls short of being wholly perfect it renders tyranny and cruelty intolerable, easy, and almost irresistibly tempting." Injustice is injury, and an unrighteous law is an evil power even before it has ripened into unrighteous acts. Protection in such a case is but the compromise of conscience with selfishness. The recognition of justice makes protection unnecessary. We hold, then, that the Married Women's Property Act of last Session, though it effects an important amendment of the law, is faulty in detail, and unsound in principle. The only measure which can satisfy us is one which shall secure to women the same rights to their own property and earnings which are enjoyed by men.

On the next day (the 23rd of September) the Conference met again. The room was so densely crowded that the audience had to adjourn to the Theatre of the Literary Society, as many persons were unable to find seats. Another paper, by Mrs. Meredith, was read, on the "Formation of a Disqualified Class of Criminal Female Offenders." Miss Emily Faithfull read a paper on "Special Training for Women." The meeting then adjourned. In the afternoon, a well-attended meeting was held to hear the Report of the Married Women's Property Committee. Lady Bowring took the chair. The Rev. A. Steinthal read the Report. Mr. Hodgkin moved that the Report be adopted. Miss Tod seconded the motion, which was carried.

Mr. Hare moved:—

That this meeting, being convinced that the Married Women's Property Act of last Session, though effecting an important amendment of the law, is faulty in detail and unsound in principle, urges upon all fellow-workers in this movement continued exertions for the passing of such a measure as shall secure to married women the same rights to their own property and earnings as are enjoyed by married men.

Dr. Pankhurst seconded the motion, which was carried unanimously.

Mr. Hancock moved the next resolution, which was as follows:—

That the following persons be appointed the Central Executive Committee for the ensuing year:—Lady Amberley, Jacob Bright, Esq., M.P., Mrs. Jacob Bright, Mrs. Butler, Miss Becker, Thomas Cholton, Esq., William Cobbe, Sir C. W. Dilke, M.P., Rev. Alfred Dene, LL.D., Rev. Septimus Hansard, Thos. Hare, Esq., Miss Hacking, Dr. W. B. Hodgson, Mrs. Hodgson, J. Boyd Kinnear, Esq., William Moore, Herbert Mozley, Esq., Dr. Pankhurst, F. Penington, Esq., Mrs. Penington, Mrs. Sutcliffe, Mrs. Henslegh Wedgwood, and Miss Wolstenholme, with power to add to their number.

Mr. Herbert Mozley seconded the resolution, which was carried.

Mrs. M'Sarrin moved:—

That the best thanks of this meeting be given to the officers of the Social Science Association for the use of their room.

Miss Wolstenholme seconded the motion, remarking that she wished also to draw the attention of the meeting to the fact that their Committee could never have succeeded in the manner they had done had it not been for the Social Science Association, who had done by far the larger portion of the work. The Bill of Mr. Shaw Lefevre was drafted by the Law Amendment Section of the Social Science Association, and without their aid nothing practicable could have been done.

The resolution was carried.

On the 24th, a large meeting composed of ladies exclusively, assembled to advocate the repeal of the Contagious Diseases Act. This meeting was not held, however, in connection with the Social Science Congress. The chair was taken by Mrs. Pennington, of London, who stated that she had received letters from Miss Nightingale and Miss Carpenter in favour of the object of the meeting. The following ladies spoke:—Mrs. Nicol, Mrs. Butler, of Liverpool; Mrs. Duncan McLaren, Mrs. Richardson, of Newcastle; Mrs. Reid, of Newcastle; Miss Wigham and Miss Tod. The following resolution was adopted:—

That this meeting strongly protests against the appointment of a Royal Commission to inquire into the working of the Contagious Diseases Acts, feeling convinced that the real ground of objection to them cannot be reached by any such tribunal, and deeply deploring the delay caused by the appointment of this commission, decides that a memorial be presented to Mr. Gladstone praying for the immediate suspension of these Acts, and requesting the executive committee to take the needful steps for its presentation.

Another resolution was carried :—

That the following ladies, with power to add to their number, be appointed the executive committee for the ensuing year— namely, Mrs. Butler, Liverpool; Mrs. Jacob Bright, Manchester; Mrs. Nichol, Edinburgh; Mrs. Reid, Newcastle; Mrs. Blackburn, Newcastle; Mrs. McLaren, Edinburgh; Miss Estlin, Bristol; Miss Merryweather, Liverpool; and Miss March Phillips, Cheltenham.

On the last day of the Ladies' Conference a paper, by Miss Newsome, was read, on "Women as Inspectors of Schools," which called forth much discussion; by Mrs. Baines, on "The Training of Domestic Servants;" by the Rev. F. A. Morris, on "The Rights and Wrongs of Women;" also a letter from the Ladies' Sanitary Association, offering 10*l*. as a prize for the best pamphlet on sanitary subjects as connected with a manufacturing population. As the wording was vague, it was resolved to let the matter stand over till further information was obtained. Lady Bowring made some remarks on Technical Schools, and Miss Tod described the Ladies' Institute at Dublin.

A vote of thanks was given to Lady Bowring, and the Conference terminated.

It is understood that no Ladies' Conferences will be held in future, as it seems to draw ladies away from the regular work of the sections. We are of opinion that the common discussion of public affairs among ladies and gentlemen should be encouraged as much as possible, therefore in spite of the great success of the Conference we are glad it is not to be repeated.

WOMEN AND THE WAR.

IN France women protested against the war before it broke out. The International Association of Women have protested against its continuance.

The following protest was circulated in London yesterday, and is being extensively signed, the names being forwarded to Mrs. G. Butler, 280, South Hill, Park Road, Liverpool, the initiative being taken by the International Association of Women:—" The horrors of war now being waged between two nominally Christian nations have awakened us more fully to the terrible opposition there is between the deliberate destruction of human life and the spirit and teaching of Christianity. While rendering all honour to the noble efforts now being made for the relief of the wounded, we, women of England, desire also to aid the still nobler work, and to further the still nobler object —the extinction of war; and we earnestly and respectfully proffer to those in power, who are responsible for the continuance of the present war, our petition, urged in the name of God, and in behalf of our friends in France and Germany, for the cessation of this awful struggle, and for the carrying out, at the earliest possible moment, the great project which will contribute largely to assuage the wounds of humanity—a general disarmament.—*Daily News*, September 16.

A GREAT number of ladies in England have formed local committees in aid of the wounded. In fact almost all the ladies in England have been engaged in making bandages and picking lint.

The ladies who have not been thus engaged are the exception.

Some scores of ladies, including many Sisters of Mercy,

have gone to give personal aid in attending to the wounded. One English lady, it is said, has been given the rank of a major in the Prussian army as a reward for her services.

In Germany women have been doing men's work, or the harvest would have been lost. The Correspondent of the *Echo* says:—

> On looking from my window before I sat down to write, I saw women in the harvest field cutting and tying the ripe wheat crop; women discharging the cargo of brown coals which a long boat had brought down the Elbe from the mines of Teplitz; women mowing green food for horses, and carrying heavy loads of the luxuriant grass to the stables of the little town in baskets strapped to their backs; at the same glance I could see other women engaged in selling fruit, vegetables, and milk. This is, to my mind, a very striking evidence of the exhausting nature of the struggle in which Germany is engaged. The manhood of the nation has gone to the Rhine.

It is said that 300 societies for aiding the wounded have been formed in Germany. The Crown Princess of Prussia constantly visits the hospitals. A Correspondent of the *Times* thus describes the effect of a visit:—

> As she passed along and stopped and spoke to each, the invalid laid himself back on his pillow with an expression of absolute *bien être*, and for the moment seemed to find something more than an anodyne for his pain. Her passing along the wards applied the most infallible of tests to the cases. If her presence did not smooth the pain wrinkles out of a man's face, or bring something like tranquillity to his drawn mouth, and cause a flash of light to his eyes, you were quite sure to hear he was in an extremely bad way. Nor was it with the wounded alone she seemed the animating spirit of the place. Nurses and doctors and convalescents walking about all addressed her with the same cordial familiarity—only tempered by their evident reverence and love.

She also causes provisions to be supplied to the families of poor men who have gone to the war.

As the trains of wounded soldiers come in, women give them food and wine without regard to nationality.

Dr. Elizabeth Garrett, who has been to Sedan, writes to the *Times* to say there is plenty of material in aid of the wounded, but a great lack of persons to distribute these necessaries. She estimates that five nurses are required where one is now employed. This is not the fault of women, as Colonel Lloyd Lindsay, the Secretary of the Central Aid Committee, has discouraged the volunteering of nurses.

The French government at the beginning of the war accepted only forty volunteer nurses, and refused the offer of many hundred women to serve in that capacity.

In short women having attempted in vain to prevent or stop the war, are doing all they can to mitigate its dreadful consequences.

BOARDING OUT PAUPER ORPHANS.

The following letter has been received by Miss Preusser—

August 16*th*, 1870.

MADAM—I am desired by Mr. Goschen to reply to several inquiries which you have made, as to the probability of steps being taken by the Poor Law Board to give effect to the wishes and suggestions expressed in the memorial which has been addressed to the President on the subject of boarding out pauper children.

The deep interest shown by a great portion of the public, and especially by ladies, in the best means of training pauper children so as to free them in after life from the depressing associations which have usually surrounded their early days, has been a source of sincere gratification to Mr. Goschen, because he has felt that the practical manner in which the subject has been approached, affords ample evidence that there is an unaffected desire on the part of many of those who have addressed him, to lend a personal and practical assistance in the great work to which allusion has been made.

He desires me to state that it would be, in his opinion, a serious loss to the public interest if means should not be found to utilise the services which so many persons, competent to tender them, are willing to place, without stint, at the disposal of the authorities who have charge of the administration of the Poor Laws, and that he has considered, with much anxiety, what might be the best mode of taking advantage of the zealous offers which are made of personal labour in organising and superintending the boarding out of pauper children.

Some legal doubts and difficulties have hitherto stood in the way of carrying out that most important branch of the system, which contemplates the removal of children from urban unions to country homes. I am desired to state that those doubts and difficulties have now been settled, and that a general order is already in type which will enable Boards of Guardians, under certain conditions, to enter into arrangements with committees duly authorised for that purpose, for the boarding out of orphan and deserted pauper children. I am to add that the views and suggestions which have been put before the President of the Poor Law Board from various quarters, have been most fully considered in the framing of the regulations which will in a few days be published. You are doubtless aware that Mr. Goschen caused very careful inquiry to be made into the practise of boarding out children prevalent in Scotland. The result of that inquiry has shown that under certain conditions, great good may be attained from the adoption of the system, but it is also apparent that very careful precautions must be taken against certain chances of abuse to which the practise is undoubtedly exposed. Mr. Goschen has been unwilling to sanction any plan until he is able to see his way to such a combination of responsible management with voluntary effort, as appeared likely to afford the indispensable security. Mr. Goschen will not fail to cause a copy of the conditions and regulations on which he considers it his duty to insist, to be sent to you the moment they are issued, as he is as anxious as you or any of your memorialists can be, that full and immediate advantage should be taken of the disposition manifested in so many quarters to lend a helping hand in the great work of education, and redeeming the vast number of poor orphan children committed to the charge of public authorities.

     I have the honour to be your obe dient servant,

To Miss A. Preusser.   W. R. KENNEDY.

MISS RYE has just returned from Canada having disposed of all her last batch of children, except ten very young ones, who are left at the Home. Miss Rye states that she could dispose of any number of boys or girls, of nine or ten years of age, in service in farm-houses.

THE EARL OF DERBY ON THE EMPLOYMENT OF WOMEN.

ON the occasion of the opening of the tenth session of the Liverpool School of Science, Lord Derby said in the course of his speech:—

There is one other point I wish to notice, and that is that all teaching given in this School of Science, whether by lectures or classes, or in any other way, women are as freely admitted as men. (Hear, hear.) I am not going into any controverted topic. The question of what branches of industrial occupation women are fitted to succeed in is one which, in my mind, can only be settled by actual experiment, but then the experiment ought to be fairly tried, and the result ought not to be prejudged. (Hear, hear.) There is a very simple alternative in the matter. Any work of an industrial or scientific kind which women are fitted to do they ought not to be excluded from doing—(hear, hear)—any work which they are not fit to do they will exclude themselves from doing. (Laughter and applause.) You do not require—if I may take such an illustration—to make it a matter of law or a social custom that no man shall go into the business of a blacksmith who is not so many inches round the arm, because you are sure that men whose arms are weak will not go into that business; so I say, shutting out women from any work for which they feel or think themselves competent, or refusing them, if they desire it, the necessary training for that occupation—in effect, shutting them out, though only in an indirect manner—seems to me rather a mean and unworthy piece of policy. I am very glad that in this institution no countenance is given to that feeling.

MISCELLANEOUS.

THE Bishop of Salisbury on his first visitation at the cathedral, said :—

The Bill for legalizing the marriage of a man with his deceased wife's sister would in all probability soon pass unless the women of England, whose question it more especially was, took it up and petitioned against it, of which petitions, as far as regarded Wilts and Dorset, he himself should be happy to take charge.

THE COMMITTEE of the Refuges for Destitute Children which now receive 400 boys, are anxious to raise the number of girls received to 200. On the occasion of opening a new wing recently added to the girls' Home, the Earl of Shaftesbury remarked :—

He thought that the institution met one of the crying necessities of the present day; for wherever he went he perpetually heard complaints of the want of a due supply of domestic servants. There was plenty of the raw material for servants; but what they wanted was the finished article such as this institution supplied. There was another thing to be borne in mind. They ought to do everything they could to enable women to get a subsistence for themselves. The proportion of women to men was very large. By the last census there were not less than 600,000 more women than men, of whom a large number must pass through the world alone and depend upon their own exertions for a livelihood. It was therefore of importance to put them in the way of getting an honest and decent livelihood, such as the Refuge would enable them to get.

PRESIDENT GENERAL GRANT is a practical women's rights man in the distribution of appointments.—*New York Herald*.

THE DEGREE of "Bachelor" of Laws has been conferred on a married lady in America. Mrs. Kepley, the lady in question, is the wife of Mr. H. B. Kepley, a practising lawyer of Effingham, in Chicago. Having for some years had a desire to be admitted to the Bar, she commenced at her own home reading various legal text books. Wishing to take a thorough course, she, with the full consent of her husband, went to Chicago, entered the law department of the University, and pursued the regular course of study prescribed by that institution to the end, and then passed a creditable examination. She obtained her diploma, but in consequence of a recent decision of the Supreme Court was unable to obtain a certificate to practise.—*Law Times.*

DUTCH apothecaries are in consternation at a decree opening the examination of apothecaries to women.

A WOMAN'S rights journal has been established at San Francisco, California, called the *Pioneer*. There are now women's journals in England, France, Germany, Portugal, Italy, Holland, in several States of America, and India.

Index

Amos, Prof. Sheldon, *Difference of Sex as a Topic of Jurisprudence and Legislation* (reviewed), 271
Anderson, Elizabeth Garrett, 122, 225
Art schools, Edinburgh, 30
Artists, Rosa Bonheur, 125
Assolant, Alfred, *Le Droit des Femmes* (Rights of Women) (reviewed), 174

Becker, Lydia, letter on Married Women's Property Act, 283; letter to *Times* on women's suffrage, 193
Bernard, Mrs. E.G. Bayle, review of Mrs. Margaret Oliphant's *Historical Sketches of the Reign of George III*, 75
Blackwell, Elizabeth, and medical education, 48
Boarding out, Boucherett, Louisa, "Practical Suggestions on Boarding Out," 4; Kennedy, W.R., letter on, 305
Bonheur, Rosa, 125
Boucherett, Jessie, "Future Plans," 1
Boucherett, Louisa, "Practical Suggestions on Boarding Out," 4
Bryce, James, endowments for girls' education, 110

Cambridge University, local examinations, 29, 109
Carpenter, Mary, Female Training School, 112; Honorary Member of Social Science Congress, 49
Children, pauper, emigration, 230
Clayland's Debating Society, London, *Mr. Mill's Subjection of Women from a Woman's Point of View* (reviewed), 82
Club, Women's, and Institute, 51
Cobbe, Frances Power, letter to *The Animal World* on women's suffrage, 295
Contagious Diseases Act, Ladies Association for the Repeal of, 51, 118
Crippen, Rev. T.G., "The Testimony of Holy Scripture Concerning the Social Status of Women," 127

Deceased Wife's Sister Bill, 17, 207
Derby, Frederick Stanley, Earl of, employment of women, 306
Destitute girls, 117, 307
Divorce, Kelly case, 88

Edinburgh University, medical education, 27, 126, 224, 292
EDUCATION, Aubrey Institute, Notting Hill, London, 226; Carpenter, Mary, Female Training School, 112; co-education, Rev. C.H. Johnstone on, 292; "College Education for Women," by Emily Shirreff, 262; educational boards, women on, 225; endowed schools for girls, 289; endowments, Association for Promoting the Application of Endowments to the Education of Women, 30, for girl's education, 110, 223; Hatfield, Miss, donation for women's college, 293; North London Collegiate School, 290; technical, 41, 115, 116; university classes for women, 27; University College, London, lectures for women, 287; University of Stockholm, 30
Elections, municipal, 33
Emigration, of pauper children, 230; and Maria Rye, 50, 188, 231, 306
EMPLOYMENT, clerk, United States government, 120; exhibition of women's work, 293; farming, 58, 126, "A Plea for Women Farmers," 9, farmwork for women and girls, 69, peasantry of Cumberland and Westmorland, 41; gentlewoman's self-help, 164; *Industrial Employment of Women in the Middle and Lower Ranks* by John Duguid Milne (reviewed), 269; mending, 52; printing, letter by Charles Wilson Felt, 45; silk-reeling, Mrs. Povall, 49; Society for Promoting the Employment of Women, letter by Louisa Elizabeth Locke King, 40; women, Lord Derby on, 306
Englishwoman's Review, "Future Plans," by Jessie Boucherett, 1

Felt, Charles Wilson, letter on printing as employment for women, 46
Food Journal: A Review of Social and Sanitary Economy (reviewed), 81
France, married woman's property, 91; women and change in government, 275; women and the war, 248

Garrett, Elizabeth, medical woman, 122, 225
Germany, medical education, 112
Historical Sketches of the Reign of George III by Margaret Oliphant (reviewed by Mrs. E.G. Bayle Bernard), 75
Hitchin College, Cambridge University, 29, 108, 287
Hobhouse, Mr. Arthur, on Married Woman's Property Bill, 60, 82
India, 232
International Woman's Association, 233
Ireland, women's suffrage meeting, Dublin, 194

Jex-Blake, Sophia, Edinburgh School of Medicine, 27
Johnstone, Rev. C.H., on co-education, 292

Kennedy, W.R., letter on boarding out of pauper orphans, 305
King, Louisa Elizabeth Locke, on Society for Promoting the Employment of Women, 39

Lamport, Charles, Pauperism and Self-Help (reviewed), 273
Law, *Difference of Sex as a Topic of Jurisprudence and Legislation* by Prof. Sheldon Amos (reviewed), 271; jurors, Wyoming, U.S., 122, 232; lawyers, women, U.S., 232, 307
Leggett, Mrs., medical student, 291
London University, examination for women, 224, 285

Macrae, David, *The Americans at Home: Pen and Ink Sketches of American Men, Manners, and Institutions* (reviewed), 275
Marriage, breach of promise actions, 68; wife starving, 250
Married women's property, Act, 237; Wolstenhome, Elizabeth, on act, 297; Bill, 12, 38, 72, 85, 211, 235, 256, 276; Dublin Society for bill, 88; Hobhouse, Mr. Arthur, on bill, 60, 82; *Echo* on, 63; France, 91; *Manchester Women's Suffrage Journal* on, 123
Medical education, 48; Edinburgh University, 27, 126, 224, 292; Germany, 112; Mrs. Leggett, 291; petition to Parliament, 112; Russia, 225; University of Stockholm, 30; Sweden, 30, 291
Medical Society, Female, 226
Medical women, Anderson, Elizabeth Garrett, 123, 225; Webster, Margaret M., 291

Mill, John Stuart, *Mr. Mill's Subjection of Women from a Woman's Point of View* by Clayland Debating Society (reviewed), 82
Milne, John Duguid, *Industrial Employment of Women in the Middle and Lower Ranks* (reviewed), 269

North London Collegiate School, 290

Oliphant, Margaret, *Historical Sketches of the Reign of George III* (reviewed by Mrs. E.G. Bayle Bernard), 75
Oxford University, local examinations, 29, 110, 285

Parry, Love Jones, M.P., letter on women's suffrage, 193
Pauperism and Self-Help by Charles Lamport (reviewed), 273
Poor Law, wife starvation, 252
Poor Law Guardians, women as, 230
Povall, Mrs., silk-reeling in South Africa, 49

Religion, "Testimony of Holy Scripture Concerning the Status of Women" by Rev. T.G. Crippen, 127
Russia, medical education, 225
Rye, Maria, and emigration, 50, 118, 231, 306

Shirreff, Emily, "College Education for Women," 262
Social Science Congress, at Newcastle, 295; Mary Carpenter, Honorary Member, 49
South Africa, employment in, silk-reeling, 49
Stockholm, University of, medical education, 30
SUFFRAGE, WOMEN'S, bill, text, 107; *Daily News* on, 171; Manchester Women's Suffrage Society, *Journal*, 62, 123; meetings: Bath, 97, Birmingham, 101, Bristol, 97, Crewe, 98, Dublin, 194, Edinburgh, 91, Frome, 127; Municipal Franchise Bill, 18; National Society for, 102, 190; objections to, 55, 62; Parry, Love Jones, M.P., letter on, 193; petitions, 108, 199, 293; Taylor, Clementia, letter on, 192; Taylor, Henry, on, 59
Sweden, medical education, 30, 291

Taylor, Clementia, letter on women's suffrage, 192
Taylor, Henry, on women's suffrage, 59

United States, *Americans at Home: Pen and Ink Sketches of American Men, Manners, and Institutions* by David Macrae (reviewed), 275; employment of government clerks, 120; jurors, women, 122, 232; lawyers, women, 232, 307
University College, London, lectures for women, 287

War, Frenchwomen and the, 248, 303
Webster, Margaret M., medical woman, 291
Wolstenhome, Elizabeth C., on Married Women's Property Act, 283, 296

Women, *Texts on Woman's Normal Position* (reviewed), 173
Women's rights, *Le Droit des Femmes* by Alfred Assolant (reviewed), 174; journals, 308

For Product Safety Concerns and Information please contact our EU representative GPSR@taylorandfrancis.com
Taylor & Francis Verlag GmbH, Kaufingerstraße 24, 80331 München, Germany

www.ingramcontent.com/pod-product-compliance
Lightning Source LLC
Chambersburg PA
CBHW070232230426
43664CB00014B/2280